Samuel R. Brown

Colloquial Japanese

Or, conversational sentences and dialogues in English and Japanese, together with an English-Japanese index to serve as a vocabulary, and an introduction on the grammatical structure of the language

Samuel R. Brown

Colloquial Japanese
Or, conversational sentences and dialogues in English and Japanese, together with an English-Japanese index to serve as a vocabulary, and an introduction on the grammatical structure of the language

ISBN/EAN: 9783337087074

Printed in Europe, USA, Canada, Australia, Japan

Cover: Foto ©Paul-Georg Meister /pixelio.de

More available books at **www.hansebooks.com**

COLLOQUIAL JAPANESE,

OR

CONVERSATIONAL SENTENCES

AND

DIALOGUES

IN

ENGLISH AND JAPANESE,

TOGETHER WITH

AN ENGLISH-JAPANESE INDEX

TO SERVE AS

A VOCABULARY,

AND

AN INTRODUCTION

ON THE

GRAMMATICAL STRUCTURE OF THE LANGUAGE.

BY

REV. S. R. BROWN, A. M.

———

SHANGHAI:
PRESBYTERIAN MISSION PRESS.
1863.

PREFACE

This work was commenced without the remotest view to publication. That part of it which is arranged alphabetically, had been written and rewritten and laid aside, when some friends happening to see it, suggested that it might be useful to other students of the Japanese language, if it were published. Still it might never have gone to the press, but for the offer of a mercantile friend in this country, to bear the expense of its publication. It was then, that the idea of adding some dialogues; an English-Japanese index; and a grammatical introduction suggested itself. The author has not hesitated to avail himself of all possible aid from the works of others within his reach. Collado's Ars Grammaticæ Japonicæ 1632. Rodriguez' Grammaire Japonaise, 1825. The Japanese-Portuguese Dictionary, 1603; and the work by M. J. R. Donker Curtius, edited by M. L. J. Hoffman, Leipsic, 1857; have been his most valuable aids, more especially the two last named.

It is but just to add, that as this book is printed at Shanghai, the author has not been able to correct the proofs, and the printer has been compelled to rely upon his own corrections from the copy. A list of the most important errata will, however, accompany the volume.

The author is constrained to tender his most grateful acknowledgements, to W. Keswick Esq., through whose spontaneous, munificence this work is published; and if it facilitate the studies of those who desire to obtain a knowledge of the language of this interesting people, the end of its publication will so far have been accomplished.

CONTENTS.

	Page
I. Preface	
II. System of Notation.	
III. Introductory Remarks on Japanese Grammar	i—lxii
IV. Sentences in English and Japanese Colloquial	1—172
V. Dialogues	173—196
VI. Weights and Measures, Money &c.	197—200
VII. English–Japanese Index	203—243

SYSTEM OF NOTATION

FOR

ROMANIZING JAPANESE WORDS.

The system adopted in this volume, has been submitted to the judgement of gentlemen who are engaged in the study of this language, and may be regarded as having received the approval of those who are most likely hereafter to produce other, and no doubt, better works on the Japanese language.

The author has divided the syllables in the alphabetically arranged part of this work, and omitted the hyphens in the Dialogues, so that both modes of writing may have a fair trial. The Katakana character being placed under each Romanized syllable, the reader will be enabled thereby to see the euphonic changes that take place in speech, and the Japanese reader will be able to see at the same time, how the sounds are represented by Roman letters. The services of a native teacher will also be rendered available, by his seeing at once, how the idea is expressed in his own tongue. A little practice, will suffice to enable any one to read the Romanized Japanese readily.

Let it be observed that there are but five vowel sounds in the Japanese language, which are the same in all positions, and are represented by, a, e, i, o, and u. The sounds of these vowels are invariably as follows, viz. A, like a in *Ah*! E. like ey in *they*, or ay in *may*. I, like i in *machine*, or ee in *bee*. O, like o in *no*. U, like oo in *fool*.

When any of these vowels are doubled, although there must be two Japanese syllables to represent it, yet in practice, the result is merely the prolongation of the single vowel sound, as, aa,=ah long. Ee=ay long. Ii=ee long. Oo=oo as in *door*. Uu,=oo prolonged as if *fool* were spelt *foo-ool*.

The most difficult sounds for a foreigner to acquire correctly, are those of nga, nge, ngi, ngo, ngu; of sz, tsz, and hi(ヒ). But when ng is an initial sound, it does not differ from ng final, in any English word, as *sing*, for instance. It is only necessary to transpose it from its position, after a vowel, to one before a, e, i, o, or u. Sz is simply the articulation of s and z, in close consecution. Tsz is but the articulation of its three letters. Neither Sz, nor Tsz, has any vowel sound after the final z. The sound of z must terminate the syllable. This at least is the pronunciation at Yedo, and Kanangawa. When hi (ヒ) is a word by itself, the final vowel i, is heard, and it sounds like the English pronoun *he*. But when it precedes another syllable commencing with a consonant, the vowel i ceases to be vocalized, and is only whispered. Thus, h'to, a man, is to be pronounced, not shto, as many do, but first the syllable *he* must be whispered, and then *to*, is to be enunciated in quick succession. To represent this suppression of the vowel in *hi* (ヒ) an apostrophe is put in the place of i after h, (h'.) The vowel i undergoes the same suppression to a whisper, after k, very often, especially before mutes. as, k'ta, for kita, he came. The vowel u, also is but whispered in ku (ク) when that syllable is followed by another commencing with k, or s, or, sh, as, Watak'shi, for Watakushi, l. Hiak'kin, for Hiakukin, a hundred catties. Asak'sa, for Asakusa, name of a district, or ward in Yedo.

When the syllable tsz (ツ) stands before a syllable in the same word commencing with t, sh, p, or k, it becomes a mere reduplication of t, sh, p, or k, Thus ニツポン is pronounced nippon. ホツキン is pronounced Hok'kin. ケツシテ, is pronounced kesh'shte, or kes'shte. カツパ, is pronounced kappa, &c. The syllable ri [リ] before テ, te, becomes likewise a reduplication of t, as, arite アリテ atte. The same occurs when ri [リ] precedes [タ] ta. as, アリタ atta.

When シ, shi precedes a mute in the same word, the i is suppressed, as, sh'ta. sh'kashi, instead of shita, and shikashi.

Vowel Combinations.

Ai, oi, ei, and ui, are proper diphthongs, and both vowels are distinctly heard. But, au, ou, and eu, often become oö in pronunciation. Thus, チガフタ is pronounced chinoöta, omou [ヲモフ], omoö; and meu, mioö; shi-yau, is pronounced sh'oö; and seu, sh'oö, wau, woö [ワウ].

Interchangeable Syllables.

フ	occurs with the sound of				ウ, u.
ハ	,,	,,	,,	,,	,, ワ, wa.
ホ	,,	,,	,,	,,	,, オ, o.
ヲ	,,	,,	,,	,,	,, オ, o.
ヒ	,,	,,	,,	,,	,, イ, i.

SYSTEM OF NOTATION

Diacritical marks over Consonants.

It will be seen by examining the following Syllabary, that twenty of them undergo a change in sound which is indicated by the marks [ʼ] or [°] placed at the right hand of the character. These marks are called ningori by the Japanese. Thus ハ, ha, with the ningoro, becomes ハ゛, ba, or ハ゜, pa. &c.

Accentuation.

The penultimate syllable receives the primary accent in polysyllabic words, unless the penultimate vowel is suppressed, and then the antepenultimate is accented. The secondary accent is thrown back two removes from the syllable that receives the primary accent. e.g. Shiránu, Wákaránu. Wakárimásh'ta. In the last word the penultimate vowel being suppressed, the accent is on the antepenult.

Words of different meanings being composed of the same syllables, might be mistaken for one another, are distinguished by difference of accent. The following are examples:—

Accented on the Penult.	Accented on the Ultimate.
Jishin, one's self.	Jishin, an earthquake.
Hana, a flower.	Hana, the nose.
Kasa, an umbrella.	Kasa, a venereal ulcer.
Kawa, a river.	Kawa, a skin.
Umi, the sea.	Umi, pus.
Uchi, to strike.	Uchi, a *house*.
Mushi, vapor.	Mushi, insects and reptiles.

Hashi, a bridge, is distinguished from hashi, chopsticks, by the suppression of the final i in the last, thus hash', signifies chopsticks. Moyéru, accented on the penult, signifies, to burn, (intrans.) as Hi nga moyéru, the fire burns, but if the last syllable receives the accent, it signifies to germinate.

Japanese syllables are written in two ways, called the Katakana, and the Hirangana. Hirangana, signifies the cursive or easy, flowing style of writing, and Katakana, the one-sided or half (written) character, Kana alone etymologically signifies, a borrowed name, or fictitious name, referring to the fact that the characters of the syllabary were borrowed from the Chinese language, as mere representatives of sound, without regard to their sense.

KATAKANA SYLLABARY.

イ = i.	レ = re	コ ゴ = ko, ngo.
ロ = ro.	ソ ゾ = so, dzo or zo.	エ = ye or e.
ハ バ パ = ha, ba, pa.	ツ ヅ = tsz, dz.	テ デ = te, de.
ニ = ni.	ネ = ne.	ア = a.
ホ ボ ポ = ho, bo, po.	ナ = na.	サ ザ = sa, za or dza.
ヘ ベ ペ = he, be, pe.	ラ = ra.	キ ギ = ki, ngi.
ト ド = to, do.	ム = mu.	ユ = yu.
チ ヂ = chi, ji.	ウ = u.	メ = me.
リ = ri.	ヰ = i.	ミ = mi.
ヌ = nu.	ノ = no.	シ ジ = shi, ji.
ル = ru.	オ = o.	ヱ = ye or e.
ヨ = wo or o.	カ ガ = ku, ngu.	ヒ ビ ピ = hi, bi, pi.
ワ = wa.	ヤ = ya.	モ = mo.
カ ガ = ka, nga.	マ = ma.	セ ゼ = se, ze.
ヨ = yo.	ケ ゲ = ke, nge.	ス ズ = sz, dz.
タ ダ = ta, da.	フ ブ プ = fu, bu, pu.	ン = n final, or ng.

INTRODUCTORY REMARKS
ON THE
GRAMMAR
OF THE
JAPANESE LANGUAGE.

The object of the writer is to give such hints on the grammatical forms of words and their construction into sentences, as will enable the student to investigate sentences by the analytic-synthetical process. It were unphilosophical to attempt to assimilate the Grammar of the Japanese to the forms of the Latin, or any other occidental language, for it has a method peculiar to itself, and all that needs to be done is to elucidate that method.

As in all other languages, so in this, there **are** classes of words which are usually denominated parts of speech.

PARTS OF SPEECH.

These are Verbs, Nouns, Personal and Interrogative Pronouns, **Adjectives**, Adverbs, Conjunctions, Postpositions, corresponding to our Prepositions, Interjections, and Constructive Particles.

Sec. I. VERBS REGULAR AND IRREGULAR

In order to conjugate a Japanese verb, it is necessary first to ascertain its root form, which is the base on which all its other forms are constructed. Hence we observe that all verbal roots, except in a few anomalous cases, end in the vowel sound I = English *ee* in bee, or E = *a* in name, and for convenience sake, verbs may be divided into regular and irregular.

Regular verbs are those in which the final vowel of the root I or E remains unchanged in the formation of the future tense, and in the formation of passive, negative, and causative verbs.

Irregular verbs are those whose root terminates in I, and the vowel in the above cases, passes into the more open sound of A or O.

Examples of Irregular Verbs.

Verb.	Root.	Future	Passive.	Causative.	Negative.
Kiku, *to hear*,	Kiki	Kikoō	Kikareru	Kikaseru	Kikanu.
Motsz, *to take up*,	Mochi / Moti	Motsoō	Motareru	Motasz	Motanu.
Korosz, *to kill*,	Koroshi	Korosoō	Korosareru	Korosaszru	Korosanu.
Shiman, *to finish*,	Shimai	Shimawoō	Shimawareru	Shimawaszru	Shimawanu.
Utsz, *to strike*,	Uchi	Utsoō	Utareru	Utaseru	Utanu.
Kuū, *to eat*,	Kui	Kuwoō	Kuwareru	Kuwaseru	Kuwanu.
Omou, *to think*,	Omoi	Omowoō	Omowareru	Omowaseru	Omowanu.
Narau, *to learn*,	Narai	Narawoō	Narawareru	Narawaseru	Narawanu.

N.B.—In verbs whose root has a vowel immediately before the terminal vowel, there is a *W* sound inserted before the strengthened *I*, when it becomes *A* or *O*, to prevent a hiatus; *e.g.* kai-fut kawoō; omoi, omowanu; and kuū kuwanu.

The reason of the change of *I* into *O* in the future of irregular verbs is as follows. In the written language, the future tense of all verbs is formed by adding ン *n* to the roots of regular verbs, and to those of irregular verbs after the final *I* of the root has passed into *A*. Hence from ake, to open, a regular verb, we have ake-n=aken for the future, which in the spoken language becomes akeo, or akeyoō. From the regular verb root mi, to see, we have min, which in the spoken language becomes mioō or miyoō in the future. In the case of the irregular verb ari, to be, we have for the future, first, ari changed into ara, and then, the ン *n* added making aran; but this in the spoken language becomes arau, and according to a euphonic law, the combination au is pronounced oō; and eu is pronounced eō. Thus アフ, グウ, オフ, オウ, are all pronounced oō; and エフ, and エウ, are pronounced eō, or eoō. See remarks on euphonic changes of vowels and consonants.

The oral language delights in courteous expressions, and one of the most remarkable features of the polished style of speech is the use of long words, and circumlocutions. Thus ari means to be, and aru is or are. But these simple forms are not used in polite conversation; at least they are never used in addressing or speaking of a person to whom one desires to show respect. In that case ari becomes arimaszru, or by elision, arimas', or more politely gozarimaszru, or gozarimas'. The verbal root mashi, which is affixed to all verbs, seems to be derived from ma a space or interval, and shi, root of szru, to do, to make or occupy, to occupy a space, or to be, and it is conjugated like any other verb. It is the only part of the compound that is subject to conjugation, the first part of it being always a simple root. Thus nomi to drink, nomimaszru, or nomimas', present indicative, hanashi to speak, hanashimaszru, or hanashimas', present indicative. This verb mashi, in the future becomes mashoō. According to the principle which is explained above, the written form of the future would be mash'an; but in the oral language N is replaced by U', ﾖ or ｳ which would give mashi-a-u, or mash'-ya-u, the I sound still being retained as a Y, to obviate the hiatus, and the written ya-u according to the law of euphony is pronounced yoŏ, or oŏ. Hence the future of nomimas' is ノミマシヤウ nomimash'oŏ. These remarks will suffice to explain the future form when as in polite speaking a verb receives the affix mashi (mas' or maszru).

Sec. II. THE IMPERATIVE.

The Imperative is the simplest form of the verb. In regular affirmative verbs, the mere verbal root, and in irregular affirmative verbs, the root with its terminal vowel I changed into E; is the imperative.

Examples.

	VERB.	ROOT.	IMPERATIVE.
Reg.	Akeru, to open,	Ake,	Ake, or Akeyo, or Akero.
Irr.	Yuku, to go,	Yuki,	Yuke, or Yukeyo.
Reg.	Miru, to see,	Mi,	Mi, or Miyo, or Miro.
Irr.	Aruku, to walk,	Aruki,	Aruke, or Arukeyo.

In the last forms of the Imperative given above, the syllables yo and ro, affixed to the simple Imperative, seem to be interjections answering very much to our O! as when we say, O see! though there appears to be no special force given to the Japanese expression by the addition of these syllables.

Sec. III. ATTRIBUTIVE FORM OF VERBS.

When a verb is used to modify the meaning of another word like an adjective, it always terminates in the vowel sound u=ｳ or ﾌ; sz =ス; or tsz=ﾂ. It is probable that in ancient times the syllables ス and ツ may have been pronounced su, and tsu, or tu. Many even now as Mr. Hoffman and his French translator, M. Leon Pagès represent ス by sou and ツ by tsou. It may be that in some districts of Japan, these two syllables are pronounced with the pure vowel sound u; but it certainly is not so in Yedo and its vicinity. If the present pronunciation were that of the learned gentlemen above named, it would only be necessary to say that the attributive form ends in u.

In accordance with this rule, to make the attributive form, regular verbs in I and E change I into iru or uru, and E into eru or uru; while Irregular verbs change I into u.

Verbs in the attributive form are also used in place of our infinitive mode. Hence this is sometimes called the substantive form of the verb.

For an example of this form, used infinitively, see 145. Karada wo ungokasz wa, to exercise the body &c. There Karada wo, the body, is the direct object of the verb Ungokasz, a causative verb in the attributive form derived from ungoku, to move; ungokasz, to cause to move, to bestir. The clause is isolated by the particle wa from the rest of the sentence which is its predicate. A similar construction, but one in which the verb in the attributive form, Musaboritoru, is used attributively to modify a noun, Koto, is seen in 144. Musaboritoru Koto, Lit. the extorting act, or the act of extortion. So also in 1269 Yomu Koto, and Kaku Koto. Yomu and Kaku are both used as adjectives modifying the noun Koto, Lit. the reading act, and the writing act, or the acts of reading and writing. Again in 60, Nippon de ts'kuremash'tani mono. Ts'kuremas' is a passive verb, in the attributive form, from the root ts'kuri, to make, and here signifies *made*. Hence literally the sense is, Japan made cloths. *i. e.* Cloths made in Japan. See also Toru Koto in 78. Toru is the attributive form from the irregular verbal root tori, to catch. Hence literally toru koto, the catching act, or act of catching, naranu is impossible, or that which cannot be. In 1224, Mamoru is the attributive form from the irregular verbal root mamori, and used as an infinitive, Mamoru, to see to, or to take charge of.

Sec. IV. Gerundives.

Among the simpler forms of the verb, derived immediately from the root, is the gerundive, which consists of the root with *te* or *de* added to it. *e. g.* Arukite, or by the elision of the k, Aruite, is the gerundive from Aruki, to walk.— Tadznete is the gerundive from Tadzne, to inquire.—Kûte is the gerundive from Kiki, to hear, or to inquire.

The nature and signification of the Japanese Gerundive, in te or de may be better understood by a reference to the use of the postposition de, with nouns and pronouns. When we say, as in 600, Doko no machi de— In what street—? De is the index of the locative relation of michi. In 133, Oshi no h'to nga te–mane de oshiemas', Dumb people talk by signs, de after temane is the index of the instrumental relation of te-mane, which signifies, manual signs. In 811, Kome de, *i. e.* in or by means of rice, de denotes the same relation of Kome, as the material with which the rents are paid to the Taikun. So in 28, Kashi to moôsz ki de, of a wood called Kashi, de denotes the instrumental relation of ki, as the material of which axehelves are made. In 365, Nani hodo de, at, or for how much? de is again the index of the locative relation of nani hodo, which means, what price? In 398, Nokoradz de, *i. e.* in all, or in all without exception, de marks the same relation. In 523, Watak'shi wa h'tori de *i. e.* I by (my) one person; de is the index of the modal relation of h'tori. In

283, Hosoo de of small-pox; de is the index of the causal relation. In 202, Bō de, i. e. with a club, de is the index of the instrumental relation. The same is true of De in 1085. Kami de, with paper. In 1189 Dochira de, and Doko de, i. e. where, in what place? de is the index of the locative relation.

From these examples we discover that de **with** nouns (and the same is true of pronouns) indicates the locative, modal, or instrumental relation of those nouns, answering to the questions Where? When? How? From **or** With what? When te or de (these **are** the same) is joined to a verbal root, and forms a gerundive, it denotes the **same** relations, and the action expressed by the verbal element of **the gerundive, is** characterized as a locative, modal, or instrumental **determination** connected with, and subordinate to another action following it. In other words, the gerundive expresses **an** action or operation done, as the mode, time, or manner in which, **or** the cause, means, or instrument by which some other action, expressed by **a** subsequent verb, **is performed**.

Thus, e. g. in 44 and 45, Yaite shimae, and Taite shimae. The gerundives Yaite=Yakite from Yaki to burn; and Taite=Takite from Taki to set on fire. Both denote the manner in which the action of **the** following verb shimae, imperative form of shimai, to finish, **to** put an end to, is to be performed, i. e. it is to be done by burning, **and** by setting on fire. In other words each gerundive is the modal determinative of the following verb, Shimae. In 216, Ano o kata wa **ude** wo kujūte oraremas', or iru, he has broken his arm. Kujūte is **a** gerundive from Kujiki, to break, and oraremas' or iru is the continuative verb, **to** be,—Kujūte denotes the condition in which the person spoken of, **is or** continues **to** be, viz. that of having broken his arm.

In 1048, Tadaima hajimete o me ni kakarimash'ta, This is **the first time** I have had the honor to see you. Hajimete **is** the gerundive form of Hajime, to begin, and denotes **the** time when the act **of seeing was** done. Lit: Now beginning, I have met your eye. 1178, Kore (4) wo ts'kutte (3) shimash'ta (2) toki (1) wa. **Lit.** When, I have finished (2) making(3) this. (4) Here ts'kutte is the gerundive from ts'kuri, to make, and modifies the verb shimash'ta, by showing in what the finishing consists, viz; in making. So in the shorter form of the same sentence, ts'kutte shimattara, the gerundive performs the **same office**, 359. Ano (1) h'to (2) no chichi (3) wa moto(4)-de (5) wo iremash'te; (6) akinai (7) wo hajime (8) sasemash'ta. (9) Lit: That (1) man's (2) father, (3) the original (4) outlay (5) putting in, (6) trade (7) to begin (8) caused (9) him to do. Here iremash'te is the polite form of irete from ire, **to** put in, and shows by what means the father set up his son in business, viz. by putting **in** the capital, (moto-de-wo).

Verbs whose roots have more than one syllable, and ending in Ki generally drop the K in the gerundive form. Thus, Yukite, Kikite, S'kite, and Ts'kite, become Yuite, Kūte, Szite, and Tszite.

Verbs in ri and chi change rite, and chite of the gerundive into tte. Thus, arite becomes atte; narite, natte; tachite, tatte; yorite, yotte; Mochite, motte; orite, otte.

Irregular verbs in mi and bi, in the spoken language, form their gerundives by dropping the final I, and changing m or b into n before the gerundive termination de. Thus;—

Yomi, *to read*, becomes, Yom'de, pronounced Yonde.
Yobi, *to call*, becomes, Yob'de, pronounced Yonde.
Ayumi, *to walk*, becomes, Ayum'de, pronounced Ayunde.
Muszbi, *to tie*, becomes, Muszb'de, pronounced Musznde.
Erami, *to select*, becomse, Eram'de, pronounced Erande.

Irregular verbs in ai and oi, (アヒand オヒ) drop the vowel I and insert u (ウor ア) in its place; and then au (アフor アウ) becomes oŏ, to which the gerundive termination te is added, Thus;—

Ai (アヒ), to meet, makes the gerundive Oŏte.
Narai (ナラヒ), to learn ,, ,, ,, Naroŏte.
Warai (ワラヒ), to laugh ,, ,, ,, Waroŏte.
Omoi (オモヒ), to think ,, ,, ,, **Omoŏte**.

Sec. V. The Conjunctive Form of the Verb.

By the conjunctive form, we mean such verbal expressions as in English are connected to the principal verb of a sentence or proposition, by the conjunctions, **when, as,** while, &c, and modify the principal verb, by their adverbial sense, denoting time present, or a past time considered as present:—*e. g* When I stand up, my feet pain me. In Japanese, Watak'shi wa tateba, ashi nga itamimas'. Here tateba signifies, When (I) stand up, and is an adverbial clause modifying the principal verb itamimas', to be in pain. Tateba is the conjunctive form of the irregular verb Tachi. This form is made by affixing ni [ニ] Eng. in, or at, and wa to the root tachi=tati. After its final I has been changed to E. [see below] ni-wa (ニハ), by elision of the I, becomes n'-wa, and that is equivalent to m'-wa, which by a law of euphony is pronounced *ba*. Hence tata-ni-wa signifies in the act of standing, or on standing up=When (I) stand up. So from Nari to become, we have Nareba, when it becomes, and from Maze, to mix, we get mazeba, when [we] mix. In place of the regular verbal root in e or i, the attributive form terminating in cru, uru, iru, is sometimes taken for the formation of the conjunctive. Thus, instead of se ba, the conjunctive form from the root shi, to do, we sometimes have szreba from szru, and instead of miba from mi, to see, we have mire ba from miru; from tatsz, to stand, we have tatszreba, and from madzru we get madzreba.

I final of irregular roots is changed into e, whence with ba **following** results the ending eba.—*e. g.*

Yuki, to go, Yukeba.
Tachi (=tati) to stand up, Tateba.
Nari, to be, Nareba.
Shiri, to know, Shireba.
Nakeri, not to be, Nakereba.
Tori, to take, Toreba.

For Irregular verbs, instead of the form just explained, the attributive form of the verb, with **ni** [ニ] or ni wa (ニハ) is also used. Thus miru ni is the locative of Miru, the fact of seeing, which is the attributive form of the verb mi, to see. Miru ni wa, therefore, signifies on seeing, **or** at the sight of, or when one sees.

Sec. VI. THE CONDITIONAL FORM.

This is made by appending ni–wa to the future of **the** written language. Thus from Yuki, **to** go, the future is Yukan. To this add the locative postposition ni, and the isolative wa, and we get Yukan–ni–wa, and from **nari**, to be, the future naran. Appending ni–wa to the **latter** we have Naran–ni–wa. These combinations, both in speaking and writing, become by resolution Yukaba, and Naraba, and signify, If one is to go, and If one is to be. As regular verbs in e have their written future in en, by the same combination we get first from tate, to erect, taten–ni–wa; from Ake, **to** open, aken–ni–wa, and from nare, to become, naren–ni–wa, which thus become taten'ba, aken'ba and naren'ba, and again by the same method of contraction tateba, akeba, nareba. See note, infra.

Note. Japanese Teachers know nothing of the rationale **of these** formations, and constantly affirm that the conjunctive **tateba is the** same in sense as the conditional, and that Yukaba and Yukeba **have** the same signification; but Mr. Hoffman has ably and clearly demonstrated the distinction as above given. Indeed it is remarkable how many obscure points in the structure **of** Japanese words **have** been elucidated by one **who** has derived all his knowledge **of Japanese** from the study **of** books.

Sec. VII. THE CONCESSIVE FORM.

The English expressions corresponding **to** this form of the verb are connected with the principal assertion by such words and phrases as though, although, for as much as, whereas, in as much as, **even** when, notwithstanding, seeing that. The word which in Japanese **is** constantly used to express the concessive sense is mo ㊀ or tomo ト㊀ In the sentence sore wa dare mo shiranu ka? Who does not know that? the principle is seen on which the concessive is formed. Mo, in this sentence, is not easily translateable, but it gives force to the interrogative **pronoun dare**, much as if we should say, Let it be who it may, or whosoever it may be, does he not understand that? ama-ngumo attemo furanu. Though there are rain-clouds, it does not rain. Here mo affixed to the gerundive atte has the sense of though or although. Or the sentence might be rendered, Even granting the presence of rain-clouds, it does not rain.

We may therefore in accordance with this principle, present the following table of verbal forms.

Kiki wa, the act of hearing.	Kiku	mo or tomo, though hearing.
Miru wa, the act of seeing.	Miru	mo or tomo, though seeing.
Arukuwa, the act of walking.	Aruku	mo or tomo, though walking.
Kiku ni wa, on hearing.	Kikuni	mo or tomo, even on hearing.
Miru ni wa, on seeing.	Miruni	mo or tomo, even on seeing.
Aruku ni wa In walking.	Arukuni	mo or tomo, even in walking.
Kikite, or Kiite or Kiite wa By hearing.	Kiite mo, though hearing, or even if one hears.	
Mite or Mite wa, by seeing. Mite mo, though seeing, or even if one sees.		
Aruite or Aruite wa by walking. Aruite mo, though or even by walking, or if one walks.		
Kikeba (=Kiki-ni-wa) When one hears. Kikedomo (= Kike-ni-tomo) even when one hears.		
Mireba (=Miru-ni-wa) When one sees. Miredomo (= Mire-ni-tomo) even when one sees.		
Arukeba, (=Aruku-ni-wa) When one walks. Arukedomo (Aruke-ni-tomo) even when one walks.		

The last of these three combinations Kike domo &c results from the contraction of Kike, and ni, and tomo. Just as ni–wa makes ba, so n–t of ni–tomo produces the d in domo.

Instead of domo, iyedomo [イヘド, or モイヱドモ] is sometimes employed. Iedomo, or Iyedomo is the concessive form of the verb ū, to say, and signifies, Though it be said, or Though it be called. This verb always has before it an appositive complement, denoting how the thing is called, or what is said, with the postposition ト to. See sentence 1183. "What is that musical instrument called"? Anonari mono wa, nani to iu ka? Literal translation ano=that narimono musical instrument, or sounding thing wa isolative particle, separating what goes before from what follows it, nani, what, (appositive complement of iu; to, postposition, index of the foregoing appositive complement; iu, do (they, indefinite subject of iu) call, attributive and predicative form of the present indicative; Ka interrogative particle. The longer form of the Japanese sentence is a more exact translation of the English. Nani to ju mono de gozarimas' Lit. What called thing is it? Iu with its appositive complements nani to is here attributive to mono thing. If the appositive is a verb, it is, in the oral language, put in the attributive form. Thus, Yuku to iu signifies he says or they say that he is going or they are going, and Yuku to iedomo signifies, lit. though one says that he is going, and is equivalent to "though he goes, or "though they go". It should be observed that the supposition relates to the present, and not to future time, and is therefore purely conssive in sense, not conditional.

SEC. VIII. Past Tense Form of Affirmative.

The preterite tense is formed by the addition of ta to the simple verbal root. Ta is derived, as M. Hoffman has ably demonstrated, from the combination of te and ari. Thus te—ari, becomes tari, and this, dropping the last syllable becomes ta. The te in tari is a gerundive ending, and hence the verb to which ta is affixed to form the preterit tense, is necessarily in the gerundive form, with ari appended to it. Thus totte-ari from tori, to catch, becomes tottari, and this again by elision of the final syllable ri becomes totta. The polite form consists of the verb-root tori—mashi—ta, which combined becomes torimash'ta, the I finaf of the verb-root mashi being elided before ta. Torimash'ta thus signifies have or has caught, or did catch. In like manner we get the following:—

From Atte= Atte gerundive from the r. r. Ari, we have **Atte—Ari=** Attari= Atta.
" Arimash'te, v. r. Arimashi, we have Arimash'te—Ari= Arimash'ta.
" Gozarimash'te v. r. Gozarimashi we have Gozarimash'te—ari= Gozarimash'ta.

These three words are the same in signification, and may mean either has been, or has had, for the radical of each of them is ari, which is the precise equivalent of the Chinese 有, a word which has both meanings.

In the higher or polite style of conversation, it is common to **avoid using the** shorter and simpler forms of expression, and instead **of** using atta for have had, the Japanese would say arimash'ta **or gozarimash'ta.** Instead also of using a single word for the **preterit, they** make use of a compound expression, consisting of **a verbal root,** denoting the principal action to be expressed, followed by **an auxiliary verb, in the preterit tense.**

Thus in 325. "He arrived there late", the shorter mode of expression is seen to be Osoku, (late,) tszita. Tszita is the preterit of Ts'ki, which by elision becomes Tszi, the Z reappearing where its elision had before been marked by an apostrophe. Tszi—te=Tszite, the gerundive, and Tszite—ari=Tszita. But the more polite mode of saying the same is ts'ki [v. r.] nasaremash'ta, preterit tense of nasareru, to do. Lit. arrive-did=did-arrive=arrived. Thus oide nasaremash'ta and itta, mean the same, namely, went or came, or **has gone or has** come. Itta, is probably a corruption of yuita=yukita. Ikita is frequently heard in the vulgar dialect of Kanagawa, meaning has gone, **or** went. By the elision of K it would become iita, and this might easily pass into itta, **just as arita** is always pronounced

Table Showing the Formation of the Past Tense of Affirmative Verbs.

Root.	Gerundive.	Components of the Past-Tense.	Resultant.
Deki, *to finish,*	Dekite,	Dekite—ari,	Dekita or Dekimash'ta.
De, *to issue,*	Dete,	Dete—ari,	Deta or Demash'ta.
Kikazari, *to dress well,*	Kikazate,	Kikazate—ari,	Kikazatta, or Kikazarimash'ta.
Nare, *to be accustomed,*	Narete,	Narete—ari,	Nareta, or Naremash'ta.
Narabe, *to put in order,*	Narabete,	Narabete—ari,	Narabeta, or Narabemash'ta.
Nari, *to sound,*	Natte,	Natte—ari,	Natta, or Naremash'ta.
Szngure, *to excel,*	Szngurete,	Szngurete—ari,	Szngureta, or Szngurenash'ta.
Szsznri, *to persuade,*	Szsznde,	Szsznde—ari,	Szsznda, or Szsznimash'ta.
Sashi, *to point to,*	Sash'te,	Sash'te—ari,	Sash'ta, or Sashimash'ta.
Sashiatari, *to be perimerd,*	Sashiatte,	Sashiatate—ari,	Sashiatatta, or Sashiatarimash'ta.
Noriwatari, *to transport by ship,*	Noriwatatte,	Noriwatatte—ari,	Noriwatatte, or Noriwatarimash'ta.
Nomikomi, *to swallow,*	Nomikonde,	Nomikonde—ari,	Nomikonda, or Nomikomimash'ta.
Mushiri, *to black,*	Mushitte,	Mushitte—ari,	Mushitta, or Mushimash'ta.
Imashime, *to prohibit,*	Imashimete,	Imashimete—ari,	Imashimeta, or Imashimemash'ta.
Horobi, *to go to,*	Horobite,	Horobite—ari,	Horobita, or Horobimash'ta.
Tsznori, *to increase,*	Tsznotte,	Tsznotte—ari,	Tsznotta, or Tsznorimash'ta.
Harai, *to scatter,*	Haratte,	Haratte—ari,	Haratta, or Harimash'ta.
Ke, *to kick,*	Kete,	Kete—ari,	Keta, or Kemash'ta.
Ori, *to break,*	Otte,	Otte—ari,	Otta, or Orimash'ta.
Taske, *to assist,*	Taskete,	Taskete—ari,	Tasketa, or Taskemash'ta.
Momi, *to shampoo,*	Monde,	Monde—ari,	Moda, or Momimash'ta.
Ikikaeri, *to revive, come to life,*	Ikikaette,	Ikikaette—ari,	Ikikaetta, or Ikikaemash'ta.
Ikikaeshi, *to resuscitate,*	Ikikaesh'te,	Ikikaesh'te—ari,	Ikikaesh'ta, or Ikikaeshimash'ta.
Nari, *to be, or become,*	Natte,	Natte—ari,	Natta, or Narimash'ta.
Shi, *to do,*	Sh'te,	Sh'te—ari,	Sh'ta, or Shimash'ta.
Soradamari, *to dissemble,*	Soradamatta,	Soradamatta—ari,	Soradamatta, or Soradamarimash'ta.
Sori, *to be warped or bent,*	Sotte,	Sotte—ari,	Sotta, or Sorimash'ta.
Tasshi, *to perfect.*	Tassh'te.	Tassh'te-ari,	Tassh'ta, or Tasshimash'ta.

atta. So also O oki nasaremash'ta is the polite way of saying what is just as fully expressed by oita=okita, *i. e.* has put. Tori nasaremash'ta is also equivalent to totta=torita, *i. e.* has taken away. See 945, "The doctor has bled (*i. e* has taken away blood from) him twice". Also in 1267, Watashi nasaremash'ta, have paid, is equivalent to watash'ta. Numerous examples of this kind will be noticed in the pages of this book.

Sec. IX. Past Continuative Form.

There is no single word that conveys the idea of an action **still** going on in past time, or the imperfect tense. But it is done by means of a gerundive followed by the verb I or Ori in the preterit tense. Thus Watak'shi wa sakujitsz hon wo yonde orimashta tokini, Sajiu uchi e mairimash'ta. "While I was reading a book yesterday, Sajiu came to the house". Here Yonde orimash'ta express exactly the sense of the imperfect tense Eng. *was reading*. The remark of M. Hoffman that the Japanese verb has no imperfect tense is therefore incorrect, unless he means to say that the Imperfect could not be expressed by one word.

The Gerundive, in this combination, is according to its true nature and office, a modal limitation of the preterit verb after it, showing in what state, condition, or operation the subject was or continued to be [orimash'ta] at some past time. The Gerundive therefore fills the place of the English present participle, like *drinking* in the phrase *was drinking*. Ori, root of Orimash'ta, or otta, is derived from I [丨 or 井] a place, or seat, a residence, and therefore signifies **to reside**, **to remain permanently**. Thus, the phrase Yedo ni szmatte oru or orimas', signifies, **He is** living at Yedo. Lit. **In** Yedo **dwelling** [he] resides= He lives in Yedo.

Examples of the Imperfect Tense.

Mite orimash'ta, *was seeing*.
Nonde orimash'ta, *was drinking*.
Kiite orimash'ta, *was hearing*.

Itte = Yunte orimash'ta, *was saying*.

Itte = Yuite orimash'ta, *was going*.
Tatte orimosh'ta, *was standing*.
Szwatte orimash'ta, *was sitting*.
Motte orimash'ta, *was taking or holding*.
Nite orimash'ta, *was lying down*.
Shimatte orimash'ta, *was finishing*.
Sh'te orimash'ta, *was going*.

Okite orimash'ta, *was getting up*.
Kite orimash'ta, *was dressing*.
Maitte orimash'ta, *was coming or going*.
Tszde orimash'ta, *was loading*. (as in a ship).
Angatte orimash'ta, *was ascending*.
Orite orimash'ta, *was descending*.
Totte orimash'ta, *was taking away*.
Hiroite orimash'ta, *was picking up*.
Dash'te orimash'ta *was taking out*.
Shimete orimash'ta, *was shutting*.
Kaite orimash'ta, *was writing*.

Sec. X. The Potential Form.

Uncertainty in the mind of the Speaker as to any fact transpiring in present time, which in English is expressed by the auxiliary *may* or *may be* is expressed in Japanese by the present indicative or attributive form of the verb, with the dubitative particle Ka after it followed by the appositive particle to (卜) and some verb signifying, to think, as dzongimas' or omoimas' *e g.* kita no hoŏ ni kuro ngumo nga atszmatte orimas' kara, Yedo no hoŏ wa ima ame nga f'tte orimas'ka to omoimas'. As black clouds are collected in the north, I think it *may be raining* at Yedo. Here f'tte orimas'ka expresses entire uncertainty in the speaker's mind whether it rains or not. If he said f'tte orimas' to omoimas', it would imply his decided opinion that it *did rain*.

The same with a little less of uncertainty might also be expressed by the future f'tte orimash'oŏ, without to omoimas'.

Uncertainty in regard to a past event is likewise expressed by the combination of a preterit, with the future of ari, and the termination of the tense is ta-aroŏ=taroŏ. Thus Sakujitsz o me ni kakattaroo signifies, He may have seen him yesterday. Sakuban ittaroŏ. He may have gone last evening. Washi (1) wa ushi [2] no shingai (3) wo Kanō-zan [4] e motte (5) ittaroŏ. The eagles (1) may have carried [5] the bullock's (2) carcase (3) to Kanozau, (4) Omai michi de komattaroŏ. You may have been in straits on the road [from not knowing the way or otherwise] The future potential denoting uncertainty, with a slight degree of expectation that the event referred to will take place, is expressed by the indicative future with the interrogative particle ka following it, together with to omoimas' or to dzonjimas'. If these last words are omitted, the future alone is sufficient, though it expresses more of certainty than the former. Mioŏ nichi fune ni norimash'oŏ ka to omoimas'. I may embark to-morrow. Mioŏ nichi fune ni norimash'oŏ, I shall probably embark to-morrow. The future in Japanese essentially denotes uncertainty, in as much as all events that have not yet transpired are regarded as contingencies that may or may not occur. Hence this tense is used as already stated, when the discourse relates to something in past time, if the speaker does not know whether it has taken place or not. A more strictly potential form of the verb, *viz:* one denoting ability to do, or the possibility of an action, is the same as that of passive verbs. Thus:—

Mieru	from Miru *to see*		may mean	*can see, or visible.*
Hanasareru	,, Hanasz *to speak,*	,,	,,	*can speak or utterable.*
Arukareru	,, Aruku *to walk,*	,,	,,	*can walk.*
Urareru	,, Uru *to sell,*	,,	,,	*can sell or saleable.*
Kawareru	,, Kau *to buy,*	,,	,,	*can buy or purchaseable.*

No explanation of this singular fact has been met with by the writer in works ancient or modern on Japanese grammar. There is no difficulty in seeing why the element E ye used for passive forms should be equally available in producing a potential form denoting ability to do, for e, eru, like its corresponding Chinese 得 [toku] signifies may or can, and is used in Chinese as frequently in this sense as in that of to get or to obtain.

It is not so easy to understand why the passive form made by are, and the potential should be the same; as for **example**, why uraréru or uraremas' should sometimes mean to be **sold**, and at others, to be able to sell. Kawareru or Kawaremas' **to be** bought, or at another time, to be able to buy. The following hypothesis may perhaps account for this identity of form, with difference of meaning. Are may be considered as the potential of ari, to be, produced as shown in this section above, by substituting e [得] for the terminal **vowel** I, after the manner of passive verbs of the first order. But e **means** can, as often as to get or receive. Hence from uru, to sell, we **have** by combination uru-are=urare, which may signify to be able to be selling, or can sell; but if, on the other hand, are be regarded as a passive from ari, to be, then urare will signify **to be sold**, and urare then will have a passive signification. Something in the context will often show which of these significations is to be given to a verb in this form. All verbs in this form derived from intransitive roots are potential in sense. To bear this in mind will save the student from much perplexity, in deciding whether he has before him a potential or a passive form. Thus in the sentence, Ano h'to wa yama e noborareru, He can ascend the mountain. Nobareru is seen to be intransitive, because the postposition e=to, or direction towards is required after the noun yama, the complement of the **verb**.

Sec. XI. The Disiderative Form of the Verb.

The Japanese has a mode of converting verbs into adjectives, expressing the desire to do what is signified by the verb. This is done by **affixing** the word tai or toō to a verbal root. Tai=taki by the elision **of** K, and toō=taku, the same elision taking **place**, and bringing the vowels A and U together, which a law of euphony **requires** to be pronounced oō Thus uri v.r. signifying to sell becomes uritoō, *i. e.* desirous to sell. Moōshi v.r. to speak, **becomes** moōshitoō, desirous to speak, nobose. v.r. to send up, becomes nobosetai or nobosetoō, desirous to send up, mi v.r. to see, becomes mitoō or mitai desirous to see; and so any verbal root may be made to assume this form, and **change** of sense. The form **in tai**, an adjective in the attributive form, **is** either conclusive **of** the sense, *i. e.* it is used as a **predicate verb, or is** used as an adjective before a noun. The form **in** toō, however, is but a verbal **predicate** adjective, and must have an equivalent to the verb "to be" expressed after it, on **the same prin**ciple that warui may **end a** proposition, **or** qualify a **noun; but** waruku=waruū used predicatively **must have a verb signifying** "to be" after it. See the section on adjectives. For examples of the **desiderative form of verbs, or desiderative verbal adjectives**, see Dialogue I. 1. O hanashi mooshitai koto nga aru. Lit. There is something of which **I wish to** speak, or of which it is desirable to speak. The phrase O hanashi-mooshitai being a compound attributive adjective belonging to the noun Koto. In Dialogue III. 1. O kiki mooshitoŏ gozarimas' **I wish to** consult, or I am desirous to consult, mooshitoŏ as a predicate adjective, takes the verb gozarimas' as **a copula after it.** Again, in Dialogue I. 22, "**Mihon nga** mitai" "I wish to see the musters,'. Mitai completes the **sense** as a predicate **verb. See also** Dialogue IV. 11. Uritoŏ gozarimas', where uritoŏ is **a predicate** adjective, and requires the copula gozarimas' after it. Besides this, verbs with **the affix** taku, taki, or tai, are conjugated in the indicate, conjunctive, concessive, and conditional modes, as will be seen hereafter. see Section. 22. Paradigm. V.

Sec. XII. Passive Form of Verbs.

The Japanese methods of forming passive verbs are peculiar; for while they are pa>sive in signification, they are still active in their forms of conjugation.

The element which **sometimes** serves to express the notion of passivity, is the regular **verb ye or** e (エ) Chinese 得 to get. The attributive form of e is eru, or yuru, its gerundive ete, and its preterit eta. Verbs formed by this as the passive element, signify to get, receive or appropriate to one's self, an action proceeding from without, which **action** is denoted by the verbal root to which e is affixed. Both in **form and** nature these are active verbs, for which in occidental languages, passive or reciprocal verbs **are** used. We need therefore only consider the derivation of passive **verbs, since their** conjugation is the same as that of active **verbs.**

There are three modes of derivation.

1. Passive verbs of the **first** order.

Irregular transitive verbs **may become passive** by substituting the **verbal** element e or **ye [エ] in place of the** terminal vowel I of the root.

Thus from Yomi act. v.r. *to read* we get Yomi pass. v.r. & Yomeru, *to be read*.
",, Ori act. v.r. *to break* ,, Ore, pass. v.r. & Oreru, *to be broken*.
,, Yaki act. v.r. *to burn* ,, Yako, pass. v.r. & Yakeru, *to be burned*.
,, Ts'kuri act. v.r. *to make* ,, Ts'kure, pass. v.r. & Ts'kureru, *to be made*.
,, **Ari** act. v.r. *to be* ,, Are, pass. v.r. attributive form not used.

These passive **verbs, and others** similarly formed, when used attributively as adjectives, frequently have the force of the **Latin** adjective in *bilis* or the English adjective ending in *ble*, **as** visible, legible &c. **Thus, Yomeru** hon wa, means a legible **book.** Yakeru pan wa, bakeable, bread, or bread that is in the process of baking. **Oreru** take wa, a bamboo that is bent, and is likely to break. See §. 10. on the potential form of verbs. For the use of Ts'kure, Tskuremas', See 60 p. 8. Ts'kuremas' tammono wa, made or manufactured cloths.

The simple root, is used with an adjective following it, precisely like the Latin supine in u. See e.g. 1 p. 1. toke yaszi, i.e. easy to be untied, where teke is the passive verbal root, from toki to untie, or disentangle.

2. Passive verbs of the second order.

Regular verbs which for the most part have monosyllabic roots, annex the passive element e (エ) to the root. Thus, Mi, root of the verb signifying to see, becomes Mie, Mieru, or Miemas', to be seen, or intransitively to appear. See 530. Watak'shi wa (as to my-self) kas'ka ni (in the distance) fune nga (the ship) miemas' (is seen, or is visible). From **ni (r.r.)** to boil, we have nie (r.r.) and nieru, or niemas' to be boiled, **or is** boiled. See the negative form of this **verb** in 1052.

In a few cases, the verbal root undergoes a strengthening **of its** final vowel, which is changed into **a or** o, and then e is added to form the passive verbal root. Thus kiki **(r.r.)** to hear becomes kikoe (r.r.) from which we have kikoeru and kikoemas to be heard, or intransitively to sound, e. g. ano tera no kane nga koko made kikoemas'. Lit. That temple's bell to this place is heard. Kikoemas' signifies, it gets a hearing, or it sounds, or it **can** be heard.

The word arayuru seems to be derived in this way from ari, to be, or to have existence. Ari is first changed to ara, and then yuru, one of the attributive forms of e [エ] is added to ara, making arayuru. This word is **in common** use, in this, its attributive form, as an adjective. Thus **arayuru** mono, signifies, The things that have existence. **i.e. all things, or** all the things [in a particular locality]. **Arayuru Hotoke, all** the Buddhas, Arayuru kami, all the gods, Arayuru h'to **all men.**

3. Passive verbs **of the third** order.

These are far the most numerous. Most transitive verbs form their passives by adding are the passive of ari "to be", to their active attributive forms, uniting the two according to **the principles of** Japanese etymology. If the active verb **is** irregular [See §.1] its attributive **form** ends in u, sz, or tsz, but if regular, it ends in **ru.** When therefore **u** comes before the passive element **are, u** being a less open vowel than a is suppressed before **it, and** instead **of** u-are, we have **are as** Yomu-Yomare. Tateru, **Taterare.** When the attributive form **active ends in sz** (su) or tsz [tsu], the combination becomes sare and tare, s or sz disappearing like u before the vowel a. Thus from utsz, to beat, we have utare to be beaten; and from korosz to kill, **we** have korosare, **to** be killed. The passive forms here given, it **must be remembered, are only the** passive verbal **roots.** The appropriate endings for the various tenses are to be annexed to them.

The v.r. *are* has no such attributive form as *areru* now in use, but we suppose it to exist, or to have been in use originally, and this hypothesis will be confirmed by the attributive passive forms in the following list of verbs,

ACTIVE ATTRIBUTIVE			PASSIVE ATTRIBUTIVE.
Hiku *to lead*,	add areru becomes		Hikareru *to be led*.
Motsz *to lift*,	,,	,,	Motareru *to be lifted*.
Umu or M'mu *to give birth*,	,,	,,	Umareru *to be born*.
Ou *to follow*,	,,	,,	Owareru *to be followed*.
Yobu *to summon*,	,,	,,	Yobareru *to be summoned*.
Yomu *to read*,	,,	,,	Yomareru *to be read*.
Akeru *to open*,	,,	,,	Akerareru *to be opened*.
Tateru *to erect*,	,,	,,	Taterareru *to be erected*.
Korosz *to kill*,	,,	,,	Korosareru *to be killed*.
Kau *to buy*,	,,	,,	Kawareru *to be bought*.
Tskuru *to make*,	,,	,,	Tskurareru *to be made*.
Nomu *to drink*,	,,	,,	Nomareru *to be drunk*.
Toru *to take away*,	,,	,,	Torareru *to be take away*.
Kuru *to bite*,	,,	,,	Kuwareru *to be bitten*.
Tsuru *to angle*,	,,	,,	Tsurareau *to be caught with hook & line*.
Tszreu *to accompany*	,,	,,	Tszrerareru *to be accompanied*.
Angeru *to promote*,	,,	,,	Angerareru *to be promoted*.
Otosz *to drop*,	,,	,,	Otosareru *to dropped*.
S'kuu *to rescue*,	,,	,,	Skurareru *to be rescued*.
Watasz *to transport*,	,,	,,	Watarareru *to be transported*.
Uru *to sell*,	,,	,,	Urareru *to be sold*.
Eru *to get*,	,,	,,	Erareru *to be gotten*.
Ushinau *to lose*,	,,	,,	Ushinawareru *to be lost*.

Of course none but transitive verbal roots can become passive. An intransitive verb may apparently assume a passive form, but in that case it is potential in sense. See. § 10.

Sec. XIII. NEGATIVE VERBS.

Theory of their Negative Element.

The Japanese language associates negation with the predicative verb. It denies that some action, situation, condition or quality is inherent in, or found in connection with the subject, but not the absolute existence of the subject. On this principle there are no such words as nobody, or nothing, nor are there any originally negative verbal roots. The power of attribution, or predication resides in the verbal element *i* root of the verb *iru*, the continuative *to be*, or in *shi*, root of *szru*, *to be* or *to do* Chinese 為. Now the negative element is *n*, seen in **nai** = is *not*. (compare the Latin non, ne, nec, and the English not, no &c) If then we prefix this negative element to the verbal root *i* we get *n-i* = *ni not to be*, a negative verbal root whose attributive or present indicative form is *nu* = *is not*.

In like manner from *shi*, by prefixing *n*, we get *n-shi*, and as *n* with *t* becomes *d*, so *n* with *sh'* becomes *dz'*, and *n-shi* becomes *dzi*, whose attributive form is dz [perhaps originally, dzn or du]. Neither dz nor *nu* is used separately but both are added to roots of affirmative verbs to make them negative, *Dz* is more commonly used in books of the higher style, and *nu* in the oral language. Still dz is **not** unfrequently met with in the spoken language. A common word is nokoradz, a negative from nokori, to except, or leave out. Nokoradz therefore signifies not excepting, without excepting.

Consonants are, so to speak, the bones-the skeleton of words; and vowels the more perishable parts, that are constantly undergoing changes. Hence in *na*—not, the vowel may be regarded as that part of the word which suffers change, while the *n* is the durable part of the syllable. Thus from naki or naku, the forms nōo and nōote are derived, in which everything but the initial letter *n* is lost. This mutation of vowel sounds is a very common phenomenon in most, if not all languages, and very noticeable in the Japanese.

Sec. XIV. Mode of Forming Negative Verbs.

Regular verbs attach *dz* or *nu* immediately to their roots (ending always in *e* or *i*. See §. I) or to the honorific appended verbal root *mase* in polite conversation, and thus is produced the negative attributive form.

Affirmative.			Negative.
Thus Ake.	v.r.	to open, becomes	Akenu or Akemasenu.
Se	v.r.	to do, ,,	Senu or Shimasenu.
Mi	v.r.	to see, ,,	Minu or Mimasenu.
Tate	v.r.	to set up, ,,	Tatenu or Tatemasenu.
Tabe	v.r.	to eat, ,,	Tabenu or Tabemasenu.
Ne	v.r.	to go to bed ,,	Nenu or Nemasenu.
Mise	v.r.	to show, ,,	Misenu or Mimasenu.
Hikae	v.r.	to restrain, ,,	Hikaenu or Hikaemasenu.
Nikume	v.r.	to incubate, ,,	Nikumenu or Nikumemasenu.
Nade	v.r.	to stroke, ..	Nadenu or Nademasenu.
Nadame	v.r.	to appease ,,	Nadamenu or Nadamemasenu.
Mite	v.r.	to be full, ,,	Mitenu or Mitemasenu.

It will be seen that the honorific affix *mase*, itself a verbal root, is affixed to the root form of the verb to which it is joined. This is the case with all verbs regular or irregular, active, passive, transitive or intransitive, so that by taking away mase, or mas', or maszru, or mashi or mash'te from any verb, the remaining part of the word must be its root.

In irregular verbs, in their simplest form, the final *i* of the root undergoes a strengthening and becomes *a* whence result the negative endings *adz* and *anu*. *Adz* is less used than *anu* in the colloquial. See § 1. paragraph 3, where this characteristic of **irregular verbs** is alluded to.

Table of Irregular Negative Verbs.

Affirmative.		Negative.
Kaki v.r. to write,	becomes	Kakanu or Kakimasenu
Tachi=Tati r.r. to stand	,,	Tatanu or Tachimasenu
Uchi=Uti r.r. to strike,	,,	Utanu or Uchimasenu
Ari v.r. to be,	,,	Aranu or Arimasenu
Nari v.r to be,	,,	Naranu or Narimasenu.
F'ki v.r. to blow,	,,	F'kanu or F'kimasenu.
Ougami v.r. to pray,	,,	Ougamanu or Ougamimasenu.
Nomi v.r. to drink.	,,	Nomanu or Nomimasenu.
Harae v.r. to pay,	,,	Harawanu or Haraimasenu
Okori v.r. to be excited,	,,	Okoranu or Okorimasenu.
Ougori v.r. to be proud,	,,	Ongoranu or Ongorimasenu.
Odori v.r. to dance,	,,	Odoranu or Odorimasenu.
Nuri v.r. to paint,	,,	Nuranu or Nurimasenu
Kaeri v.r. to return,	,,	Kaeranu or Kaerimasenu.
H'ki v.r. to lead,	,,	H'kanu or H'kimasenu.
Odoshi v.r. to intimidate,	,,	Odosanu or Odoshimasenu
Naki v.r. to cry,	,,	Nakanu or Nakimasenu.
Mawashi v.r. to cause to turn,	,,	Mawasanu or Mawashimasenu.
Hiroi v.r. to pick up,	,,	Hirowanu or Hiroimasenu.
Yurumi v.r. to loosen,	,,	Yurumanu or Yurumimasenu.
Hirumi v.r. to faint,	,,	Hirumanu or Hirumimasenu.''
Hodokoshi v.r. to attribute,	,,	Hodokosanu or Hodokoshimasenu.
Nengai v.r. to beg,	,,	Nengawanu or Nengaimasenu.
Tóokari v.r. to be far from,	,,	Toŏkaranu or Toŏkaradz.

Sec. XV. Negative Imperative Form.

The negative imperative is made by affixing the negative element *na* to the affirmative attributive. Thus, from

Szru, *to do*, we have, Szruna, *do not do*.
Tataku, *to strike* ,, Tatakuna, *do not strike*.
Nasaru, *to be doing* ,, Nasaruna, *do not be doing*.
Toru, *to take away* ,, Toruna, *do not take away*.

In polite conversation, instead of the short imperative form given above, Nasaruna, or Nasarimas'na is placed after a verbal root, and serves as a sort of auxiliary verb to that root which denotes the action forbidden. Thus, instead of Miruna, do not see, Mi nasaruna, or Mi nasaremas'na would be the better expression in addressing an equal or a superior. Tori nasaruna, would be said rather than the simple Toruna, do not take away.

Sec. XVI. The Negative Preterit Form.

The preterit form of regular negative verbs, is made by affixing *nanda* to the simple root, or to the same increased by the honorific affix *mashi* which is itself a verbal root. In common parlance *mase* is more frequently heard than *mashi*, but the latter is more correct and in better taste. If the verb is irregular the final *i* of the root, is changed to *a* (See Section I. Paragraph. 3).

Table of Negative Preterit Verbs.

From :—

Ts'ke, *reg. v.r. to apply*, we have, Ts'kenanda or Ts'kemashinanda.
Tobi, *irreg. v r. to fly*, „ „ Tobananda or Tobimashinanda.
Same, *reg. v.r. to cool*, „ „ Samenanda or Samashinanda.
Same, „ „ *to waken*, „ „ Samenanda or Samashinanda.
Mayoi, *irreg. v.r. to be at a loss*, „ „ Moyowananda or Mayoimashinanda
Yurushi, „ „ *to pardon*, „ „ Yurusananda or Yurushimashinanda.
De, *reg. v.r. to go out*, „ „ Denanda or Demashinanda.
Kuri *irreg. r.r. to overhaul as a rope.*, „ Kurunanda or Kurimashinanda.
Konomi, „ „ *to desire*. „ „ Konomananda or Konomimashinanda

The foregoing negative preterit form is less used in conversation than the following, in which *nakatta* is placed after the simple regular verbal root, or added to the irregular verbal root when its final *i* has been changed to *a*. Nakatta is itself a compound of naku, the adverb **not**, and atta, the preterit of the verb ari, to be, and hence nakatta signifies has not been or has not. It is therefore used as a negative auxiliary verb. Each of the verbs in the foregoing table may be put in the negative preterit form as follows:—

Ts'ki *reg. v.r. to apply*, and Ts'ki nakatta, *has not applied*.
Tobi *irreg v.r. to fly*, „ Tobinakatta, *has not flown*.
De *reg. v.r. to go or come out* „ Denakatta, *did not go or come out*.

Sec. XVII. Negative Future Forms.

Of these there are two. By the first method mai, is appended to the affirmative attributive form, if it contain no more syllables than the root of the verb, otherwise the excess is dropped before **mai**.

The affix mai is a negative verb signifying not to be, derived **from** maji (madzi) by the elision of j. Maji is given in the old dictionaries as a negative future ending without explanation. Mr. Hoffman maintains that it is compounded of ma space, and nasi not to be. But it would seems more readily derived from the combination of ma,–dzi (= n–shi). The meaning is the same whichever derivation be adopted, but the **etymology** here suggested is more direct, because the **sounds** represented by ji and **dz, are so** nearly identical as to be **easily** interchanged, and as dzi, signifies, not to be (See §. 13.) the theory of Mr. Hoffman respecting the regular ending **dz,** receives corroboration by the present hypothesis.

The second method of forming the negative future, **consists** in placing de **aroŏ after** the negative attributive form in **nu.**

De thus becomes a locative post-position giving a gerundive force to the form in nu, which precedes it. Thus "nomanu dearoŏ" would mean, he will not be in the act of drinking, or brielfly he will not drink. The future of Japanese verbs simply predicts, but never expresses determination as in English.

Future Forms in Mai.

Naru *to become,*	Narumai, *will not become.*
Narimas', ,,	Narimas'mai., ,, ,,
Aru, *to be,*	Arumai, *will not be.*
Arimas' ,,	Arimas'mai ,, ,, ,,
Miru, *to see,*	Mimai, *will not see.*
Mimas',	Mimas'mai, ,, ,,
Ttasz, *to accomplish,*	Ttaszmai, *will not accomplish.*
Ttashimas' ,,	Ttashimas'mai,,, ,, ,,
Kikoeru, *to be heard,*	Kikoemai, *will not be heard.*
Kikaemas', ,, ,,	Kikoemas'mai ,, ,, ,,
Katadzkeru. *to put aside*	Katadzkemai *will not put aside.*
Katadzkemas', ,, ,,	Katadzkemas'mai ,, ,, ,,
Katayoru, *to get aside*	Katayorumai, *will not get aside.*
Korobu, *to fall to ruin*	Korubumai, *will not fall to ruin*
Korobimas' ,, ,,	Korobimas'mai, ,, ,, ,,
Ochiru, *to fall down,*	Ochimai, *will not fall down,*
Ochimas' ,, ,,	Ochimas'mai ,, ,, ,,
Szru, *to do,*	Semai or Szmai *will not do*
Shimas', *to do,*	Shimas'mai, ,, ,, ,,
Arau, *to wash,*	Araumai, *will not wash.*
Arimas' ,, ,,	Araimas'mai, ,, ,, ,,
Wabiru, *to intercede,*	Wabirumai *will not intercede.*
Omou, *to think,*	Omoumai *will not think.*
Omoimas', ,,	Omoimas'mai,,, ,, ,,
Semitoru, *to take by conquest*	Semitorumai *will not take by conquest.*
Semitorimas' ,, ,, ,,	Semitorimas'mai ,, ,, ,,
Semeru, *to attack.*	Sememai *will not attack.*
Sememas',, ,,	Sememas'mai ,, ,, ,,
Semeiru, *to enter by force.*	Semeirumai *will not enter by force.*
Semeirimas' ,. ,, ,,	Semeririmas'mai ,, ,, ,,

On examining the foregoing list of verbs it will be seen that there is a difference among them in the mode of forming the negative future. **Thus** from aru, whose root is ari, also a dissyllable, we have aru-mai, or arimas'mai, for the future. The compound root of arimas' (arimaseru, アリマスル) is arimashi, consisting of four syllables. From miru, on the contrary, we get minai for the negative future, mai being appended immediately to the root mi, which is a monosyllable. So likewise from ochiru, kikoeru, and semeru we have the futures *Ochimai, kikoemai, and sememai, of which Ochi, kikoe and seme **are** the roots. It appears therefore that in every case, mai is preceeded by as many syllables as there are in the root of the verb, whether it be simple or compound. Hence we derive the following rule viz: mai is affixed to the attributive form of verbs, when that form has **no** more syllables than the root, but if it has more, the excess is dropped from the end of the attributive form, and then mai is added to produce the negative future. There appear to be a few anomalous verbs, in which the terminal vowel of the root, becomes e or o, in the negative future, the negative attributive, and the conjunctive forms. Thus, ki, the root of kuru, to come, instead of giving kimu in the negative attributive, becomes konu, not to come. The negative future is ko-mai, instead of ki-mai, and the negative conjunctive is koneba. Shi the root of szru, sz, to do, has for its negative attributive senu, for its negative future semai, and seneba for the negative conjunctive.

Sec. XVIII. Negative Gerundive.

In books, and in the colloquial language at Miako, a negative gerundive in *de* is much used, but not in Yedo and its vicinity. The gerundive of books is derived from the root of regular verbs, by adding de, and from the root of irregular verbs by first changing the terminal vowel I to A, and then annexing de. In the miako dialect the vowel I is inserted between the A and de, or in regular **verbs, an** I **is** inserted after the terminal I of the root before de. Thus from mi regular verbal root, to see, we have in the written language, mide, not seeing, and miide in the Miako dialect.

From tori, to take, irreg. *e.r*, we have torade, in books, and toraide not taking, at Miako. The latter form is frequently met with in books written in the colloquial style, or books for the common people.

At Yedo, however, instead of mide, not seeing, minaide, or midzni, is used. Instead of Torade, Toradz-ni or Toranaide is used. The phrases minai-to and toranai-to, are also used to the same intent, and signify by not seeing and by not taking.

---

*The remark of Rodriguez that the form *motome mai* is vicious, is incorrect. **The** future form *motomurumai* is wrong.

Sec. XIX. Negative Conjunctive Forms.

The negative conjunctive form for the present tense, like the affirmative, ends in *eba*. It is derived from the regular verbal root in *ni*, (See § 13. Paragraph second), which according to § 5. being irregular, changes the final I into E before ba (ni—wa) thus making eba. From nomi, irreg.v.r. to drink, we have noma before the negative element ni in its root form, making nomani irreg. neg. *v.r.* and then the final I is changed to E, and ba (ni—wa) is added thus forming nomaneba, meaning, when one does not drink, which may relate either to present or future time. *e.g.* Anoh'towa sakewo nomaneba, midaremasenu. When he does not drink saki, he does not make disturbance. In conversation we often hear, nomanuto or nomadzuiwa or nomanaito, as well as nomaneba all having the same meaning. See Dialogue III, p. 184 No. 6. Hakono uchi wo namari de haraimaseneba &c. When, or in case that you do not line the boxes with lead &c. Omae no sh'taku nga dekineba, yukaremasen', since you are not ready, I cannot go. Omae sh'taku nga dekineba, yukaremasen', as you are not ready, we cannot go. No (*ノ*) being omitted in the latter sentence makes the difference in the subject of yukaremasen. Dekineba, dekidzwa, and dekinakereba, may also be used with reference to a future time. Thus mioō nichi sh'taku nga dikineba, yukare mai. We might substitute dekidzwa, or dekinakereba for dekineba in the preceeding sentence without changing the sense. The form in eba may likewise refer to past time. Thus, sakunen kono shingotowo shimawaneba, konnen dzehi shimawoō. Since I did not finish this work last year I shall finish it this year at all events. The compound verb shimawa-nakatta, with kara (because or since) after it, would have the same signification as shimawaneba, so also, instead of dekineba, or dekidzwa, or dekinakereba, the expression dekinakattaraba (= deki-nakatta araba) may be used with the same meaning.

Sec. XX. Negative Conditional Form.

The negative conditional of books is not unfrequently made by placing wa after the negative gerundive of the written language as nomadewa, toradewa, mide wa. If one does not drink, or take, or see. The more common colloquial expression for the negative presuppositive or conditional, at Yedo, would be noma nakereba, tora nakereba, mi-nakereba, or nomanu naraba, toranu naraba, miru naraba, or nomimaseneba, torimaseneba, mimaseneba. See Dialogue II, p. 179, N. 7. Watak'shi wa kiu ni toiya e yarimaseneba, &c. If I do not immediately send some money to the wholesale dealers &c. See also 585. Kaishi nasuraneba. If you do not pay &c. kaisanu naraba or kaisanakereba would express the same

Naraba is the conditional form of nari, to be, derived from **naran**, future indicative, and ni–wa–ba, meaning, if it be.

Nakereba is the conditional form of the verb keri with the negative element na prefixed. Keri is never used alone, but is found in composition with other words, as keredomo, though it be, *i.e.* although it is difficult to decide what keri means; but in the colloquial of the present day, it appears to signify, to be. The **remark** of Rodriguez that it is used to denote past time, can hardly **be** sustained, either by the usage of Japanese writers or speakers.

Sec. XXI. NEGATIVE CONCESSIVE FORM.

This like the affirmative is made by **the affix tomo or domo**(トモ or ドモ) added to the negative r.r. after its final vowel I has been changed to E. *e.g.* mine domoshiru. Though I do not see (it), I know (it) kikane domo, shiru, Though I do not hear (it) I know (it). The form made by to iyedomo (トイヘドモ) is also used, in books. Thus kare kitaradz to iedomo, ware kokoroni kakedz, Though he does not **come,** I care not. The same colloquially would be expressed thus, ano h'to nga kimasenu to iutomo watak'shi kokoro ni kakenu.

Sec. XXII. PARADIGMS OF VERBS.

With the exception of the desiderative verb, all Japanese verbs are conjugated alike. Even the desiderative verb but slightly differs from others in this respect. Hence two paradigms might serve as examples for the student, but for the sake of convenience we shall furnish an examples of a substantive, an active, a passive, a causative, a desiderative, and a negative verb.

MODES.

This is confessedly **a** complicated subject, but **since grammarians,** even to this day, disagree in respect to the conjugation **of the English verb, it** need not be wondered at, if there should **be diversity of** opinion as to that of the Japanese. The reader will recollect **that** the language of this country, has as yet received but little **attention** from philologists, and no one can boast of more than a limited acquaintance with it.

All that the writer of these remarks can venture to say on the topic now under consideration, is that there appear to be seven modes belonging to the Japanese verb. *viz:* the indicative, the conjunctive, the concessive, the conditional, the potential, the imperative, and the participial under which last we include the infinitive, the participle **and** the gerund or gerundive. **Some grammarians, we** are aware, deny that the infinitive and participle are modes of the verb, conceiving them to be essentially devoid of all modality, but without stopping to discuss the question, it is believed that these distinctions will be intelligible, and the paradigms more useful with than without them.

TENSES.

The Japanese verb has three tenses, the present, past and future, together with a separate continuative form of each, in the indicative mode. The latter differ from the former three, just as in English, I am writing, I was writing, I shall be writing, differ respectively from, I write, I wrote, and I shall write.

PERSON AND NUMBER.

The distinction of three grammatical persons, which prevails in occidental languages, and is so strictly observed, that the verb must be associated with them by means of conjugative terminations, namely the distinction of the person speaking, spoken of, and spoken to, is altogether foreign to the Japanese. Hence the verb does not admit of endings to indicate them. The same is true of number.

When speaking of or to a person of quality, the honorific prefix *o* (御) is placed before the verb, or if it be the verb aru (to be), *go* (御) is prefixed, and the long form **gozarimas'**, or gozarimaszru, in full, is used. If the verb have an auxiliary, *o* is placed before the principal verb, and the auxiliary is *nasaru* or *nasareru* (to do) in some of its forms, as O yomi nasaremas'ka? Do you, or does he read? But this evidently bears no resemblance to grammatical person in verbs.

The folloing paradigms are intended to present the forms used in speaking, not those of books, except so far as they may happen to be the same in both.

PARADIGM I.
Principal parts.

Ari, *irreg.* **v.r.**   To be, or *exist.*
Aru, Arimaszru or gozarimas.   Attributive form, *is* or *to be* or *being*
Atta, Arimash'ta or gozarimash'ta. Past tense form, *was* or *has been*
Atte, Arimash'te or gozarimash'te, Gerundive form, *Being*

INDICATIVE MODE.

Pres. Aru, Arimas' or Gozarimas'
Past. Atta. Arimashta or Gozarimashta.
Fut. Aroö, Arimashoö or Gozarimashoö or like the present.

CONJUNCTIVE MODE.

Pres. Areba. Arimaszreba or Gozarimaszeba.
Past. Attareba, Aremash'tareba. Gozarimash'tareba.
Fut. like the present.

Concessive Mode.

Pres. Aredomo, Arimaszredomo, and sometimes Attemo.
Past. Attaredomo, Arimash'taredomo.
Fut. Aroō or Arimashoō, keredomo.

Conditional Mode.

1. *That of Uncertainty.*

Pres. Araba, Arunaraba, Arimasnaraba.
Past. Attaraba, or Attara, Attanaraba, or Arimash'taraba.
Fut. Like the present, or Arōo mononara.

2. *That of the assumed hypothesis contrary to the fact.*

Pres. Areba. Arimaszreba or Gozarimaszreba.
Past. Attaraba, Attara, Attanaraba, Arimash'taraba.
Fut. Not used.

Potential Mode.

1 *That of ability*, not used.

2 *That of uncertainty.*

Pres. Aruka, or Arimas'ka, with ト = to and オモウ = omo-ō or ゾンヂマス = dzonjimas' following, meaning, *to think.*
Past. Attaroōka or Arimash'taroōka, followed by omoō or dzonjimas',
Fut. Aroōka, or Arimash'oōka   "   "   "   "

Participial Mode.

*1. *The infinitive, not used.*

2. *The participle*, used attributively, Aru, Arimas, with **a noun**
3. *The gerundive*,   Atte, Arimash'te.   [following.

Note. **The verb ari** has not the continuative tenses of the indicative, and is otherwise defective. The imperative mode is not used

PARADIGM II.

Of the regular Active verb, Miru to see.

Principal Parts.

Mi. *v.r. to see.*
Miru, Mimas', O mi nasaru, Attributive **form** *to see* or *sees* or *seeing.*
Mita, Mimash'ta, or Omi nasareta. Past tense indicative *saw has seen.*
Mite, Mimash'te, or Omi nasarete, Gerundive form, *by seeing* or *seeing.*

---

* If there is a proper infinitive the author has not been able to discover it. Aru koto is not an infinitive mode of the verb, koto is a noun and aru a participial adjective. The phrase means, an existing act, thing or fact.

Indicative Mode.

Pres. Miru, Mimas, O mi nasaru, or Omi nasaremas'
Do. Con. Mite iru, Mite orimas, Mite oide nasaru.
Past. Mita, Mimash'ta, Omi nasareta, or nasaremash'ta.
Do. Con. Mite ita, Mite arimash'ta, or Mite oide nasaremash'ta.
Fut. Miyŏo, Mimashoŏ, **Miru** de arŏo, O mi nasaremashŏo.
Do. Con. **Mite iyoŏ, Mite** orimashoŏ, or **Mite oide nasaremashŏo.**

Conjunctive Mode.

Pres. Mireba, Mimaszreba, **or O mi** nasareba.
Past. Mitareba, Mimash'tareba, **or O** mi nasaretareba.
Fut. *Like the present.*

Concessive Mode.

Pres. **Miredomo,** Mimaszedomo, Mitemo, **or O mi nasaretemo,** or O mi nas'temo.
Past. **Mitaredomo,** Mimash'taredomo, **or O mi nas'taredomo.**
Fut. *Like the present.*

Conditional Mode.

1. *Of uncertainty, or mere presupposition.*

Pres. Mireba, Mimaszreba, **or O** mi nasareba *i. e. If you see.*
Past. Mitaraba, Mitanaraba, Mimash'tanaraba, O mi nasaretara.
Fut. *Like the present*, or **Miyŏo** mono nara.

2. *Of the* assumed *hypothesis contrary to the fact.*

Pres. **Mireba,** Mimaszreba, **O mi** nasareba *i. e. If I saw.*
Past. **Mitara, Mimash'tara, or O mi** nasaretara *i. e. If I had seen.*
Fut. *Wanting.*

Potential Mode.

1. *Of Ability.*

Pres. Mirareru, **Miraremas', Miru koto nga dekiru** O mi nasaru koto nga **dekiru.**
Past. Mirareta, **miraremash'ta, or** O mi nasaru kotonga dekimashta.
Fut. Mirareyoŏ, miraremash'oŏ, O mi nasaru kotonga dekimash'oŏ.

2. *Of uncertainty or* possibility.

Pres. Miruka, mimas'ka, or mite iruka, mite o ide nasaruka (to omou).
Past. Mitaka, mimash'taka, or o mi nasaremash'taka, **(to** omou).
Fut. Miyoŏka, mimash'oŏka, or miru de arooka (to **omou).**

Imperative Mode.

Miro, mi nasare, or mi nasai, o mi nasaremash'.

PARTICIPIAL MODE.

1. *The infinitive pres.* mi with ni = to, to express a purpose **as mi ni.**
   Do. Miru or mimaizru, used as a verbal noun *to see.*
   Do. Fut. Miyoŏ, or mimash'oŏ to szru, a proximate future.
2. *The participle,* Miru or mimaszru, used attributively, or with a postposition as miru ni wa, *on, or while seeing.* This may refer to past, present or future time.
3. *The gerundive,* Mite, nimash'te, or o mi nas'te, contraction for nasarete.

Note. With the postpositions, kara, yori or nochini, as mite kara or mite yori, it would mean after seeing, either in past or future time, Mite preceeding another verb would sustain **the** same relation to it, as **the** word *fighting* in the English sentence *He died fighting* does **to the** verb died *i.e.* purely a gerundive relation.

PARADIGM III.

Of a Passive Verb. Korosare *v.r. to be* **killed.**

Principal parts.
- Korosare, *v.r.* Koroshi–are, the passive **element.**
- Korosareru, Attributive form, *is killed.*
- Korosareta, Past tense Indicative, *was or has been* **killed.**
- Korosarete, Gerundive, *by being killed, or being* **killed.**

INDICATIVE MODE.

Pres. Korosareru, Korosaremaszru, or Korosaremas'.
Do. Con. Korosarete iru or orimas = *He is in the state of one killed.*
Past. Korosareta Korosaremash'ta = *He was or has been killed.*
Do. Con. Korosarete ita or orimash'ta = *He was in the state of one killed.*
Fut. Korosareyoŏ or Korosareraidearoŏ = *He will be killed.*

CONJUNCTIVE MODE.

Pres. Korosarereba, *Since he is killed.*
Past. Korosaretareba, Korosaretara.
Fut. *Like the present.*

CONCESSIVE MODE.

Pres. Korosaruredomo or Korosaretemo.
Past. Korosaretaredomo, Korosareta, keredomo.
Fut. *Like the present.* **or** Korosareyoŏ keredomo **Korosareru de aroŏ** Keredomo.

CONDITIONAL MODE.

Pres. Korosarereba or Korosarareba, Korosareru nara.
Past. Korosaretaraba or korosaretara.   [nara.
Fut. *Like the present,* or Korosareyoo nara or Karosareru de aroo

POTENTIAL MODE.

1. **Of** Ability.

Pres. Koroseru, korosemas'.
Past. Koroseta, korosemash'ta.
Fut. Koroseyoŏ, korosemash'oŏ **or** Koroseru de aroŏ.

2. Of *Uncertainty*.

Pres. Korosarete iru or imaska or orimas'ka (to omou) or korosareruka (to omou)
Past. Korosare taroōka, korosarete arimashoo ka.
Fut. Korosareyoōka, Korosareru de aroōka.

IMPERATIVE MODE.
Wanting in the colloquial, in books korosareyo

PARTICIPIAL MODE.

1. *Infinitive*, ni, denoting the object or purpose,
2. *Participle*, as an attributive, followed by a noun, or taking, an object after it, or governed by a postposition.

Pres. Korosareru, **Korosaremaszru.**
Past. Korosareta, **Korosaremash'ta,** used attributively.
Fut. Korosareyoō-to szru, Do.

3. *Gerundive*. Korosarete Korosamash'te.

PARADIGM IV.

The *Causative verb* Miseru, *to show, or cause to see.* Derived from mi *to see*, and se, root of the verb szru *to do or cause*.

Principal Parts.
- Mise, *v.r. to show*.
- Miseru, attributive form, *showing, shows or to show*.
- Miseta, past tense indicative, *showed or has shown*.
- Mite, gerundive, *by showing or showing*.

INDICATIVE MODE.
Pres. **Miseru,** misemas'zru, or misemas'.
Do. Con. Misete iru or misete orimas',
Past. Miseta. Misemashta, o mise nasaremash'ta.
Do. Con. **Misete** ita or orimashta, misete oide nasaremash'ta.
Fut. **Miseyoō, Misemash'oō,** o mise nasaremashoō.
Do. Con. **Misete iyoō, misete** orimash'oō, misete oide nasaremash'oō,

CONJUNCTIVE MODE.
Pres. Misereba Misemaszreba, o **mise nasareba.**
Past. Misatareba, Misemash'tareba, **o mise** nasaretareba.
Fut. *Like the present.*

CONCESSIVE MODE.
Pres. { Miseredomo, o mise **nasaretemo, or O mise** nasattemo.
        { Misetemo, misemash'temo.
Past. Misetaredomo. **O mise** nasaretaredomo.
Fut. Miseyoō **keredomo, Omise** moōsoō **to** szredomo.

CONDITIONAL MODE.
Pres. **Misereba,** Miseru nara or naraba, misetara = Misete araba.
Past. **Misetaraba,** Misetanaraba, Misemash'ta naraba.
Fut. **Miserunara,** miserataraba, miseru naraba or miseyoō mononara.

POTENTIAL MODE
1. *Of Ability.*

Pres. Miserareru, miserаremas', miserukoto nga dekiru.
Past. Miserareta, Miseraremash'ta.
Fut. Misereyoŏ, Miseraremash'oŏ.

2. *Of Uncertainty.*

Pres. Misete iru ka, or orimas'ka (to omou).
Past. Misetaroŏ, or Misete arimash'oŏ, with ka following & (to omou).
Fut. Miseyoŏka or Misemash'oŏka (to omou).

IMPERATIVE MODE.

Misero, Mise nasai, Mise nasare, O mise nasaremash'.

PARTICIPIAL MODE.

1. *The infinitive* to express a purpose, Mise ni.
2. *The participle,* used attributively, Miseru Misemaszru.
   Do. with a postposition, as Miseruniwa, *on seeing.*
   Do. past, Miseta, Misemash'ta, used attributively.
   Do. fut. Miseyoŏ to szru. „   „   „
3. *The gerundive.* Misete, Misemash'te or o mise nasarete, **or o mise nas'te.**

PARADIGM V.

Desiderative *verb,* Mitai, *to be desirous to see.*

Principal parts.
{ Mitaku, root **form.** — Mi *v.r.* **taku.**
Mitai, attributive or predicate **form, pres.** indicative.
Mitakatta, Past **tense** indicative.
Mitakute, Gerundive form, also, Mitoŏte.

INDICATIVE MODE.

Pres. Mitai, or Mitoo gozarimas'.
Do. Con. Mitakute iru, or Mitoŏte iru.
Past. Mitakatta, Mitoŏ atta, **or** Mitoŏ gozarimash'ta.
Do. Mitaku omoote ita, or orimash'ta.
Fut. *Like the present.*

CONJUNCTIVE MODE.

Pres. Mitai ni,
Past. Mitakatta **ni.**
Fut. *Wanting.*

CONCESSIVE MODE.

Pres. Mitai keredomo, Mitaku temo.
Past. Mitakatta keredomo.
Fut. **Like** *the present,* **also,** Mitaku wa aredomo.

Conditional Mode.

Pres. Mitakuba, Mitai, naraba, Mitakereba,
Past. Mitakatta naraba.
Fut.   Like the present.

Potential of Uncertainty.

Pres. Mitakaroŏ. (*He may wish to see*).
Past. Mitakattaroŏ (*He may have wished to see*).

Participial Mode.

1. *Infinitive,* Wanting.
2. *Participle,* used attributively Pres. Mitai, Past, Mitakatta.
3. *Gerundive,* Mitakute, or Mi'toote.

Note. Any Active verb may be made a desiderative one by the affix tai.

To express regret at not having done something, or to say what one would have done, under a certain condition, that did not exist, there is a singular pharse in common use, made up of a verb in the future or past indicative and the words mono wo *e.g. If I had seen it, I would have bought it,* Watak'shi wa mitara, katta mono wo, or kawoŏ mono wo. Again, *If his father had been alive, things would not have come to this pass.* Moshi chichi nga itara, koŏ wa naru maimono wo, or *If his father were alive, he would put things to rights again.* Moshisoni chichi nga itara, mata tate naosz koto mo aroo monŏ wo. This, if it can be called a mode of the verbs, is the true subjunctive, to be always employed in the apodosis of a sentence whose protasis contains a verb in the conditional mode of the assumed antithesis.

PARADIGM VI.

Negative Verb, Kakanu, *writes not or does not write.*
Derivation, Kaki. *irreg. v.r.* affirmative,–nu. See. § 13.

Kakani, *v.r.* not used separately.
Kakanu, attributive and predicate form, *writes not.*
Kakananda or Kakimasenanda *did not write or has not written.*
Kakanaide, **Kakadzni,** at Miako kakaide Gerundive, *not writing.*

Indicative Mode.

Pres. Kakanu, Kakimasenu, Kakanai.
Do. Con. Kakadzni, iru or orimas' Kakanai de iru.
Past. Kakananda, Kakimasenanda, Kakanakatta.
Do. Con. Kakadzniita, or orimash'ta Kakanaide ita.
Fut.   Kaku mai Kakimas'mai Kaki wa shimai.
Do. Con. Kakadzniyoŏ or orimashoŏ, when a person is the subject, and kakadzni aroo, or kakadzni aru dearoa, or kakanaide aroŏ, when the subject is a thing.

Conjunctive Mode.

Pres. Kakaneba, Kakimaseneba, Kakanu kara, kakanai kara.
Past. Kakadzareba Kakanakatta kara kakanakereba.
Fut. Kaku mai kara, Kakimasmai kara kakiwashimai kara.

Concessive Mode.

Pres. { Kakaredomo, Kakimasenedomo.
{ Kakadztomo Kakanutomo.
Past. { Kakanandaredomo, Kakimasenandaredomo.
{ Kakanakattaredomo.
Fut. Kakumai keredomo, Kakiwashimai keredomo.

Conditional Mode.

Pres. { Kakaneba, kakanu nara or naraba.
{ Kakanai naraba, kakanakereba
Past. { Kakanandareba, Kakanakereba.
{ Kakanakattareba, Kakanakatta **naraba**.
Fut. *Like the present.*

Potential Mode.

1 *Of Ability.*

Pres. { Kakenu or Kakienu Kakemasenu,
{ Kaku koto dekimasenu Kakenai.
Past. { Kakenanda, kakemasenanda,
{ Kakenakatta Kakienakatta.
Fut. { Kakimai or Kakiemai Kakinakaroŏ
{ Kakemas'mai, or kakiemas'mai.

2 *Of Uncertainty.*

Pres. { Kakanaika or kakanuka, kakanaideiru ko?
{ Kakadz ni iru (to omou).
Past. { Kakanandaroŏ kakanakatta de aroŏ,
{ Kakanai de arimashoŏ.
Fut. Kakumaika Kakimas'maika (to omou, following.)

Imperative Mode.

Kakuna. Kakimas'na.

Participial Mode.

1 *Infinative,* Wanting.

2 *Participle.*

Pres & Fut.. Kakanu, used attributively.
Past. Kakananda.

3 *Gerundive.*

Kakaushidz. kakadzni, and at Miako, kakaide.

REMARKS ON THE PARADIGMS.

1. They are intended chiefly to present the conjugative forms derived from the verbal roots, as their base. The periphrases by which modes may be indicated, are idioms belonging rather to the province of the lexicographer, than that of the grammarian.

2. The conditional mode is usually characterized by the word moshi (Chin. 若), *i. e.* if, or granting that, preceding it, and when both the conditional and conjunctive forms are the same, which must always be the case, in regular verbs in E, (See §.§. 5 and 6,) this presuppositive particle distinguishes the one from the other.

3. The author is of the opinion that the so called infinitives of the old Portuguese grammarians, (such as, miru koto, *to see*, and mita koto, *to have seen*,) are not proper infinitives. They are substantive phrases, composed of the noun koto, and a verb modifying it. See. 203. Koto e kuru koto wo iyangarimas', Lit. He refuses the act of (Kuru) coming. *i. e.* He will not come. See also 941. Aratameru koto wo itashimasenu. Here aratameru koto wo, is a phrase constituting the direct object of the transitive verb itashimasenu, or seru. In 144, musaboritoni koto wa, *i. e.* Extortion, or the act of taking away wrongfully, is the subject of the sentence. Although these and similar expressions might be best rendered in English, by infinitives, yet this is not their office in the Japanese construction. For a proper infinite governing a direct object, and at the same time being subject of a proposition, see, 145. Karada wo ungokazs wa &c. Lit. To exercise the body, or to bestir the body, &c.

Rodriquez and Collado also give the form miru to, as the infinitive, but this is even more objectionable than those in koto, because *to* (ト) in this position, is a conjunction, most frequently equivalent to the English conjunction *that*.

Besides the infinitive given in the paradigms, expressing a purpose (as mi ni, *to see*,) there is a phrase composed of a verb in the attributive form, followed by the noun *tame*, a purpose; and the postposition ni signifying *for*, which often answers to our infinitive. See. 1208. Dare nga tetsz wo *uru tame ni* motte iru ka? Uru tame ni, here rendered *for sale*, when analyzed, is, ni═for, dame═ the purpose of, Uru═*selling*, *old English*, *for to sell*. Uru is a verb in the attributive form qualifying the noun tame, which, again, is governed by the postposition ni.

The subject infinitive in English, is often expressed in Japanese by the gerundive with wa or by the conjunctive mode. *e.g.* Yubi wo k'tte wa [or kireba] itoö gozarimas To cut ones finger is painful. The literal signification of K'tte wa, and kireba, when one cuts. Watak'shi yori sh'ta no h'to wo utte wa [or Uteba], iyashii waza de aroö. It would be a mean act to strike a man inferior to myself. Here Uttewa, and Uteba, mean *were I to strike*, *should I strike* **or** *to strike*. But though in a free translation, these verbs would be put in the English infinitive, yet in the Japanese they are by no means infinitives. The literal rendering of the first example would be, *When I eat* [conjunctive mode] *my finger it is painful*, and the second would be literally, *when I strike* [conjunctive] *a man inferior to myself, it will be a mean act*.

Utszwa, the form given in the paradigms for the infinitive as an abstract noun, might be inserted in the above sentence, **and** then to render it literally, *to strike*, would be correct.

4 The participles mirn h'to, mirn mono, and mita h'to, mita mono, of Rodriquez and Collado are rejected for reasons similar to those which have been given for setting aside their so called infinitives in *to* and *koto*. When we come to speak of the mode of constructing relative propositions, the nature of these expressons will appear.

Sec. XXIII, Nouns.

Japanese nouns are indeclinable. Being without inflections, their relations to other words are indicated either by position or by postpositions such as ni, e or ye, no, kara, yori, de, &c. or by what we call constructive particles, as wa (ハ) nga (ガ) and wo (ヲ). Wa, which is merely an isolative particle, serving to separate a word or clause, from the words that follow it, is not a sign of the nominative, though it frequently stands between the subject and its predicate. As a proof that, it is not a case sign, we may refer to an instance **in** which it is superadded even to wo, which marks the direct object of a verb. See 724. Kataki ni szru mono wo ba, anata kore wo kawaingare, &c; The first phrase ending with woba is equivalent to enemies **and** literally rendered it would be, as to enemies, love ye these, **&c.** Ba = wa with the ningori (バ) separates the words before it from those following it, as a substantive phrase, in apposition with the pronoun sore wo which is the direct object of the verb kawaingare, to love. Wa is a sort of vinculum around a collection of words which here is the direct object of a verb, and serves to give definiteness to this group of words, distinguishing it from the other elements of the proposition. Sec. 754. Mina warui koto no uchi **de** wa, *Of all bad things* &c. This particle is not generally translateable, but may, to express its force, be sometimes rendered *as to*, *In regard to*, Latin quoad, French quant à. Nga or ga (ガ) is used for the same purpose, except that it seems to be more emphatically definitive. See 3. Ichidora nga *i.e. a dollar precisely*. The difference between wa and nga is scarcely translateable, but is to be expressed by the tone of the speaker's voice, rather than by any corresponding words **in** English. The native ear at once percives the difference, and a foreigner can acquire the use of these particles, only by practice and much familiarity with the Japanese usage. The native teachers say that wa is a kind of cordon drawn around a word or words, as if to isolate it or them, as a distinct subject of thought, and that nga is used when one or more objects are singled out being present or conceived to be present, spoken of specifically. Thus, if a Japanese should say of a certain lot of teas in Yĕdo, *Here are the musters*, his expression for *the musters*, would be, Mihon wa, *i. e. the musters*, as separated from the original packages, but, if a buyer taking one of the samples should say he liked it, his expression would be Kono *mihon nga* ki ni irimas'. The idea would then be, that that particular sample suited him. See Dialogue I Nat. 6, and For. 9. where these expressions are used.

The attributive (possessive or genitive) relation is denoted by the postposition no (ノ,) for which the Chinese equivalent is 之, See 2. Akangane no deru to koro wa, Lit.=Copper's issuing place *i. e.* the place whence it comes. Nga (ガ) is used for the same purpose, after either nouns or pronouns. See 735. watak'shi nga kimono. *My clothes*, the same as watak'shi no kimono. Examples of this use of no and nga are too numerous to require further references.

Whenever wo [ヲ] is used it is placed after the direct object of a verb. A verb, therefore, with such a complement may be known to be transitive. But it must not be supposed that a transitive verb, or one that would be transitive in English, always takes wo as the index of its direct object. On the contrary, it sometimes takes wa, sometimes woba=wo wa, sometimes nga and sometimes neither, after its direct regimen, See 970. Are no szru koto wa mireba, or Ano h'to no okonai wa mireba, &c. Here, szru koto wa, and okonai wa, both meaning conduct, are the direct objects of mireba Lit. *when I see*, The verb miru, *to see*, usually governs its direct regimen, with wo. Nga likewise may follow the direct regimen of a verb. See 456. Washi wa sono ri nga wakaranu. I cannot understand the rationale of that It is abundantly evident, then that wa and nga are not essentially case signs. Wo only, is, when used, invariably the sign of the complement of a transitive verb. But even this may be replaced by wa, or, nga, or all the three omitted.

The other relations of nouns, are expressed by words which we call postpositions, answering to our prepositions, See § 28.

NUMBER.

The noun is the same in form for both the singular and plural. When, however, it is desired to express the plural number, the noun is sometimes repeated, as H'to, *a man* H'to-bito, *men* Iro, *a sort* Iro-iro, *sorts* Shina, *an article*, Shina-jina *articles*, Shima, *an island*, Shima jima *islands* Kuni, **a** *country*, Kuni nguni. *countries*. This doubling of the word, signifies more than mere plurality, for it carries with it the idea of multitude, and sometimes of universality. Thus, Kuniguni means *all countries*, and Iro-iro, *many kinds*. Besides this method of making plurals, there are certain words appended to nouns and pronouns, to denote plurality. Such are ra (ラ,) Chinese 等, signifying a class, or kind, Domo (ドモ,) Chinese 共 together, collectively; tachi [タチ,] Chinese 達, all over every; ngata — kata, (ガタ,) Chinese 方, side or region; shiu (シウ,) Chinese 衆 a sign of the plural, and nado.

Examples.

SINGULAR	PLURAL
Yakunin, *an officer of government.*	Yakunin-tachi, *officers.*
H'yak'sh'o, *a farmer*,	H'yak'sh'o ra, *farmers.*
Ko, *a child*,	Ko-domo, *children.*
Neko, **a** *cat*,	Neko-domo *cats.*
Kerai. *a retainer.*	Kerai-domo, *retainers.*
Daimio, *a noble,*	Daimio-ngata, *nobles.*
Tonosama, *a feudal lord*,	Tonosoma-ngata, *lords.*
Onango, *a woman*,	Onango-shiu, *women.*

The word rui, (Chinese 類.) meaning a kind or species is frequently attached to names of inanimate objects, to denote plurality. Thus on the sign-board of a paper dealer, we often see "Kami rui shina-jina", "*All sorts of paper*". A noun already made plural by domo sometimes receives ra in addition, as kodomo-ra, *children*. This word at least, is often **so** used.

The plural signs, **are not** used indiscriminately, **but** varied according to the degree of respect **with** which the persons addressed, **or** spoken of, are regarded. Beginning with that which denotes the least degree, they may be arranged in the following order of ascent to the highest 1. Domo, 2. Ra, 3 Tachi, 4 Shiu, 5 Ngata. Rui, applied to names of things or persons, and Nado, which is used in the same way, seem to be devoid of any such distinction.

GENDER

Nouns in this language are essentially without **gender.** When it is necessary to indicate sex, the prefixes O for the **male, and** Me for **the** female are put before the noun; as Ushi, *a* **beef,** Oushi, *a bull*, and Meushi *a cow*, Tori, **a** *fowl*, Ondori = O-no-tori, *a cock,* Men dori = me-no-tori, *a hen.*

Sec. XXIV. PRONOUNS.

The Japanese like the Chinese language, delights **in the** use of nouns and adjectives of quality, as personal pronouns.

The emperor, for the pronoun of the first **person, uses** (朕) **Shin,**
which may signify, subtle, recondite. The **Taikun, or** any nobleman of high rank, would use Yo. (余 or 予) when addressing **inferiors, and** Watak'shi if speaking to a superior. **To a friend** they
would say Sessh'a(拙者) meaning I. Officers of government would
use Sessh'a and watak'shi, in like circumstances. **Washi is** use by
persons of inferior station, when speaking to those under **them. The**
meaning of Watak'shi, is still uncertain. It is the word most generally
used for the first person. Washi and Ore are used by the common
people for **I.**

For the **second person,** the emperor is addressed by the courtiers,
with Shin, meaning your majesty. Addressing his attendants, the
emperor uses Nanji, which is derived by contraction from na-mochi,
having a name, or illustrious. **The** Taikun in addressing high daimos
such as the Sankio, **for the** pronoun **of** the second person says
Kikoō which is merely the Chinese 貴公, Honorable Lord, English,
My Lord. To most of the princes, inferior to the Sankio, he would
say Sono-koō. Lit. that side, or quarter. The servants of a daimio,
addressing their liege lord, would say Watak'shi, **for I, und** Kimi,
Lord, or Gozen, Your presence, **or** Tonosama, for you. **To a friend**
or superior the usual address **is** Anata, for the pronoun **of the** second
person. Damios' retainers **and officers** of Government **(yakunins)** use
the same term, in speaking **to those** of their **own class,** but if speaking
to an inferior, *temai* is the pronoun used. **Temae signifies,** "before
(my) hand", Omae' which is **of the** same **import of Gozen, is used**
among **the** common people when addressing **each other, especially, at**
entertainments, where the wine flows freely. **It is also used as a**
pronoun of less respectful import than **Anata.**

The personal pronouns most commonly heard, are **Watak'shi, Washi,**
and Ore, for the **first** person, Anata, Sonohoō, Omae and **Temae, for**
the second, and Ano **o kata,** Ano-kata, Ano h'to or Are wa, for **the**
third. Sama is **often added to** those for the second person, and **in**
the vulgar dialect **is contracted into san as** Omae san, Anata san.

Politeness of address has **been so long** and carefully studied among
the Japanese, that they **are very careful to** select the proper terms,
in conversation, and nothing **is** more offensive to their taste, or more
significant of bad breeding than carelessness, or neglect in **this** matter.

Pronouns Properly so Called

Most of these are derived from primitive **adverbs of** place. The
following **is a list of** these adverbial roots.

1. Wa (ワ), **which** denotes the central point of space, the conceived
position **of the person** speaking, or the place of the **I or** me.

2. A (ア), somewhere else, a place less definitely marked **than wa.**

3. **Ka** (力), a place definitely determined, & at some distance—*there*.
4. Ko (ヱ), a place near at hand, and determined,—here.
5. Yo (ヨ), a place exterior to another—yonder. [there.
6. So (ソ), a place already referred to, or conceived of as such—
7. Da or Do, interrogative elements, *where?* Compare **ich** in *who? which? what? whence?* and *qu* in the Lat. *quis? quo? quere?*

These adverbs of place, in composition with **other** words **from** pronouns, and pronominal adjectives. Pronouns **are so** formed by adding *re* (レ) to the adverbial root, with two or **three** exceptions, *Re* is the last syllable of *are*, to be from *ari*, *e. r.* the final vowel being strengthened into *e*. The pronominal adjectives are made by adding *no* or *nga* to these adverbial roots. Thus we have Ware, in **books**, signifying I, and Wanga, my. Wutak'shi, and Washi in the colloquial used for the pronoun of the first person, are probably derived from the same root *wa*.

From A, Are, *He, she* or *that*, and Ano, pronl. adj. *that.*
" Ka, Kare, *He,* or *she* or *that,* and Kano, " " *that.*
" Ka, Kore, *This* and Kono, " " *this.*
" So, Sore, *That* and Sono, " " *that.*
" Da, Dare, *Who?* and Dareno, " " *Whose?*
" Do, Dore, *Which?* **and** Dono, " " *Which?*

The word Donata, *Who?* **is derived from Dono** and **Kata.** Lit. *which side?*

Nani or Nan, (Chinese 何,) is an interrogative pronoun, meaning *what*. Used attributively, it is Namo, *what?* Idzre also is **a common** word for *which?* and Idzreno, the attributive form of the same, as Idzre no h'to, *which man?*

REFLEXIVE PRONOUNS.

Mi, (Chinese 身) the body, or person, is a noun much used where in English a reflexive pronoun would be employed, and is either of the first, second, or third person. See 21. From Mi, is derived Midz kara [= mi-no-kara] Chinese 自 which signifies, of one's self *i. e.* one's self personally. Onore is a reflexive pronoun derived from Ono each and ore I, and hence signifies, one's self individually. From Ono, or perhaps from Onore, is derived Onodzkara, and signifies, from or by **one's** self individually. The following Chinese reexive pronouns are also in common use. **Ji.** [自] and Jishin [自身] both signify one's self. Ji man no h'to, **is** "*a man who prides himself*", Jishin no koto, an affair belonging to one's **self.** Jibun, [自分] is also **used in** the same sense as Jishin.

RECIPROCAL PRONOUNS.

There seem **to be no proper** reciprocal pronouns Reciprocity of action is expressed either by adverbs, or by *ai*, root of the verb isgnifying to meet, used as the first part of a compound verb, which si thus made to express an action and its mutual character.

The adverbs most commonly used for this purpose are, Tangaini, or Aitangai ni, Soŏ hoŏ [雙方] and Rioŏhoŏ, [兩方], The last two literally mean both sides or two sides. *Ai* is an element of very many compound words, conveying the idea of reciprocity or mutual participation, as, Aishiru, *to know each other*, Aiszszmeru, *to counsel each other*, Aideshi, *a fellow pupil*, Aikotoba, *a pass-word i. e.* one to be given to each other, and Aikuchi, *mutual assent*.

RELATIVE PRONOUNS.

These are also wanting in the Japanese language. The office of the relative pronoun is to connect an adjective proposition with the leading one. Compare the English sentence, *The prudent man looks to the future*, with *The man, who is prudent, looks to the future*. In the latter, the adjective proposition, *who is prudent*, is developed from the verbal adjective *prudent*, and by means of the relative pronoun *who* as a connecting word, it occupies, the place of that adjective in the first sentence. The genius of the Japanese language, as it has no relative pronouns, makes it necessary that a sentence of that description, should assume the construction in which the adjective is used attributively before its noun. Hence *The man who comes*, would be expressed, in Japanese, by the words Kuru h'to wa, and *The man who came*, by k'ta, or kimash'ta h'to wa. A verb is thus used attributively with a noun, which in English, would be the antecedent of a relative pronoun the subject of that verb.

The noun tokoro, precisely like the Chinese, 所 the place, or the place where, is also used as a substitute for the relative pronoun Thus, *the act of doing*, is szru koto, the person *who does*, szru h'to, and *that which a man does*, is h'to noszru to koro. Tokoro in this use of it, may be in any of the relations (cases) that a noun sustains and therefore in the analysis of a sentence containing it, it may have case signs, like any other noun, and yet when rendered into English, it will be converted into the compound relative pronoun, *that or those, which* or *what*, or the simple relative *which*, Watak'shi no shireru tokoro de gozarimas', *It is what I know*. Inishie yori mochiiru tokoro no nen-ngo de gozarimas. They [certain Chinese characters] are the year-names used from ancient times. Mochiiru to korono=those which were used. See Dialogue, II. 30 p. 183 "Omai no iu tokoro wa &c. *what you say &c.*

Sec. XXV ADJECTIVES.

Adjectives of Japanese origin, have one of two forms, when used attributively, or before a noun, *viz*, that ending in ki (キ) or that in ua [ナ].

Na, is the first syllable of the word, naru, *to be*, and according to M. Hoffman, the radical vowel of ki, *riz, i*, is the verb, *to be*. Analogy would favor this conclusion, for as na, and ki have the same office, and produce the same effect, they should have in themselves the same meaning. Besides, the predicative use of the adjective ending **in** ki, as we shall see below, strongly corroborates M. Hoffman's view.

These endings ki and na are affixed to the radical form of the adjective, as Nanga, *r* Nangaki—Nangai, *long*. Yawaraka, *r*. Yawarakana, *soft*.

The two terminations are not, however generally interchangeable. Some adjectives take one, and some the other. Usage, and a **good** dictionary will decide which is proper.

Examples of Adjectives.

Taka,	root.	Takaki,	or	Takai,	[by elision of k.]		*High*.
Samu,	„	Samuki,	or	Samui,	„	„	*Cold*.
Atsz,	„	Atszki,	or	Atszi,	„	„	*Thick*.
Usz,	„	Uszki,	or	Uszi,	„	„	*Slender*.

In conversation, the *k* is usually, though not always elided. In books written in a familiar style, the same elision often takes place.

Examples of Adjectives in Na.

Tairaka,	root,	Tairakana,	*Level*.
Tash'ka,	„	Tash'kana,	*True or reliable*.
Taōyaka,	„	Taōyakana,	*Flexible, and graceful*.
Akiraka,	„	Akirakana,	*Bright, clear*.

There are also three ways in which the adjective is used predicatively.

1. It may have the form in *ki*, as before. An adjective which concludes a proposition, or sentence ends always in *ki*, or *i*, if *k* be elided, and when so used it includes in itself the copula, or verb *to be e.g.* See 997. the second form of the sentence. Kono shikata wa yasashii. *This work is easy*, or *This is easy work*. Comparing it with the longer and more polite form immediately above it, we see that the copula gozarimas', of the first, is omitted in the second, and unless the ki=i which terminates yasashii be the verb to be, the sentence has no copula. Yasashii, therefore, includes the copula in itself.

It was probably this peculiarity of Japanese construction the induced Rodriquez to call adjectives occupying this position in the proposition; adjective verbs. When the copula is in the past or future tense, the verb aru is developed distinctly as an affix to the **adjective**. Thus arewa yorosh'katta, *That has been, or was good*. **and** Arewa yorosh'karoō, *That will be* **good or** *well*.

2. When a separate word is used for the copula, as aru, **naru**, or shi, the predicate adjective ends in ku, as are wa yorosh'ku, or yoroshiu, gozarimas', *That is good* or *well*, or again;

3. When usage does not admit of the termination ku, **the root form of the adjective, with the locative de after it, precedes** the copula, as, are **wa** yawaraka de gozarimas'. It is not true, therefore, that the **form in** ku is always adverbial, though many adverbs have this **termination**. On the contrary, wherever this form precedes a substantive verb, it is an **adjective**. The common morning salutation O hayoŏ, in its full expression, is O hayoŏ gozarimas', *You are early Sir*, and here hayoŏ, which is the same as hayaku =(hayau, =hayoŏ,) is a predicate adjective. So, also, Waruku natta, signifies, *has become bad, or has been and now is bad*, and here too **waruku** is an adjective. But when **the verb** following **this** form is not **a substantive** verb, the word ending in ku is an adverb, as, **Osoku mairimash'ta,** *came late*, Waruku okonaimash'ta, *Conducted badly*.

Adjectives in ki, are also used as concrete nouns *e.g.* shiroki, *white*, and Shiroki wa **nga**, or **wo**, *the white* [ones]. Furuki wo s'tete, *abandoning or rejecting the old*. In conversation the *k* is elided and no [ノ] added to the adjective, **to form** concrete nouns, as Furui no wo s'tete, **atarashii no wo** totta. *Rejecting the old, he took the new*. Furui no **nga ki ni irimasen'**, *The old* [ones] *do not suit me*.

To find the root of an adjective, reject the termination *ki* or *iku* or *na*. Adjectives which cannot take the termination, *ki* are **transformed into** concrete nouns, by simply affixing the attributive particle no [ノ] to the root, as, Taira, *r* Taira no wa, nga, **or wo**, *The level or even* [ones]. Some adjectives may take either the termination **na** or *ki*, as Yawarakana, **and** yawarakai.=yawarakaki.

Abstract **nouns, are also derived from** adjectives by **annexing the** syllable sa [サ] **to the root,** as Nanga. *r*. Nangasa, *length*. **Aka,** *r*. Akasa *redness*. Hiro, *r*. Hirosa, *breadth*, Sa is propably a contraction for shi, to be [是]. and the separative and definitive particle wa [ハ].

Adjectives of Chinese origin, are simply Chinese words transferred to this language, and made attributive in their meaning, by means of the particle no [ノ] following them, when the noun to which they belong is a word of **Japanese** orgin as, Nippon no h'to, a Japanese Fuji no yama, Lit. the no-two **mountain,** the peerless mountain. But when both **the adjective, and the noun to** which it **belongs are** Chinese, **no is omitted, as, Nippon jin, a** Japanese and Fuji san, **The matchless mountain. Here the Chinese** and Japanese languages are **not** at variance, **in respect to the relative** positions of the adjectives and noun. **But when either one, or both words** is of Japanese origin the **particle no [ノ]must be placed between the** adjective and the noun.

By this means any noun may be made to perform the office of an attributive adjective, as, Akangano no mono, *a copper article*. Rash'a no kimono, *Woolen clothes*.

Adjectives signifying deprivation, and corresponding to English adjectives having the termination less, are formed by placing nako, or nai preceded by no (ノ) after the noun denoting that of which deprivation has taken place, Thus, chichi, a father, and chichi no nai, fatherless, Haha no nai, motherless; Soko no nai, bottomless; F'ta no nai oke, a tub without a cover

Adjectives signifying resemblances in quality, kind, or nature, to some thing, are formed by adding the termination shiki, or rash'ki, to a noun. *e.g.* kodomo, a child, or children, and kodomorash'ki purerite. Otoko, a male, Otokorashiki, like men, or manly, Onango, a woman, Onangorash'ki, like women, womanly, or effeminate. Otona, an adult male. Otonash'ki, manly, like a grown up man H'torash'ki like human beings, *i.e.* human, not like brutes. Kimirash'ki, like princes or princely. Shiki, signifies, such as, or like, and perhaps ra in rash'ki is only the plural sign, affixed to the preceding noun. M. Hoffman considers it to be derived from ari, to be, the final vowel being strengthened into *a*, but upon the supposition that ra is the sign of the plural, the meaning of H'torash'ki would be, like the human species, or like mankind. *i.e.* human. Adjectives, of this description may be formed from nouns, interjections, and verbal roots; as, Bakarash'ki, foolish, from the noun baka. Kanash'ki, or kanash'ii, from kana! alas! and meaning, sad, or lamentable, and airash'ki, lovely, from ai, to love.

Quere. May not the common word medzrash'ki, or medzrashii, be derived from me, the eye, tszou to attract, and sh'ki like, or such, as, together signifying, such [a thing] as attracts the eye, *i.e.* something rare or novel?

A large **number of** adjectives **is derived** by adding beki **to** their attributive form, *e.g.* Tattomer, to respect, and tattomu beki, **respect**ble, Warau or waroŏ, to laugh, and waroŏ beki, laughable or **ridiculous**, Sz to do, and szbeki, possible. Aru, to be, and aru beki, [that which ought to be] proper, or suitable. Beki is the attributive form of an adjective derived from be, a contraction of mube, or m'be [Chinese 可]. English, *may* or the adjective termination, *ble*. The ancient Portuguese dictionary defines it to mean, *with reason*, *In truth;* adjectives formed **by** means of this element often include the idea of duty, or necessity.

COMPARISON OF ADJECTIVES.

Degrees of comparison, **are expressed** by **a method** common to the Tartar and Japanese languages. **In** order to express the comparative, relative or the real comparative, **a** quality is simply attributed to an object, as having a relation to another object, with which the first is compared. The object, therefore, with which the comparison is made, is regarded as the starting point from which the attribution of the equality in question is made. Hence it is marked by the postposition yori, from, or proceeding from. Thus to say *A tempo is larger than a zeni*, the Japanese expression would be, Tempo wa zeni yori oöki. Lit. Starting from a zeni, [as the point or object with which the comparison is made,] a tempo is large.

The comparative degree may also be expressed by verbs signifying to exceed. For examples, see Index, under the word *Better*, & references.

The comparison of absolute equality, is made by means of hodo [ほド"], a noun signifying quantity· *e.g.* Nami wa, yama hodo takai, *The waves are as high as mountains.* or *The waves are mountain* [quantity or measure] *high.*" The same is expressed by yoö ni after the name of the object with which the comparison is made. Thus, Ishi yoö ni katai. [It] *is hard as a stone.* See 646. Lit. *It is hard in the manner of a stone.* The superlative absolute, is made by prefixing itatte [Chinese 甚], hanahada, ma, or some other intensive adverb to the adjective. Thus, Itatte warui, signifies extremely bad. Hanahada kuroi, very black, and Ma shiroi, very white. Ma is a primitive word, found in Makoto, truth or reality, Masash'ki reliable, [from masa, abstract noun, and sh'ki], and Masari, and Mashi, to exceed, to excel, to be better, which is likewise composed of masa and ari. Hanahada is given in the Portuguese dictionary, as an adverb signifying greatly.

The superlative relative, is made by prefixing Ichi, one, Ichi no, Dai, ichi no, or Ichiban, to an adjective, as; Ichi ban yoroshii, *The best*.

The idea of excess in a quality, is expressed by Amari *v.r.* to be excessive, before an adjective, as, Amari osoi, too late. Amari, tszyoi, too strong, or by placing szngiru, which means also, to be excessive, after an adjective, as, h'ayaszngiru, too early, or too fast, Taka szngiru, too tall.

Numeral Adjectives.

1. *Cardinal numbers.*

The primitive cardinal numbers are 1 H'to, 2 Fta, 3 Mi, 4 Yo, 5 Itsz, 6 mu, 7 Nana, 8 Ya, 9 Kokono, 10 Toö. and anciently the enumeration was continued by saying. Toö (10) Amari (plus) H'to Toöamari F'ta, and so on, to 19 inclusive, and then 20 was Hatachi. Lit. Twice 10. misoji, (三ツ于) 30, Yosoji, 40 Isoji,=Itsz-so-ji, 50. Musoji, 60. Nana-soji, 70, Yasoji, 80, Kokono-soji, 90, Momo, 100, Chi, 1.000, Yorodz, 10.000. The form now in use, H'totsz, is equivalent to H'to no, and thus the syllable tsz=no, is added to all the primitive numbers above, up to Kokono, 9. inclusive. Thus,

1. Htotsz.
2. F'tatsz.
3. Mitsz.
4. Yotsz.
5. Itsztsz.
6. Mutsz.
7. Nanatsz.
8. Yatsz.
9. Kokonotsz.
10. Toö.

GRAMMAR.   xliii

These were in use before the Chinese system of weights, and measures, and notation of periods of time was introduced into Japan. Since then, two systems, one Japanese and the other purely Chinese, have existed side by side, or have been intermingled with each other. Still the two are not applied indiscriminately. Japanese numbers are used before words of Japanese origin, and Chinese numbers before words of Chinese extraction, when the number does not exceed 10.

Comparative Table of Numbers

CHINESE.		JAPANESE.	
1. Ichi,	(一).	1. H'totsz.	
2. Ni,	(二).	2. F'tatsz.	
3. San,	(三).	3. Mitsz.	
4. Shi,	(四).	4. Yotsz.	
5. Go,	(五).	5. Itsztsz.	
6. Rok',	(六).	6. Mutsz.	
7. Sh'chi,	(七).	7. Nanatsz,	
8. Hachi,	(八).	8. Yatsz.	
9. Ku,	(九).	9. Kokonotsz.	
10. Jiu,	(十).	10. Too	
100. H'yak'	(百).		
1000. Sen,	(千).		
10000. Man, or Ban,	(萬)		

The number of hundreds, thousands, or tens of thousands is expressed by a numeral before the hundreds, thousands &c. as S'am b'yaku 300, Sh'chi zen, 7,000. Rok'man, 60,000 &c.

ORDINAL NUMBERS.

These are the Chinese numerals Ichi, ni, san, &c. followed by ban [番] which signifies *an order of succession*. Thus, Ichiban, first, Niban second, Samban, third, &c. and Go jiu ban, fiftieth.

The same is also expressed by prefixing Dai [第] to the same numerals, with no [ノ], or ban no, following them when used attributively, Dai ichi, first, Dai ichi no, or Dai ichi ban no, first. When only three things are to be enumerated, as the three vols. of a book, the first is called j'oō [上], the second, Chiu [中], and the third Ge [下], or using Japanese words of the same import, Kami, Naka, and Shimo; or Saki, the first, Tszgi, the next, or second, and Ato, the last, or third. When used attributively, all these must be followed by no [ノ]. The first, in order of time, is expressed by Hajime, *v. r. to begin*, with no [ノ] after it. Hajime no toshi, the first year [of a period] Hajime no h'to, the first man.

REDUPLICATIVE NUMBERS.

These are made by prefixing the Chinese numerals to the word bai. [陪], which means *doubled*, Thus Ichi bai, is one doubled or 2. Ni bai is two doubled, or 4, Sam bai, is three doubled or 6, or 2 times 1, 2 times 2, and 2 times 3.

Still another method of expressing reduplication, is to add the original Japanese numeral to e [へ, Chinese 重], which signifies *superaddition* Thus, Il'to e means a single one; F'ta e, twofold. Mi e, threefold. Yo e, fourfold. &c. Ya e, eightfold, has come to be used indefinitely for *mainifold*, as, Ya e no hana; A manifold flower, or one whose petals overlie each other in many superadditions, like that of the flowering cherry, or the double rose.

DISTRIBUTIVE NUMBERS.

These are formed by placing Dztsz (ヅ ツ) signifying, at a time, at once, after the Japanese numerals so far as they extend, and after that to the Chinese. Thus H'totsz dztsz signifies, one at a time, or one by one. F'tatsz, dztsz, two at a time and so on. H'yaku dztsz, a hundred at once. When persons are enumerated, H'tori, F'tari, or Mitari are used before dztsz, so that, H'tori dztsz, F'tari dztsz &c, signify one person at a time. Two persons at a time and so on. The phrase ate ni, from the verb ateru, and ni, is also used as synonymous with dztsz, and may replace it, after the aforesaid numerals. See. 171.

ITERATIVE NUMBERS.

These are either Japanese or Chinese. The Japanese are formed by prefixing the primitive numerals H'to, F'ta &c to tabi. which signifies, a time, and the Chinese by prefixing the Chinese numerals, to the word do [度] which means the same as tabi, Thus, we have two sets of words, having the same signification.

JAPANESE.	CHINESE.
H'to tabi, *once*.	Ichi do, *once*.
F'ta tabi, *twice*,	Ni do, *twice*.
Mi tabi, *thrice*,	San do, *thrice*.
Yo tabi, *four times*,	Shi do, *four times*.
Itsz tabi, *five times*,	Go do, *five times*.
Mu tabi, *six times*,	Rok' do, *six times*.
Nana tabi, *seven times*,	Sh'chi do, *seven times*.
Ya tabi *eight times*,	Hachi do, *eight times*.
Kono tabi, **nine times**,	Ku do, *nine times*.
To tabi, **ten** *times*,	Jiu do, *ten times*.
Jiu ichi tabi, *eleven times*,	Jiu ichi do, *eleven times &c*.

It will be observed that Chinese numerals are used even before tabi, for numbers higher than 10.

FRACTIONAL NUMBERS.

½ Ham bun (*Chinese*, 半分).
⅓ Sam bu no ichi, *i.e. one of three parts*.
¼ Shi bu no ichi, $\frac{1}{7}$ Jiu ichi bu no ni,
⅕ Go bu no ichi, $\frac{1}{100}$ H'yaku bu no ichi.
⅗ Go bu no san, $\frac{1}{1000}$ Sen bu no ichi.
⅛ Hachi bu no ichi, $\frac{1}{10000}$ Ichi man bu no ichi.
1/10 Jiu bu no ichi, $\frac{2}{10000}$ Ichi man bu do s'an.

In **all** fractional expressions, the denominator precedes the particle **no (ノ)**, and the numerator follows it.

NUMERATIVE AUXILIARIES.

The **Japanese**, in common with other Asiatics, **especially** the Chinese, make use of certain auxiliary words, in the **enumeration** of concrete objects, which form a part of the numerical expression **of** those objects. By these auxiliaries, objects are divided into classes, according to their external appearance. Some of the auxiliaries are used solely for such and such an object, and others are applied to the names of a large number. Usage regulates their application and it does not admit of any positive rule. It is evident that this is **a** peculiarity of the Japanese language and not borrowed from China, because, though the Chinese numerative auxiliaries are most commonly used, yet there are Japanese words for the same. These auxiliaries, bear a resemblance in meaning, though **not in** their grammatical use, to the English words, piece, and **stick**, in the phrases, *A piece of cloth, A stick of wood.*

These phrases, in Japanese, would be, Tanamono ittan, *i.e.* Of cloth one piece, and Ki ip'pon, *i.e.* Of trees one root, or a tree, or, a stick of wood. In the **first**, tan is the numerative auxiliary, and in the second, pon=hon. The Chinese equivalent of tan is 反, and that of **pon or** hon is, 本. The numerative auxiliaries **for various** classes of objects, must be learned by usage, rather than by rule. The following are a few of them, with the specification of their proper objects.

Hon, 本 for things long and slender, **as**, Fude ip'pon, **One** *pencil.*

H'ki, 匹 for quadrupeds, as, **Kuma ip'piki,** *One bear.*

Mai, 枚 for things thin **and flat, as,** Tempo ichi mai, *One Tempo.*

K'yaku, 脚 for articles of furniture having feet, as, T'skue ik'k'yaku *one desk.*

Soō, 艘 for boats and other sailing craft, as, Kobune is'soō, *One boat.*

Riu. 粒 for kernels of grain, as Kome ichiriu, *One* **kernel of rice.**

Tszbu, Jap. Do. as, Morokoshi h'to tszbu, *One kernal of corn.*
Wa, 羽 for birds, as Niwatori ichi wa, *One fowl.* [medicine
Zai, 剤 for a parcel of medicine as, K'szri ichi zai, *One packet of*
Tszmami Jap. for a pinch of any thing; as, Tabako h'to tszmami, *A pinch of tobacco.*
Se, 脊 for saddles, as, Kura is'se, *One saddle,*
Soŏ, 雙 for pairs of screens, as, Bioŏbu is'soo, *A pair of screens.*
Furi, Jap. for a sword as, Katana h'to furi, *One sword.*
Kasane, Jap. for suits of clothing, as, Kirui h'to kasane, *A suit of clothes.*
Ken, 軒 for houses and shops, as, Iye ik'ken, *One house.*
Tomai, Jap. for store houses, as, Kura h'to tomai *One godown.*
Soku, 足 for all foot-gear, as, Tabi is'soku, *A pair of stockings*
Ma 間 for apartments, as Nedokoro h'to ma, *One bedroom.*
Ch'oŏ, 掉 for norimono and sedan chairs, as, Norimono itch'oŏ, *One norimon.*
Satsz, 冊 for vols. of a book. as, Hon is'satsz, *One volume.*
Ch'oŏ, 挺 for tools with handles, as Nokongiri itch'oŏ, **One saw.**
Tszngai, Jap. for pairs of animals, Tori h'to tszngai, *A pair of birds.*
Rioŏ, 輪 for wheel carriages, as, Kur'ma ichi rioŏ. *One cart.*
J'oŏ 疊 for mats, **as,** Tatami ichi j'oŏ, *One mat.*

NOTATION OF TIME.

There are four terms which signify a day, *viz.* Ka, Hi, Jitsz and Nichi. Ka and Hi are purely Japanese. The other two are of Chinese origin, being different pronunciations of the same Chinese character 日.* These all originally denote the natural day, or the time from sunrise to sunset. But nichi has been appropriated to the designation of the civil day, and is so used in Japanese Almanacs [Koyomi]. In common parlance, the term Chiu ya (晝夜) or Hiru-yoru expresses the whole astronomical day.

---

*Jitsz is the pronounciation brought from China, about the commencement of the Western Tsin dynasty, or A. D. 284, according to the Japanese Chronologists, and Nichi is a pronounciation of 日 imported when Buddhism was introduced from China, at the close of the Chin dynasty, three centuries latter.

GRAMMAR xlvii

The different parts of the day, are named as follows, viz.

Yoake, *day break*.　　　　Hingure or Kure ngata **evening**
Hi-no-de, *sunrise*.　　　　　*twilight dusk*.
Asa, *morning*.　　　　　　　Yunbe or ban, *evening*.
Hiru, or Nichiu, *noon*,　　　Yoru or Yo-naka, *midnight*.
Hiru mai, *forenoon*.　　　　Machiru, or mappiru, *midday*.
Hiru Sangi. *afternoon*.

The term Jitsz 日 is confined to the designation of certain days as Gau-jitsz 元日 the first day of the year Sakujitsz yesterday. Is'sakujitsz, day before yesterday, or Senjitsz a former **day**. Nichi is also used for the same purpose though not in reference to **days** that are past, as Ken nichi 今日, to-day Mioŏ nich 明日 to-morrow and Mioŏ ngo nichi, 明後日 day after to-morrow.

In counting days without reference to their order, the cardinal numbers, Ichi, ni, San, &c. may be prefixed to nichi, for all numbers except **4**, and those in which 4 occurs. Shi 四 nichi 日 **are** never joined to each other, because Shi (=4) and shi 死 death have the same pronounciation, and to avoid the unpleasent association, Yok'ka, is used instead of Shi nichi, meaning 4 days.

The designations of the days of the month are as follows:—

viz. 1. Tszitachi　　11. Jiu ochi nichi.　21. Nijiu ochi nichi.
　　 2. Fts'ka.　　　12. Jiu ni nichi.　　22. Nijiu ni nichi.
　　 3. Mik'ka.　　　13. Jiu san nichi　 23. Nijiu san nichi.
　　 4. Yok'ka　　　14. Jiu Yok'ka　　 24. Nijiu yok'ka.
　　 5. Its'ka.　　　15. Jiu go nichi.　　25. Nijiu go nichi.
　　 6. Muika.　　　16. Jiu roku nichi.　26. Nijiu roku nichi.
　　 7. Nano ka.　　17. Jiu sh'chi nichi. 27. Nijiu sh'chi nichi.
　　 8. Yoŏ ka.　　 18. Jiu hachi nichi. 28. Nijiu hachi nichi.
　　 9. Kokono ka. 19. Jiu ku nichi.　　29. Nijiu ku nichi.
　　10. Toŏ ka　　 20. Hats'ka.　　　　30. Misoka.

Tszitachi signifies, the moon's rising, or the first of the new moon, Inisoka, is compouneded of Mi (3) So (10) and **ka (a day).** *i. e.* 30th day. Hatsz in hats'ka=20.

Substituting Ichi nichi, for Tszitachi, San jiu nichi for inisoka, in the table above, the same terms **are** used as cardinal numbers, in counting days.

With **the** same substitutions, they become ordinal numbers, by adjoining **the word** *me* 日 toka or nichi. *e.g.* Nano ka me wa yaszmibi de gozarimas'. The seventh day is a day of rest. Muika me ni deki angarimash'ta. He finish it on the 6th day (from a given date.) *i. e.* He finished it in seven days.

Hours.

The civil day is divided into 12 portions, from midnight to midnight.

There are two methods of naming the 12 divisions (hours) of the day. The first is identical with the Chinese method, and was probably introduced into Japan at the same time with Chinese letters. According to this, the hours are called after the 12 signs of the Zodiac.

In the second method, the hours are numbered, not forward from 1 to 12. but singularly enough, in retrogression from 9 to 4. which being repeated gives twice six, or twelve hours for the day. Both these modes of counting the hours are in use among the common people, but the introduction of watches into Japan induces those who carry them to prefer the numbers, to the names of the signs of the zodiac.

When the names of the zodiacal signs are used to designate hours, the 12th part of a day is called a Koku, but when numbers are used it is called a Doki,

The two modes of naming the hours of the day, may be presented as follows:—

1st hour. Ne no koku, The hour of the *rat.* Kokonotsz doki, or 9th. hour, *i.e.* 10. P. M. to 12. M.

2nd hour. Ushi no koku, The hour of the *bull.* Yatsz doki, or 8th, hour, *i.e.* 12 M. to 2. A. M.

3rd hour. Tora no koku. The hour of the *tiger.* Nanatsz doki, or 7th, hour, *i.e.* 2. A. M. to 4. A. M.

4th hour. U no koku. The hour of the *hare.* Mutsz doki, or 6th hour, *i.e.* 4. A. M. to 6. A. M.

5th hour. Tatsz no koku. The hour of the *dragon.* Itsztsz doki, or 5th, hour, *i.e.* 6. A. M. to 8. A. M.

6th hour. Mi no koku. The hour of the *serpent.* Yotsz doki, or 4th. hour, *i.e.* 8. A. M. to 10. A. M.

7th hour. M'ma no koku. The hour of the *horse.* Kokonotsz doki, or 9th hour, *i.e.* 10. A. M. to 12. Noon.

8th hour. Hitszji no koku. The hour of the *goat.* Yatsz doki, or 8th hour, *i.e.* 12 M. to 2 P. M.

9th hour. Saru no koku. The hour of the *monkey.* Nanatsz doki, or 7th hour, *i.e.* 2. P. M. to 4. P. M.

10th hour. Tori no koku. The hour of the *cock.* Mutsz doki, or 6th hour, *i.e.* 4 P. M. to 6. P. M.

11th honr. Inu no koku. The hour of the *dog.* Itsztsz doki, or 5th hour, *i.e.* 6. P. M. to 8. P. M.

12th honr. I no koku. The hour of the *boar.* Yotsz doki, or 4th hour, *i.e.* 8 P. M. to 10 P. M.

The corresponding European hours are here given, to show **what** they would be if the hours of the astronomical day were of equal length. This is not, however, the fact. On the contrary, for the purposes of civil life, they vary according to the increase or diminution of the natural day at different seasons of the year. Hence there are but two days in the year, viz. those at the equinoxes in which the hours of the day and night are of equal length, or in which they coincide with the hours of our day. In Japanese almanacs, the astronomical day is divided into 100 koku 刻 or minute parts, and thus a koku is equal to 14 minutes and 24 **seconds**. The koku is again subdivided into 100 bun 分 so that a **bun** is 8 and $\frac{64}{125}$ seconds.

The almanacs give the length of each day in koku and halves of koku. But since the natural day, and natural night are each divided into 6 doki, the doki of a summer's day must be much longer than that of a night at the same season, and vice versâ. The practice is to call sunrise Mutsz doki, or 6 o' clock, or more commonly Ake mutsz, the opening 6th hour and sunset kure-mutsz, or **the** darkening sixth hour. Japanese clocks are made so as to be set two or three times a month, in order to give the hours of the day and night according to this arrangement.

ENUMERATION OF MONTHS AND YEARS.

The Japanese name for **a** month is **ts'ki**, Lit. moon, and the Chinese 月, is pronounced Ngetsz or **Ngatsz**. The months of a year in their order are named **as** follows:—

1st. Sh'oo ngatsz. *Chinese* 正月. 7th. Sh'chi ngatsz. 七月

2nd. Ni Ngatsz. 二月. 8th. Hachi ngatsz. 八月

3rd. San Ngatsz. 三月. 9th. Ku ngatsz. 九月

4th. Shi Ngatsz. 四月. 10th. Jiu ngatsz. 十月

5th. Go Ngatsz. 五月. 11th. Jiu ichi ngatsz. 十一月

6th. Roku Ngatsz. 六月. 12th. Jiu ni ngatsz. 十二月

An intercalary month takes **the** numerical **part of its** name from **the** month immediately preceding. Thus **in** 1862 there was an intercalary 8th month of 30 days, immediately after the regular 8th month of 29 days. The general name for intercalary months is Urudzki, from Uru, 閏, supernumerary, and ts'ki, a moon or month. **The intercalary** month of 1862 **was** called **uru** hachi ngatsz.

Months are enumerated by means of the Japanese cardinal numbers before the Japanese word ts'ki, as far as the 10th month, or if the Chinese name for a month is used the Chinese numerals must be used before it, and its pronunciation then is ngetsz, not ngatsz. *e.g.*

H'to tski,	Ichi ngetsz,	or Ik ka	↑ ngetsz, *One month.*
F'ta ts'ki,	Ni ngetsz,	or Ni ka	„ ngetsz, *Two months.*
Mi ts'ki,	San ngetsz,	or San ka	„ ngetsz, *Three months.*
Yo ts'ki,	Shi ngetsz,	or Shi ka	„ ngetsz, *Four months.*
Itsz ts'ki.	Go ngetsz,	or Go ka	„ ngetsz, *Five months.*
Mu ts'ki,	Rok ngetsz.	or Rok ka	„ ngetsz, *Six months.*
Nana ts'ki	Sh'chi ngetsz.	or Sh'chi ka	„ ngetsz, *Seven months.*
Ya ts'ki,	Hachi ngetsz.	or Hak' ka	„ ngetsz, *Eight months.*
Kokono ts'ki,	Ku ngetsz,	or Ku ka	„ ngetsz, *Nine months.*
To ts'ki,	Jiu ngetsz,	or Jik' ka	„ ngetsz, *Ten months.*
———	Jiu ichi ngetsz, or	Jiu ik' ka	„ ngetsz, *Eleven months.*
———	Jiu ni ngetsz,	or Jiu ni ka	„ ngetsz, *Twelve months.* &c.

Years are enumerated by prefixing the Chinese cardinal numbers to the Chinese word Nen, (a year), or the Japanese numerals to the Japanese word toshi, (year), for any number not exceeding ten, after which the Chinese numbers must be used, except, (as in the enumeration of days) where the number four occurs, when yo takes the place of shi (四 4,) even before the Chinese Nen. This deserves to be noted as an exception to the general rule that Chinese numerals are used with Chinese nouns, and Japanese numerals with Japanese nouns. Thus, Yo toshi, and Yo nen are both used for 4 Years.

The term *me*, 目 is also employed after toshi and nen, to convert the numerals that immediately precede them into ordinal numbers. It is also used for the same purpose, after ts'ki and ngetsz. *e.g.* Kommodoru Periuri Nippon e mairimash'ta yori, jiu nen me ni narimas'. It is the tenth year since Commodore Perry came to Japan. Jiu ni ngetsz me wa toshi no owari de gozarimas'. The twelfth month is the end of the year. Yo ts'ki me ni kairimash'oŏ. He will return in the fourth month (from a given date).

Sec. XXVII Adverbs.

Adverbs are either primitive or compound, and may be arranged etymologically under the following classes.

1 *Primitive adverbs*, such as, Ma more, or truly, verily; Kioŏ to-day.

2. *Adverbs ending in Ku*, derived from adjectives, as Hayaku, from Haya, root of the adjective Hayai; early.

3. *Compounds of verbal roots*, as Tachi-machi, lit. standing and waiting, *i.e*, instantly, at once.

4. *Compounds of adjectives and nouns;* as, Choŏ-do, lit. exact measure, exactly.
5. *Compounds of verbal roots and nouns;* as, I-ma, the present interval, i e. now.
6. *Compounds of a nouns,* or pronoun and postposition, as, Ato de; afterwards, Sore de, at that, or at that rate; Sokode, thereupon.
7. *Compounds of an adverb and the radical of an adjective,* as mohaya, already, or with a negative following; no longer.
8. *Compounds of adjectives and the postposition ni,* as, ooki ni, greatly.
9. *Compounds of demonstrative adjectives and nouns,* as, Kon-nichi, to-day, lit. this day.
10. *Compounds of several parts of speech;* as, Nam-ben-de-mo, at how many soever times, over and over again, Doŏde-mo. In what manner soever, however.
11. *Gerundives,* as, Sashiatatte, in a direct or pointed manner, Sadomete, certainly, or positively. Hajimete, at first, Kaite, = kakite, in writing, i.e. not orally. Most of the above compounds are adverbial phrases, but are none the less adverbs in their office, and are often best rendered by an English adverb. It may assist the learner to adopt the usual division of adverbs into classes, according to the nature of the modification which they denote, and give a list of some of each. This division is the logical one, in contradistinction to that given before.

1. *Adverbs of time,* or those which answer to the question When? or How often?

a. *Of present time.* Ima, now. Tadaima, just now. Mada, still. Kioŏ, and kon nichi, to-day. Tachi machi, instantly, Szugu ni, immediately.

b. *Of past time.* Saku jitsz, yesterday. Mo haya, already. Saki hodo, just now. Moŏ s'koshi saki ni, a little while ago. Ima made, or I-rai, hitherto, or heretofore. Kara, and yori, since. I-zen, Ato, Saki, and Mae or Mai, ago. Mukashi, in former times, Saku nen, last year. Saku ngetsz, last month.

c. *Of time to come.* Kore kara, henceforth, Kono-i-ngo, hereafter. Ots'ke, by and by. Hayaku, soon. Ash'ta, Mioŏ-nichi, to-morrow. Mioŏ-ngo-nichi, and Asatte, day after to-morrow. Akuru toshi, Mioŏ-nen, Rai-nen, next year. Rai ngetsz next month. Mioŏ-asa, to-morrow morning. Mioŏ-ban, to-morrow evening. Mioŏ-nichi no hiru, to-morrow noon.

d. *Of relative time,* Hayaku, early. Osoku, late. Atsde, afterwards. Mai ni, before. Uchi ni, whilst, Sono toki, then. Toki, when.

e. *Of absolute time.* Itszdemo, always. Tszni. (with a negative verb,) never.

2 *Adverbs of place.* answering to the question, Where? Whither? Whence? Asoko, or As'ko, there, or yonder As'ko e, thither.

As'ko kara thence. **Achi, Achira, there.** Achi e, or Achira e, thither Achi kara, or Achira kara, thence. Kochi, Kochira, here. Kokoni, and kokode, here. Kochi e, Kochira e, Kokoe, hither. Koko kara, Kochi kara, Kochira kara, hence. Aru tokoro ni, somewhere. Uchi ni, in. Sotoni, out. Doko-demo, wherever. **Hoka e, Yoso e, away.** Sh'osh'o, every where. Koko no uchi ni, hereabout. **Ue e, upward,** Sh'ta e, downward. Mawari ni, around Kosh'ko ni, there.

3. *Adverbs of number*, answering to the question, How often? H'to **tabi,** and Ichido, once. F'ta tabo and ni do, twice. Nitabi, and **san do, thrice,** &c. Mare ni, seldom. Tamasaka ni, rarely. Kasanete, and **mata,** or F'ta tabi, again.

4. *Adverbs of degree*, or those which answer to the question, How much? Hanahada, very, or very much. Amari, too, too much, excessively Bakari, only, and **about** *i.e.* more or less. Tooku, far. Takaku, high. Sh'kuku, low. Tada-bakari, merely. Chitto, somewhat. Itatte, very, extremely. Ooki ni, much, greatly. Mattaku entirely. Taingai, and Taitei, generally. Ara ara, in the main. *i.e.* not minutely, or particularly. No koradz, **without exception. Yooyooto** scarcely, with difficulty. Fusoku ni, **insufficiently. Kotongotoku,** altogether. Soro-soro to, liesurely, moderately.

5. *Adverbs of manner*, answering to the question, How?

a. Of quality. Yoku or yorosh'ku, well, Waruu, or **Waruku, badly** Jiki ni, quickly. Shidzkani, slowly. Hayaku **fast.** Yooi ni or yas'ku, easily. Ukengatte, willingly. Ayamatte, accidentally, **or by** mistake. Kuwashiku, minutely, particularly. **Sassoku,** directly. Yawarakani soft.

b. Of Affirmation. **Hai,** yes. **Tash'ka** ni, surely. Kes'hte, positively. **Makoto** ni, **truly,** really, **Yangate,** of course. Ketszj'oo sh'te, doubtless. Ukengai nashi **ni,** without doubt. Mochiron, unquestionably.

c. Of Negation. Iiye, no. In some regions Iiya, no. Fu (Chinese 不 not, the first element in Chinese negative compounds, as Fusoku, Chinese 不足 not enough **The termination of** negative **verbs,** nu, and dz.

d. Of doubt. Ookata, probably, perhaps. **Taingai on the whole,** probably. Satewa, if so, in that case.

Sec. XXVIII. Postpositions.

These are the same in nature and office as prepositions in other languages, but as they are always placed after the words to which they relate, we call them postpositions. This is merely an external definition, and though so far correct, it does not indicate **their internal nature.** Postpositions are from words which express **only the** relations of things either external or internal to the human mind. The external relations being physical are obvious to the senses, but the internal belong to the province of the intellect. Both are however, subject to the same analysis, because the mind supposes a close resemblance between the external and the intellectual world. Hence it is that postpositions, for the most part, express equally well the external or physical, and the internal or intellectual relations of things. The number of possible relations is almost infinite, and yet they **are** all expressed by comparatively a very small number of postpositions; without confusion or mistake. In some languages, relations are also expressed by cases. The language which has no cases, must have more prepositions or postpositions. The Japanese language is on this account rich in postpositions. They are either simple and primitive, or compound and derived. Those of most frequent occurrence in speech, are for the most part monosyllabic. A much **greater** number, are either derived from these alone, or from verbal roots, and nouns with **the** addition of monosyllabic postpositions. **A few** are given here, **as** specimens of the above named classes.

1. *Simple postpositions.*

Ni. In or at, denoting rest in and into.
Ni. To; sign of the dative relation.
Ni. On; at rest on.
Ni. By; of the agent.
De. At, of place, or With; instrumental.
De. Of; index of the relation of the material to the thing made.
To. With; of accompaniment.
No. Of; index of the genitive relation.

E, or Ye. To, or towards; after verbs of motion.
E, or Ye. At; denoting temporary rest.
Kara. From; or after, of time or place.
Yori. From, or Since; of place or time.
Motte. With; instrumental gerundive from the verbal root, mochi, to take.
Made. Till, or until.

2. *Compound or derived postpositions.*

Nite, At, or in. Gerundive from ni v.r. to be in, De denoting the same local relation is from nete, by contraction.
Ue ni. Upon, Above. from Ue, the upper side, and ni, on.
Sh'ta ni. Under, Beneath, from Sh'ta, the bottom, and ni, at
Ushiro ni. Behind. from Ushiro,

the rear, and **ni, in.**
Soba ni. Beside, from Soba, the side, and ni, at.
Mae or Mai. Before, of place or time; from ma, the eye, and e the direction.
Omote ni. Before, In front of; from Omote, the face or front, and ni, in.

Hoka ni. Besides. from Hoka, outside of some limit, and ni, in.
Aida ni. Between; from Aida, an interval of space or time and ni, in.
Mukoō ni. Beyond; from Mukoō, the opposite quarter, and ni, in.
Konata ni. This side of; from Kono kata and ni, on this side.
Temai, or Temae ni. This side of; from Te, hand, and mae, before.
Tame ni. For, (expressing purpose or end,) For the sake of, from tame a purpose, or final cause. and ni.
Kawari ni. Instead of; from kawari v.r. to exchange, and ni, in.
Tonari. Near, Next to; properly an adj. as are *near* and *next* in English.

Uchi ni, Within. Uchi, interior and ni, in.
Soto ni. Without. Sote, exterior, and ni.
Nochi ni. After, of time, from nochi, Chinese 後, and ni, in. Always of the future.
Toötte. Through. Gerundive from Toöri, v.r. to go through.
Tsz. Through. Chinese 通.
Mawari ni, Around, from Mawari, v.r. to go round about, and ni,
Yoko ni. Across. Athwart; from Yoko, a transverse position or direction and ni, in.
Naka ni. In the midst of. Among. Into; from Naka, middle, and ni.
Uchi ni. Among. Amongst.
Nokosh'te. Except, Gerundive, from Nokoshi, v.r. to leave out.

Sec. XXIX. CONJUNCTIONS.

Conjunctions properly speaking connect only propositions. Those particles which merely connect words, are prepositions or postpositions. as, Two *and* two are four, all *but* one died. Of two connected propositions, one is either independent of the other, or forms an integral part of the same. In the former case the conjunction is called coördinative. In the latter, subordinative. It is not intended here to give more than a few specimens of each class.

1. COÖRDINATIVE CONJUNCTIONS.

These express logical relations of thought, and the logical relations between independent thoughts can only be those of causility and antithesis. Hence there are but three kinds of coordinative conjunctions, viz. copulative, adversative, and causal.

1 *Copulative conjunctions.* And, both-and, neither-nor.

The Japanese puts *to* (ト) where we use *and*, to connect two nouns that are the complex subject of a single verb, forming a sentence which is capable of resolution into two propositions. To (ト) conveys the idea of association, or companionship in this case, nearly or quite as much as when it is a postposition meaning *with. e.g.* See 718. Shishi *to* torawa &c. Lions *and* tigers &c.

To (ト) repeated is also used as a copulative conjunction (if *and* in such a case may be so called) when it connects the two subjects of the same verb, in the manner of a complex subject as, Kono h'to *to*, ano h'to *to*, kioŏ-dai de gozarimas'. This man *and* that, are brothers. Mo (と) signifies also. Mo (と) repeated signifies *both—and*, when there are two subjects, and two affirmative verbs. *e.g.* Ha mo yoroshi-i, koŏ-ki mo yoroshii. Both the (tea) leaf, and the flavor are good. Here the verb *to be* is repeated in yoroshii. On the other hand, if the verb or verbs following mo (と) repeated, are negative verbs, Mo—mo, signifies neither nor. *e.g.* Bım boo no h'to *mo* kanemochi *mo* joŏ-ngoŏ wa nongareon *Neither* the rich *nor* the poor can escape death.

When the sentence has but one subject and two predicative verbs the use of the copulative conjunction may be obviated, by putting the first verb into the gerundive form, ending in te, de or sh'te. But it is a mistake to suppose that either te, sh'te, or de is a conjunction as some have done. *e.g.* Yedo e itte, mimash'ta. He went to Yedo *and* saw it. Lit. Going to Yedo, he saw it. This construction deserves particular attention.

• 2. *Adversative conjunctions*, But, **but** yet, nevertheless, notwithstanding, &c.

Nga has the force **of** but, after finite **verbs.** See 313. Are wa kokoro-dzashi wa yoroshi-i nga. machingoŏta. He meant well (lit. his intention was good,) but he was mistaken. See also, 279. and Dialogue I. *N.* 4. Keredomo and haredomo But. Nevertheless. These are concessive forms of the verbs keri and Nari, but used **as** conjunctions in this sense. See 542, and Dialogue II. *F.* 22, and *F.* 24. The elliptical sentence, Nevertheless he is innocent, would be expressed thus, Naredomo tszmi nga nai.

The concessive form of the verb is sufficient, without a conjunction, to express the adversative sense, for which we use though, although, nevertheless, and notwithstanding, *e.g.* Dachoŏ wa hane nga aredomo, tobu koto nga dekinu. The ostrich has wings, but it cannot fly. or Notwithstanding the ostrich has wings it cannot fly.

3. *Disjunctive conjunctions.* Aruiwa (or, or else) Hi wo moyasz ni wa, takingi arujwa szmiwo ts'kaimas'. We use kindling-wood **or** else charcoal in lighting a fire. Tatoe wo motte, aruiwa otoshi-banashi wo itash'te &c. By means of illustrations, or by making jokes, &c.

Ka repeated, signifies or, as **in** the double question, **Is it high water or low?** Michi shiwo ka, h'ki shiwo ka**?** In **an** assertion, it would signify either—or, or whether or; but then Ka **must** not conclude the sentence. Hiru ka, kini sk'oshi mawatta ka to omou, **I** think it is *either* noon, *or* a little after noon. Michi shiwo ka, h'ki shiwo ka to kikimash'ta. He inquired *whether* it was high water *or* low. Oŏkata repeated may have the meaning of or, See, 648.

4. *Causal Conjunctions*

a. Causative Conjunctions. **Kara** following the member of the sentence which assigns the cause. **Sec. 25.** 26. 673. Yue and yue ni and Niyotte, all signifying *because*, or *for*, are used for the same purpose, and in the same position.

b. Illative Conjunctions, of such as precede the member which expresses an effect or consequence. *e.g.* Then, therefore, consequently, hence, thereupon, &c.

Soösh'te kara. Sore da kara. Then. Kore ni yotte, Sore ni yotte, on this account or on that. Kono yueni sore yue ni, consequently. Sore kara, therefore, Soko de, thereupon, These are adverbial phrases, used as conjunctives.

II. SUBORDINATIVE CONJUNCTIONS.

These introduce a clause or proposition as a member or factor (subject, attribute, object) of another proposition. They are, as it were, the inflections of the subordinate proposition, shewing its relation to the main proposition.

1. Those which merely introduce the subordinate proposition, expressing an abstract idea *To* (├) that. Anoh'towa shinimash'ta *to* (├), omoimas'. I think *that* he is dead.
Ka, whether, anoh'to wa fune ni norimash'te itta *ka* mo shirimasen'. I do not know whether he went by ship. Ka, if. Ano h'to wa shini wa, Shinai *ka* to, kikimash'ta. I asked if he was dead. In the last example *to* (├) after ka, is an appositive particle, showing that all the words which precede it, are the complement of kikimash'ta (=asked) and that they conjointly are explanatory of, and in apposition with some word understood meaning *question*, so that the sentence in full would be, I asked (the question) if he was dead.

Wherever the words of another are quoted, or one's own are repeated by way of narration, *to* (├) is placed after the quotation, or the words repeated, in the same way as above, and for the same purpose.

This is a particle of frequent recurrence whether in the oral or written language, and in often the most difficult to understand.

2 Subordinative **conjunctions** of time, corresponding to the English words, **when, while** or **whilst,** before, after, till, or until, since, &c.

Toki, when; is a noun meaning time, used as a conjunction. Yedo e yukimash'ta toki, **Rokungo no kawa ni midz nga mashimash'ta.** When I went to Yedo, the waters in the river Rokungo were high. Kara, after a gerundive signifies *after*, or *when*. Tabete kara, yukimash'ta. He went after eating, or when he had eaten.

Uchi ni, Whilst. Yedo ni orimash'ta uchi ni, kaji nga arimash'ta. There was a conflagration, whilst I was in Yedo.

Mai ni, before. Watak'shi wa mairanu mai ni, shingoto wo sh'te shimaimash'oö. I shall finish my business before I return.

Made, until. Gai koku no h'to wa koko e mairimas' made. wa.

Yokohama ichi men ni, no de gozarimash'ta. Until foreigners came here, Yokohama was all a field.

Yori, since. Mairimash'te yori, ano tokoro wa hirakemash'ta. That place has been opened, since they came.

3. *Subordinative conjunctions of place*, meaning where, whither, whence, wherever, &c.

Anata no shinuru *tokoro de*, watak'shi mo mata as'ko ni shinimash'oŏ. Where thou diest I will die. Here *tokoro de*, is the conjunctive phrase, and as'ko ni—there, its corelative. Doko e, whither. Doko e yukimash'ta ka, shiranu. I do not know whither he has gone. Doko kara, whence, Doko kara kimash'ta ka, shirimasen', I know not whence it came. Doko e with mo following, signifies *wherever*. Doko e okimash'te *mo*, kamaimasenu. It is immaterial where you put it.

4. *Subordinative conjunctions of manner*, meaning; as, as if, so that.

Toŏri ni, as. Anata no os'shiaru toŏri ni, itashimash'ta. I have done as you directed. Yoŏ ni. As if. Bioŏki no yoŏ ni miemas'. He looks as if he were sick. Yoŏ ni may also signify *so that*. H'tobito no osoreru yoŏ ni okonaimash'ta. He behaved so that people **were** afraid of him.

5 *Subordinative conjunctions of causality*, meaning; because, since, whereas. &c.

A. *Of the actual cause.* Kara, because, or whereas. Hoshi wa taisoŏ toŏi kara, chiisaku miemas'. The stars appear small, because they are very distant.

B. *Of the adversative cause*, or concession. This is expressed **by** the concessive form of the verb, in mo or domo.

C. *Of the final cause or purpose.* Tame ni, that. Yakunan wo nongareru tame ni, kimono **wo** kaete kimash'ta. He changed his dress that he might escape from danger.

D. *Of the possible cause*, denoted by; if, unless, except. Moshi, with an affirmative verb following it, is if; with a negative verb, unless, except. Moshi sono fune nga kono kuni e ts'ku nara, oŏki ni kanemoŏke wo itashimas'. If that ship reaches this country I shall make a great deal of money. Moshi naru take hayaku kaira**nai** to, watak'shi nga shimpai itashimas'. If you do not come back **as** soon as possible I shall be anxious.

6. *Subordinative conjunctions of intensity.* As—as, **then, and** the, repeated before the comparative degree of adjectives.

To onaji yoŏ na, as—as. Ano h'towa chichi to onaji yoŏna kanemochi de gozarimas'. He is *as* rich **as** his father. Yori, than. Ano deshi **wa sono** shish'oŏ yori sai **nga** gozarimas. That pupil has **more natural talent than his** teacher. **Oŏi** *hodo* yoi. *The* more, *the* better.

Sec. XXX. Interjections.

A few, the most common in speech are given below. Aa! Ah! Alas! Expressive of sorrow **or** displeasure, **as**; Aa, soŏ **itte wa** warui! Ah! you ought not to say so! Ee! Expressive of anger as, Ec, sore wa ikenai! That never will do!

Sate-sate. Expressive of admiration or regret, like the English O! or Oh! as, Sate-sate komatta ame! O what a disagreeable rain!

Satemo satemo, similar to the preceding, as; Satemo satemo hanga itai! Oh! How my tooth aches! Yare-yare, expressive of surprise, as, Yare-yare, ano h'towa shinimash'ta ka! Indeed! He is dead! The final word ka, is a contraction of cana, alas! much used in books, not a note of interrogation, Naru hodo! This is an exclamation often heard in conversation. And though difficult to analyze it seems to be nearly equivalent to our *Ah! Indeed!* expressive at once of surprise, and satisfaction, as if the remark that drew it forth corresponded to what might have been expected. Show a Japanese some philosophical instrument and he will answer Naru hodo! to every explanation you may give of the apparatus. Literally the phrase would seem to mean, *As much as possible.*

CHAPTER II.

SYNTAX.

The first chapter has occupied so much more space than was anticipated at the outset, that it will be impossible, without unwarrantably increasing the size of this volume, to treat extensively of the subject of syntax. The structure and use of the several parts of speech, having been discussed, it remains now to speak very briefly of the structure of sentences.

Sec. I. SIMPLE PROPOSITIONS.

The most general rule for the construction of a simple proposition, in the Japanese language, is, to place the subject at the beginnig and the verb at the end of the sentence. The other words, by which it may be expanded, follow the rule, that every modifying word, must stand immediately before the word which it modifies.

Thus, an attributive adjective stands before the noun to which it belongs, and a predicate adjective before the copula; a noun in an oblique case, before the postposition that marks its relation to some other word: an adverb, before the verb or adjective which it modifies: and both the direct and indirect complement of a verb, stand before the verb, as being adjuncts that modify its meaning.

Sec. II. COMPOUND SUBORDINATIVE PROPOSTIIONS.

The simple proposition may be taken as the model on which compound subordinative propositions are formed, for the subordinate proposition, stands in a *grammatical* relation to the leading proposition,

that is, it is a member or factor of some syntactical combination.
There are but three kinds of subordinate propositions.

    I. SUBSTANTIVE PROPOSITIONS.
    II. ADJECTIVE PROPOSITIONS.
    III. ADVERBIAL PROPOSITIONS.

These respectively occupy the place, and follow the construction of the parts of speech after which they are severally named.

I. SUBSTANTIVE PROPOSITIONS represent either, the subject, the complementary object, the supplementary object, the quoted sentiment, or the quoted question, and in each of these cases, the substantive proposition stands before the leading one.

Case 1. Subject. example; *Omai no iu tokoro wa*, mottomo de gozarimas'. *What you say*, is quite right.

Case 2. Complementary object, *Watak'shi no ari-dake wo yaroō*. I will give, *as much as I have*, or *what I have*.

Case 3. The quoted thought or sentiment. *Soō de aru to*, hanashimash'ta. He said *that it was so*.

Case 4. The quoted question. *Soō ka to*, kikimash'ta. He asked *Is it so?* i.e. He asked *if it was so?* Remark. The particle to (ト) which marks a quoted thought, assertion, or question, is always followed by a verb of *saying*, *thinking*, *knowing*, **or** *perceiving* and the like, in the leading proposition.

II. ADJECTIVE PROPOSITIONS or those which occupy the place **and** follow the construction of an adjective. In English, this proposition in its full form, is introduced by a relative pronoun, referring to a noun, the subject of the leading proposition, as, The *man*, *who* told me, is dead. The proposition, *who told me*, modifies the subject (man) of the leading proposition, like an adjective. Adjective propositions in English, and other languages that have relative pronouns, arise from an attributive participial or verbal adjective, developed to a proposition. Thus, *the speaking man* is equivalent to *the man who speaks*. As the Japanese has no relative pronouns, to serve as conjunctives, the participial mode of speaking, is universally adopted, where we use the developed adjective proposition. The adjective proposition is employed, as follows; viz:—

First, to modify the subject of the leading proposition, and therefore precedes it *e.g. Oōzaka ni orimas' akindo wa*, kane-mochi de gozarimas'. The merchants, *who live in Oōzaka* are rich men. Akiredo is the subject, and Oōzaka, no **orimas'**, the adjective proposition modifying it.

Secondly, to modify the complementary **o**bject, in which case it immediately precedes the object. *e.g. Oyaji no tometa kanewo*, mina ts'kai-ts'kushimash'ta. He has spent all the money *that his father accumulated*.

Thirdly, to modify the supplementary object, which it likewise precedes. *e.g. Shin-ki ni-tatta* uchi ni szmatte orimas'. He is living in the *house* [sup. obj.] *which he has newly built.*

III. ADVERBIAL PROPOSITIONS. They are so called because they modify the **verb of the** leading proposition, and **they arise from adverbs, or adver**bial phrases, developed to propositions. Thus from *suddenly*, is developed *before he was aware*, and from *during life, while I live*. Adverbial propositions express the modification of *place, time, manner, cause*, and *intensity* and must precede the leading proposition

1. Adverbial propositions of place. *Anata no orimas tokoro ni,* watak'shi mo orimash'oō. *Where you live* I will live.

2. Adverbial **propositions of time.** See. 1179, In the longer form **of the sentence, the word toki, [time]** stands at the end of the adverbial proposition. In the shorter **form,** the verb of the adverbial proposition, shimattara, is in the conjunctive mode, fut. tense, and no **other word denoting** time is required.

3. **Adverbial** propositions of manner. *Watak'shi no iu toōri ni.* korewo shiro. Do this, *as I tell you. Soku shi-szru yoō ni,* butta. He struck [him], *so that he died immediately.*

4. **Adverbial** propositions of the cause, introduced in English by, *as,* **because,** *since, if, unless, although. Tangai* **ni** *nakama-doshi* **nareba,** men-men kokoro-dzashi wo hanash'ta. *As they were of the same mind,* they told each other their intention. (Said of two frogs who met on a journey). Here the verb **nareba,** the conjunctive **mode** of nari, to be, supplies the place of a conjunction, and according to **its nature express** the adverbial sense. See. Chap. I. §. 5. The **same** mode, would also be used, where *since,* introduces an adverbial proposition in English.

The *Actual* cause *Ano h'to wa nibui kara,* Oshietemo tozi ni h'to ni naru mai. He will never be a man, by teaching, *for he is so stupid.*

The *possible* cause. *Soō nas'te kudasareba.* aringatoō gozarimas'. *If you will kindly do so,* I shall be much obliged. See. Dialogue. I. No. 21. The word kudasareba, in the text, ought to be kudasaraba, in the conditional mode. The Japanese, however, constantly, confound the two forms.

The *adversative cause,* or concession. ***Kikimash'ta** keredomo,* wa karimasenanda, *Although I heard,* I did not understand it.

A negative verb in the conditional mode, gives the sense of unless or except; as, Dashimasen' naraba, uri haraimas. If you do not take it up, (*lit. out*) I shall sell it to reimburse myself. See Dialogue 1. F. 22.

5. Adverbial **propositions of** intensity. Maszmasz kiu-kutsz ni natta, sono uede iyoiyo h'to nga oōku narimash'ta. The more they were oppressed, **the more they** multiplied. Oōi hodo yoi. The

more, the better. See. 509. 500. 948. 949. 970. and 1065.

Remark. The adverbial proposition of manner, cause, **means**, is often characterized by the gerundive form of the verb. Thus in the common expression, Motte koi, motte is the gerundive form of mochi, to take, and the two words signify taking, (the thing), or take (the thing) and (koi) come. *i.e.* Bring. Doku wo nonde, shinimash 'ta, He drank poison and died, or, He died (in what manner or from what cause?) from drinking poison. Nashi ngajiku sh'te, ochimas'. The pear becomes ripe and falls off, or, The pear becoming ripe, falls off. Yoso ngoto no yo, ni o kiki nasarete wa, meiwaku ni dzonjinas'. Hearing us if it were something foreign (or extraneous) to yourselves, you will experience a delusion, or If you hear &c. Here the proposition ending with *nasarete wa*, is expressive of a conditional cause. The gerundive with wa, often has this force. See remarks on the nature of the gerundive, Chap. 1. §. 4.

In both the simple and compound subordinative propositions, the universal principle of construction seems to be, that all modifiers, whether words or subordinate propositions, should stand before those which they modify. When, as is sometimes the case, the subject and predicate verb of the leading proposition are separated, the subject is put at the beginning and the verb at the end of the compound proposition, probably for the sake of emphasis. The leading verb never changes its place.

Sec. 3. Compound Coordinative Propositions.

The simple propositions included in the compound coordinative proposition, are constructed in the manner described in the first section of this chapter. Coordination is a combining of two distinct propositions into one. They still express distinct thoughts. The relations of thoughts are logical, and these relations are only those of causality and antithesis. The more copulative combination expresses no relation between the propositions combined, but only a common relation, either adversative or causal, to a third proposition. Hence it admits of more than two members. The three relations in which the parts of a coördinating proposition stand to **each** other are.

1. The *copulative*, or that in which two assertions **are** simply coupled together, as, The man walked *and* the boy ran.

2. The *adversative*, or that in which one is opposed **to** the other, as, Oranges do not grow in hig**h** latitudes, but they do within the tropics.

3. The *causal*, or that by which we account for one assertion, by means of another.

1. The copulative relation, is in Japanese, expressed by pauses,

rather than by conjunctions. Thus, Watak'shi wa kukimas', anata wa yomimas. I write (and) you read. In this omission of the conjunction, the Japanese corroborates the fact that such a combination, expresses no logical relation between the two connected assertions, but is merely a coupling of them together. Inochi wa mijikai, sz be ki koto wa ooi. *Life is short, and there is much to be done*, is a closer resemblance of two independent thoughts, while yet, they sustain no logical relation to each other.

The merely copulative combination may consist of two or more propositions, all equally emphatic, and the more so, if conjunctions are omitted. This combination is looser and more imperfect than the antithetic and causal.

2. The adversative combination: *e.g.* Mungi wa makadz ni haemasenu nga, h'to nga makimas'. Wheat does not grow wild, but men plant it. Here the adversative proposition is placed last, while the conjunction nga, but, is joined to the end of the other.

Ts'chi nga hoshii keredomo, te nga kakaru. The soil is desirable, but it requires labor. This is a restrictive combination, and the same order of propositions is preserved, with keredomo, but, but yet, as their connective.

Lastly, there is the disjunctive **combination**; *e.g.* Watak'shi wa achira e yukimash'oŏ ka, aruiwa anata nga kochira e mairimas' ka ni itashimash'oŏ. Either I shall go there, or else you will come here.

In such a combination the order of propositions is changeable at pleasure.

As might be expected from the nature of coördinative propositions, there is far less regularity in their construction, than in compound subordinative propositions, because the relation between the members is not grammatical but logical.

SENTENCES IN ENGLISH
AND
JAPANESE COLLOQUIAL.

A

1. *A bow-knot is easy to untie.*
   Hi-za o-ri ni mu-sz-bu to to-ke ya-sz-u go za-ri-ma-s'.
   ヒザ オリ ニ ムスブ ト トケ ヤスウ ゴ ザリマス
   Do. Hi-za o-ri ni mu-sz-bu to to-ke ya-sz-i.
   ヒザ ヲリ ニ ムスブ ト トケ ヤスイ

2. *A copper-mine is called doûzan.*
   A-ka nga-ne no de-ma-s' to-ko-ro wa do-o-za-n to mo-o-shi-ma-s'.
   アカ ガ子 ノ デマス トコロ ハ ドウザン ト モウシマス
   Do. A-ka nga-ne no de-ru to-ko-ro wa do-o-za-n to i-u.
   アカ ガ子 ノ デル トコロ ハ ドウザン ト イウ

3. *A dollar is the fixed price.*
   I-chi do-ra nga ji-o-o ne-da-n de go za-ri-ma-s'.
   イチ ドラ ガ ジャウ 子ダン デ ゴ ザリマス
   Do. I-chi do-ra nga ji-o-o ne-da-n da.
   イチ ドラ ガ ジャウ 子ダンダ

4. *A child neglected grows worse and worse.*
   Ko-do-mo wa s'-te-te o-ki-ma-s' to shi-da-i ni wa-ru-ku na-ri-ma-s'.
   コドモ ハステテ オキマス ト シダイニ ハルクナリマス
   Do. Ko-do-mo wa s'-te-te o-ku to shi-da-i ni wa-ru-ku na-ru.
   コドモ ハステテ ヲク ト シダイ ニ ハルク ナル

5. *Any body can do that.*
   So-re wa do-na-ta de mo de-ki-ma-s'.
   ソレ ハ ドナタ デモ デキマス
   Do. So-re wa da-re de mo de-ki-ru.
   ソレ ハ ダレ デモ デキル

6. *Another vessel has arrived.*
   Ho-ka no fu-ne nga ts'-ki-ma-sh'-ta.
   ホカ ノ フ子 ガ ツキマシタ
   Do. Ho-ka no fu-ne nga tsz-i-ta.
   ホカ ノ フ子 ガ ツイタ

7. *A new law was published yesterday.*
   Sa-ku ji-tsz shi-n ki ni ha-t-to wo ta-te-ra-re-ma-sh'-ta.
   サクジツ シンキニハツトヲ タテラレマシタ
Do. Sa-ku ji-tsz shi-n ki ni ha-t-to wo ta-te-ra-re-ta.
   サクジツ シンキニハツトヲ タテラレタ

8. *Any thing will do.*
   Na-ni de mo yo-ro-shi-u go za-ri-ma-s'.
   ナニデモ ヨロシウ ゴザリマス
Do. Na-ni de mo yo-i.
   ナニデモヨイ

9. *Are you well?*
   Go ki ngen yo-ro-shi-u go za-ri-ma-s' ka?
   ゴキゲン ヨロシウ ゴザリマス カ
Do. Ka-wa-ru ko-to wa na-i ka?
   カハルコト ハナイカ

10. *Are you ready?*
    A-na-ta sh'-ta-ku wa yo-ro-shi-u go za ri-ma-s' ka?
    アナタ シタク ハ ヨロシウ ゴザリマス カ
Do. O-ma-e sh'-ta-ku wa i-i ka?
    オマエ シタク ハイイカ

11. *Are your children all at home?*
    A-na-ta no ko-do-mo shi-u wa o u-chi de go za-ri-ma-s' ka?
    アナタノ コドモ シウ ハオウチデ ゴザリマス カ
Do. O-ma-e no ko-do-mo wa mi-na u-chi ni i-ru ka?
    オマエノ コドモ ハ ミナ ウチニイルカ

12. *Are you married?*   (to a superior.)
    Go shi-n-zo wa go za-ri-ma-s' ka?
    ゴ シンゾ ハ ゴザリマスカ
Do. O-ma-e ka-mi-sa-n wa a-ri-ma-s' ka?   (to an equal.)
    オマエ カミサン ハ アリマス カ
Do. Te-ma-e wa ni-o-o-bo-o nga a-ru ka.   (to an inferior.)
    テマエ ハ ニヤウボウガ アルカ

13. *Are they your own?*
    Ana-ta go ji-bu-n no de go za-ri-ma-s' ka?
    アナタ ゴジブンノデ ゴザリマスカ
Do. O-ma-e ji-shi-n no ka?
    オマエ ジシンノカ

14. *Are you sure of it?*
    A-na-ta ta-sh'-ka ni sh'-t-te o i-de na-sa-ri-ma-s' ka?
    アナタ タシカ ニシツテオイデナサリマスカ
Do. O-ma-e ta-sh'-ka ni sh'-t-te i-ru ka?
    オマエ タシカ ニシツテイルカ

15. *Are you coming back again?*
    A-na-ta ma-ta o i-de na-sa-ri-ma-sh'-o-oka?
    アナタ マタオイデナサリマ シヤウカ

Do. O-ma-e ma-ta ki na-sa-ru ka?
オマエ マタ キ ナサルカ

16. *Are you at work by the day or by the job?*
O-ma-e shi-ngo-to wo i-ri ni sz-ru ka, u-ke a-i ni sz-ru ka?
オマエ シゴト ヲイリニスル カ ウケアイニスルカ

17. *Are potatoes to be had here?*
Ja-nga-ta-ra i-mo wa ko-ko de ka-wa-re-ma-s'ka?
ジヤガタラ イモ ハ ココデ カワレマスカ

Do. Ja-nga-ta-ra i-mo wa ko-ko de ka-wa-re-ru ka?
ヤガタラ イモ ハ ココデ カワレルカ

18. *Are you not ashamed?*
Ha-dz-ka-shi-u wa go za-ri-ma-se-nu ka?
ハヅカシウ ハゴザリマセス カ

Do. Ha-ji wo shi-ra-nu ka?
ハジ ヲ シラスカ

19. *As many as you please*
O no-dzo-mi shi-da-i ni i-ku-tsz de mo.
オノヅミ シダイニイクツデモ

Do. No-dzo-mi shi-da-i ni i-ku-tsz de mo.
ノヅミ シダイニイクツデモ

20. *As quick as a wink, do it.*
Ma-ba-ta-ki no ma ni na-sa-re-ma-sh'.
マバタキ ノマニ ナサレマシ

Do. Ma-ba-ta-ki no ma ni shi-ro.
マバタキ ノマニ シロ

21. *As long as you do so you will not get well.*
A-na-ta mi no o-ko-na-i no na-o-ri-ma-se-nu u-chi wa, ya-ma-i wa na-o-ri-ma-se-nu.
アナタ ミ ノ オコナイ ノ ナヲリマセス ウチ ハ ヤマイ ハ ナヲリマセス

Do. O-ma-e mi no o-ko-na-i no na-o-ra-nu u-chi wa, ya-ma-i wa na-o-ra-nu.
オマエ ミ ノ オコナイ ノ ナヲラス ウチ ハ ヤマイ ハ ナヲラス

22. *Ask him; he knows all about it.*
A-no o ka-ta ni o ki-ki na-sa-re; yo-ku sh'-t-te o i-de na-sa-re-ma-s'.
アノ オカタニ オキキ ナサレ ヨク シツテオイデ ナサレ マス

Do. A-no h'-to ni ki-ke; yo-ku sh'-t-te i-ru.
アノ ヒト ニキケ ヨク シツテイル

23. *At your leisure.*
O te tsz-ngo-o shi-da-i ni.
オ テツゴウ シダイニ

Do. Te tsz-ngo-o shi-da-i ni.
テ ツゴウシダイニ

24. *At whose expense has this been done?*
Ko-re wa do-no o ka-ta nga ka-ne wo da-sh'-te ts'-ku-ra-re-ma-sh'-ta ka?
コレハドノオカタガカ子ヲダシテツクラレマシタカ

Do. Ko-re wa da-re nga ka-ne wo da-sh'-te ts'-ku-ra-re-ta ka?
コレハダレガカ子ヲダシテツクラレタカ

25. *Averaging them at $300 each, I will take them, for they are not of the same quality.*
Ko-re wa fu-do-o nga go za-ri-ma-s' ka-ra, na-ra-sh'-te sa-m bi-ya-ku do-ra dz-tsz ni wa-ta-k'-shi ka-i-ma-sh'-o-o.
コレハフドウガ ゴザリマスカラ ナラシテ サンビヤクドラヅツ ニワタクシカイマシャウ

Do. Ko-re wa fu-do-o nga a-ru ka-ra, na-ra-sh'-te sa-m bi-ya-ku dz-tsz ni ka-wo-o.
コレハフドウガ アルカラ ナラシテ サンビヤクヅツニカヲフ

26. *Avoid that man, for he tells lies.*
A-no h'-to wa i-tsz-wa-ri wo mo-o-shi-ma sz-ru ka-ra, o he-da-te na-sa-re.
アノヒトハイツワリヲモウシマスルカラオヘダテナサレ

Do. A-no h'-to wa i-tsz-wa-ri wo i-u ka-ra, ha-bu-ke.
アノヒトハイツワリヲイフカラハブケ

27. *Awake me at 6 o'clock to morrow morning.*
Mi-o-o a-sa mu-tsz do-ki ni wa-ta-k'-shi wo o o-ko-shi na-sa-re-te ku-da-sa-re.
メヤウアサムツドキニワタクシ ヲオオコシ ナサレテクダサレ

Do. Mi-o-o a-sa mu-tsz do-ki ni wa-ta-k'-shi wo o-ko-se.
メヤウアサムツドキニワタクシヲオコセ

28. *Axe-helves, and spear-handles are made of a wood called ka-shi.*
Yo-ki no e to, ya-ri no e wa, ka-shi to mo-o-sz ki de ts'-ku-ri-ma s'.
ヨキノエトヤリノエハ カシトモウスキデツクリマス

Do. Yo-ki no e to ya-ri no e wa, ka-shi to i-u ki de ts'-ku-ru.
ヨキノエトヤリノエハカシトイフキデツクル

29. *Aye; at your service.*
Ha-i, Ka-sh'-ko-ma-ri-ma-sh-ta.
ハイカシコマリマシタ

B

30. *Back your cart up to the door.*
Ku-r'ma wo ka-do-ngu-chi ni mo-do-se.
クルマヲカドグチニモドセ

31. *Be still (of noise.) Be still (talking.)*
   Shi-dz-ka ni o shi-na sa-re. O da-ma-ri na-sa-re.
   シヅカニオシナサレ。オダマリナサレ
Do. Shi-dz-ka ni shi-ro. Da-ma-re.
   シヅカニシロ。ダマレ

32. *Be a good boy.*
   Sz-na-wo ni na-sa-i-ma-sh'.
   スナヲ ニナサイマシ
Do. O-to-na-sh'-ku shi-ro.
   オトナシクシロ

33. *Be quick, or you will lose it.*
   Ha-ya-ku na-ke-re-ba, u-shi-na-i ma-s'.
   ハヤク ナケレバウシナイマス
Do. Ha-ya-ku na-ke-re-ba u-shi-no-o.
   ハヤクナケレバウシナフ

34. *Be on the look out for it.*
   O ki wo ts'-ke-te mi-te o i-de na-sa-re.
   オキヲツケテミテオイデナサレ
Do. Ki wo ts'-ke-te mi-te i-ro.
   キヲツケテミテイロ

35. *Begin where you left off.*
   O ya-me na-sa-re-ta to-ko-ro yo-ri o ha-ji-me na-sa re.
   オヤメナサレタトコロヨリオハジメナサレ
Do. Ya-me-ta to-ko-ro yo ri ha-ji-me-ro.
   ヤメタトコロヨリハジメロ

36. *Be there exactly at the time.*
   So-no ko-ku-nge-n ni ta-ngu-wa-dz a-chi-ra ni ma-t-te o i-de na-sa-re.
   ソノコクゲンニタガワヅアチラニマツテオイデナサレ
Do. So-no ko-ku-nge-n ni chi-nga-i na-ku, a-chi-ra ni ma-t-te i-ro.
   ソノコクゲンニチガイナクアチラニマツテイロ

37. *Besides this how much do you want?*
   Ko-no ho-ka ni i-ku-ra o i-ri na-sa-re-ma-s' ka?
   コノホカニイクラオイリナサレマスカ
Do. Ko-no ho-ka ni i-ku-ra i-ru ka?
   コノホカニイクライルカ

38. *Bring a light.*
   A-ka-ri wo mo-t-te o i-de na-sa-re.
   アカリヲモツテオイデナサレ
Do. A-ka-ri wo mo-t-te ko-i.
   アカリヲモツテコイ

39. *Bring a chair.*
   ..-sz wo mo-t-te o i-de na-sa-re.
   イスヲモツテオイデナサレ

Do. Ki-yo-ku-ro-ku wo mo-t-te ko-i.
キヨクロクヲ マツテ コイ

40. *Bridges are built and the poor are aided, in Japan, with the money derived from fines.*
Ni-p-po-n de wa ka-ri-o-o no ka-ne de ha-shi wo ts'-ku-ra-re-ma-s', hi-n mi-n wo s'-ku-wa-re-ma-s'.
ニツポンデハ カリヤウノカ子デ ハシ ヲ ツクラレマス ヒンミン ヲ スクワレマス

41. *Bring it here.*
Ko-chi-ra-e mo-t-te o i-de na-sa-re.
コチラエモツテオイデ ナサレ

Do. Ko-chi-ra e mo-t-te ko-i.
コチラエモツテ コイ

42. *Brush away those cobwebs.*
So-no ku-mo no sz wo ha-ra-e.
ソノ クモ ノスヲ ハラエ

43. *Brush my shoes.*
Wa-ta-k'-shi no ku-tsz wo mi-nga-ke.
ワタクシノクツ ヲ ミガケ

44. *Burn it up.*
Ya-i-te o shi-ma-e na-sa-re.
ヤイテ オシマエ ナサレ

Do. Ya-i-te shi-ma-e.
ヤイテ シマエ

45. *Burn up the rubbish.*
Go-mi wo ta-i-te shi-ma-e.
ゴミ ヲ タイテ シマエ

46. *Buy me an umbrella & rain-coat.*
Wa-ta-k'-shi no ka-sa to mi-no wo ka-t-te ki-te ku-da-sa-re.
ワタクシ ノ カサ ト ミノ ヲ カツテキテ クダサレ

Do. Wa-ta-k'-shi no ka-sa to mi-no wo ka-t-te ko-i.
ワタクシ ノ カサ ト ミノ ヲ カツテコイ.

47. *Burning the dead is called kwasoo*
Shi-ni-ma-sh'-ta h'-to wo ya-ku ko-to wo k'-wa-so-o to mo-o-shi-ma-s'.
シニマシタヒトヲ ヤク コト ヲ クワソウ トモウシマス

Do. Shi-n-da h'-to wo ya-ku ko-to wo k'-wa-so-o to i-u.
シンダ ヒトヲ ヤク コト ヲ クワソウトイフ

C

48. *Call a servant.*
Ko-dz-ka-i wo yo-n-de ku-da-sa-re.
コヅカイ ヲ ヨンデ クダサレ

Do. Ko-dz-ka-i wo yo-n-de ko-i.
コヅカイ ヲ ヨンデ コイ

49. *Call at the least twenty coolies.*
　　Ni-n-so-ku wo ni ji-u ni-n ni ka-ke-nu yo-o ni yo-n-de ku-da-sa-re.
　　ニンソクヲ ニジウニンニカケヌ ヨウニヨンデクダサレ
Do.　Ni-n-so-ku wo ni ji-n ni-n ni ka-ke-nu yo-o ni yo-n-de ko-i.
　　ニンソク ヲ ニジウニンニカケ ヌ ヨウニヨ ンデコイ

50. *Can he read?*
　　A-no o ka-ta wa yo-mu ko-to nga de-ki-ma-s'-ka?
　　アノオカタハ ヨムコト ガデキマスカ
Do.　A-no h'-to wa yo-mu ko-to nga de-ki-ru ka?
　　アノヒトハ ヨムコトガデキルカ

51. *Can you not spare me one of those Japanese pencils?*
　　A-na-ta so-no fu-de wo i-p-po-n wa-ta-k'-shi ni ku-da-sa-re-ma-se-nu ka?
　　アナタソ ノ フデヲ イッポン ワタクシ ニクダサレマ セ スカ
Do.　O-ma-e so-no fu-de wo i-p-po-n wa-ta-k'-shi ni ku-re-nu ka?
　　オマエソ ノフデヲイッポンワタクシ ニ クレヌカ

52. *Can you find out how this is made?*
　　Ko-re wa do-o sh'-te ts'-ku-t-te go za-ri- ma-s' ka, o ka-n-nga-i na-sa-re-te shi-re-ma-s' ka?
　　コレ ハドウシテツ クツテゴザリマスカ オカンガイ ナサルテシレマスカ
Do.　Ko-re wa do-o sh'-te ko-shi-ra-e-ta ka, ka-n-nga-i-te shi-re-ru ka?
　　コレ ハドウシテコシラエタ カ カンガ イテシ レ ルカ

53. *Can I do any thing to help you?*
　　A-na-ta, na-n zo o s'-ke mo-o-shi-ma-sh'-o ka?
　　アナタ ナンゾヤスケ モウシ マシオカ
Do.　O-ma e na-n zo te-tsz-da-wo-o ka?
　　オマエナンゾテツダヲウカ

54. *Can you not find me one like that?*
　　A-na-ta wa-ta-k'-shi ni so-no yo-o-na shi-na wo h'-to-tsz ta-dz-ne-te ku-da-sa-re-ma-se-nu ka?
　　アナタワタクシニソノヨウナシナ ヲヒトツタヅネ テクダサレマセスカ
Do.　O-ma-e wa-ta-k'-shi ni so-no yo-o-na shi-na wo h'-to-tsz ta-dz-ne-te ku-re-nu ka?
　　オマエワタクシニソノヨウナシナヲヒトツタヅ ネテクレヌカ

55. *Can you mend this?*
　　A-na-ta ko-re wo o na-o-shi na-sa-ru ko-to wa de-ki-me-s' ka?
　　アナタ コレ ヲヲナオシナサル コト ハデキマスカ
Do.　O-ma-e ko-re wo na-o-sz ko-to wa de-ki-ru ka?
　　オマエコレ ヲナヲスコト ハデキルカ

56. *Carry this back.*
　　Ko-re wo o mo-chi na-sa-re-te o ka-e-ri na-sa-re.
　　コレ ヲ オモチ ナサレテ オカエリ ナサレ
　Do.　Ko-re wo mo-t-te ka-e-re.
　　コレ ヲ モッテ カエレ

57. *Carry this letter to Mr.——.*
　　Ko-no te-nga-mi wo——— sa-ma e mo-t-te o i-de na-sa-re-te
　　コノ テガミ ヲ　　　　サマ エ モッテ オイデ ナサレテ
　　ku-da-sa-re.
　　クダサレ
　Do.　Ko-no te-nga-mi wo——— sa-ma e mo-t-te yu-ke.
　　コノ テガミ ヲ　　　　サマ エ モッテ ユケ

58. *Carry this box in.*
　　Ko-no ha-ko wo u-chi e i-re-ro.
　　コノ ハコ ヲ ウチ エ イレロ

59. *Carry it this side up.*
　　Ko-no ho-o wo u-e ni sh'-te mo-t-te yu-ke.
　　コノ ホウ ヲ ウエ ニ シテ モッテ ユケ

60. *Cloths imported from foreign countries, can be sold cheaper than those made in Japan.*
　　Ni-p-po-n de ts'-ku-re-ma-s' ta-m-mo-no yo-ri, ga-i ko-ku ka-ra
　　ニッポン デ ツクレマス タンモノ ヨリ ガイ コク カラ
　　wa-ta-ri-ma-s' ta-m-mo-no wa ya-sz-ku u-ra-re-ma-s'.
　　ワタリマス タンモノ ハ ヤスク ウラレマス

61. *Come day after tomorrow.*
　　Mi-o-o ngo ni-chi o i-de na-sa-re.
　　メヤウ ゴ ニチ オイデ ナサレ
　Do.　Mi-o-o ngo ni-chi ki na-sa-e.
　　メヤウ ゴ ニチ キナサエ

62. *Comb your hair.*
　　Ka-mi wo ku-shi de o na-de ts'-ke na-sa-re.
　　カミ ヲ クシ デ オナデ ツケ ナサレ
　Do.　Ka-mi wo ku-shi de na-de ts'-ke-ro.
　　カミ ヲ クシ デ ナデ ツケロ

63. *Come early tomorrow morning.*
　　Mi-o-o a-sa ha-ya-ku o i-de na-sa-re.
　　メヤウ アサ ハヤク オイデ ナサレ
　Do.　A-sh'-ta no a-sa ha-ya-ku ki na-sa-e.
　　アシタ ノ アサ ハヤク キナサエ

64. *Come quick; here is a large snake.*
　　O ha-ya-ku o i-de na-sa-re, o-o-ki-na he-bi nga i-ma-s'.
　　オハヤク オイデ ナサレ オヲキナ ヘビ ガ イマス
　Do.　Ha-ya-ku ko-i; o-o-ki-na he-bi nga i-ru.
　　ハヤク コイ オオキナ ヘビ ガ イル

65. *Come whenever you please.*
   I-tsz ni-te mo o-bo-shi-me-shi shi-da-i ni o i-de na-sa-re.
   イツニテ モ オボシ メシ シダイニオイデ ナサレ
Do. I-tsz ni-te mo yo-i to o-mo-o to-ki ni ki na-sa-e.
   イツニテ モ ヨイト オモフ トキニキ ナサエ

66. *Come let us take a ride.*
   M'-ma ni o no-ri na-sa-re-te, wa-ta-k'-shi do-mo to o i-de na-sa-re.
   ウマニオノリ ナサレテ ワタクシドモ トオイデ ナサレ
Do. M'-ma-ni no-t-te wa-ta-k'-shi do-mo to yu-ki na-sa-e.
   ウマニノッテ ワタクシドモ トユキ ナサエ

67. *Come let's see who is the strongest.*
   Wa-ta-k'-shi do-mo to chi-ka-ra ku-ra-be wo sh'-te go ra-n na-sa-re.
   ワタクシドモ ト チカラクラベ ヲシテ ゴラン ナサレ
Do. Wa-ta-k'-shi do-mo to chi-ka-ra ku-ra-be wo sh'-te, mi na-sa-e.
   ワタクシドモ ト チカラクラベ ヲシテ ミ ナサエ

68. *Come let's take a walk.*
   Wa-ta-k'-shi do-mo to o a-so-bi ni o i-de na-sa-re.
   ワタクシドモ トオアソビニオイデ ナサレ
Do. Wa-ta-k'-shi do-mo to a-so-bi ni yu-ki na-sa-e.
   ワタクシドモ トアソビニ ユキ ナサエ

69. *Come again some other time.*
   Ta ji-tsz ma-ta o i-de na-sa-re.
   タジツ マタオイデ ナサレ
Do. Ma-ta ko-n-da ki na-sa-e.
   マタ コンダ キ ナサエ

70. *Come again soon.*
   Ma-ta ki-n ji-tsz ni o i-de na-sa-re.
   マタ キンジツニオイデ ナサレ
Do. Ma-ta so-no u-chi ni ko-i.
   マタ ソノウチニ コイ

71. *Come, go with me.*
   Wa-ta-k'-shi to to-mo-ni o i-de na-sa-re.
   ワタクシ トトモニオイデ ナサレ
Do. Wa-ta-k'-shi to to-mo-ni yu-ke.
   ワタクシ トトモニ エケ

72. *Come, make up your mind what you will do.*
   A-na-ta na-ni wo na-sa-ri-ma-sh'-o-o ka, ha-ya-ku o ki-me na-sa-re.
   アナタナニヲ ナサリマシャウカ ハヤクオキメ ナサレ

72. Na-ni wo sz-ru ka, ha-ya-ku ki-me-ro.
ナニヲ スルカ ハヤク キメロ

73. *Come now, altogether; up with it.*
Mi-na k'-te, to-mo ni o-shi a-nge-ro.
ミナ キテ トモニ オシ アゲロ

74. *Come now, tell me all about it.*
I-ma, wa-ta-k'-shi ni ku-wa-sh'-ku o ha-na-shi na-sa-re.
イマ ワタクシニ クワシク オ ハナシ ナサレ

Do. I-ma, wa-ta-k'-shi ni no-ko-ra-dz ha-na-se.
イマ ワタクシニ ノコラズ ハナセ

75. *Consider that matter well.*
So-no ko-to wo yo-ku ka-n-nga-e-te go ra-n na-sa-re.
ソノコトヲ ヨク カンガエテ ゴランナサレ

Do. So-no ko-to wo yo-ku ka-n-nga-e-te mi-ro.
ソノコトヲ ヨク カンガエテ ミロ

76. *Count the eggs in that basket.*
So-no ka-ngo no ta-ma-ngo wo ka-dzo-e-te go ra-n na-sa-re.
ソノカゴ ノ タマゴ ヲ カゾエテ ゴランナサレ

Do. A-no ka-ngo no ta-ma-ngo wo ka-dzo-e-te mi-ro.
アノカゴ ノ タマゴ ヲ カゾエテ ミロ

77. *Cover those boxes with oil-paper, so that they will not get wet.*
A-no ha-ko no nu-re-nu yo-o-ni to-o yu wo ka-ke-te o-ke.
アノハコ ノ ヌレヌ ヤウニ トヲユ ヲ カケテ オケ

78. *Cranes & geese abound in the fields of Japan, but it is forbidden to catch them.*
Tsz-ru to ga-n wa ni-p-po-n no ta ni ta-ku-sa-n o-ri-te o-ri-
ツル ト ガン ハ ニッポン ノ タニ タクサン オリテ オリ
ma-s' nga, to-ru ko-to wa go ch'-o ji de go za-ri-ma-s'
マス ガ トル コト ハ ゴテウジ デ ゴザリマス

Do. Ni-p-po-n no ta ni, tsz-ru to ga-n wa ta-n-to i-ru nga, go
ニッポン ノ タニ ツル ト ガン ハ タント イル ガ ゴ
ch'-o ji da ka-ra, to-ru ko-to wa na-ra-nu.
テウジ ダ カラ トル コト ハ ナラヌ

79. *Crape is made by tightly twisting the silken threads.*
Chi-ri me-n wa ki-nu i-to ni o-o-ku yo-ri wo ka-ke-te ts'-ku-
チリメン ハ キヌイト ニ オヲク ヨリ ヲ カケテ ツク
ri-ma-s'.
リマス

Do. Chi-ri me-n wa i-to ni ta-n-to yo-ri wo ka-ke-te ts'-ku-ru.
チリメン ハ イトニ タントヨニ ヲ カケテ ツクル

80. *Cut it in two.*
K'-t-te f'-ta-tsz ni na-sa-re-ma-sh'.
キッテ フタツ ニ ナサレマシ

Do. K'-t-te f'-ta-tsz ni shi-ro.
キッテ フタツ ニ シロ

81. *Cuttle-fish are considered a delicacy in Japan.*
   Ni-p-po-n de wa ta-ko-wa ko-o bu-tsz ni o-mo-wa-re-ma-s'
   ニッポンデ ハ タコ ハ コウブツ ニオモワレマス
   Do. Ni-p-po-n de wa ta-ko wa ko-o bu-tsz ni o-mo-wa-re-ru.
   ニッポンデ ハ タコ ハ カウブツ ニオモワレル

D

82. *Did you say so?*
   A-na-ta wa so-no to-o-ri ni o-se-ra-re-ma-sh'-ta ka?
   アナタ ハ ソノ トオリ ニ オオセラレ マシタ カ
   Do. O-ma-e so-no to-o-ri ni i-t-ta-ka?
   オマエ ソノ トオリ ニ イッタカ

83. *Did you tell him so?*
   A-na-ta wa-no o ka-ta ni sa-yo-o ni o-s'-shi-ya-ri-ma-sh'-ta ka?
   アナタ ハ アノオカタ ニ サヤウニ オッシャリマシタ カ
   Do. O-ma-e a-no h'-to ni so-no yo-o ni ha-na-sh'-ta ka?
   オマエ アノ ヒト ニ ソノ ヤウニ ハナシタ カ

84. *Did you ever see an elephant?*
   A-na-ta wa i-ma ma-de ni dzo-o wo go ra-n na-sa-re-ma-sh'-ta ka?
   アナタ ハ イママデ ニ ヅウ ヲ ゴラン ナサレマシタ カ
   Do. O-ma-e wa i-ma ma-de ni dzo-o wo mi-ta ka?
   オマエ ハ イママデ ニ ヅウ ヲ ミタ カ

85. *Did you hear the bell ring?*
   Ka-ne nga na-ri-ma-sh'-ta nga o ki-ki na-sa-re-ma-sh'-ta ka?
   カ子 ガ ナリマシタ ガ オキキ ナサレマシタ カ
   Do. Ka-ne nga na-t-ta nga ki-i-ta ka?
   カ子 ガ ナッタ カ キイタ カ

86. *Did you hear the clock strike?*
   To-ke-i no ka-ne nga na-ri-ma-sh'-ta nga o ki-ki na-sa-re-ma-sh'-ta ka?
   トケイノカ子 ガ ナリマシタ ガ オキキ ナサレマシタ カ
   Do. To-ke-i no ka-ne nga na-t-ta nga ki-i-ta ka?
   トケイノカ子 ガ ナッタ ガ キイタ カ

87. *Did you hear him say so?*
   A-no h'-to no a-no ha-na-sh'-ta ko-to wo, o ki-ki na-sa-re-ma-sh'-ta ka'.
   アノ ヒト ノ アノ ハナシタ コト ヲ オキキ ナサレマシタ カ
   Do. A-no h'-to no a-no ha-na-sh'-ta ko-to wo ki-i-ta ka?
   アノ ヒト ノ アノ ハナシタ コト ヲ キイタ カ

88. *Dinner is ready.*
　　Hi-ru go ha-n no sh'-ta-ku wa mo-o yo-ro-shi-u go za-ri ma-s'.
　　ヒルゴハンノシタクハモウヤロシウゴザリマス
　Do. Hi-ru me-shi no sh'-ta--ku nga mo-o i-i.
　　ヒルメシノシタクガモウイイ

89. *Divide this into five parts.*
　　Ko-re wo i-tsz ni o wa-ri na-sa-re.
　　コレヲイツニオハリナサレ
　Do. Ko-re wo i-tsz ni wa-ri na-sa-e.
　　コレヲイツニハリナサエ

90. *Do you smoke?*
　　Ta-ba-ko wo o no-mi na-sa-re-ma-s' ka?
　　タバコヲオノミナサレマスカ
　Do. Ta-ba-ko wo no-mu ka?
　　タバコヲノムカ

91. *Do this first: afterwards the other.*
　　Ko-re wo sa-ki ni na-sa-re-te, ho-ka no wo a-to de na-sa-re-ma-sh'.
　　コレヲサキニナサレテホカノヲアトデナサレマシ
　Do. Ko-re wo sa-ki ni sh'-te, ho-ka no wo a-to de shi-ro.
　　コレヲサキニシテホカノヲアトデシロ

92. *Do you like Indian corn?*
　　A-na-ta wa to-o mo-ro-ko-shi wo o s'-ki de go za-ri-ma-s ka?
　　アナタハトウモロコシヲオスキデゴザリマスカ
　Do. O-ma-e wa to-o mo-ro-ko-shi wo s'-ki ka?
　　オマエハトウモロコシヲスキカ

93. *Do as you please.*
　　A-na-ta no o-bo-shi-me-shi ni na-sa-re-ma-sh'.
　　アナタノオボシメシニナサレマシ
　Do. O-ma-e no o-mo-o to-o-ri ni na-sa-i.
　　オマエノオモフトヲリニナサイ

94. *Do it as well as you can.*
　　Ki-ri-o-o no o-yo-bu da-ke na-sa-re-ma-sh'.
　　キリヤウノオヨブダケナサレマシ
　Do. Se-i i-p-pa-i ni shi-ro.
　　セイイッパイニシロ

95. *Do you speak English?*
　　A-na ta wa I-ngi-ri-sz no ko-to-ba wo o ts'-ka-e na-sa-re-ma-s' ka?
　　アナタハイギリスノコトバヲオツカエナサレマスカ
　Do. O-ma-e I-ngi-ri-sz no ko-to-ba wo ts'-ka-e-ru ka?
　　オマエイギリスノコトバヲツカエルカ

96. *Do figs grow in this country?*
　　Ko-no ku-ni ni i-chi-ji-ku no ki nga ha-e-ma-s' ka?
　　コノクニニイチジクノキガハエマスカ

96. Ko-no ku ni ni i-chi-ji-ku ki nga ha-e-ru ka?
コノ クニニ イ チジク キガ ハエル カ

97. *Do you remember how it was?*
A-re wa do-o i-ta-sh-ta ko-to de go za-ri-ma-s' ka, o-bo-e-te
アレ ハ ドウイタシタ コトデ ゴ ザリマス カ オボエテ
o i-de na-sa-re-ma-s' ka?
オイデ ナサレマスカ

Do. A-re wa do-o sh'ta ko-to ka, o-bo-e-te i-ru ka?
アレ ハ ドウ シタ コト カ オボエテイル カ

98. *Do the Japanese make pistols?*
Ni-p-po-n h'to wa ta-ne-nga-shi-ma wo ko-shi-ra-i-ma-s' ka?
ニッポン ヒト ハ タネ ガシマ ヲ コシライマス カ

Do. Ni-p-po-n h'to wa ta-ne-nga-shi-ma wo ts'-ku-ru ka?
ニッポン ヒト ハ タネ ガシマ ヲ ツクル カ

99. *Do you know any thing about this.*
Ko-no ko-to wo s'-ko-shi wa go zo-n-ji de go za-ri-ma-s' ka?
コノコト ヲ スコシ ハ ゴ ゾンジデ ゴ ザリマス カ

Do. Ko-no ko-to wo s'-ko-shi wa sh'-t-te i-ru ka?
コノコト ヲ スコシ ハ シッテイル カ

100. *Do you know what is good for a cold?*
H'-ki ka-ze no k'-sz-ri wo sh'-t-te o i'-de na-sa-re-ma-s' ka?
ヒキ カゼ ノ クスリ ヲ シッテオイデナサレマス カ

Do. H'-ki ka-ze no k'-sz-ri wo sh'-t-te i-ru ka?
ヒキ カゼ ノ クスリ ヲ シッテイル カ

101. *Do you really need it?*
A-na-ta ko-re wa ma-ko-to ni i-ri yo-o de go za-ri-ma-s' ka?
アナタ コレ ハ マコト ニ イリヨウデ ゴ サリマス カ

Do. Ta-sh'-ka ni i-ri yo-o ka?
タシカ ニ イリヨウ カ

102. *Do this the first thing to-morrow morning.*
Mi-o-o a-sa ko-re wo sa-ki ni na-sa-re-ma-se.
ミヤウアサ コレ ヲ サキ ニ ナサレマセ

Do. A-sz no a-sa ko-re wo sa-ki ni shi-ro.
アス ノ アサ コレ ヲ サキ ニ シロ

103. *Does this silk fade?*
Ko-no ki-nu no i-ro wa sa-me-ma-s' ka?
コノ キヌ ノ イロ ハ サメマス カ

Do. Ko-no ki-nu no i-ro wa sa-me-ru ka?
コノ キヌ ノ イロ ハ サメル カ

104. *Does your watch keep good time?*
A-na-ta no to-ke-i wa yo-ku a-i-ma-s' ka?
アナタ ノ トケイ ハ ヨクアイマス カ

Do. O-ma-e no to-ke-i wa yo-ku a-u ka?
オマヘ ノ トケイ ハ ヨク アフ カ

105. *Does he live there still?*

105. A-no o ka-ta wa ma-da a-so-ko ni sz-ma-t-te o i-de na-sa-re-ma-s' ka?
アノオカタ ハ マダ アソコ ニ スマツテオイデ ナサレ マスカ

Do. A-no h'-to wa ma-da a-s'-ko ni sz-ma-t-te i-ru ka?
アノ ヒト ハ マダ アスコ ニ スマツテ イル カ

106. *Do not touch that.*
So-re ni te wo o ts'-ke na-sa-ru-na.
ソレニ テ ヲ オツケ ナサルナ

Do. So-re wo i-ji-ru-na.
ソレ ヲ イジルナ

107. *Do not play too hard.*
A-ma-ri sa-wa-i de o a-so-bi na-sa-ru-na.
アマリ サワイ デ オアソビ ナサルナ

Do. A-ma-ri sa-wa-i de a-so-bu-na.
アマリ サワイデ アソブナ

108. *Do not come here again.*
Mo-o f'-ta-ta-bi ko-ko ni o i-de na-sa-ru-na.
モウ フタタビ ココ ニオイデ ナサルナ

Do. Mo-o f'-ta-ta-bi ko-ko e ku-ru-na.
モウ フタタビ ココ エ クルナ

109. *Do not let it get wet.*
O nu-ra-shi na-sa-re-ma-s'-na.
オ ヌラシ ナサレ マスナ

Do. Nu-ra-sz-na.
ヌラスナ

110. *Do not mind what he says.*
A-no h'-to no mo-o-sa-re-ru ko-to ni o ka-ma-i na-sa-ru-na.
アノ ヒト ノ モウサレル コト ニ オカマイ ナサルナ

Do. A-re nga i-u ko-to ni ka-ma-u-na.
アレ ガ イフ コト ニ カマウナ

111. *Do not take up so much room.*
So-no yo-o ni ha-ba wo na-sa-re-ma-s'-na.
ソノ ヤウニ ハバ ヲ ナサレ マスナ

Do. So-o ha-ba wo sz-ru-na.
ソウ ハバ ヲ スルナ

112. *Don't throw away a single kernel of that bird-seed.*
So-no ki-bi h'-to tsz-bu mo o s'-te na-sa-ru-na.
ソノ キビ ヒトツブ モ オステ ナサルナ

Do. So-no ki-bi h'-to tsz-bu mo s'-te-ru-na.
ソノ キビ ヒトツブ モ ステルナ

113. *Do not waste a bit of it.*
S'-ko-shi mo o tsz-i-ya-shi na-sa-ru-na.
スコシ モ オツイヤシ ナサルナ

Do. S'-ko-shi mo tsz-i-ya-sz-na.
スコシ モ ツイヤスナ

114. *Do not be in such a hurry.*
   So-no yo-o ni o i-so-ngi na-sa-ru-na.
   ソノ ヤウニオイソギ ナサルナ
Do.   So-no yo-o ni se-ku-na.
   ソノヤウニセクナ

115. *Do not leave the door open.*
   To wo a-ke ha-na-sh'-te o i-de na-sa-ru-na.
   トヲアケ ハナシテオイデ ナサルナ
Do.   To wo a-ke ha-na-sh'-te de-ru-na.
   トヲアケ ハナシテ デルナ

116. *Do not let it burn: stir it.*
   Ko-nge-nu yo-o ni o ka-ki ma-wa-shi na-sa-re.
   コゲヌヤウニオカキ マワシ ナサレ
Do.   Ko-nge-nu yo-o ni ka-ki ma-wa-se.
   コゲヌヤウニ カキ マワセ

117. *Do not put it off any longer.*
   Ma-ta o no-ba-shi na-sa-ru-na.
   マタオノバシ ナサルナ
Do.   Ma-ta no-ba-sz-na.
   マタ ノバスナ

118. *Do not be discouraged.*
   O a-ki na-sa-ru-na.
   オアキ ナサルナ
Do.   A-ki-ru-na.
   アキルナ

119. *Do not swallow the pits.*
   Ta-ne wo o no-mi ko-mi na-sa-ru-na.
   タネヲオノミコミ ナサルナ
Do.   Ta-ne wo no-mi ko-mu-na.
   タネ ヲ ノミ コムナ

120. *Do not be so long about it.*
   So-no yo-o ni h'-sa-sh'-ku o ka-ka-ri na-sa-ru-na.
   ソノヤウニヒサシクオ カカリ ナサルナ
Do.   So-no yo-o ni na-nga-ku ka-ka-ru-na.
   ソノ ヤウニナガク カカルナ

121. *Do not lose your place.*   (in reading.)
   A-na-ta no o yo-mi na-sa-re-ta to-ko-ro wo o wa-sz-re na-sa-ru-na.
   アナタノ オヨミ ナサレタ トコロ ヲ オワスレ ナサルナ
Do.   Yo n-da to-ko-ro wo wa-sz-re-ru-na.
   ヨンダ トコロ ヲ ワスレルナ

122. *Do not soil that map.*
   So-no e-dz wo o yo-ngo-shi na-sa-ru-na.
   ソノエズヲオ ヨゴシ ナサルナ

122. So-no e-dz wo yo-ngo-sz-na.
ソノ エズ ヲ ヨゴ スナ

123. *Do not take that child's play-things.*
A-no ko-do-mo no mo-chi-a-so-bi wo o to-ri na-sa-ru-na.
アノ コドモ ノ モチ アソビ ヲ オトリ ナサルナ

Do. A-no ko-do-mo no mo-chi-a-so-bi wo to-ru-na.
アノ コドモ ノ モチ アソビ ヲ トルナ

124. *Do not go there; you may get hurt.*
A-so-ko e o i-de na-sa-ru-na; ke-nga wo sz-ru to a-bu-no o go za-ri-ma-s'.
アソコ エ オイデ ナサルナ ケガ ヲ スルト アブノ フゴ ザニマス

Do. A-s'-ko e yu-ku-na; ke-nga wo sz-ru to a-bu-na-i.
アスコ エ ユクナ ケガ ヲ スルト アブナイ

125. *Don't wake up the baby.*
Sh'o ni no me wo o sa-ma-shi na-sa-ru-na.
セウニ ノ メ ヲ オサマシ ナサルナ

Do. Ko no me wo sa-m i-sz-na.
コノ メ ヲ サマスナ

126. *Do you not see into it get?*
Ma-da o wa-ka-ri na-sa-re-ma-se-nu-ka?
マダ オ ワカリ ナサレマ セヌカ

Do. Ma-da wa-ka-ra-nu ka?
マダ ワカラヌカ

127. *Do not ride too fast down hill.*
Ya-ma wo o-ri-ru ni wa m'-ma nga ha-ya sz-ngi-ru ha-shi-ra-se na-sa-ru-na.
ヤマ ヲ オリル ニ ハ ウマ ガ ハヤ スギル ハシ ラセ ナサルナ

Do. Ya-ma wo ku-da-ru ni wa m'-ma nga ha-ya sz-ngi-ru ha-shi-ra-se-ru-na.
ヤマ ヲ クダル ニ ハ ウマ ガ ハヤ スギル ハ シラセルナ

128. *Dont bring that here; away with it.*
So-re wo ko-ko e mo-t-te o i-de na-sa-ru-na; ho-ka e o ya-ri na-sa-re.
ソレ ヲ ココ ヘ モッテ オイデ ナサルナ ホカ ヘ オヤリ ナサレ

Do. So-re wo ko-ko e mo-t-te ku-ru-na, ho-ka e ya-re.
ソレ ヲ ココ ヘ モッテ クルナ ホカ ヘ ヤレ

129. *Do not take the whole, leave some for him.*
No-ko-ra-dz o to-ri na-sa-ru-na; a-no o ka-ta ni no-ko-sh'-te o o-ki na-sa-re.
ノコラズ オトリ ナサルナ アノ オカタ ニ ノコシテ オオキ ナサレ

129. Mi-na to-ru-na; a-no h'-to ni no-ko-sh-te o-ke.
ミナ トルナ アノヒト ニノコシテ オケ

130. Do not trade with that man; he is sure to take you in.
A-no h'-to to ka-u-e-ki wo na-sa-ru-na; ta-sh'-ka ni a-na-ta wo
アノヒト ト カウヱキ ヲナサルナ タシカ ニアナタ ヲ
da-ma-shi-ma-sz-ru.
ダマシマスル

Do. A-no h'-to to ka-u-e-ki wo shi na-sa-ru-na; ta-sh'-ka ni o-
アノヒト ト カウヱキ ヲ シ ナサルナ タシカ ニオ
ma-e wo da-ma-s'.
マヘ ヲ ダマス

131. Do not call him off from his work again.
A-no h'-to no ma-nga ka-ke-ru ka-ra mo-o o-yo-bi na-sa-re-
アノヒト ノ マガ カケル カラ モウ オヨビ ナサレ
ma-sz-na.
マスナ

Do. A-no h'-to no ma-nga ka-ke-ru ka-ra, mo-o yo-bu-na.
アノヒト ノ マガ カケル カラモウ ヨブナ

132. Do not cross my threshold again without leave.
Wa-ta-k'-shi no yu-ru-shi-ma-se-nu u-chi wa, ka-sa-ne-te ji-f'-
ワタクシ ノ ユルシマセヌ ウチ ハ カサネテ ジフ
ku wo o ma-ta-ngi na-sa-ru-na.
ク ヲ オ マタギ ナサルナ

Do. Wa-ta-k'-shi no yu-ru-sa-nu u-chi wa f'-ta-ta-bi ji-f'-ku wo
ワタクシ ノ ユルサヌ ウチ ハ フタタビ ジフク ヲ
ma-ta-ngu-na.
マタグナ

133. Dumb people talk by signs.
O-shi no h'-to nga te ma-ne de o-shi-e-ma-s'.
オシ ノ ヒト ガ テ マ子 デ オシエマス

Do. O-shi no h'-to nga te ma-ne de o-shi-e-ru.
オシ ノ ヒト ガ テ マ子 デ オシエル

134. Dyers are called ko-o-ya sho-ku-nin.
So-me mo-no sz-ru h'-to wa ko-o-ya sh'-yo-ku-ni-n to mo-o
ソメ モノ スル ヒト ハ コウヤ シヨクニン ト モウ
shi-ma-s'.
シマス

Do. So-me mo-no sz-ru h'-to wa ko-o-ya sh'-yo-ku-ni-n to i-u.
ソメ モノ スル ヒト ハ コウヤ シヨクニン トイフ

E

135. Each country has its own laws.
O no o-no no ku-ni wa ji ko-ku no ha-t-to nga go za-ri-ma-s'.
オノオノ ノ クニ ハ ジコク ノ ハット ガ ゴザリマス

135. O-no o-no no ku-ni wa ji ko-ku no ha-t-to nga a-ru
オノオノノクニハジコクノハットガアル

136. *Earthquakes are frequent here.*
Ko-no to-ko-ro wa ji shi-n nga o-ri o-ri go za-ri-ma-s'.
コノトコロハジシンガオリオリゴザリマス

Do. Ko-no to-ko-ro wa ji shi-n nga o-ri o-ri i-ta-shi-ma-s'.
コノトコロハジシンガオリオリイタシマス

137. *Empty this box.*
Ko-no ha-ko no na-ka no mo-no wo a-ke-te ku-da-sa-re.
コノハコノナカノモノヲアケテクダサレ

Do. Ko-no ha-ko no na-ka no mo-no wo a-ke-ro.
コノハコノナカノモノヲアケロ

138. *England & China have been at war three times.*
I-ngi-ra-n wa Ka-ra to mi ta-bi ka-s-se-n ni o-yo-bi-ma-sh'-ta.
イギランハカラトミタビカッセンニオヨビマシタ

Do. I-ngi-ra-n wa Ka-ra to sa-n do ta-ta-ka-t-ta.
イギランハカラトサンドタタカッタ

139. *Ever since I came here, I have been unwell.*
Wa-ta-k'-shi ko-ko-ni ma-i ri-ma-sh'-te yo-ri ki-bu-n nga a-shi-a go za-ri-ma-s'.
ワタクシココニマイリマシタヨリキブンガアシウゴザリマス

Do. Wa-ta-k'-shi ko-ko-ni k'-te ka-ra ki-bu-n nga wa-ru-ku na-t-ta.
ワタクシココニキテカラキブンガワルクナッタ

140. *Every body knows that.*
So-re wa do-na-ta mo go zo-n-ji, de go za-ri-ma-s'.
ソレハドナタモゴゾンジデゴザリマス

Do. So-re wa da-re mo sh'-t'-te i-ru.
ソレハダレモシッテイル

141. *Every Japanese may wear one short sword at pleasure.*
Wa-ji-n mi-na mi-na wa-ki za-shi wo i-p-po-n sa-shi-ma-s' ko-to-wa kæt-te shi-da-i ni na-ri-ma-s'-
ワジンミナミナワキザシヲイッポンサシマスコトハカッテシダイニナリマス

Do. Ni-p-po-n ji-n wa mi-na mi-na wa-ki-za-shi wo i-p-po-n sa-sz ko-to wa ka-t-te shi-da-i ni-na-ru.
ニッポンジンハミナミナワキザシヲイッポンサスコトハカッテシダイニナル

142. *Evil deeds run a thousand leagues; but good deeds do not go out of one's door.* (a proverb)
A-ku ji wa se-n ri wo ha-shi-ru, ko-o ji wa mo-n wo i-de-dz.
アクジハセンリヲハシルコウジハモンヲイデズ

143. *Evil left to itself grows worse and worse.*
A-sh'-ki wo s'-te-te o-ki-ma-s' to shi-da-i ni tsz-no-ri-ma-sz-ru.
アシキヲステテオキマストシダイニツノリマスル

143. A-sh'-ki wo s'-te-te o-ku to shi-da-i ni tsz-no-ru.
アシキ ヲ ステテオク ト シデイ ニ ツノル

144. *Extortion is very wrong.*
Mu-sa-bo-ri-to-ru ko-to wa ha-na-ha-da mu-do-o no i-ta-sh'
ka-ta de go za-ri-ma-s'.
ムサボリトル コト ハ ハナハダ ムトウ ノ イタシ
カタ デ ゴ ザリマス

Do. Mu-sa-bo-ri-to-ru ko-to wa ha-na-ha-da mu-do-o no sz-ru-ko-to
ムサボリトル コト ハ ハナハダ ムドウ ノ スル コト

145. *Exercise of the body is its medicine.* (a proverb.)
Ka-ra-da wo u-ngo-ka-sz wa mi no k'-sz-ri de go za-ri-ma-s'.
カラダ ヲ ウゴカス ハ ミ ノ クスリ デ ゴ ザリマス

Do. Ka-ra-da-wo u-ngo-ka-sz wa mi no k'-sz-ri ni na-ru.
カラダヲ ウゴカス ハ ミ ノ クスリ ニ ナル

F.

146. *Feed my horse well, he is growing thin.*
Wa-ta-k'-shi no m'-ma-nga ya-se-ru ka-ra ta-k'-sa-n ku-wa-se-ro.
ワタクシ ノ ムマ ガ ヤセル カラ タクサン クハセロ

147. *Few persons say so.*
So-no yo-o ni mo-o-sz h'-to wa s'-ku-no-o go za-ri-ma-s'.
ソノ ヨウニ モウス ヒト ハ スクノウ ゴ ザリマス

Do. So-no yo-o ni i-u h'-to-wa s'-ku-na-i.
ソノ ヨウニ イウ ヒト ハ スクナイ

148. *Feel this, how soft it is.*
Ko-re ni sa-wa-t-te go ra-n na-sa-re; ya-wa-ra-ka de go za-ri-ma-s'.
コレ ニ サハツテ ゴラン ナサレ ヤハラカ デ ゴ ザ
リマス

Do. Ko-re ni sa-wa-t-te mi na-sa-i; ya-wa-ra-ka-i.
コレ ニ サハツテ ミ ナサイ ヤハラカイ

149. *Fill it up.*
I-p-pa-i o i-re na-sa-re.
イツパイ ヲ イレ ナサレ

Do. I-p-pa-i i-re-ro.
イツパイ イレロ

150. *Fill it half full.*
Ha-m-bu-n o i-re na-sa-re.
ハンブン ヲ イレ ナサレ

Do. Ha-m-bu-n i-re-ro.
ハンブン イレロ

151. *Fill it a little more than half full.*
Ha-m-bu-n yo-ri s'-ko-shi yo-ke-i o i-re na-sa-re.
ハンブン ヨリ スコシ ヨケイ ヲ イレ ナサレ

151. Ha-m-bu-n yo-ri s'-ko-shi yo-ke-i i-re-ro.
ハンブン ヨリ スコシ ヨケイイレロ

152. *Find my hat, & bring it here*
Wa-ta-k'-shi no ka-mu-ri mo-no wo ta-dz-ne-te k'-te ku-da-sa-re.
ワタクシ ノカムリモ ノヲタヅ子テクテ クダサレ

Do. Wa-ta-k'-shi no ka-mu-ri mo-no wo ta-dz-ne-te mo-t-te ko-i.
ワタクシ ノカムリモノヲ タヅ子テモッテコイ

153. *Fix it to suit yourself.*
No-zo-mi shi-da-i ni o o-ki na-sa-re.
ノゾミ シダイニオオキ ナサレ

Do. Ka-t-te shi-da-i ni o-ke.
カッテ シダイニオケ

154. *Fry some, and boil the rest.*
S'-ko-shi ya-i-te, a-to wa o ni na-sa-re.
スコシヤイテアト ハヲニ ナサレ

Do. S'-ko-shi ya-i-te, a-to wa ni na-sa-i.
スコシヤイテアト ハニ ナサイ

155. *For whom are you making this?*
Ko-re wo do-na-ta ni o ta-no-ma-re de o ts'-ku-ri na-sa-re-ma-s' ka?
コレヲ ドナタニヲタノマレデヲックリ ナサレマスカ

Do. Ko-re wo da-re ni ta-no-ma-re-te ts'-ku-ru ka?
コレヲ ダレニ タノマレテ ックル カ

156. *Fuel is cheaper in Japan than in China.*
Ka-ra yo-ri Ni-p-po-n de wa sz-mi ta-ki-ngi wa ya-sz-u go-za-ri-ma-s'.
カラ ヨリ ニッポンデ ハスミタキギ ハヤスウ ゴザリマス

Do. Ka-ra yo-ri Ni-p-po-n de wa sz-mi ta-ki-ngi nga ya-sz-i.
カラ ヨリ ニッポンデ ハスミタキギ ガ ヤスイ

157. *Furl the sail.*
Ho wo o-ro-se.
ホ ヲ ヲロセ

158. *Furniture is not seen in Japanese parlors.*
Ni-p-po-n no za-sh'-ki no u-chi-ni wa do-o-ngu nga mi-e-ma-se-nu.
ニッポン ノザシキノウチニ ハ ドウグ ガ ミエ マセヌ

Do. Ni-p-po-n no za-sh'-ki no u-chi-ni wa do-o-ngu nga mi-e-nu.
ニッポン ノザシキノ ウチニハ トウグ ガ ミエヌ

159. *Get the horse ready.*
M'-ma no sh'-ta-ku wo shi-ro.
ムマ ノ シタク ヲ シロ

160. *Get my attendants ready.*
Wa-ta-k'-shi no to-mo no sh'-ta-ku wo shi-ro.
ワタクシ ノ トモ ノ シタク ヲ シロ

161. *Get it done before I come back.*
Wa-ta-k'-shi no ka-e-ru ma-e-ni sh'-te o shi-ma-e na-sa-re.
ワタクシ ノ カエル マエニ シテ オ シマエ ナサレ

Do. Wa-ta-k'-shi no ka-e-ru ma-e--ni sh'-te shi-ma-e.
ワタクシ ノ カエル マエニ シテ シマエ

162. *Get out of my way.*
Wa-ki e o yo-ri na-sa-re-te ku-da-sa-re.
ワキ エ オ ヨリ ナサレテ クダサレ

Do. Wa-ki e yo-re.
ワキ エ ヨレ

163. *Get up quick.*
Ha-ya-ku o o-ki na-sa-re-ma-se.
ハヤク オヲキ ナサレマセ

Do. Ha-ya-ku o-ki na-sa-i.
ハヤク ヲキ ナサイ

164. *Get me an ink-stone.*
Sz-dz-ri i-shi wo mo-t-te k'-te ku-da-sa-re.
スズリイシ ヲ モッテ キテ クダサレ

Do. Sz-dz-ri i-shi wo mo-t-te ko-i.
スズリ イシ ヲ モッテ コイ

165. *Get me a ruler.*
J'-o-o-ngi wo mo-t-te k'-te ku-da-sa-re.
ヂャウギ ヲ モッテ キテ クダサレ

Do. J'-o-o-ngi wo mo-t-te ko-i.
ヂャウギ ヲ モッテ コイ

166. *Get your dinner first, and then go.*
Sa-ki e o hi-ru go ha-n wo a-nga-t-te o-yu-ki na-sa-re.
サキ エ オヒル ゴ ハン ヲ アガッテ オユキ ナサレ

Do. Sa-ki--e hi-ru me-shi wo ta-be-te, yu-ke.
サキ エ ヒル メシ ヲ タベテ ユケ

167. *Give this to me.*
Ko-re wo wa-ta-k'-shi ni ku-da-sa-re-ma-sh'.
コレ ヲ ワタクシ ニ クダサレ マシ

Do. Ko-re wo wa-ta-k'-shi ni ku-da-sa-i.
コレ ヲ ワタクシ ニ クダサイ

168. *Give him as much as he wants.*
A-no o ka-ta ni i-ku-ra de-mo i-ru ho-do o a-nge na-sa-re.
アノ オカタ ニ イクラ デモ イル ホド オアゲ ナサレ

Do. A-no h'-to ni i-ku-ra de-mo i-ru ho-do ya-ri na-sa-i.
アノ ヒト ニ イクラ デモ イル ホド ヤリ ナサイ

169. *Give him two thirds of it.*
　　Sa-m bu ni a-no o ka-ta ni o a-nge na-sa-re.
　　サンブ ニアノオカタ ニオ アゲ ナサレ
Do.　Sa-m bu ni a-no h'-to ni ya-ri na-sa-i.
　　サンブ ニアノヒト ニヤリ ナサイ

170. *Give me a receipt for this money.*
　　Wa-ta-k'-shi ni ko-no ka-ne no o u-ke-to-ri nga-ki wo ku-da-sa-re-ma-se.
　　ワタクシ ニコノ カ子 ノオウケトリ ガキ ヲ クダサレマセ
Do.　Wa-ta-k'-shi no ko-no ka-ne no u-ke-to-ri wo ku-da-sa-i.
　　ワタクシ ノコノ カ子 ノウケトリ ヲ クダサイ

171. *Give each of those boys a tempo.*
　　A-no o-to-ko no ko-do-mo ni to-o h'-ya-ku wo i-chi ma-i dz-tsz o ya-ri na-sa-re.
　　アノオトコノ コドモ ニトウヒャク ヲ イチ マイヅツ オヤリ ナサレ
Do.　A-no o-to-ko no ko-do-mo ni h'-ya-ku se-n wo i-chi ma-i dz-tsz ya-re.
　　アノオトコノ コドモ ニヒャクセン ヲ イチ マイヅツ ヤレ

172. *Give this to your master.*
　　Ko-re wo o-ma-i no da-n-na ni a-nge na-sa-i.
　　コレ ヲ オマイ ノ ダンナ ニアゲ ナサイ

173. *Go and eat your meal.*
　　Go ze-n o a-nga-ri ni o yu-ki na-sa-re.
　　ゴゼン オアガリ ニオユキ ナサレ
Do.　O me-shi wo ta-be ni yu-ke.
　　オメシ ヲタベニユケ

174. *Go to bed.*
　　O shi-dz-ma-ri na-sa-re.
　　オシヅマリ ナサレ
Do.　Ne na-sa-i.
　　子 ナサイ

175. *Go & find out what that is.*
　　A-re wa na-ni de go za-ri-ma-s' ka i-t-te go ra-n na-sa-re.
　　アレ ハ ナニデ ゴ ザリマス カイツテ ゴ ラン ナサレ
Do.　A-re wa na-n da ka, i-t-te mi na-sa-i.
　　アレ ハ ナンダ カイツテ ミ ナサイ

176. *Go & come back immediately.*
　　Sz-ngu ni i-t-te o i-de na-sa-re-ma-sh'.
　　スク ニイツテオイデ ナサレ マシ
Do.　Sz-ngu ni i-t-te ko-i.
　　スク ニイツテコイ

177. *Go and put this back.*
Ko-re wo mo-to no to-ko-ro e o o-ki na-sa-re.
コレヲモトノトコロヱオヲキナサレ

Do. Ko-re wo mo-to no to-ko-ro e o-ke.
コレヲモトノトコロヱオケ

178. *Go and help weigh the sugar*
A s'-ko e i-t-te sa-to-o wo ha-ka-ri ni ka-ke-ru te-tsz-da-i wo shi-ro.
アスコヱイツテサトウヲハカリニカケル テツダイヲ シロ

179. *Go and get this pail mended.*
Ko-no te o-ke wo na-o-sa-se ni mo-t-te yu-ke.
コノテヲケヲナヲサセニモツテユケ

180. *God governs all things in heaven and earth.*
Te-n chi ba-n mo-tsz to-mi-ni Ka-mi nga o sa-me ra-re-ma sz-ru.
テンチバンモツトモニカミガヲサメラレマスル

181. *Grind that Indian corn.*
Ko-no mo-ro-ko-shi wo hi-i-te ko ni shi-ro.
コノモロコシヲヒイテコニシロ

182. *Guilty persons are afraid of others.*
Tsz mi a-ru mo-no wa h'-to wo o-so-re-ma sz-ru.
ツミアルモノハヒトヲオソレマスル

183. *Gunpowder is made of saltpetre, charcoal, and sulphur.*
E-n-sh'-o-o wa sh'-o-o-se-ki to sz-mi to i-wo-o de ts'-ku-ri-ma-s'.
ヱンシヤウハシヤウセキトスミトイワウデ ツクリマス

Do. E-n-sh'-o-o wa sh'-o-o-se-ki to sz-mi to i-wo-o de ts'-ku-ru.
ヱンシヤウハシヤウセキトスミトイワウデ ツクル

H.

184. *Had you not better take the other.*
Ho-ka no wo ts'-ka-i-ma-sh'-te wa yo-ro-shi-u go za-ri-ma-se-nu-ka?
ホカノヲツカイマシテハヨロシウゴサリマセヌカ

Do. Ho-ka no wo ts'-ka-t-te-wa yo-ro-sh'-ku na-i ka?
ホカノヲツカツテハヨロシクナイカ

185. *Hand me an envelope.*
J'-o-o bu-ku-ro wo i-chi ma-i ku-da-sa-re.
ジヤウブクロヲイチマイクダサレ

Do. J'-o-o bu-ku-ro wo i-chi ma-i ku-re-ro.
ジヤウブクロヲイチマイクレロ

186. *Hark! what noise is that?*
O ki-ki na-sa-re! A-no hi-bi-ki wa na-ni de go za-ri-ma-s' ka?
オキキナサレ アノ ヒビキ ハ ナニテ ゴザリムス カ
Do. Ki-ke! A-no hi-bi-ki wa na-ni ka?
キケ アノ ヒビキ ハ ナニカ

187. *Hark! what is that?*
O ki-ki na-sa-re! A-re wa na-ni de go za-ri-ma-s' ka?
オキキナサレ アレ ハ ナニデ ゴザリマス カ
Do. Ki-ke! A-re wa na-ni ka?
キケ アレ ハ ナニカ

188. *Has your father got well.*
A-na-ta no chi-chi no go bi-o-o-ki wa yo-ro-shi-u go-za-ri-ma-s' ka?
アナタノ チチ ハ ゴビヤウキ ハ ヨロシウ ゴザリマスカ
Do. O-ma-e no chi-chi no bi-o-o-ki wa yo-i ka?
オマイ ノ チチ ノ ビヤウキ ハ ヨイ カ

189. *Have you any work for me to do Sir?*
Da-n-na wa-ta-k'-shi no i-ta-sz shi-ngo-to nga go za-ri-ma-s' ka?
ダンナハ タクシノイタス シゴト ガ ゴザリマスカ

190. *Have dinner ready by the time divine service is over.*
Wa-ta-k'-shi do-mo no o-nga-mi wo shi-ma-u ma-de-ni go ha-n no sh'-ta-ku wo sh' te o-ke.
ワタクシトモ ノ オガミヲ シマフ マデニ ゴハンノ シタクヲ シテオケ

191. *Have you not done this yet?*
Ko-re wa ma-da de-ki a-nga-ri-ma-se-nu ka?
コレ ハ マダ デキ アガリマセヌカ
Do. Ko-re wa ma-da de-ki a-nga-ra-nu ka?
コレ ハ マダ デキ アガラヌカ

192. *Have you any more.*
A-na-ta ma-da go za-ri-ma-s'-ka?
アナタ マダ ゴザリマスカ
Do. O-ma-e ma-da a-ru ka?
オマエ マダ アルカ

193. *Have you done with this?*
Ko-re wo ts' ka-t-te o shi-ma-i na-sa-re-ma-sh'-ta ka?
コレヲ ツカツテ オシマヒ ナサレマシタカ
Do. Ko-re wo ts'-ka-t-te shi-ma-t-ta ka?
コレヲ ツカツテ シマツタカ

194. *Have you ever been to Nagasaki?*
I-ma-ma-de ni Na-nga-sa-ki e o i-de na-sa-re-ta ko-to wa go za-ri-ma-s' ka?
イママデニ ナガサキ エ オイデ ナサレタ コト ハ ゴザリマスカ

194. I-ma ma-de ni Na-nga-sa-k͟i e i-tta ko-to wa a-ru ka?
イマ マ デ ニ ナガ サキ エ イッタ コト ハ アル カ

195. Have you found your spoon?
A-na-ta no sa-ji wo o ta-dz-ne i-da-sa-re-ma-sh'-ta ka?
アナタ ノ サジ ヲ オタヅネ イダサレ マシタ カ

Do. O-ma-e no sa-ji wo sa-nga-shi da-sh'-ta ka?
オマエ ノ サジ ヲ サガシ ダシタ カ

196. Have you gained or lost by it?
A-na-ta so-re de to-ku wo na-sa-re-ma-sh'-ta ka, so-n wo, na-sa-re-ma-sh'-ta ka?
アナタ ソレ デ トク ヲ ナサレ マシタ カ ソン ヲ ナサレ マシタ カ

Do. O-ma-e so-re de to-ku wo sh'-ta ka, so-n wo sh'-ta ka?
オマエ ソレ デ トク ヲ シタ カ ソン ヲ シタ カ

197. Have you kept an account of expenditures all along?
A-na-ta ko-re ma-de no ki-n ngi-n no de-nga ch'-o-me-n ni hi-ka-e-te go za-ri-ma-s' ka?
アナタ コレ マデ ノ キンギン ノ デガ テウメン ニ ヒカエテゴ ザリ マス カ

Do. O-ma-e ko-re ma-de no ki-n ngi-n no de nga ch'-o-me-n ni ka-ki to-me-te a-ru-ka?
オマエ コレ マデ ノ キンギン ノ デガ テウメン ニ カキ トメテ アル カ

198. Have you any objection to it?
So-re wa a-na-ta no o ki ni i-ri-ma-se-nu ka?
ソレ ハ アナタ ノ オキニ イリ マセス カ

Do. So-re wa o-ma-e no ki-ni i-ra-nu-ka?
ソレ ハ オマエ ノ キニ イラス カ

199. Have an eye to those coolies occasionally to-day.
Ko-n ni-chi ko-no ni-n-so-ku no sz-ru ko to wo o-ri o-ri o mi ma-wa-ri ku-da-sa-re.
コン ニチ コノ ニンソク ノ スル コト ヲ オリオリ オ ミ マワリ クダサレ

Do. Ko-n ni-chi ko-no ni-n-so-ku no sz-ru ko-to wo to-ki do-ki mi ma-wa-ri na-sa-e.
コン ニチ コノ ニンソク ノ スル コト ヲ トキ ドキ ミ マワリ ナサエ

200. Have your seeds come up?
O ma-ki na-sa-re-ta ta-ne wa me nga de-ma-sh'-ta ka?
オ マキ ナサレタ タ子 ハ メ ガ デ マシタ カ

Do. O-ma-e no ma-i-ta ta-ne wa me nga de-ta ka?
オマエ ノ マイタ タ子 ハ メ ガ デタ カ

201. He is dead. (of a superoir)
A-no o-ka-ta wa o na-ku-na-ri na-sa-re-ma-sh'-ta.
アノ オカタ ハ オ ナクナリ ナサレ マシタ

E

201. A-no h'-to wa shi-na-re-ta (or) sh'-ki-o   (of a commoner)
アノヒトハシナレタ シキヨ
Do. Ta-i ku-n wa ko-o ki-o a-so-ba-sa-re-ma-sh'-ta. (of the
タイクンハ ゴウキヨアソバサレマシタ
Tai-kun)
Do. Da-i-mi-o wa go se-i ki-o na-sa-re-ma-sh'-ta. (of a Daimio)
ダイメウハ ゴセイキヨナサレマシタ

202. *He struck me with a club.*
A-no sh'-to nga wa-ta-k'-shi wo bo-o de ta-ta-ki-ma-sh'-ta.
アノヒト ガ ワタクシ ヲ ボウデタタキマシタ
Do. A-no sh'-to nga wa-ta-k'-shi wo bo-o de bu-t-ta.
アノヒト ガ ワタクシ ヲ ボウデブッタ

203. *He will not come here.*
A-no sh' to wa ko-ko-e ku-ru ko-to wo i-ya-nga-ri-ma-s'.
アノヒト ハ ココエクル コト ヲ イヤガリマス
Do. A-re wa ko-ko e ku-ru ko-to wo i-ya-nga-ru
アレハ ココエクル コト ヲ イヤガル

204. *He is gone to Yedo.*
A-no o ka-ta wa Ye-do e o i-de na-sa-re-ma-sh'-ta.
アノ オカタ ハ エドエオイデ ナサレマシタ
Do. A-no h'-to wa Ye-do e yu-ki-ma-sh'-ta.
アノヒト ハ エド エユキマシタ

205. *He keeps two horses.*
A-no o ka-ta wa m'-ma wo ni h'-ki ka-t-te o-ki na-sa-re-ma-s'.
アノオカタハムマヲ ニヒキ カッテオキナサレマス
Do. A-no h'-to wa m'-ma wo ni h'-ki ka-t-te o-ku.
アノヒトハムマヲ ニヒキ カッテオク

206. *He is making money fast.*
A-no o ka-ta wa ji-ki ni ka-ne wo mo-o-ke-ru ko-to wo na-
アノオ カタ ハ ジキニ カ子 ヲ モウケル コト ヲ ナ
sa-re-ma-sz-ru.
サレマスル
Do. A-no h'-to wa ji-ki ni ka-ne wo mo-o-ke-ru ko-to wo sz-ru.
アノヒト ハ ジキニ カ子 ヲ モウケル コト ヲ スル

207. *He is to have his trial to day.*
A-no h'-to wa ko-n ni-chi gi-m mi wo u-ke-ra-re-ma-s'.
アノヒト ハ コン ニチ ギン ミ ヲ ウケラレマス
Do. A-re wa ki-o gi-m mi wo u-ke-ru·
アレ ハ ケウ ギン ミ ヲ ウケル

208. *He looks like a Chinese.*
A-no h'-to wa To-o ji-n ni ni-te i-ru yo-o n' mi-e-ma-s'.
アノヒト ハ トウヂンニ ニテイルヤウ ニ ミエマス
Do. A-re wa To-o ji-n ni ni-te i-ru yo-o ni mi-e-ru.
アレ ハ トウ ヂンニニテイルヤウ ニ ミエル

209. *He is a spendthrift.*
A-no o ka-ta wa fu-shi-ma-tsz de go za-ri-ma-s'.
アノオカタハフシマツデゴザリマス
Do. A-no h'-to wa fu-shi-ma-tsz.
アノヒトハフシマツ

210. *He is fond of opium.*
A-no o-ka-ta wa a-he-n wo sz-i-te ta-be-ra-re-ma-s'.
アノオカタハアヘンヲスイテタベラレマス
Do. A-no h'-to wa a-he-n wo sz-i-te ta-be-ru.
アノヒトハアヘンヲスイテタベル

211. *He has spent all his money.*
A-no o ka-ta wa ka-ne wo mi-na ts'-ka-i ha-ta-shi-ma-sh'-ta.
アノオカタハカ子ヲミナツカヒハタシマシタ
Do. A-no h'-to wa ka-ne wo mi-na ts'-ka-i ts'-ku-sh'-ta.
アノヒトハカ子ヲミナツカヒツクシタ

212. *He has the fever and ague.*
A-no o ka-ta wa o-ko-ri no ya-ma-i de go za-ri-ma-s'.
アノオカタハオコリノヤマヒデゴザリマス
Do. A-no h'-to wa o-ko-ri wo wn-dz-ro-o-te i-ru.
アノヒトハオコリヲウヅラフテイル

213. *He is a well-bred man.*
A-no o ka-ta wa re-i ngi nga ta-da-shi-n go za-ri-ma-s'.
アノオカタハレイギガタダシウゴザリマス
Do. A-no h'-to wa re-i ngi wo yo-ku sh'-t-te o-ri-ma-s'.
アノヒトハレイギヲヨクシツテオリマス

214. *He does not know good manners.*
A-no o ka-ta wa re-i ngi wo shi-ri-ma-se-nu.
アノオカタハレイギヲシリマセヌ
Do. A-no h'-to wa re-i ngi wo shi-ra-nu.
アノヒトハレイギヲシラヌ

215. *He is a very bad man.*
A-no o ka-ta wa ha-na-ha-da a-ku ni-n de go za-ri-ma-s'.
アノオカタハハナハダアクニンデゴザリマス
Do. A-re wa ha-na-ha-da a-sh'-ki h'-to.
アレハハナハダアシキヒト

216. *He has a broken arm.*
A-no o ka-ta wa u-de wo ku-ji-i-te o-ra-re-ma-s'.
アノオカタハウデヲクヂイテオラレマス
Do. A-no h'-to wa u-de wo ku-ji-i-te i-ru.
アノヒトハウデヲクヂイテイル

217. *He has put his wrist out of joint.*
A-no h'-to wa te ku-bi no ho-ne wo chi-nga-i na-sa-re-ma-sh'-ta.
アノヒトハテクビノホ子ヲチカイナサレマシタ

217. A-no h'-to wa te ku-bi no ho-ne wo chi-nga-i-ta.
アノヒト ハ テクビ ノ ホ子 ヲ チ ガイタ

218. *He is ashamed of it.*
A-no o ka-ta wa so-re de ha-ji wo o shi-ri na-sa-re-ma-s'.
アノオ カタ ハ ソレ デ ハヂ ヲオ シリ ナサレマス

Do. A-no h'-to wa so-re de ha-ji wo shi-ru.
アノヒト ハンレ デ ハヂ ヲ シル

129 *He is an American, not a Japanese.*
A-no o ka-ta wa A-me-ri-ka no h'-to de Ni-p-po-n no h'-to
アノオ カタ ハ アメリカ ノ ヒト デ ニツポン ノ ヒト
de go za-ri-ma-se-nu.
デ ゴザリマセス

Do. A-re wa A-me-ri-ka no h'-to de Ni-p-po-n no h'-to de
アレ ハ アメリカ ノ ヒト デ ニツポン ノ ヒト デ
wa na-i.
ハナイ

220. *He has not done this right.*
A-no o ka-ta wa ko-re wo ts'-ku-ru ko-to wa yo-ro-sh'-ku go
アノオ カタ ハ コレ ヲ ツクル コト ハ ヨロシク ゴ
za-ri-ma-se-nu.
ザリマセヌ

Do. A-no h'-to wa ko-re wo ts'-ku-ru ko-to wa yo-ro-sh'-ku na-i.
アノヒト ハ コレ ヲ ツクル コト ハ ヨロシクナイ

221. *He is an impudent fellow.*
A-no h'-to wa ha-ji wo shi-ra-nu.
アノヒト ハ ハヂ ヲ シラヌ

222. *He has a new jacket.*
A-no o ka-ta wa a-ta-ra-shi-i ha-o-ri nga go za-ri-ma-s'.
アノオ カタ ハ アタラシイ ハヲリ ガ ゴザリマス

Do. A-no h'-to wa a-ta-ra-shi-i ha-o-ri nga a-ru.
アノヒト ハ アタラシイ ハヲリ ガ アル

223. *He said I might go.*
A-no o ka-ta nga wa-ta-k'-shi ni i-t-te mo yo-i to o-s-shi-ya-
アノオ カタ ガ ワタクシ ニイツテモ ヨイト オツシヤ
ri-ma-sh'-ta.
リマシタ

Do. A-no h'-to nga wa-ta-k'-shi ni i-t-te mo yo-i to i-t-ta.
アノヒト ガ ワタクシ ニイツテモ ヨイトイツタ

224. *He has gone home.*
O ta-ku e o ka-i-ri na-sa-re-ma-sh'-ta.
オタクエオ カイリナサレマ シタ

Do. U-chi e ka-i-t-ta.
ウチ エカイツタ

225. *He was here just now.*
Sa-ki ho-do ko-ko ni o i-de na-sa-re-ma-sh'-ta.
サキ ホド ココ ニオイデ ナサレマシタ

Do. Sa-k'-ki ko-ko ni i-ta.
サツキ ココ ニイタ

226. *He is as bad as ever.*
Se-n no to-o-ri wa-ru-u go za-ri-ma-s'.
センノトウリ ワルウ ゴザリマス

Do. Se-n no to-o-ri wa-ru-i.
センノトウリ ワルイ

227. *He has a bad cold.*
A-no o ka-ta wa sh-o-o-ka-n wo wa-dz-ra-t-te o i-de na-sa-re-ma-s'.
アノオカタ ハ シヨウカンヲ ワズラツテオイデナサレマス

Do. A-no h'-to wa sh-o-o-ka-n wo wa-dz-ra-t-te i-ru.
アノヒト ハ シヨウカン ヲ ワズラツテイル

228. *He has a bad cough.*
A-no o ka-ta wa se-ki nga o-mo-o go za-ri-ma-s'.
アノオカタ ハ セキ ガ オモヲ ゴザリマス

Do. A-no h'-to wa se-ki nga o-mo-i.
アノヒト ハ セキ ガ オモイ

229. *He is a clever boy.*
A-no o ko wa ha-tsz-me-i de o i-de na-sa-re-ma-s'.
アノオコ ハ ハツメイデオイデ ナサレマス

Do. A-no ko wa ri-ko-o mo-no.
アノコ ハ リコウ モノ

230. *He comes here seldom.*
Ta-ma ni ko-ko ni o i-de na-sa-re-ma-s'.
タマニ ココ ニオイデ ナサレマス

Do. Ta-ma ni ko-ko o ku-ru.
タマニ ココ エ クル

231. *He is only pretending.*
A-no o ka-ta wa to-bo-ke-ta ko-to ba-ka-ri na-sa-re-ma-s'.
アノオカタ ハ トボケタ コト ベカリ ナサレマス

Do. A-re wa to-bo-ke-ta ko-to ba-ka-ri sz-ru.
アレ ハ トボケタ コト ベカリ スル

232. *He and I differ in opinion about that.*
A-no ko-to wa wa-ta-k'-shi no o-mo-o to a-no o-ka-ta no o-mo-i na-sa-ru to wa chi-nga-i-ma-sz-ru.
アノコト ハ ワタクシ ノ オモフ ト アノ オカタ ノ オ オモイナサル ト ハ チガイマズル

Do. A-no ko-to wa wa-ta-k'-shi no o-mo-o to a-no h'-to no o-mo-o to chi-nga-i-ma-s'.
アノ コト ハ ワタクシ ノ オモフ ト アノ ヒト ノ オ モフ ト チ ガイマス

233. *He is the most polite man I am acquainted with.*
Wa-ta-k'-shi no dzo-n-ji-ma-sh'-ta u-chi de wa a-no o ka-ta
ワタクシ ノ ゾンチマシ タ ウチ デ ハ アノ オカタ

nga i-chi-ba-n re-i ngi ta-da-shi-u go za-ri-ma-s'.
ガ イ チ ベン レイ ギ タタシウ ゴ ザリマス

Do. Wa-ta-k'shi sh'-t-ta u-chi de wa a-no h'-to nga i-chi-ba-n
ワガクシ シッタウチ デ ハ アノヒト ガ イ チ バン
re-i ngi nga ta-da-shi-i.
レイギ ガ タダシイ

234. *He is so stupid, he will never learn any thing.*
A-no o h'-to wa gu-do-n de go za-ri-ma-s' ka-ra, tsz-i-ni o-bo-
アノオヒト ハ グドンデ ゴザリマス カラ ツイニオボ
e-ru ko-to wa de-ki-ma-s' ma-i.
エルコト ハ デキマス マイ

Do. A-re wa gu-do-n yu-e tsz-i-ni o-bo-e-ru ko-to wa de-ki ma-i.
アレ ハ グドンユエ ツイ ニ オボエル コト ハ デキ マイ

235. *He does not understand his business well.*
A-no o ka-ta wa ka-ngi-o-o no mi-chi wo wa-ki-ma-e-te o-
アノオカタ ハ カギャウノ ミチ ヲ ワキマエテオ
ra-re-ma-se-nu.
ラレマセス

Do. A-no h'-to wa ka-ngi-o-o no mi-chi wo shi-ra-nu.
アノヒト ハ カギャウノ ミチ ヲ シラス

236. *He is so sick that he cannot live long.*
A-no o ka-ta wa go bi-o-o shi-n de go za-ri-ma-s' ka ra, o
アノオ カタ ハ ゴ ビャウ シンデ ゴ ザリマス カ・ラオ
na-nga i-ki wa de-ki-ma-s' ma-i.
ナガイキ ハ デキマス マイ

Do. A-no h'-to wa bi-o-o shi-n da ka-ra na-nga-ku wa i-ki-ra-
アノヒト ハ ビャウシン ダ カラ ナガ ク ハ イキラ
re ma-i.
レマイ

237. *He was covered with mud from head to foot.*
A-no o ka-ta wa a-ta-ma ka-ra a-shi ma-de ni do-ro ma-bu-
アノオ カタ ハ アタマ カラ アシ マデ ニ ドロ マブ
re ni o na-ri na-sa-re-ta.
レニオ ナリ ナサレタ

Do. A-no h'-to wa a-ta-ma ka-ra a shi ma-de ni do-ro ma-bu-
アノヒト ハ アタマ カラ アシ マデ ニ ドロ マブ
re ni na-t-ta.
レニ ナッタ

238. *He is always in mischief.*
A-no h'-to wa he-i ze-i wa-ru-i i-ta-dz-ra wo i-ta-shi-ma-s'.
アノヒト ハ ヘイゼイ ワルイ イタズラ ヲ イタシマス

Do. A-no h'-to wa tsz-ne ni wa-ru-i i-ta-dz-ra wo sz-ru.
アノヒト ハ ツ子ニ ワルイ イタズラ ヲ スル

239. *He cannot do such a thing as this well; it is not in him.*
A-no o ka-ta wa chi-e nga ta-ri-nu yu-e ko-no to-o-ri ni wa
アノ オカタ ハ チエ カ タリヌ ユヱ コノ トヲリ ニ ハ
de-ki-ma-se-nu.
デキマセヌ

Do. A-re wa gu-ma-i da ka-ra ko-no to-o-ri ni wa de-ki-nu.
アレ ハ グマイ ダカラ コノ トヲリ ニ ハ デキヌ

240. *He is a late riser.*
A-no o ka-ta wa a-sa-ne wo i-ta-shi-ma-s'.
アノオカタハ アサ子 ヲ イタシマス

Do. A-re wa a-sa-ne-bo wo sz-ru.
アレ ハ アサ子ボウ スル

241. *He gets up before day-break.*
A-no o ka-ta wa yo a-ke ma-e ni o o-ki na-sa-ru.
アノオカタハ ヨ アケ マヘ ニ オオキ ナサル

Do. A-no h'-to wa yo a-ke ma-e ni o-ki-ru.
アノ ヒト ハ ヨ アケ マヘ ニ オキル

242. *He gets up by sun-rise.*
A-no o ka-ta wa hi no de ni o o-ki na-sa-ru.
アノ オカタ ハ ヒ ノ デ ニ オオキ ナサル

Do. A-no h'-to wa hi no de ni o-ki-ru.
アノ ヒト ハ ヒ ノ デ ニ オキル

243. *He spends money foolishly.*
A-no o ka-ta wa mu-da ni ku-ne wo o ts'-ka-i na-sa-ru.
アノ オカタ ハ ムダ ニ カ子 ヲ オツカイ ナサル

Do. A-no h'-to wa mu-da ni ka-ne wo ts'-ka-u.
アノ ヒト ハ ムダ ニ カ子 ヲ ツカウ

244. *He is too strong for you.*
A-no o ka-ta wa a-na-ta ni ku-ra-be-ma-sz-ru to chi-ka-ra nga
アノ オカタ ハ アナタ ニ クラベマスル ト チカラ ガ
tsz-yo, sz-ngi-ma-sz-ru.
ツヨス ギマスル

Do. A-no h'-to wa o-ma-e ni ku-ra-be-ru to chi-ka-ra nga tsz-
アノ ヒト ハ オマヱ ニ クラベル ト チカラ ガ ツ
yo sz-ngi-ru.
ヨ スギル

245. *He says he is unwilling.*
Ko-no-ma-nu to o-s'-shi-ya-ri-ma-s'.
コノマヌ トオッシャ リマス

Do. I-ra na-i to i-u.
イラナイトイフ

246. *He cares for nobody.*
A-no o ka-ta wa ho-ka no h'-to ni ka-ma-i-ma-se-nu.
アノ オカタ ハ ホカノ ヒト ニ カマイマセヌ

Do. A-no h'-to wa ho-ka no h'-to ni ka-ma-wa-nu.
アノ ヒト ハ ホカ ノ ヒト ニ カマワヌ

247. *He deserves a flogging.*
A-no o ka-ta wa ta-ta-ka-re na-sa-re-te mo yo-ro-shi-u go za
アノオカタハタタカレナヰレテモヨロシウゴザ
ri-ma-s'.
リムス

Do. A-re wa ta-ta-ka-re-te mo i-i.
アレハタタカレテモヨイ

248. *He knows what he is about.*
A-no o ka-ta wa ko-ko-ro e a-t-te na-sa-re-ma-s'.
アノオカタハココロエアッテナサレスマ

Do. A-no h'-to wa ko-ko-ro e a-t-te sz-ru.
アノヒトハココロエアッテスル

249. *He will not lose by it.*
So-no ko-to de ke-s'-sh'-te so-n wo i-ta-shi-ma-se-nu.
ソノコトデクッシテソンヲイタシマセス

Do. A-no ko-to de ke-s'-sh-te so-n wo shi-ma-se-nu.
アノコトデクッシテソンヲシマセス

250. *He cares little for dress.*
A-no o ka-ta wa i-ru-i no ko-to ni a-ma-ri o ka-ma i na-sa-
アノオカタハイルイノコトニアマリオカマイナサ
re-ma se-nu.
レマセヌ

Do. A-no h'-to wa ki-mo-no ni a-m-ri ka-ma-wa-nu.
アノヒトハキモノニアマリカマハス

251. *He is always well dressed.*
A-no o ka-ta wa he-i ze-i yo-ro-shi-i i-f'-ku wo o-ki na-sa-
アノオカタハヘイゼイヨロシイイフクヲオキナサ
re-ma-s'.
レマス

Do. A-no h'-to wa tsz-ne ni i-i ki-mo-no wo ki-ma-s'.
アノヒトハツ子ニイイキモノヲキマス

252. *He is drunk every day.*
A-no o ka-ta wa ma-i ni-chi sa-ke ni ta-be yo-t-te o i-de na-
アノオカタハマイニチサケニタベヨッテオイデナ
sa-ru.
サル

Do. A-no h'-to wa ma-i ni-chi sa-ke ni yo-t-te i-ru.
アノヒトハマイニチサケニヨッテイル

253. *His opinion and yours are the same.*
A-no o ka-ta wa o-mo-o to a-na-ta no o-mo-o to o-na-ji-ko-to
アノオカタハオモフトアナタノオモフトオナジコト
de go za-ri-ma-s'.
デゴザリマス

Do. A-no h'-to no o-mo-o to o-ma-e to o-na-ji-ko-to.
アノヒトノオモフトオマヘトオナジコト

254. *He denies that he did it.*
A-no o ka-ta wa i-ta-shi-ma-se-nu to o-s'-shi-ya-ri-ma-s'.
アノオカタ ハ イタシマセヌ ト オッシヤリマス
Do. A-no h'-to wa shi-ma-se-nu to i-i-ma-s'.
アノヒト ハ シマセヌ ト イイマス

255. *He confesses that he did it.*
A-no o ka-ta wa i-ta-shi-ma-sh'-ta to a-ra-wa ni mo-o-shi-ma-sh'-ta.
アノオ カタ ハ イタシマ シタ ト アラハ ニ モウシ マシタ
Do. A-no h'-to wa i-ta-sh'-ta to a-ki-ra-ka ni i-t-ta.
アノヒト ハ イタシタ ト アキラカ ニ イッタ

256. *He is said to be rich.*
A-no o ka-ta wa bu-nge-n de go za-ri-ma-s' to mi-na nga mo-o-shi-ma-s'.
アノオカタ ハ ブゲン デ ゴザリマス ト ミナ ガ モ ウシマス
Do. A-no h'-to wa cho-o-ja to mi-na i-i-ma-s'.
アノヒト ハ テウジヤ ト ミナ イイマス

257. *He is a new comer.*
A-no o ka-ta wa ha-ji-me-te o i-de na-sa-re-ta o ki-ya-ku de go za-ri-ma-s'.
アノオカタ ハ ハジメテ オイデ ナサレタ オ キヤク デ ゴ ザリマス
Do. A-no h'-to wa ha-ji-me-te k'-ta ki-ya-ku ji-n.
アノヒト ハ ハジメテ キタ キヤクジン

258. *He has blue eyes.*
A-no o ka-ta no me wa a-i i-ro de go za-ri-ma-s'.
アノオカタ ノ メ ハ アイイロ デ ゴザリマス
Do. A-no h'-to no me wa a-i i-ro ni mi-e-ru.
アノヒト ノ メ ハ アイイロ ニ ミエル

259. *He is a hard man to deal with.*
A-no h'-to to u-ri ka-i sz-ru ko-to wa mu-dz-ka-shi-u go za-ri-ma-s'.
アノヒト ト ウリカイ スル コト ハ ムヅカシウ ゴ ザ リマス
Do. A-no h'-to to u-ri ka-i wa shi ni-ku-i.
アノヒト ト ウリカイ ハ シ ニクイ

260. *He has been gone all day.*
A-no o-ka-ta wa ki-o-o wa i-chi ni-chi o ru-sz de go za-ri-ma-sh'-ta.
アノオカタ ハ キヤウ ハ イチ ニチ オルス デ ゴ ザリ マシタ
Do. A-no h'-to ki-o-o wa i-chi ni-chi u-chi ni o-ri-ma-se-na-n-da.
アノヒト キヤウ ハ イチ ニチ ウチ ニ オリマセナンダ

261. *He has gone back.*
A-no o ka-ta wa a-chi-ra-e o ka-i-ri na-sa-re-ma-sh'-ta.
アノオカタ ハ アチラヱオカイリナサレマシタ
Do. A-no h'-to wa a-chi e ka-i-t-ta.
アノヒト ハ アチヱカイッタ

262. *He fell flat on his back.*
A-no o ka-ta wa a-wo-no-ke ni o ko-ro-bi na-sa-re-ta.
アノオカタ ハ アヲノケニオコロビナサレタ
Do. A-no h'-to wa a-wo-no-ke ni ko-ro-n da.
アノヒト ハ アヲノケ ニ コロンダ

263. *He does not live here now.*
A-no o ka-ta wa i-ma ko-ko ni sz-ma-t-te o-ra-re-ma-se-nu.
アノオカタ ハ イマココニスマッテオラレマセヌ

264. *He (a child) wants to play all the time.*
A-no o ko wa i-tsz-de-mo yo-ku o a-so-bi na-sa-re ta-nga-ru.
アノオコ ハ イツデモ ヨクオアソビナサレ タガル
Do. A-no ko-do-mo wa i-tsz-de mo yo-ku a-so-bi ta-nga-ru.
アノ コドモ ハ イツデ モ ヨクアソビタガル

265. *He was born deaf and dumb.*
A-no o ka-ta wa m'-ma-re ts'-ki o-shi de go za-ri ma-s'.
アノオカタ ハ ウマレ ツキ オシデ ゴザリマス
Do. A-re wa m'-ma-re ts'-ki o-shi da.
アレ ハ ウマレ ツキ オシダ

266. *He has not been here to-day*
A-no o ka-ta wa ko-n ni-chi ma-da ko-ko ni o i-de na-sa-
アノオカタ ハ コン ニチ マダ ココ ニ オイデ ナサ
re-ma-se-nu.
レマセヌ

267. *He lives there all alone.*
A-no o ka-ta wa h'-to-ri a-so-ko ni sz-ma-t-te o i-dena-sa-re-
アノオカタ ハ ヒトリ アソコ ニ スマッテオイデナサレ
ma-s'.
マス
Do. A-no h'-to-wa h'-to-ri a-s'-ko ni sz-n-de i-ru.
アノヒト ハ ヒトリ アソコ ニ スンデイル

268. *He does not understand this business.*
A-no o ka-ta wa ko-no sh'-yo-ku wo o shi-ri na-sa-re-ma-se-nu.
アノオカタ ハ コノシヨクヲオシリ ナサレマセヌ
Do. A-no h'-to wa ko-no sh'-yo-ku wo shi-ra-nu.
アノヒト ハ コノシヨク ヲ シラヌ

269. *He has been arrested for theft.*
A-no o ka-ta wa nu-sz-mi wo i-ta-shi-ma-sh'-ta ka-ra me-shi
アノオカタ ハ ススミ ヲイタシマシタ カラメシ
to-ra-re-ma-sh'-ta.
トラレマシタ

Do.　A-re wa do-ro-bo-u-sh'-ta ka-ra shi-ba-ra-re-ta.
　　　アレ ハ ドロボウシタ カラ シバラレタ

270. *He is sick of his bargain.*
　　　A-no o ka-ta wa te wo u-t-ta ka-ra ko-o k'-wa-i i-ta-sh'-te o-
　　　アノオカタ ハ テ ヲウッタカラ コウ クワイ イタシテ オ
　　　ra-re-ma-s'.
　　　ラレマス

Do.　A-no h'-to wa te wo u-t-ta ka-ra ko-o k'-wa-i sh'-te i-ru.
　　　アノヒト ハ テ ヲ ウッタカラ コウクワイ シテイル

271. *He is near sighted.*
　　　A-no o ka-ta wa ki-n nga-n de go za-ri-ma-s'.
　　　アノオカタ ハ キンガン デ ゴ ザリマス

Do.　A-no h'-to wa chi-ka me-da.
　　　アノヒト ハ チカ メダ

272. *He is the worst man I ever knew.*
　　　Wa-ta-k'-shi no dzo-n-ji-ma-sh'-ta u-chi de wa a-no o ka-ta
　　　ワタクシ ノ ゾンジマシタウチ デ ハ アノオカタ
　　　nga i-ta-t-te wa-ru-u go za-ri-ma-s'.
　　　ガ イタッテワルウ ゴ ザリマス

Do.　Wa-ta-k'-shi no sh'-t-ta u-chi de wa a-no h'-to nga i-chi-
　　　ワタクシ ノ シッタウチ デ ハ アノヒト ガ イチ
　　　ba-n wa-ru-i.
　　　バンワルイ

273. *He does well for so small a boy.*
　　　A-no ko-do-mo wa chi-i-sa ke-re-do-mo yo-ku yo-o nga ta-ri
　　　アノ コドモ ハ チイサ ケレドモ ヨク ヨフ ガ タリ
　　　ma-s'.
　　　マス

Do.　A-no ko-do-mo wa chi-i-sa-i nga yo-ku ya-ku ni ta-tsz.
　　　アノ コドモ ハ チイサイ ガ ヨク ヤク ニ タツ

274. *He has run through all his property.*
　　　A-no o ka-ta wa ka-za-i wo no-ko-ra-dz ts'-ka-i ts.-ku-shi-ma-
　　　アノオ カタ ハ カザイ ヲ ノコラズ ツカイ ツクシマ
　　　sh'-ta.
　　　シタ

Do.　A-no h'-to wa ka-za-i wo no-ko-ra-dz ts'-ka-t-te shi-mo-o-ta.
　　　アノヒト ハ カザイ ヲ ノコラズ ツカッテ シモウタ

275. *He is in the right, they are in the wrong.*
　　　A-no o ka-ta no o-bo-shi-me-shi to-o-ri nga yo-ro-shi-u go za-
　　　アノオカタ ノ オボシメシ ドヲリ ガ ヨロシウ ゴ ザ
　　　ri-ma-s'. A-no o ka-ta nga-ta no o-bo-shi-me-shi wa so-o i
　　　リマス アノオ カタ ガタノ オボシメシ ハ ソウイ
　　　i-ta-shi-ma-s'.
　　　イタシマス

Do.　A-no h'-to no o-mo-i do-o-ri nga yo-i-A-no h'-to ta-chi no
　　　アノヒト ノ オモイ ドウリ ガ ヨイ アノ ヒトタチ ノ

o-mo-o to-ko-ro wa chi-nga-u.
オモフトコロ ハ チガウ

276. *He thinks a great deal of his horse.*
A-no o ka-ta wa go ji bu-n no m-ma wa chi-n ch'-o i-ta-sa-re-ma-s'.
アノオカタ ハ ゴ ジブン ノ ムマ ハ チンチヤウ イタ
サレマス

Do. A-no h'-to wa ji bu-n no m'-ma wo da-i ji ni sz-ru.
アノコト ハ ジブン ノ ムマ ヲ ダイジニ スル

277. *He thinks nothing of getting dead drunk.*
A-no o ka-ta wa sa-ke ni yo-i-ma-s' to sh'-o ta-i na-ku na-ri-ma-s' ko-to-mo-na-ni mo ka-ma-i-ma-se-nu.
アノオカタ ハ サケ ニ ヨイマスト シヤウタイナク ナ
リマス コトモナニモ カマイマセヌ

Do. A-no h'-to wa sa-ke ni yo-o-to sh'-o ta-i na-i nga na-ni mo ka-ma-wa-nu.
アノヒト ハ サケ ニ ヨウト シヤウタイナイ ガナニ モ
カマワヌ

278. *He is deeply in debt, and likely to fail.*
A-no o ka-ta wa sh'-ya-k'-ki-n nga ta-i so-o ni go za-ri-ma-s' ka-ra, no-chi ni wa bu-n sa-n wo i-ta-shi-ma-sh'-o-o.
アノオカタ ハ シヤクキン ガ タイソウニ ゴ ザリマス
カラ ノチニ ハ ブンサン ヲ イタシマシヤウ

Do. A-no h'-to wa sh'-ya-k' ki-n nga o-o-i ka-ra no-chi ni wa bu-n sa-n wo sz-ru de a-ro-o.
アノヒト ハ シヤクキン ガ オホイ カラ ノチニ ハ
ブンサン ヲ スル デアロヲ

279. *He was once poor but now has become rich.*
A-no o ka-ta wa sa-ru ko-ro hi-n j'-a de go za-ri-ma-sh'-ta nga, i-ma de wa fu-u ki-ni na-ri-ma-sh'-ta.
アノオカタ ハ サル コロ ヒンシヤデ ゴ ザリマシタ
ガ イマデ ハ フウキニ ナリマシタ

Do. A-no h'-to wa sa-ru ko-ro hi-n j'-a de a-t-ta nga i-ma de wa f'-ku sh'-a ni na-t-ta.
アノヒト ハ サル コロ ヒンジヤデアッタ ガ イマデ
ハ フクシヤ ニ ナッタ

280. *He is a learned man.*
A-no o ka-ta wa ha-ku nga-ku de go za-ri-ma-s'.
アノオカタ ハ ハク ガク デ ゴ ザリマス

Do. A-no h'-to wa ha-ku nga-ku da.
アノヒト ハ ハク ガクダ

281. *He does not care what he says.*
A-no o ka-ta wa e-n ri-o na-shi ni o-s'-shi-a-ri-ma-s'.
アノオカタ ハ エンリヨナシ ニ オッシヤリマス

Do. A-re wa e-n ri-o na-shi ni i-u.
アレハ エンリヨナシ ニ イフ

282. *He is blind of one eye.*
A-no o ka-ta wa ka-ta-me de go za-ri-ma-s'.
アノオカタハカタメデゴザリマス
Do.   A-no h'-to wa me-k-ka-chi da.
アノヒトハ メツカチダ

283. *He died of small pox.*
A-no o ka-ta wa ho-o-so-o de o na-ku-na-ri na-sa-re-ma-sh'-ta.
アノオカタハホウソヲデオナクナリ ナサレマシタ
Do.   A-re wa ho-o-so-o de shi-n-da.
アレハ ホウソヲデシンダ

284. *He has lost all his property.*
A-no o ka-ta wa ka-za-i wo mi-na na-ku sa-re-ma-sh'-ta.
アノオカタハカザイヲ ミナナクサレマシタ
Do.   A-re wa ka-za-i wo mi-na na-ku sh'-ta.
アレハカザイヲ ミナ ナクシタ

285. *He is a stingy fellow.*
A-no o ka-ta wa shi-wo-o go za-ri-ma-s'.
アノオカタハシウフゴ ザリマス
Do.   A-re wa shi-wa-i.
アレ ハシワイ

286. *He has sprained his ankle.*
A-no o ka-ta wa a-shi-ku-bi wo ku-ji-ki-ma-sh'-ta.
アノオカタハアシクビヲ クジキマシタ
Do.   A-re wa a-shi-ku-bi wo ku-ji-i-ta.
アレハアシクビヲ クジイタ

287. *He was fined one and one-half kobans for buying stolen property.*
A-no o ka-ta wa nu-sz-bi-to no mo-no wo ka-i-ma-sh'-ta yu-
アノオカタハススビトノモノ ヲカイマシタ ユ
e k'-a-ri-o ki-n i-chi ri-o ni bu to-ra-re-ma-sh'-ta.
エクワリヤウキンイチリヤウニブ トラレマシタ
Do.   A-no h'-to wa do-ro-bo no mo-no wo ka-t-ta ka-ra, ka-ri-
アノヒトハドロボウノ モノヲ カツタカラクワリ
o ki-n i-chi ri-o ni bu. to-ra-re-ta.
ヤウキンイチリヤウニブ トラレタ

288. *He writes a good hand.*
A-no o ka-ta wa no-o j'-o-de go za-ri-ma-s'.
アノオカタハ ノウジヨデゴ ザリマス
Do.   A-re wa mo-ji wo yo-ku ka-ku.
アレ ハモンジヲ ヨクカク

289. *He keeps house himself.*
A-no o ka-ta wa ka-na-i no ko-to wo h'-to-ri de na-sa-re-ma-s'.
アノオカタハカナイノ コトヲ ヒトリデナサレマス
Do.   A-re wa ka-na-i no ko-to wo h'-to-ri de sz-ru.
アレハ カナイノコトヲヒトリデ スル

290. *He has gone ashore.*
A-no o ka-ta wa o-ka ni o a-nga-ri na-sa-re-ma-sh'-ta.
アノオカタ ハ オカ ニ オ アガリ ナサレマシタ
Do. A-no h'-to wa o-ka ni a-nga-t-ta.
アノヒト ハオカ ニ アガッタ

291. *He is always losing his pocket-book.*
A-no o ka-ta wa o-ri o-ri ka-mi-i-re wo na-ku-sa-re-ma-s'.
アノオカタ ハ オリオリ カミイレ ヲ ナクサレマス
Do. A-no h'-to wa o-ri o-ri ka-mi-i-re wo na-ku-sz.
アノヒト ハオリオリ カミイレ ヲ ナクス

292. *He looks very like his brother.*
A-no o ka-ta wa a-ni sa-ma ni yo-ku ni-te o i-de na-sa-re-ma-s'.
アノオ カタ ハ アニ サマ ニ ヨク ニテオイデ ナサレマス
Do. A-re wa a-ni ni yo-ku ni-te i-ru.
アレ ハ アニニヨク ニテイル

293. *He said to be poor.*
A-no o ka-ta wa hi-n-ki-u de go za-ri-ma-s' to, h'-to ni i-wa-re-ma-s'.
アノオ カタ ハ ヒンキウ デ ゴ ザリマス ト ヒト ニイワレマス
Do. A-re wa bi-m-bō-o da to h'-to ni i-wa-ru-ru.
アレ ハ ビンボウ ダ ト ヒト ニイワルル

294. *He has been a great traveller.*
A-no o ka-ta wa sh'-o ko-ku wo hi-ro-ku o me-ngu-ri na-sa re-ta h'-to de go za-ri-ma-s¹.
アノオ カタ ハ シヨ コク ヲ ヒロクオ メグリ ナサ レタヒト デ ゴ サリマス
Do. A-re wa ku-ni-ngu-ni wo hi-ro-ku ma-wa-t-ta h'-to da.
アレ ハ クニグニ ヲ ヒロクマワッタヒトダ

195. *He lives over the river.*
A-no o ka-ta wa ka-wa no mu-ko-o ni o i-de na-sa-re-ma-s'.
アノオカタ ハ カワ ノ ムカフ ニオイデナサレマス
Do. A-re wa ka-wa no mu-ko-o ni i-ru.
アレ ハ カワ ノ ムカフ ニイル

296. *He is not of age.*
A-no o ka-ta wa ma-da o-to-na ni o na-ri na-sa-re-ma-se-n'.
アノオ カタ ハ マダ オトナ ニ オナリ ナサ レマ セン
Do. A-re wa ma-da o-to-na ni na-ra-nu.
アレ ハ マダ オトナ ニナラヌ

297. *He has played a trick upon us.*
A-no o ka-ta wa ta-wa-mu-re ni wa-ta-k'shi wo o da-ma-shi
アノオカタ ハ タワムレニ ワタクシ ヲ オダマシ

na-sa-re-ma-sh'-ta.
ナサレマシタ

297. A-re wa j'-o-o da-n ni wa-shi wo da-ma-sh'-ta.
アレハジヤウダンニワシヲダマシタ

298. *He sells them at a great profit.*
A-no o ka-ta wa so-re wo u-ri-ma-sh'-te ta-i-so-o o mo-o-ke
アノオカタハソレヲウリマシテタイソウオマフケ
na-sa-re-ma-s'.
ナサレマス

Do. A-re wa ko-re wo u-t-te ta-i-so-o mo-o-ke-ru.
アレハコレヲウツテタイソウモフケル

299. *He has become used to it.*
A-no o h'-to wa so-re ni na-re-te o shi-ma-i na-sa-re ma-sh'-ta.
アノオヒトワソレニナレテオシマイナサレマシタ

Do. A-re wa so-re ni na-re-te shi-ma-i-ta.
アレハソレニナレテシマツタ

300. *He is very careful of his horse.*
A-no o ka-ta wa m'-ma wo ta-i-se-tsz ni yo-o ji-n na-sa-re-
アノオカタハムマヲタイセツニヨフジンナサレ
ma-s'.
マス

Do. A-re wa m'-ma wo da-i-ji ni yo-o ji-n wo sz-ru.
アレハムマヲダイジニヨフジンヲスル

301. *He can undersell us.*
A-no h'-to wa wa-ta-k'-shi do-mo yo-ri ya-s'-ku u-ru ko-to nga
アノヒトハワタクシトモヨリヤスクウルコトガ
de-ki-ma-s'.
デキマス

Do. A-re wa wa-shi yo-ri ya-s'-ku u-ru ko-to nga de-ki-ru.
アレハワシヨリヤスクウルコトガデキル

302. *He is a middle aged man.*
A-no o ka-ta wa chi-u ne-n de go za-ri-ma-s'.
アノオカタハチウネンデゴザリマス

Do. A-re wa chi-u ne-n mo-no da.
アレハチウネンモノダ

303. *He owes more than he is worth, and will finally be bankrupt.*
A-no o ka-ta wa ji-bu-n no shi-n-da-i yo-ri sh'-a-k'-ki-n nga
アノオカタハジブンノシンダイヨリシヤクキンガ
yo-ke-i de go za-ri-ma-s', ka-ra tsz-i-ni wa ji-mo-tsz i-ta-
ヨケイデゴザリマスカラツイニハジメツイタ
shi-ma-sh'-o-o.
シマシヤウ

Do. A-re wa shi-n-da-i yo-ri sh'-a-k'-ki-n nga yo-ke-i da ka-
アレハシンダイヨリシヤクキンガヨケイダカ

ra shi-ma-i-ni tsz-bu-re-ru de a-ro-o.
ラ シマイニ ツブレル デ アラフ

304. *He has no right to do it.*
A-no o ka-ta wa so-re wo na-sa-re-te wa mi-chi-nga chi-nga-i ma-sh'-o-o.
アノオ カタ ハ ソレ ヲ ナサレテ ハ ミチ ガ チガイ マシャウ

Do. A-re wa so-re wo sh'-te wa mi-chi nga chi-nga-o.
アレ ハ ソレ ヲ シテ ハ ミチ ガ チガフ

305. *He injures himself by drinking sake.*
A-no o ka-ta wa sa-ke wo o no-mi na-sa-re-te ka-ra-da nga i-ta-mi-ma-s'.
アノオ カタ ハ サケ ヲオ ノミ ナサレテ カラダ ガ イタミマス

Do. A-re wa sa-ke wo no-n-de ka-ra-da nga i-ta-mu.
アレ ワ サケ ヲ ノンデ カラダ ガ イタム

306. *He is a good hand at this business.*
A-no o ka-ta wa ko-re wo na-sa-ru ko-to nga j'-o-o-dz de go za-ri-ma-s'.
アノオ カタ ハ コレ ヲ ナサル コト ガジャウズ デ ゴ ザリマス

Do. A-re wa ko-re wo sz-ru ko-to nga-j'-o-o-dz da.
アレ ハ コレ ヲ スル コト ガジャウズ ダ

307. *He has made a good teacher.*
A-no o ka-ta wa yo-ro.sh'-ki shi-sh'-o-o ni na-ri-ma-sh'-ta.
アノオ カタ ハ ヨロシキ シシャウ ニ ナリ マシタ

Do. A-re wa yo-ki shi-sh'-o-o ni na-t-ta.
アレ ハ ヨキ シシャウニ ナッタ

308. *He lives this side of the temple.*
A-no o ka-ta wa te-ra yo-ri te-ma-i ni o-ra-re-ma-s'.
アノオ カタ ハ テラ ヨリ テマイ ニ オラレマス

Do. A-no h'-to wa te-ra yo-ri te-ma-i ni sz-ma-t-te i-ru.
アノ ヒト ハ テラ ヨリ テマイ ニ スマツテイル

309. *He lives three doors this side of the inn.*
A-no ka-ta-wa ha-ta-ngo-ya yo-ri sa-n nge-n te-ma-i ni sz-ma-t-te o-ra-re-ma-s'
アノオ カタ ハ ハタゴヤ ヨリ サンゲン テマイ ニス マツテオラレマス

Do. A-re wa ha-ta-ngo-ya yo-ri sa-n nge-n te-ma-i ni sz-ma-t-te o-ru.
アレ ハ ハタゴヤ ヨリ サンゲン テマイ ニスマツ テオル

310. *He lives ten doors beyond the custom house.*
A-no o ka-ta wa u-n-j'-o-o-sh'-o no ji-k ke-n sa-ki ni sz-ma-
アノオ カタ ハ ウンジャウショ ノ ジツケン サキ ニ スマ

| | t-te o-ra-re-ma-s'.
| | ツテオラレマス
| Do. | A-no h'to wa u-n-j'-o-o-shi'-o no ji-k ke-n sa-ki ni sz-ma-
| | アノ ヒト ハ ウンジヤウシヨノ ジツケン サキ ニ スマ
| | t-te i-ru.
| | ツテイル

311. *He lives the other side of the tea house.*
A-no o ka-ta wa ch'-a-ya no sa-ki ni sz-ma-t-te o i-de na-
アノオカタ ハ チヤヤ ノ サキ ニ スマツテオイデ ナ
sa-re-ma-s'.
サレマス

Do. A-re wa ch'-a-ya no sa-ki ni sz-ma-t-te i-ru.
アレ ハ チヤヤ ノ サキ ニ スマツテイル

312. *He let it fall and broke it to pieces.*
A-no o ka-ta nga o o-to-shi na-sa-re-ta **ka-ra** ku-da-ke-ma-sh'-ta.
アノオカタガ オオトシナサレタ カラ クダケ マシタ

Do. A-re nga o-to-sh'-ta ka-ra ko-wa-re-ta.
アレガ オトシタ カラ コハレタ

313. *He meant well, but was mistaken.*
A-no o ka-ta wa ko-ko-ro dza-shi wa yo-ro-shi-u go za-ri
アノオカタ ハ ココロ ザシ ハ ヨロシウ ゴ ザリ
ma-sh'-ta nga ma-chi-nga-i-ma-sh'-ta.
マシタ ガ マチガヒマシタ

Do. A-re wa ko-ko-ro dza-shi wa yo-ro-shi-i-nga ma-chi-ngo-o-ta.
アレ ハ ココロ ザシ ハ ヨロシイガ マチガフタ

314. *He thinks more of eating than of any thing else.*
A-no o ka-ta wa ho-ka no ko-to yo-ri ta-be-ma-s' ko-to ni mi
アノ オカタ ハ ホ カノ コト ヨリ タベマス コト ニ ミ
wo i-re-ma-s'.
ヲイレマス

Do. A-re wa ho-ka **no** ko-to yo-ri ta-be-ru ko-to ni mi **wo** i-
アレ ハ ホ カノ コト ヨリ タベル コト ニ ミ ヲイ
re-ru.
レル

315. **He did it** *on purpose.*
A-no o ka-ta wa ko-ko-ro e-te i-ta-sa-re-ma-sh'-ta.
アノオ カタ ハ ココロエテ イタサレ マシタ

Do. A-re wa wa-za-to shi-ma-sh'-ta.
アレ ハ ワザト シ マシタ

316. *He keeps his horse well.* (said of the owner.)
A-no o ka-ta wa m'-ma wo yo-ku ya-shi-na-wa-se-ma-s'.
アノ オカタ ハ ムマ ヲヨク ヤシナウセマス

Do. A-re wa m'-ma wo yo-ku ya-shi-na-u. (of the groom.)
アレ ハ ムマ ヲヨク ヤシナフ

317. *He is a respectable man.*
A-no o ka-ta wa ta-t-to-mu be-ki h'-to de go za-ri-ma-s'.
アノオカタ ハ タツトム ベキ ヒト デ ゴ ザリマス
Do.   A-re wa ta-t-to-mu be-ki h'-to da.
アレ ハ タツトム ベキ ヒト ダ

318. *He looks out well for himself.*
A-no o ka-ta wa ji-bu-n nga-t-te no yo-ro-sh'-ki ko-to wo o-mo-i na-sa-ru.
アノオカタ ハ ジブン ガツテノ ヨロシキ コト ヲ オモイナサル
Do.   A-re wa te-ma-i nga-t-te no yo-i ko-to wo o-mo-o.
アレ ハ テマイ ガツテノ ヨイコト ヲ オモフ

319. *He is a selfish fellow.*
A-no o ka-ta wa wa-nga ma-ma no mo-no de go za-ri-ma-s'.
アノオカタ ハ ワガ ママノ モノ デ ゴザリマス
Do.   A-re wa wa-nga ma-ma mo-no.
アレ ハ ワガ ママ モノ

320. *He broke the law.*
A-no o ka-ta wa ha-t-to wo ya-bu-ri-ma-sh'-ta.
アノオカタ ハ ハツトヲ ヤブリマシタ
Do.   A-re wa ha-t-to wo ya-bu-t-ta.
アレ ハ ハツトヲ ヤブツタ

321. *He thinks of nothing but making money, and cares for nothing else.*
A-no o ka-ta wa ka-ne wo fu-ya-sz ko-to ba-ka-ri o o-mo-i na-sa-re-ma-s', ho-ka no ko-to wo o ka-ma-i na-sa-re-ma-se-nu.
アノオカタ ハ カ子 ヲ フヤスコト バカリオ オモヒナサレマス ホカノ コト ヲ オカマヒナサレマ セス
Do.   A-no h'-to wa ka-ne wo ta-me-ru ko-to ba-ka-ri o-mo-t-te, ho-ka no ko-to wa ka-ma-wa-nu.
アノヒト ハ カ子ヲ タメル コト バカリオモツテ ホカノ コト ハ カマワヌ

322. *He is always finding fault.*
A-no o ka-ta wa i-tsz-de-mo h'-to no a-ya-ma-chi wo ta-dz-ne-te o-ri-ma-s'.
アノオカタ ハ イツデモ ヒトノ アヤマチ ヲ タヅ子テオリマス
Do.   A-re wa i-tsz-de-mo h'-to no a-ya-ma-chi wo ta-dz-ne-te i-ru.
アレ ハ イツデモ ヒト ノ アヤマチ ヲ タヅ子テイル

323. *He asks too much for his goods.*
A-no h'-to no shi-ro-mo-no no ne-da-n dz-ke wa ta-ka sz-ngi-ru.
アノヒト ノ シロモノ ノ 子ダンヅケ ハ タカスギル
Do.   A-re nga shi-ro-mo-no wa ne nga ta-ka-i.
アレ ガ シロモノ ハ 子 ガ タカイ

324. *He is worth 10,000 kobangs.*
A-no o ka-ta wa i-chi ma-n ri-o-o no shi-n shi-o-u de go
アノオ カタ ハ イチ マン リヤウノシン シヨウデゴ

za-ri-ma-s'.
ザリマス

Do.   A-re wa i-chi ma-n ri-o-o no shi-n shi-o-u da.
アレハイチ マンリヤウノ シン シヨウダ

325. *He arrived there late.*
A-no o ka-ta wa mu-ka-u e o-so-ku o ts'-ki na-sa-re-ma-sh'-ta.
アノオカタハム カフエオソクオツキナサレマシタ

Do.   A-re wa mu-ka-u e o-so-ku tsz-i-ta.
アレハム カフエオソクツイタ

326. *He has just gone out.*
A-no o ka-ta wa sa-ki ho-do ho-ka ni o i-de na-sa-re-ma-sh'-ta.
アノオカタハサキホド ホカニオイデナサレマシタ

Do.   A-re wa sa-ki ho-do ho-ka ni yu-i-ta.
アレハサキホドホカ ニユイタ

327. *He has just gone home.*
A-no o ka-ta wa sa-ki ho-do u-chi e o ka-i-ri na-sa-re-ma-sh'-ta.
アノオカタハサキホドフチエオカイリナサレマシタ

Do.   A-no h'-to wa sa-ki ho-do u-chi ni ka-i-t-ta.
アノヒトハサキホドウチニカイツタ

328. *He comes here often.*
A-no o ka-ta wa ta-bi ta-bi ko-ko ni o i-de na-sa-re-ma-s'.
アノオカタハタビタビココニオイデナサレマス

Do.   A-re wa ta-bi ta-bi ko-ko ni ku-ru.
アレハタビタビ ココニクル

329. *He comes here several times a day.*
A-no o ka-ta wa hi ni i-ku ta-bi mo ko-ko ni o i-de na-sa-re-ma-s'.
アノオカタハヒニイクタビモ ココニオイデナサレマス

Do.   A-re wa hi ni na-n do mo ko-ko ni ku-ru.
アレハビ ニナンド モ ココ ニクル

330. *He is an honest man.*
A-no o ka-ta wa sh'-o-o-ji-ki de go za-ri-ma-s'.
アノオカタハシヤウジキデ ゴ ザリマス

Do.   A-re wa sh'-o-o-ji-ki mo-no.
アレハシヤウジキモノ

331. *He has gone on board ship.*
A-no o ka-ta wa fu-ne e o i-de na-sa-re-ma-sh'-ta.
アノオカタハ フ子エオイデナサレマシタ

Do.   A-re wa fu-ne e i-t-ta.
アレハフ子エイツタ

332. *He has gone up the river.*
A-no o ka-ta wa ka-wa yo-ri a-nga-t-te o i-de na-sa-re-ma-
アノオカタハカハヨリ アガツテ オイデナサレマ

Do. A-re wa ka-wa yo-ri a-nga-t-te i-t-ta.
シタ
アレハカハ ヨリ アガツテイツタ

333. *He is coming this evening whether or no.*
A-no o ka-ta wa ko-m ba-n dze-hi-to-mo o-i-de na-sa-re-ma-sh'-o-o'.
アノオカタ ハ コン バンゼヒトモオイデ ナサレ マシャウ

Do. A-no h'-to wa ko-m ba-n dze-hi-to-mo ku-ru de a-ro-o.
アノヒト ハ コンバンゼヒトモ クルデ アラフ

334. *He has cheated me out of a dollar.*
A-no o ka-ta wa wa-ta-k'-shi wo da-ma-sh'-te i-chi do-ra o to-ri na-sa-re-ma-sh'-ta.
アノオカタ ハ ワタクシ ヲ ダマシテ イチ ドラ オ トリナサレマシタ

Do. A-re wa wa-ta-k'-shi wo da-ma-sh'-te i-chi do-ra to-t-ta.
アレ ハ ワタクシ ヲ ダマシテ イチ ドラ トツタ

335. *He is left handed.*
A-no o ka-ta wa hi-da-ri ki-ki de go za-ri-ma-s'.
アノオカタ ハ ヒダリ キキ デ ゴザリマス

Do A-re wa hi-da-ri ki-ki da.
アレ ハ ヒダリ キキ ダ

336. *He is a great coward.*
A-no o ka-ta wa o-ku bi-o-o de go za-ri-ma-s'.
アノオカタ ハ オクビヤウデ ゴ ザリマス

Do. A-re wa o-ku bi-o-o mo-no da.
アレ ハ オクビヤウ モノ ダ

337. *He is a good natured looking man.*
A-no o ka-ta wa ni-u-wa ni mi-e-ma-sz-ru.
アノオカタ ハ ニウワ ニ ミエマスル

Do. A-re wa ni-u-wa ni mi-e-ru.
アレ ワ ニウワ ニ ミエル

338. *He has been gone a great while.*
A-no o ka-ta wa o i-de na-sa-re-ma-sh'-ta yo-ri hi-sa-sh'-ku na-ri.ma-s'.
アノオカタ ハ オイデ ナサレマシタ ヨリ ヒサシク ナリマス

Do. A-re wa i-t-te yo-ri hi-sa-sh'-ku na-ru.
アレ ハ イツテ ヨリ ヒサシク ナル

339. *He promised to come to-day.*
A-no o ka-ta wa ko-n ni-chi ma-i-ri-ma-sz-ru to ya-ku so-ku wo i-ta-shi-ma-sh'-ta.
アノオカタ ハ コン ニチ マイリマスル トヤクソク ヲイタシマシタ

Do.　　A-re wa ki-o-ku-ru to ya-ku so-ku shi-ma-sh'-ta.
　　　　アレハ　ヲクル　トヤクソクシマシタ
340. *He was taken sick on the road.*
　　　　A-no o ka-ta wa mi-chi de o wa-dz-ra-i na-sa-re-ma-sh'-ta.
　　　　アノオカタハ三チ　デオワヅラヒ　ナサレマシタ
Do.　　A-re wa mi-chi de wa-dz-ra-t-ta.
　　　　アレハ三チ　デ　ワヅラッタ
341. *He told me all about it.*
　　　　A-no o ka-ta wa no-ko-ra-dz wa-ta-k'shi ni o ha-na-shi na-
　　　　アノオカタハ　ノコラズワタクシ　ニオハナシ　ナ
　　　　sa-re-ma-sh'-ta.
　　　　サレマシタ
Do.　　A-no h'-to wa no-ko-ra-dz wa-shi ni ha-na-sh'-ta.
　　　　アノヒト　ハ　ノコラヅ　ワシニハナシタ
342. *He was to have done it in a month.*
　　　　A-no o ka-ta wa h'-to ts-ki no u-chi ni ki-t-to de-ki-ma-s to
　　　　アノオカタ　ハヒトツキ　ノウチ　ニキットデキマス　ト
　　　　ya-ku so-ku wo i-ta shi-ma-sh'-ta.
　　　　ヤクソクヲイタシ　マシタ
Do.　　A-re wa h'-to ts'-ki no u-chi ni ki-t-to de-ki-ru to ya-ku
　　　　アレハヒトツキ　ノ　ウチ　ニキット　デキル　ト　ヤク
　　　　so-ku wo sh'-ta.
　　　　ソク　ヲシタ
343. *He is fond of fine clothes.*
　　　　A-no o ka-ta wa ki-re-i no ki-mo-no nga o s'-ki de go za-ri-
　　　　アノオ　カタハ　キレイ　ノキモノガオスキデゴザリ
　　　　ma-s'.
　　　　マス
Do.　　A-re wa ki-re-i no ki-mo-no nga s'-ki da.
　　　　アレハ　キレイノ　キモノガスキダ
344. *He had some, but has none now.*
　　　　A-no o ka-ta wa sa-ru ko-ro go za-ri-ma-sh'-ta nga, ta-da-i-ma
　　　　アノオカタ　ハサルコロゴ　ザリマシタガ　タダイマ
　　　　de wa go za-ri-ma-se-n'.
　　　　デハゴザリマセン
Do.　　A-re wa sa-ru ko-ro a-t-ta i-ma de wa na-i.
　　　　アレハ　サルコロアッタイマ　デ　ハナイ
345. *He has committed harakiri.*
　　　　A-no o ka-ta wa se-p-pu-ku wo i-ta-sa-re-ma-sh'-ta
　　　　アノオカタ　ハセツブク　ヲイタサレマシタ
Do.　　A-re wa ha-ra wo ki-t-ta.
　　　　アレハ　バラ　ヲキッタ
346. *Help me a little.*
　　　　A-na-ta s'-ko-shi wa-ta-k'-shi ni o te wo o ka-shi na-sa-re-
　　　　アナタスコシ　ハタクシ　ニオテヲオカシ　ナサレ

te ku-da-sa-re-ma-sh'.
テクダサレマシ

Do. O-ma-e chi-t-to wa-ta-k'-shi ni te wo ka-sh'-te ku-re-ro.
オマエチツト ワタクシ ニ テヲ カシテ クレロ

347. *Help me twist this string.*
Wa-ta-k'-shi i-to wo yo-ri-ma-s' ka-ra, o te-tsz-da-i na-sa-re-
ワタクシイト ヲ ヨリマス カラ オテ ツダイナサレ
te ku-da-sa-re.
テクダサレ

Do. Wa-ta-k'-shi i-to wo yo-ru ka-ra, te-tsz-da-t-te ku-re-ro.
ワタクシイト ヲ ヨル カラ テツダツテ クレロ

348. *Help him to some rice.*
A-no o ka-ta ni go ha-n wo o a-nge na-sa-re-te ku-da-sa-re.
アノオカタニ ゴ ハン ヲ オアゲナ サレテ クダサレ

Do. A-re ni wa me-shi wo ku-wa-sh'-te ku-re-ro.
アレニ ハ メシ ヲ クワシテ クレロ

349. *Here is the place for it.*
O-ki-ma-s' to-ko-ro wa ko-ko de go za-ri-ma-s'.
オキマス トコロ ハ ココ デ ゴ ザリマス

Do. O-ku to-ko-ro wa ko-ko da.
オクトコロ ハ ココデ

350. *Here is a dose of medicine.*
Ko-ko ni k'-sz-ri nga i-t-ch'-o go za-ri-ma-s'.
ココ ニ クスリ ガ イツテウ ゴ ザリマス

Do. Ko-ko ni k'-sz-ri nga i-t-ch'-o a-ru.
ココ ニ クスリ ガ イツテウアル

351. *Here it is.* (after searching.)
Ko-ko ni go za-ri-ma-s'.
ココ ニ ゴ ザリキス

Do. Ko-ko ni a-ru.
ココ ニ アル

352. *Here it is, take it as long as you require it.* (when given to be used)
Go yu-ru-ri-to o ts'-ka-i na-sa-re-ma-sh'.
ゴ ユルリト オ ツカイ ナ サレ キシ

Do. Yu-ru yu-ru to ts'-ka-e.
ユル ユル ト ツカエ

353. *His father lives at Yedo.*
A-no o ka-ta no chi-chi wa Ye-do ni sz-ma-t-te o i-de na
アノオカタ ノ チチ ハ エド ニ スマツテ オイデナ
sa-re-ma-s'.
サレマス

Do. A-re no chi-chi wa Ye-do ni sz-ma-t-te i-ru.
アレノ チチ ハ エド ニ スマツテイル

354. *His pronunciation is bad.*
A-no o ka-ta no go i-n nga wa-ru-u go za-ri-ma-s'.
アノオカタ ノ ゴイン ガ ワルウ ゴ ザリマス

Do. A-re no go i-n nga **wa-ru-i.**
アレノゴインガ ワルイ

355. *His shop is next to mine.*
A-no h'-to no mi-se wa wa-ta-k'-shi no to-na-ri de go za-ri-ma-s'.
アノヒトノ ミセ ハ ワタクシ ノ トナリ デ ゴザリマス

Do. A-re nga mi-se wa o-re no to-na-ri da.
アレガ ミセ ハ オレノトナリダ

356. *His manners are clownish.*
A-no o ka-ta no fu-u-dzo-ku wa i-na-ka mo-no de go za-ri-ma-s'.
アノオカタ ノ フウゾク ハ イナカ モノ デ ゴザリマス

Do. A-re nga fu-u-dzo-ku wa i-na-ka mo-no da.
アレガ フウゾク ハ イナカ モノダ

357. *His wife is my aunt.*
A-no o ka-ta no tsz-ma wa wa-ta-k'-shi no o ba de go za-ri-ma-s'.
アノオカタ ノ ツマ ハ ワタクシ ノ オバ デ ゴザリマス

Do. A-re no **tsz-ma wa** wa-ta-k'-shi no o ba da.
アレノツマ ハ ワタクシ ノ オバダ

358. *His mind is not on his work.*
A-no o h'-to wa na-sa-ru ko-to ni mi wo o i-re na-sa-ra-nu.
アノオヒト ハ ナサル コト ニ ミ ヲ オイレ ナサラヌ

Do. A-re wa sz-ru ko-to ni mi wo i-re-nu.
アレ ハ スル コト ニ ミ ヲ イレヌ

359. *His father set him up in business*
A-no h'-to no chi-chi wa mo-to de wo i-re-ma-sh'-te a-ki-na-i wo ha-ji-me sa-se-ma-sh'-ta.
アノヒトノチチ ハ モト デ ヲ イレマシテ アキナイ ヲ ハジメ サセマシタ

Do. A-re no chi-chi wa mo-to de wo i-re-te a-ki-na-i **wo** ha-ji-me sa-se-ta.
アレノチチ ハ モト デ ヲ イレテ アキナイ ヲ ハジメ サセタ

360. *His horse ran away with him, and he could not stop him.*
A-no o ka-ta wa m'-ma de ha-shi-ra-se-ma-sh'-ta nga, ji-shi-n de to-me-ru, ko-to nga de-ki-ma-se-na-n-da.
アノオカタ ハ ムマ デ ハシラセマシタ ガ ジシン デ トメル コト ガ デキマセナンダ

Do. A-re wa m'-ma de ha-shi-ra-se-ta nga to-me-ru ko-to nga
アレ ハ ムマ デ ハシラセタ ガ トメル コト ガ

de-ki na-ka-t-ta.
デマナカッタ

361. *His house is opposite to mine.*
A-no o h'-to no i-e wa wa-ta-k'-shi no i-e no mu-ko-o de go za-ri-ma-s'
アノオヒトノイヱハワタクシ ノイヱノ ムカオデ ゴザリマス

Do. A-re nga i-e wa wa-shi no i-e no mu-ko-o da.
アレ ガイヱハ ワシ ノイヱノ ムコウダ

362. *His wound is healed.*
A-no o ka-ta no ki-dz wa i-e ma-sh'-ta.
アノオカタノ キヅ ハイヱ マシタ

Do. A-re no ki-dz wa i-e-ta (or)na-o-t-ta.
アレノキヅ ハイヱタ ナオッタ

363. *His income is 1000 rio a month.*
A-no o ka-ta no ri-o-o bu-n no a-nga-ri-da-ka wa h'-to ts'-ki ni se-n ri-o-o dz-tsz ha-i-ri-ma-s'.
アノオカタノリヤウブンノ アガリダカ ワヒトツ キニセン リヤウヅツ ハイリマス

Do. A-re nga ri-o-o bu-n no a-nga-ri-da-ka wa h'-to ts'-ki ni se-n ri-o-o dz-tsz, ha-iru.
アレガ リヤウブン ノ アガ リタカ ハヒトツキ ニセン リヤウヅツハイル

364. *His children have their own way.*
A-no o ka-ta no ko-do-mo wa wa-nga ma-ma de go za-ri-ma-s'.
アノオカタノコドモハワガ ママデゴザリマス

Do. A-re nga ko-do-mo wa wa-nga ma-ma mo-no da.
アレガ コドモハワガ ママモノダ

365. *How do you sell this article?*
A-na-ta ko-no shi-na wa na-ni ho-do de o u-ri na-sa-re-ma-su ka?
アノタ コノシナ ハ ナニ ホド デオウリ ナサレマス カ

Do. O-ma-e ko-re wa na-ni ho-do de u-ru ka?
オマヱ コレハ ナニホド デウルカ

366. *How do you say that in Japanese.*
So-re wa Ni-p-po-n de wa na-ni to mo-o-shi-ma-s' ka?
ソレハニッポンデ ハ ナニトモウシマス カ

Do. So-re wa Ni-p-po-n de wa na-ni to i-u ka?
ソレ ハ ニッポンデ ハ ナニトイウカ

367. *How many eggs are there here.*
Ko-ko ni ta-ma ngo wa i-ku-tsz go za-ri-ma-s' ka?
ココニ タマゴ ハイクス ゴ ザリマス カ

Do. Ko-ko ni ta-ma-ngo wa i-ku-tsz a-ru ka?
ココニ タマ ゴ ハ イクツ アルカ

368. *How much did you pay for this?*
　　Ko-re wa na-ni ho-do de o ka-i na-sa-re-ma-sh'-ta ka?
　　コレ ハ ナニ ホド デ オカイ ナサレ マシタ カ
Do.　Ko-re wa i-ku-ra de ka-t-ta ka?
　　コレ ハ イクラ デ カツタ カ

369. *How is this idea expressed in Japanese?*
　　Ko-no o-mo-o ko-to wa Ni-p-po-n de wa na-ni to i-i-ma-sh'-
　　コノ オモフ コト ハ ニツポン デ ハ ナニ ト イイマシ
　　ta-ra yo-ro-shi-u go za-ri-ma-sh-'o-o ka?
　　タラ ヨロシウ ゴ ザリマシヤウ カ
Do.　Ko-no o-mo-o ko-to wa Ni-p-po-n de wa do-o i-t-ta-ra yo-
　　コノ オモフ コト ハ ニツポン デ ハ ドウ イツタラ ヨ
　　ka-ro-o ka?
　　カラフ カ

370. *How long do you want this?*
　　Ko-re wa i-tsz ma-de o i-ri yo-o de go za-ri-ma-s' ka?
　　コレ ハ イツ マデ オイリ ヨフ デ ゴ ザリマス カ
Do.　Ko-re wa i-tsz ma-de i-ri yo-o da ka?
　　コレ ハ イツ マデ イリ ヨウ ダ カ

371. *How long do you want it?*　　　　(speaking of length.)
　　Na-nga-sa na-ni ho-do o i-ri na-sa-re-ma-s' ka?
　　ナガサ ナニ ホド オイリ ナサ レマス カ
Do　Na-nga-sa na-ni ho-do i-ru ka?
　　ナガサ ナニ ホド イル カ

372. *How does he get his living?*
　　A-no o h'-to wa na-ni wo ka-ngi-yo-o ni sh'-te o ku-ra-shi na-
　　アノ オヒト ハ ナニ ヲ カギヨウ ニ シテ オ クラシ ナ
　　sa-re-ma-s' ka?
　　サレ マス カ
Do.　A-re wa na-ni wo ka-ngi-yo-o ni sh'-te ku-ra-sz ka?
　　アレ ハ ナニ ヲ カギヨウ ニ シテ クラス カ

373. *How long shall you be gone?*
　　A-na-ta i-tsz ma-de ni yu-t-te o ka-e-ri na-sa-re-ma-s' ka?
　　アナタ イツ マデ ニユツテ オカエリ ナサレ マス カ
Do.　O-ma-e-i-tsz ma-de ni i-t-te ka-e-ru ka?
　　オマエ イツ マデ ニ イツテ カエル カ

374. *How long is this house.*
　　Ko-no i-e no ke-n sz-u wa na-n nge-n go za-ri-ma-s' ka?
　　コノ イエ ノ ケンスウ ハ ナン ゲン ゴ ザリマス カ
Do.　Ko-no i-e no ke-n sz-u wa na-n nge-n a-ru ka?
　　コノ イエ ノ ケンスウ ハ ナン ゲン アル カ

375. *How wide is it?*
　　Ha-ba wa na-ni ho-do de go za-ri-ma-s' ka?
　　ハバ ハ ナニ ホド デ ゴ ザリマス カ

Do. Ha-ba wa na-ni ho-do a-ru ka?
ハバハナニホドアルカ

376. *How wide is the front entrance?* (or door)
I-e no ma-ngu-chi wa na-n nge-n ho-do go-za-ri-ma-s'?
イエノマグチハナンゲンホドゴザリマス'

Do. I-e no ma-ngu-chi wa na-n nge-n ho-do a-ru ka?
イエノマグチハナンゲンホドアルカ

377. *How long is the house from front to rear?*
So-no i-e no o-ku-yu-ki wa na-n nge-n ho-do go za-ri-ma-s' ka?
ソノイエノオクユキハナンゲンホドゴザリマスカ

Do. So-no i-e no o-ku-yu-ki wa na-n nge-n ho-do a-ru-ka?
ソノイエノオクユキハナンゲンホドアルカ

378. *How much is he worth?*
A-no o ka-ta wa shi-n sh'-o-o wa na-ni ho-do de go za-ri-ma-s' ka?
アノオカタハシンシャウハナニホドデゴザリマスカ

Do. A-no h'-to wa na-ni ho-do no shi-n sh'-o-o ka?
アノヒトハナニホドノシンシャウカ

379. *How much is this worth?*
Ko-no ne-u-chi wa na-ni ho-do ngu-ra-i de go za-ri-ma-sh'-o-o ka?
コノネウチハナニホドグラヒデゴザリマシヤウカ

Do. Ko-no ne-u-chi wa do-no ku-ra-i de a-ro-o ka?
コノネウチハドノクラヒデアラフカ

380. *How hard the wind blows?*
A-á ha-nge shi-i ka-ze de go za-ri-ma-s'?
アアハゲシイカゼデゴザリマス

Do. A-á tsz-yo-i ka-ze da?
アアツヨイカゼダ

381. *How long have you been here?*
Ko-ko ni na-ni ho-do o i-de na-sa-re-ma-sh'-ta ka?
ココニナニホドオイデナサレマシタカ

Do. Ko-ko ni na-ni ho-do i-ta ka?
ココニナニホドイタカ

382. *How long is it since you come here.*
A-na-ta ko-chi-ra e ma-i-ri-ma-sh'-te yo-ri na-ni ho-do ni na-ri-ma-s' ka?
アナタコチラエマイリマシテヨリナニホドニナリマスカ

Do. O-ma-e ko-chi-ra e ki-te yo-ri na-ni ho-do ni na-ru ka?
オマエコチラエキテヨリナニホドニナルカ

383. *How do you want this done?*
　　A-na-ta ko-re wa do-no yo-o ni ts'-ra-sh'-te yo-ro-shi-u go-za-ri-ma-sh'-o-o ka?
　　アナタ コレ ハ ドノ ヤウニ ツラシテ ヨロシウ ゴザリマシャウカ
Do.　O-ma-e ko-re wa do-o ts'-ku-t-te yo-ku-ro-o ka?
　　オマエ コレ ハ ドウ ツクッテ ヨカラフ カ

384. *How much do you want?*
　　A-na-ta na-ni ho-do o i-ri yo-o de go za-ri-ma-s' ka?
　　アナタ ナニ ホド オイリヨウ デゴザリマスカ
Do.　O-ma-e na-ni ho-do i-ru ka?
　　オマエ ナニ ホド イルカ

385. *How came you to be so late?*
　　A-na-ta na-ni go yo-o nga go za-ri-ma-sh'-te ka-yo-o ni o-so-o na-ri-ma-sh'-ta ka?
　　アナタ ナニ ゴヨウ ガ ゴザリマシテ カヤウニオソウナリマシタカ
Do.　O-ma-e na-ni nga a-t-te ko-no yo-o ni o-so i ka?
　　オマエ ナニ ガアッテ コノ ヤウニオソイカ

386. *How long shall I make it?*
　　Wa-ta-k'-shi ko-re wo na-nga-sa na-ni ho-do ts'-ku-ri-ma-sh'-o-o ka?
　　ワタクシ コレ ヲ ナガサ ナニ ホド ツクリマシヤウカ
Do.　Wa-ta-k'-shi ko-re wo na-nga-sa do-re ho-do ni ts'-ku-ro-o ka?
　　ワタクシ コレ ヲ ナガ サ ドレ ホド ニ ツクロウカ

387. *How much do I owe you?*
　　Wa-ta-k'-shi a-na-ta ni sh'-a-k'-yo-o nga na-ni ho-do go za-ri-ma-sh'-o-o ka?
　　ワタクシ アナタ ニ シャクヨウ ガ ナニ ホド ゴザリマシャウカ
Do.　Wa-ta-k'-shi o-ma-e ni ka-ri nga i-ku-ra a-ru ka?
　　ワタクシ オマエ ニ カリ ガ イクラ アルカ

388. *How many kinds of tea are there?*
　　Sz-be-te ch'-a no ru-i wa i-ku shi-na ho-do go za-ri-ma-s' ka?
　　スベテ チヤ ノ ルイ ハ イクシナ ホド ゴザリマスカ
Do　Sz-be-te ch'-a no ru-i wa i-ku shi-na ho-do a-ru ka?
　　スベテ チヤ ノ ルイ ハ イク シナ ホド アルカ

389. *How long will it be before grapes are ripe?*
　　Bu-do-o no ji-k'-shi-ma-sz wa i-tsz no ko-ro de go za-ri-ma-s' ka?
　　ブドウ ノ ジクシマス ハ イツ ノ コロ デ ゴザリマスカ

Do. Bu-do-o no ji-k'-sz no wa i-tsz ngo-ro ka?
ブドウノジクスノハイツゴロカ

390. *How did it turn out?*
A-no ko-to wa i-ka-nga na-ri-ma-sh'-ta ka?
アノコトハイカガナリマシタカ

Do. A-no ko-to wa do-o na-t-ta ka?
アノコトハドヲナッタカ

391. *How much does that weigh?*
So-no me-ka-ta wa na-ni ho-do go za-ri-ma-s' ka?
ソノメカタハナニホドゴザリマスカ

Do. So-no me-ka-ta wa i-ku-ra a-ru-ka?
ソノメカタハイクラアルカ

392. *How much ought I to give for it?*
Wa-ta-k'-shi ko-re wo na-ni ho-do ka-i-ma-sh'-te yo-ro-shi-u go za-ri-ma-s' ka?
ワタクシコレヲナニホドカイマシテヨロシウ
ゴザリマスカ

Do. Wa-shi wa ko-re-wo i-ku-ra de ka-t-te yo-i ka?
ワシハコレヲイクラデカッテヨイカ

393. *How much do you think it is worth?*
A-na-ta ko-re wo na-ni ho-do no ne-u-chi to o-bo-shi-me-sz ka?
アナタコレヲナニホドノ子ウチトオボシメスカ

Do. O-ma-e ko-re wa i-ku-ra ngu-ra-i no neu-chi to o-mo-u ka?
オマヘコレハイクラグライノ子ウチトオモフカ

394. *How much does he get a month?*
A-no h'-to wa i-chi nge-tsz ni ki-u-ki-n wo i-ku-ra o to-ri na-sa-ru ka?
アノヒトハイチゲツニキウキンヲイクラオトリナサルカ

Do. A-re wa i-chi nge-tsz ni ki-u-ki-n wo i-ku-ra mo-ra-u ka?
アレハイチゲツニキウキンヲイクラモラウカ

395. *How many are there in all?*
No-ko-ra-dz de i-ku-tsz go za-ri-ma-s' ka?
ノコラズデイクツゴザリマスカ

Do. No-ko-ra-dz de i-ku-tsz a-ru ka?
ノコラズデイクツアルカ

396. *How much does this hold?*
Ko-re ni wa na-ni-ho-do ha-i-ri-ma-s' ka?
コレニハナニホドハイリマスカ

Do. Ko-re ni wa do-re ho-do ha-i-ru ka?
コレニハドレホドハイルカ

397. *How thick the mosquitoes are?*
Ka nga o-o ku-te u-t-to-shi-u ngo za-ri-ma-s'
カガオホクテウットシウゴザリマス

Do. Ka nga o-o-ku-te u-ru-sa-i.
カガオホクテウルサイ

398. *How much does it all amount to?*
　　No-ko-ra-dz de da-i ki-n wa i-ka ho-do ni na-ri-ma-s' ka?
　　ノコラズデダイキンハイカホドニナリマスカ
Do.　No-ko-ra-dz de da-i wa i-ku-ra ni na-ru ka?
　　ノコラズデダイハイクラニナルカ

399. *How does he support himself?*
　　A-no o ka-ta wa yo a-ta-ri ni na-ni wo sh'-te o ku-ra-shi na-sa-ru-ka?
　　アノオカタハヨアタリニナニヲシテオクラシナサルカ
Do.　A-re wa na-ni wo to se-i ni sh'-te i-no-chi wo tsz-na-ngu ka?
　　アレハナニヲトセイニシテイノチヲツナグカ

400. *How far is it to Fujiyama?*
　　Fu-ji-sa-n ma-de wa i-ku ri ho-do go-za-ri-ma-s' ka?
　　フジサンマデハイクリホドゴザリマスカ
Do.　Fu-ji-sa-n e wa na-ni ho-do a-ru ka?
　　フジサンヘハナニホドアルカ

401. *How long will you be about it?*
　　I-tsz ngo-ro ma-de ni ka-ka-ri-ma-sh'-o-o ka?
　　イツゴロマデニカカリマショウカ
Do.　I-tsz ma-de ka-ka-ru ka?
　　イツマデカカルカ

402. *How many can you spare?*
　　I-ka ho-do ni i-dz-ri na-sa-re-te ku-da-sa-re-ma-sh'-o-o ka?
　　イカホドニイズリナサレテクダサレマショウカ
Do.　I-ku-ra ni i-dz-t-te ku-re-ru ka?
　　イクラニイズッテカレルカ

403. *How many days will you be about it?*
　　I-k' ka ho-do ka-ka-ri-ma-sh'-o-o ka?
　　イクカホドカカリマショウカ
Do.　I-k' ka ho-do ka-ka-ru ka?
　　イクカホドカカルカ

404. *How do you do to-day?* (Said when a person is not known to have been ill.)
　　Ko-n ni-chi wa go ki-nge-n yo-ro-shi-u o i-de na-sa-re-ma-s' ka?
　　コンニチハゴキゲンヨロシウオイデナサレマスカ
Do　Ko-n ni-chi wa ka-wa-ru ko-to wa na-i ka?
　　コンニチハカワルコトハナイカ
How do you do to-day?　(when one has been ill.)
　　Ko-n ni-chi wa go ki-bu-n wa i-ka-nga de go za-ri-ma-s' ka?
　　コンニチハゴキブンハイカガデゴザリマスカ
Do.　Ko-n ni-chi wa o ko-ko-ro yo-i ka?
　　コンニチハオココロヨイカ

405. *How long may I keep it?*
　　Wa-ta-k'-shi i-tsz o ka-ri mo-o-sh'-te o-ki-ma-sh'-te yo-ro-shi
　　ワタクシイツオカリモオシテオキマシテヨロシ

u go za-ri-ma-s' ka?
ウゴ ザリマスカ
Do. Wa-ta-k'-shi i-tsz ma-de ka-ri-te o-i-te yo-i ka?
ワタクシイツ マデ カリテオイテヨイカ

406. *Human nature is the same in all countries.*
Ba-n ko-ku to-mo-ni h'-to no m'-ma-re-ts'-ki wa o-na-ji-ko-to
バンコクトモニヒト ノウマレツキ ハ オナジコト
de go za-ri-ma-s'.
デゴ ザリマス
Do. Se-ka-i no h'-to no m'-ma-re-ts'-ki wa o-na-ji-ko-to da.
セカイ ノヒト ノウマレツキ ハ オナジコト ダ

407. *Hunting is forbidden within* 10 *ri in all directions from the Nihon bridge at Yedo.*
Ye-do no Ni-ho-n ba-shi ka-ra ji-u ri yo ho-o ka ri wo sz-ru
エド ノ ニホン バシ カラ ジウリ ヨホウ カリ ヲ スル
ko-to wa ki-n-ze-i de go za-ri-ma-s'.
コト ハ キンゼイデ ゴ ザリマス
Do. Ye-do no Ni-ho-n ba-shi ka-ra ji-u ri yo ho-o ka-ri wo sz-
エド ノ ニホン バシ カラ ジウリヨホウ カリ ヲ ス
ru ko-to na-ra-nu.
ル コトナラヌ

408. *Humble persons do not boast of their merits.*
Ke-n so-n no h'-to wa ko-o ni ho-ko-ri ma-se-nu.
ケンソン ノヒト ハ コウニ ホコリ マセヌ
Do. He-ri-ku-da-ru h'-to wa ko-o ni ho-ko ra-nu.
ヘリクダル ヒト ハ コウニ ホコ ラヌ

I.

409. *I am not well.*
Wa-ta-k'-shi wa ki-bu-n nga yo-ro-shi-u go za-ri-ma-se-n'.
ワタクシ ハ キブン ガ ヨロシウ ゴ ザリマセン
Do. Wa-ta-k'-shi nga ki-mo-chi nga wa-ru-i.
ワタクシ ガ キモチ ガ ワルイ

410. *I want it well done.*
Wa-ta-k'-shi yo-ro-sh'-ku ts'-ku-ra-se-to-o dzo-n-ji-ma-s'.
ワタクシ ヨロシク ツクラセトウ ゾンジマス
Do. Wa-ta-k'-shi yo-ku ts'-ku-ra-se-ta-i
ワタクシ ヨク ツクラセタイ

411. *I want some of each kind.*
Wa-ta-k'-shi i-ro i-ro s'-ko-shi dz-tsz i-ri-ma-s'.
ワタクシ イロイロ スコシ ズツ イリマス
Do. Wa-ta-k'-shi i-ro i-ro s'-ko-shi dz-tsz i-ru.
ワタクシ イロイロ スコシ ズツイル

I.

412. *I am a little deaf.*
Wa-ta-k'-shi wa mi-mi nga s'-ko-shi to-o-o go za-ri-ma-s'.
ワタクシ ハ ミミ ガ スコシ トヲウゴ ザリマス

Do. Wa-ta-k'-shi wa s'-ko-shi mi-mi nga to-o-i.
ワタクシ ハ スコシ ミミ ガ トヨイ

413. *I have the tooth ache.*
Wa-ta-k'-shi wa ha nga i-ta mi-ma-s'.
ワタクシ ハ ハ ガ イタ ミマス

Do. Wa-ta-k'-shi wa ha nga i-ta-mu.
ワタクシ ハ ハ ガ イタム

414. *I assure you it is not so.*
Sa-yo-o de **wa** go za-ri-ma-se-nu ma-ko-to wo o ha-na-shi-mo-o-shi-ma-s'!
サヨウデ ハ ゴザリマセヌ マコト ヲ オハナシ モ ウシマス

Do. So-o de wa na-i ho-n to wo ha-na-s'.
ソウデ ハナイ ホント ヲ ハナス

415. *I have read this book through.*
Wa-ta-k'-shi wa ko-no ho-n wo yo-mi o-wa-ri-ma-sh'-ta.
ワタクシ ハ コノ ホン ヲ ヨミ オワリマシタ

Do. Wa-shi wa ko-no ho-n wo yo-n-de shi-ma-t-ta.
ワシ ハ コノ ホン ヲ ヨンデ シマッタ

416. *I have never had any other.*
Wa-ta-k'-shi wa i-ma ma-de ni ho-ka no wa go za-ri-ma-se-na-n-da.
ワタクシ ハ イマ マデ ニ ホカ ノ ハ ゴ ザリマセ ナンダ

Do. Wa-ta-k'-shi wa **i-ma** ma-de ni ho-ka no wa na-ka-t-ta.
ワタクシ ハ イマ マデ ニ ホカ ノ ハ ナカッタ

417. *I cannot afford it.*
Wa-ta-k'-shi wa so-no yo-o ni da-sz ko-to wa de-ki-ma-se-nu.
ワタクシ ハ ソノ ヨウニ ダス コト ハ デキマセス

Do. Wa-shi wa so-n na-ni da-sz ko-to wa de-ki-na-i.
ワシ ハ ソンナニ ダス コト ハ デキナイ

418. *I cannot bear it any longer.*
Wa-ta-k'-shi mo ha-ya ka-n-ni-n na-ri-ma-se-nu.
ワタクシ モ ハヤ カンニン ナリマセス

Do. Wa-ta-k'-shi wa mo ka-n-ni-n nga na-ra-nu.
ワタクシ ハ モ カンニン ガ ナラス

419. *I would rather not go.*
Wa-ta-k'-shi wa yu-ku yo-ri yu-ki-ma-se-nu ho-o nga yo-ro-shi-i to dzo-n-ji-ma-s'.
ワタクシ ハ ユク ヨリ ユキマセス ホウ ガ ヨロ シイ ト ゾンジ マス

Do. Wa-shi wa yu-ku yo-ri yu-ka-nu ho-o nga yo-i to o-mo-o.
ワシ ハ ユク ヨリ ユカス ホウ ガ ヨイト オモウ

420. *I did not understand, although I heard it.*
Wa-ta-k'-shi wa ki-ki-ma-sh'-ta ke-re-do-mo wa-ka-ri-ma-se-na-n-da.
ワタクシハ キキマシタケレドモ ワカリマセ ナンダ

Do. Wa-shi wa ki-i-ta ke-re-do-mo wa-ka ra-na-ka-t-ta.
ワシハキイタケレドモワ カラナカッタ

421. *I think it will be so eventually*
Shi-ji-u wa sa-yo-o de go za-ri-ma-sh'-o-o to o-mo-i-ma-s'.
シジウハ サヨウデゴザリマシヨウ トオモイマス

Do. Tsz-i ni wa so-o de a-ro-o to o-mo-o.
ツイニ ハソウデアロウ ト オモウ

422. *I will not do so again.*
Wa-ta-k'-shi f'-ta-ta-bi so-no to-o-ri ni i-ta-shi-ma-se-nu.
ワタクシフタウビ ソノ トオリニイタシマセヌ

Do. Wa-shi wa f'-ta-ta-bi so-no to-o-ri ni wa se-nu.
ワシ ハ フタタビ ソノトウリニ ハ セヌ

423. *I got up this morning before day break.*
Wa-ta-k'-shi ke-sa yo-a-ke ma-e ni o-ki-ma sh'-ta.
ワタクシ ケサ ヨアケマエ ニオキマシタ

Do. Wa-shi wa ke-sa ku-ra-i u-chi ni o-ki-ta.
ワシハ ケサ クライウチニオキタ

424. *I must have this tooth out.*
Wa-ta-k'-shi wa ko-no ha wo uu-ki-ta-i to o-mo-i-ma-s'.
カタクシハ コノハヲ スキタイトオモイマス

Do. Wa-shi wa ko-no ha wo nu-ki-ta-i to o-mo-o.
ワシ ハ コノ ハ ヲ スキタイト オモウ

425. *I can do it now as well as any time.*
Wa-ta-k'-shi wa i-ma i-ta-shi-ma-s' mo no-chi ni i-ta-shi-ma-s' mo o-na-ji-ko-to de go za-ri-ma-s'.
ワタクシ ハイマイタシマス モノチニイタシマ スモ オナジコト デ ゴザリマス

Do. Wa-shi wa i-ma sz-ru mo no-chi ni sz-ru mo o-na-ij-ko-to da.
ワシ ハ イマスル モ ノチ ニ スル モ オナジコ トダ

426. *I see now that I was mistaken.*
Wa-ta-k'-shi wa sa-ki ni chi-nga-i-ma-sh'-ta nga i-ma de wa ko-ko-ro dz-ki-ma-sh'-ta.
ワタクシハ サキニチ ガイマシタガイマデ ハ コ コロズキマシタ

Do. Wa-shi wa sa-ki ni chi-nga-e-ta nga i-ma de wa ki nga-tsz-i-ta.
ワシ ハサキニ チ ガエタ ガイマデ ハ キ ガ ツイタ

427. *I came across it in the market.*
Wa-ta-k'-shi wa i-chi ni yu-ki a-aw-se-te ka-i-ma-sh'-ta.
ワタクシハイチニユキアワセテカイマシタ
Do. Wa-shi wa i-chi ni yu-ki a-wa-se-te ka-t-ta.
ワシハイチニユキアワセテカッタ

428. *I have been busy helping off with his baggage.*
Wa-ta-k'-shi wa a-no o ka-ta no ni-ngo-shi ra-i no te-tsz-da-
ワタクシハアノオカタノニゴシライノテツダ
i de i-so-nga-shi-u go-za-ri-ma-sh'-ta.
イデイソガシウゴザリマシタ
Do. Wa-shi wa a-no h'-to no ni wo ts'-ku-t-te ya-ru no de i-
ワシハアノヒトノニヲツクッテヤルノデイ
so-nga-shi ka-t-ta.
ソガシカッタ

429. *I am beginning to be a little better of my* **illness.**
Wa-ta-k'-shi no bi-o-o-ki nga i-ma-s'-ko-shi yo-ro-shi-u go za-
ワタクシノビヨウキガイマスコシヨロシウゴザ
ri-ma-s'.
リマス
Do. Wa-shi no bi-o-o-ki wa i-ma s'-ko-shi yo-ro-shi-i.
ワシノビヨウキハイマスコシヨロシイ

430. *I found them scattered here and there all along the road.*
Wa-ta-k'-shi wa a-chi ko-chi no mi-chi ni chi-t-te a-ru no wo
ワタクシハアチコチノ三チニチッテアルノヲ
yu-ki a-wa-se-te mi-ma-sh'-ta.
ユキアハセテ三マシタ
Do. Wa-shi wa a-chi ko-chi no mi-chi ni chi-t-te a-ru no wo
ワシハアチコチノ三チニチッテアルノヲ
mi-ta.
三タ

431. *I am afraid that boy will not turn out well.*
Wa-ta-k'-shi a-no ko-do-mo wa se-i ch'-o i-ta-shi-ma-sh'-te
ワタクシアノコドモハセイチヤウイタシマシテ
mo ro-ku-na mo-no ni wa na-ri-ma-s'-ma-i to o-mo-i-ma-s'.
モロクナモノニハナリマスマイトオモイマス
Do. Wa-shi wa a-no ko-do-mo wa se-i ch'-o sh'-te mo ro-ku-
ワシハアノコドモハセイチヤウシノモロク
na mo-no ni na-ru-ma-i to o-mo-o.
ナモノニナルマイトオモウ

432. *I have a charge of 10 rio against you.*
Wa-ta-k'-shi no ch'-o-me-n no o-mo-te ni a-na-ta ni ka-ne-
ワタクシノチヨメンノオモテニアナタニカネ
nga ji-u ri-o ka-shi nga shi-ru-sh'-te go za-ri-ma-s'.
ガジウリヨウカシガシルシテゴザリマス

432. Wa-shi nga ch'-o-me-n ni o-ma-e ni ji-u ri-o no ka-shi
ワシ ガ チヨメン ニオマエ ニシウリヨウノカシ
nga shi-ru-sh'-te a-ru.
ガ シルシテアル

433. *I have been here upwards of a year.*
Wa-ta-k'-shi wa ko-ko ni i-chi ne-n a-ma-ri o-ri-ma-sh'-ta.
ワタクシ ハ ココ ニイチ ネン アマリ オリマシタ
Do. Wa-shi wa ko-ko ni i-chi ne-n no yo i-ta.
ワシ ハ ココ ニイチ ネン ノ ヨイタ

434. *I have paid you up to the end of last month.*
Wa-ta-k'-shi a-na-ta ni se-n nge-tsz mi-so-ka ma-de no bu-n
ワタクシ アナタニセン ゲツ ミソカ マデ ノブン
wo a-nge-ma-sh'-ta.
ヲアゲマシタ
Do. Wa-shi wa o-ma-e ni se-n nge-tsz no-mi-so-ka ma-de no
ワシ ハオマエニセン ゲツ ノ ミソカ マデ ノ
bu-n wo ya-t-ta.
ブン ヲ ヤッタ

435. *I told you to do this long ago.* (to a servant)
Wa-ta-k'-shi ko-re wo shi-ro i-i-ts'-ke-te ka-ra hi-sa-sh'-ku
ワタクシ コレ ヲ シロ イイツケテ カラ ヒサシク
na-ru.
ナル

436. *I am sick.*
Wa-ta-k'-shi wa bi-o-o-ki go za-ri-ma-s'.
ワタクシ ハ ビヨウキ ゴ ザリマス
Do. Wa-ta-k'-shi wa bi-o-o-ki.
ワタクシ ハ ビヨウキ

437. *I don't care.*
Wa-ta-k'-shi wa ka-ma-i-ma-se-nu.
ワタクシ ハ カマイ マセヌ
Do. Wa-ta-k'-shi wa ka-ma-wa-nu (or) Wa-ta-k'-shi to-n-j'-a-ku
ワタクシ ハ カマワヌ   ワタクシ トンジャク
na-i.
ナイ

438. *I want this.*
Wa-ta-k'-shi wa ko-re wo ho-shi-u go za-ri-ma-s'
ワタクシ ハ コレ ヲ ホシウ ゴ ザリマス
Do. Wa-shi wa ko-re nga ho-shi-i.
ワシ ハ コレ ガ ホシイ

439. *I don't know.*
Wa-ta-k'-shi wa dzo-n-ji-ma-se-nu.
ワタクシ ハ ゾンジマセヌ
Do. Wa-shi wa shi-ra-nu.
ワシ ハ シラヌ

440. *I cannot tell.*
　　Wa-ta-k'-shi wa ha-na-sa-re-ma-se-nu.
　　ワタクシ ハ ハナサレマセヌ
Do.　Wa-shi wa ha-na-sa-re-nu.
　　ワシ ハ ハナサレヌ

441. *I suppose so.*
　　Wa-ta-k'-shi wa sa-yo-o ni o-mo-i-ma-s'.
　　ワタクシ ハ サヨウ ニ オモイマス
Do.　Wa-ta-k'-shi wa so-o o-mo-o.
　　ワタクシ ハ ソウオモウ

442. *I don't like this.*
　　Wa-ta-k'-shi wa ko-re wo s'-ki-ma-se-nu.
　　ワタクシ ハ コレ ヲ スキマセヌ
Do.　Wa-shi wa ko-re wo s'-ka-nu.
　　ワシ ハ コレ ヲ スカヌ

443. *I am hungry.*
　　Wa-ta-k'-shi wa ku-u f'-ku ni na-ri-ma-sh'-ta.
　　ワタクシ ハ クウ フク ニ ナリマシタ
Do.　Wa-shi wa ha-ra nga sz-i-ta.
　　ワシ ハ ハラ ガ スイタ

444. *I am going out to-day.*
　　Wa-ta-k'-shi wa ko-n ni-chi yo-so e ma-i-ri-ma-sh'-o-o to o-mo-i-ma-s'.
　　ワタクシ ハ コン ニチ ヨソ エ マイリマシヨウト オモイマス
Do.　Wa-shi wa ko-n ni-chi yo-so e yu-ko-o.
　　ワシ ハ コン ニチ ヨソ エ ユコウ

445. *I am sleepy.*
　　Wa-ta-k'-shi ne-mu-u go za-ri-ma-s'.
　　ワタクシ ネムウ ゴ ザリマス
Do.　Wa-shi wa ne-mu-i.
　　ワシ ハ ネムイ

446. *I have lost my book.*
　　Wa-ta-a'-shi no ho-n nga fu-n ji-tsz i-ta-shi-ma-sh'-ta.
　　ワタクシ ノ ホン ガ フンジツ イタシマシタ
Do.　Wa-shi no ho-n nga na-ku na-ri-ma-sh'-ta.
　　ワシ ノ ホン ガ ナクナリマシタ

447. *I am very tired.*
　　Wa-ta-k'-shi wa ha-na-ha-da ts'-ka-re-ma-sh'-ta.
　　ワタクシ ハ ハナハダ ツカレマシタ
Do.　Wa-shi wa o-o-ki ni ts'-ka-re-ta.
　　ワシ ハ オヲキ ニ ツカレタ

448. *I have not a cash.*
　　Wa-ta-k'-shi wa ze-ni nga s'-ko-shi mo go za-ri-ma-se-nu.
　　ワタクシ ハ ゼニ ガ スコシ モ ゴ ザリマセヌ

Do. Wa-shi wa ze-ni nga s'-ko-shi mo na-i.
ワシハゼニガ スコシ モナイ

449. *I have never seen him.*
Wa-ta-k'-shi wa ma-da a-no o-ka-ta-nı o me ni ka-ka-ri-ma-se-n'.
ワタクシ ハ マダ アノ ヲカタニ オメ ニ カカリマセン

Do. Wa-shi wa ma-da o-no h'-to wo mi-nu.
ワシ ハ マダ アノ ヒト ヲ ミス

450. *I am afraid to tell.*
Wa-ta-k'-shi wa i-u ko-to wo ha-ba-ka-ri-ma-s'.
ワタクシ ハ イウ コト ヲ ハバカリマス

Do. Wa-shi wa i-u ko-to wo ha-ba-ka-ru.
ワシ ハ イウ コト ヲ ハバカル

451. *I have forgotten.*
Wa-ta-k'-shi wa sh'-tsz-ne-n i-ta-shi-ma-sh'-ta.
ワタクシ ハ シッ子ン イタシマシタ

Do. Wa-shi wa wa-sz-re-ta.
ワシ ハ ワスレタ

452. *I will see to that myself.*
Wa-ta-k'-shi nga ji-shi-n de sa-shi-dz wo i-ta-shi-ma-sh'-o-o.
ワタクシ ガ ジシン デ サシズ ヲ イタシマシヨウ

Do. Wa-shi nga ji-shi-n de sa-shi-dz wo shi-yo-o.
ワシ ガ ジシン テ サシズ ヲ シヨウ

453. *I do not want any help.*
Wa-ta-k'-shi ni te-tsz-da-i wa i-ri-ma-se-n'.
ワタクシ ニ テツダイ ハ イリマセン

Do. Wa-shi ni te-tsz-da-i wa i-ra-nu.
ワシ ニ テツダイ ハ イラス

454. *I have been taking medicine.*
Wa-ta-k'-shi wa k'-sz-ri wo no-mi-ma-sh'-ta.
ワタクシ ハ クスリ ヲ ノミマシタ

Do. Wa-ta-k'-shi wa k'-sz-ri wo no-n-da.
ワタクシ ハ クスリ ヲ ノンダ

455. *I have not seen it.*
Wa-ta-k'-shi ma-da ha-i-ke-n i-ta-shi-ma-se-na-n-da.
ワタクシ マダ ハイケン イタシマセナンダ

Do. Wa-shi wa ma-da mi na-ka-t-ta.
ワシ ハ マダ ミ ナカッタ

456. *I cannot understand the rationale of it.*
Wa-ta-k'-shi wa so-no ri nga wa-ka-ri-ma-se-n'.
ワタクシ ハ ソノ リ ガ ワカリマセン

Do. Wa-shi wa so-no ri nga wa-ka-ra-nu.
ワシ ハ ソノ リ ガ ワカラス

457. *I am ashamed.*
Wa-ta-k'-shi wa ha-ji wo ka-ki-ma-s'.
ワタクシ ハ ハジ ヲ カキマス
Do. Wa-shi wa ha-ji wo ka-ku.
ワシ ハ ハジ ヲ カク

458. *I am not sure.*
Wa-ta-k'-shi wa ta-sh'-ka ni dzo-n-ji-ma-se-n'.
ワタクシ ハ タシカ ニ ゾンジマセン
Do. Wa-shi wa ta-sh'-ka ni shi-ra-nu.
ワシ ハ タシカ ニ シラヌ

459. *I shall go this evening.*
Wa-ta-k'-shi wa ko-m ba-n k'-t-to ma-i-ri-ma-sh'-o-o.
ワタクシ ハ コン バン キット マイリ マシヨウ
Do. Wa-shi wa ko-m ba-n k'-t-to yu-ko-o.
ワシ ハ コン バン キット ユコウ

460. *I have cut my finger.*
Wa-ta-k'-shi wa yu-bi- ni ki-ri-ki-dz wo ko-shi-ra-e-ma-sh'-ta.
ワタクシ ハ ユビ ニ キリキズ ヲ コシラエマシタ
Do. Wa-shi wa yu-bi ni ki-ri-ki-dz wo ko-shi-ra-e-ta.
ワシ ハ ユビ ニ キリキズ ヲ コシラエタ

461. *I have set my seal in my blood that I will not break my promise.*
Wa-ta-k'-shi wa ya-ku-so-ku wo chi-nga-i-ma-se-nu ta-me ni
ワタクシ ハ ヤクソク ヲ チガイマセヌ タメニ
ke-p-pa-n wo i-ta-shi-ma-sh'-ta.
ケッパン ヲ イタシマシタ
Do. Wa-shi wa ya-ku-so-ku wo chi-nga-e-nu yo-o ni ke-p-pa-
ワシ ハ ヤクソク ヲ チガエヌ ヨウ ニ ゲッパ
n wo sh'-ta.
ン ヲ シタ

462. *I have seen this before.*
Wa-ta-k'-sh wa ko-re wo ma-e ka-ta ha-i-ke-n i-ta-shi-ma-sh'-ta.
ワタクシ ハ コレ ヲ マエ カタ ハイケン イタシマ シタ
Do. Wa-shi wa ko-re wo ma-e ka-ta mi-ta.
ワシ ハ コレ ヲ マエ カタ ミタ

463. *I think so too.*
Wa-ta-k'-shi wa ya-ha-ri sa-yo-o ni dzo-n-ji-ma-s'.
ワタクシ ハ ヤハリ サヨウ ニ ゾンジマス
Do. Wa-shi wa ya-p'-pa-ri so-o o-mo-o.
ワシ ハ ヤッパリ ソヲヲモウ

464. *I like this best.*
Wa-ta-k'-shi wa ko-re nga i-chi-ba-n ki ni i-ri-ma-s'.
ワタクシ ハ コレ ガ イチバン キニ イリマス

464. Wa-shi wa ko-re nga i-chi-ba-n ki ni i-ru.
ワシ ハ コレガ イチバン キニイル

465. *I do not think so.*
Wa-ta-k'-shi wa sa-yo-o ni wa dzo-n-ji-ma-se-nu.
ワタクシ ハ サヨヲニ ハ ゾンジマセス

Do. Wa-shi wa so-o wa o-mo-wa-nu.
ワシ ハ ソヲ ハ オモワス

466. *I do not believe it.*
Wa-ta-k'-shi wa shi-n-ji-ma-se-nu.
ワタクシ ハ シンジマセス

Do. Wa-shi wa ma-ko-to to se-nu.
ワシ ハ マコト ト セス

467. *I don't care whether there are any or not.*
Go-za-ri-ma-sh'-te mo go za-ri-ma-se-nu de mo to-n-j'-a-ku i-
ゴザリマシテ モ ゴザリマセス デモ トンジャクイ
ta-shi-ma-se-nu.
タシマセス

Do. A-t-te mo na-ku-te mo ka-ma-wa-nu.
アッテモ ナクテモ カマワス

468. *I shall go in a month.*
Wa-ta-k'-shi wa mo h'-to ts'-ki ta-chi-ma-sh'-te ma-i-ri-ma-sh'-
ワタクシ ハ モ ヒトツキ タチマシテ マイリマシ
yo-o.
ヨウ

Do. Wa-shi wa mo h'-to ts'-ki ta-t-te yu-ko-o.
ワシ ハ モ ヒトツキ タッテ ユコウ

469. *I cannot stay here any longer.*
Wa-ta-k'-shi wa mo ko-ko ni o-ra-re-ma-se-n.
ワタクシ ハ モ ココニ オラレ マセス

Do. Wa-shi wa mo ko-ko ni wa o-ra-re-nu.
ワシ ハ モ ココニハ オラレス

470. *I have no more patience with you.*
Wa-ta-k'-shi wa a-na-ta no ka-to ni mo ko-n-ni-n nga na-ri-
ワタクシ ハ アナタ ノ カトニモ コンニンガ ナリ
ma-se-nu.
マセス

Do. Wa-shi wa o-ma-e no ko-to ni mo ka-n-ni-n nga na-ra-nu.
ワシ ハ オマエノ コトニモ カンニンガ ナラス

471. *I bathe twice a day.*
Wa-ta-k'-shi hi ni ni do dz-tsz yu wo ts'-ka-i-ma-s'.
ワタクシ ヒニニド ヅツ ユ ヲ ツカイマス

Do. Wa-shi wa hi ni ni do dz-tsz yu wo ts'-ka-u.
ワシ ハ ヒニニド ズツ ユ ヲ ツカウ

472. *I have sent a messenger.*
Wa-ta-k'-shi wa ts'-ka-i no mo-no wo ts'-ka-wa-shi-ma-sh'-ta.
ワタクシ ハ ツカイ ノ モノヲ ツカハシマシタ

672. Wa-shi wa ts'-ka-i wo ya-t-ta.
ワシハツカイヲヤッタ

673. *I have just found out what it means.*
Wa-ta-k'-shi wa ta-da-i-ma ka-n-nga-i i-da-shi-ma-sh'-ta.
ワタクシハタダイマカンガイイダシマシタ

Do. Wa-shi wa ta-da-i-ma ka-n-nga-i da-sh'-ta.
ワシハタダイマカンガイダシタ

474. *I cannot help it.* (in the sense of preventing)
Wa-ta-k'-shi wa f'-se-ngu ko-to nga de-ki-ma-se-n'.
ワタクシハフセグコトガデキマセン

Do. Wa-shi wa f'-se-ngu ko-to nga de-ki-nu.
ワシハフセグコトガデキヌ

475. *I cannot help it.* (in the sense of remedying.)
Wa-ta-k'-shi wa na-o-s' ko-to nga de-ki-ma-se-nu.
ワタクシハナヲスコトガデキマセヌ

Do. Wa-shi wa na-o-s' ko-to nga de-ki-nu.
ワシハナヲスコトガデキヌ

476. *I never said so.*
Wa-ta-k'-shi wa ma-da so-no yo-o-na ko-to wo mo-o shi-ma-se-n'.
ワタクシハマダソノヨヲナコトヲモヲシマセン

Do. Wa-shi wa ma-da so-n-na ko-to wo i-wa-nu.
ワシハマダソンナコトヲイワヌ

477. *I am surprised at that*
Wa-ta-k'-shi wa so-re wo he-n ni o-mo-i-ma-s'.
ワタクシハソレヲヘンニヲモイマス

Do. Wa-shi wa so-re wo he-n ni o-mo-o.
ワシハソレヲヘンニオモウ

478. *I forgot to wind up the clock last night.*
Wa-ta-k'-shi sa-ku-ba-n to-ke-i wo ka-ke-ru ko-to wo sh'-tsz ne-n i-ta-shi-ma-sh'-ta.
ワタクシサクバントケイヲカケルコトヲシツネンイタシマシタ

Do. Wa-shi wa yu-u-be to-ke-i wo ka-ke-ru ko-to wo wa-sz-re-ta.
ワシハユウベトケイヲカケルコトヲワスレタ

479. *I cannot lift this.*
Wa-ta-k'-shi wa ko-re wo mo-ta-re-ma-se-nu.
ワタクシハコレヲモタレマセヌ

Do. Wa-shi wa ko-re wo mo-ta-re-nu.
ワシハコレヲモタレヌ

480. *I sometimes work in the garden for amusement.*
Wa-ta-k'-shi wa ta-no-shi-mi ni to-ki-do-ki ha-ta-ke wo ts'-ku-
ワタクシハタノシミニトキドキハタケヲツク

ri-ma-s'.
リマス

480. Wa-shi-wa ta-no-shi-mi ni to-ki-do-ki ha-ta-ke wo ts'-ku-ru.
ワシハ タノシミニ トキドキ ハタケヲ ツクル

481. *I cannot tell them apart.*
Wa-ta-k'-shi wa mi wa-ke-ra-re-ma-se-nu.
ワタクシ ハ ミワケラレマセヌ

Do. Wa-shi wa mi wa-ke-ra-re-nu.
ワシ ハ ミワケラレヌ

482. *I am at a loss what to do.*
Wa-ta-k'-shi wa do-o sh'-te yo-ka-ro-o ka shi-re-ma-se-nu.
ワタクシ ハ ドウシテ ヨカロウカ シレマセヌ

Do. Wa-shi wa do-o sh'-te yo-ka-ro-o ka shi-ra-nu.
ワシ ハ ドウシテ ヨカロウカ シラヌ

483. *I will help you all I can.*
Wa-ta-k'-shi wa de-ki-ma-s' ho-do a-na-ta ni o te-tsz-da-i wo i-ta-shi-ma-sh'-o-o.
ワタクシ ハ デキマスホド アナタニオテツダイヲ イタシマショウ

Do Wa-shi wa de-ki-ru ho-do o-ma-e ni te-tsz-da-wo-o.
ワシ ハ デキル ホド オマエニ テツダヲウ

484. *I do not want so much.*
Wa-ta-k'-shi wa so-no yo-o ni ta-k'-sa-n wa i-ri-ma-se-nu.
ワタクシ ハ ソノヨウニ タクサン ハイリマセヌ

Do. Wa-shi wa ko-n-na ni i-ra-nu.
ワシ ハ コンナ ニイラヌ

485. *I think a little less will do.*
Mo-o chi-t-to he-ra-sh'-te yo-ro-shi-u to dzo-n-ji-ma-sz-ru.
モウ チット ヘラシテ ヨロシウト ゾンジマスル

Do. Mo-o s'-ko-shi he-ra-sh'-te i-i to o-mo-o.
モヲスコシ ヘラシテイイト オモウ

486. *I have taken pains with this.*
Wa-ta k'-shi wa ko-ko-ro ni ka-ke-te ko-re wo i-ta-shi-ma-sh'-ta.
ワタクシ ハ ココロニ カケテ コレヲ イタシマシタ

Do. Wa-shi wa ko-ko-ro ni ka-ke-te ko-re wo sh'-ta.
ワシ ハ ココロニ カケテ コレヲ シタ

487. *I cannot think so.*
Wa-ta-k'-shi wa sa-yo-o ni wa o-mo-wa-re-ma-se-nu.
ワタクシ ハ サヨウニ ハ ウモワレマセヌ

Do. Wa-shi wa sa-yo-o ni wa o-mo-wa-re nu.
ワシ ハ サヨウニ ハ オモワレヌ

488. *I will see to it presently.*
Wa-ta-k'-shi wa no-chi ni mi-ma-sh'-o-o.
ワタクシ ハ ノチニ ミマショウ

Do. Wa-shi wa no-chi ni mi-yo-o.
ワシ ハ ノチ ニ ミヤヨウ

489. *I will send for it.*
　　Wa-ta-k'-shi wa to-ri ni ts'-ka-wa-se-ma-sh'-o-o.
　　ワタクシ ハ トリ ニ ツカワセマシヨウ
Do.　Wa-shi wa to-ri ni ya-ro-o.
　　ワシ ハ トリ ニ ヤロウ

490. *I am sick of fish.*
　　Wa-ta-k'-shi wa sa-ka-na wo ta-be a-ki-ma-sh'-ta.
　　ワタクシ ハ サカナ ヲ タベ アキマシタ
Do.　Wa-shi wa sa-ka-na wo ku-i a-ki-ta.
　　ワシ ハ サカナ ヲ クイアキタ

491. *I have a bad memory.*
　　Wa-ta-k'-shi wa mo-no o-bo-e nga wa-ru-u go za-ri-ma-s'.
　　ワタクシ ハ モノ オボエ ガ ワルウ ゴ ザリマス
Do.　Wa-shi wa mo-no o-bo-e nga wa-ru-i.
　　ワシ ハ モノ オボエ ガ ワルイ

492. *I am a stranger here.*
　　Wa-ta-k'-shi wa ko-ko ni ri-o-sh'-ku wo sh'-te o-ri-ma-s'.
　　ワタクシ ハ ココ ニ リヨシク ヲ シテ オリマス
Do.　Wa-shi wa ko-ko ni ri-o-sh'-ku wo sh'-te i-ru.
　　ワシ ハ ココ ニ リヨシク ヲ シテイル

493. *I must change my clothes.*
　　Wa-ta-k'-shi wa ki-mo-no wo ki-ka-e-ru yo-ro-shi-u go za-ri-ma-s'.
　　ワタクシ ハ キモノ ヲ キカエル ヨロシウ ゴ ザリマス
Do.　Wa-shi wa ki-mo-no wo ki-ka-e-ru nga yo-i.
　　ワシ ハ キモノ ヲ キカエル ガ ヨイ

494. *I said so only in jest.*
　　Wa-ta-k'-shi wa sa yo-o ni j'-o-o-da-n ba-ka-ri mo-o-shi-ma-sh'-ta.
　　ワタクシ ハ サヨウ ニ ジヨウダン バカリ モウシマシタ
Do.　Wa-shi wa sa yo-o ni j'-o-o-da-n ba-ka-ri i-t-ta.
　　ワシ ハ サヨウニジヨウダンバカリイツタ

495. *I do not sell on credit.*
　　Wa-ta-k'-shi wa ka-ke-u-ri wa i-ta-shi-ma-se-nu.
　　ワタクシ ハ カケウリ ハ イタシマセヌ
Do.　Wa-shi wa ka-ke-u-ri wa se-nu.
　　ワシ ハ カケウリ ハ セヌ

496. *I have been ill for a month.*
　　Wa-ta-k'-shi wa h'-to ts'-ki wa-dz-ra-i-ma-sh'-ta.
　　ワタクシ ハ ヒトツキ ワズライマシタ
Do.　Wa-shi wa h'-to ts'-ki wa-dz-ra-t-ta.
　　ワシ ハ ヒトツキ ワズラツタ

497. *I do not want this any longer.*
Wa-ta-k'-shi wa ko-re wo mo-o i-ri-ma-se-nu.
ワタクシ ハ コレ ヲ モウイリマセス
Do. Wa-shi wa ko-re wo mo-o i-ra-nu.
ワシ ハ コレヲ モウイラヌ

498. *I cannot keep it out of my mind.*
Wa-ta-k'-shi wa ko-re wo wa-sz-ra-re-ma-se-nu.
ワタクシ ハ コレヲワスラレマセス
Do. Wa-shi wa ko-re wo wa-sz-ra-re-nu.
ワシ ハ コレヲ ワスラレヌ

499. *I am not in want of it at present.*
Wa-ta-k'-shi wa i-ma ko-re wo i-ri-ma-se-nu.
ワタクシ ハイマ コレ ヲ イリマセス
Do. Wa-shi wa i-ma ko-re wo i-ra-nu.
ワシ ハイマ コレ ヲ イラヌ

500. *I do not know when he will come.*
A-no o ka-ta wa i-tsz o i-de na-sa-ru ka dzo-n-ji-ma-se-nu.
アノオカタ ハ イツオイデ ナサル カ ゾンジマセス
Do. A-no h'-to wa i-tsz ku-ru da-ro-o ka shi-ra-nu.
アノヒト ハイツ クル ダロウ カシラヌ

501. *I bought these at auction.*
Wa-ta-k'-shi wa ko-re wo se-ri de ka-i-ma-sh'-ta.
ワタクシ ハ コレ ヲ セリ デ カイマシタ
Do. Wa-shi wa ko-re wo se-ri de ka-t-ta.
ワシ ハ コレ ヲ セリデカッタ

502. *I have done my best to teach him.*
Wa-ta-k'-shi wa i-ta-t-te mi wo i-re-te a-no h'-to wo o-shi-e-ma-sh'-ta.
ワタクシ ハ イタツテ ミ ヲ イレテ アノ ヒト ヲ オシエ マシタ
Do. Wa-shi wa i-ta-t-te mi wo i-re-te a-no h'-to wo o-shi-e-ta.
ワシ ハ イタツテ ミ ヲ イレテ アノ ヒト ヲ オシエタ

503. *I want it done in this way.*
Wa-ta-k'-shi wa ko-no to-o-ri ni ts'-ku-ra-se-to-o go za-ri-ma-s'
ワタクシ ハ コノトウリニ ツクラセトウゴ ザリマス
Do. Wa-shi wa ko-no to-o-ri ni ts'-ku-ra-se-ta-i.
ワシ ハ コノトウリ ニ ツクラセタイ

504. *I want three ichibus.*
Wa-ta-k'-shi ka-ne nga sa-m bu ho-s'-shi-i.
ワタクシ カ子 ガ サンブ ホツシイ

505. *I will stick to my word.*
Wa-ta-k'-s hi wa ya-ku-so-ku wo ka-ta-ku a-i ma-mo-ri-ma-sh'-o-o.
ワタクシ ハ ヤクソク ヲ カタク アイ マモリマシ ヨウ

505. **Wa-shi** wa ya-ku-so-ku wo ka-ta-ku ma-mo-ro-o.
ワシ ハ ヤクソク ヲ カタク マモロウ

506. *I would thank you to explain it.*
A-na-ta ko-re wo to-i-te o ki-ka-se-te ku-da sa-ra-ba a-ri-nga-to-o dzo-n-ji-ma-s'.
アナタ コレ ヲ トイテ オ キカ セテ クダ サラバ アリガ
トウゾンジマス

Do. O-ma-e ko-re wo to-i-te ki-ka-se-ru na-ra a-ri-nga-ta-i.
オマエ コレ ヲ トイテ キカ セル ナラ アリ ガタイ

507. *I have nothing to do with that.*
Wa-ta-k'-shi wa so-no ko-to ni s'-ko-shi mo ka-ka-ri **a-i** go za-ri-ma-se-n'.
ワタクシ ハ ソノ コト ニ スコシ モ カカリ アイゴ
ザリ マセン

Do. Wa-shi wa so-no ko-to ni s'-ko-shi mo ka-ka-ri a-i **wa** na-i.
ワシ ハ ソノ コト ニ スコシ モ カカリ アイ ハ ナイ

508. *I won't have any thing to do with it.*
No-chi-no-chi ni na-ri-ma-sh'-te mo, wa-ta-k'-shi wa ka-ma-i-ma-s' ma-i.
ノチ ノチ ニ ナリマシテ モ ワタクシ ハ カマイ
マス マイ

Do. No-chi ni wa-shi wa ka-ma-wa-nu.
ノチ ニ ワシ ハ カマワヌ

509. *I like this more and more the more I use it.*
Wa-ta-k'-shi wa ko-re wo ts'-ka-e na-re-te shi-da-i ni **yo-ro-**sh'-ku na-ri-ma-s'.
ワタクシ ハ コレ ヲ ツカエ ナレテ シダイ ニ ヨロ
シクナリマス

Do. Wa-shi wa ko-re wo ts'-ka-e na-re-te da-n da-n yo-ku na-ru.
ワシ ハ コレ ヲ ツカエ ナレテ ダンダンヨクナル

510. *I like this more and more the more I eat it.*
Wa-ta-k'-shi wa ko-re wo ta-be na-re-te shi-da-i ni s'-ki ni na-ri-ma-s'.
ワタクシ ハ コレヲ タベ ナレテ シダイ ニ スキ ニ ナ
リマス

Do. Wa-shi wa ko-re wo **ta-be** na-re-te da-n-da-n s'-ki ni na-ru.
ワシ ハ コレヲ タベ ナレテ ダンダン スキニ ナル

511. *I cannot reach so high.*
Wa-ta-k'-shi wa so no yo-o ni ta-ka-ku-te wa to-do-ku ko-to nga de-ki-ma-se-n'.
ワタクシ ハ ソノ ヨウニ タカ クテ ハ トドク コト
ガ デキ マセン

Do. Wa-shi wa so-no yo-o ni ta-ka-ku-te wa o-yo-bu ko-to **nga** de-ki-nu.
ワシ ハ トノ ヨウ ニ タカクテ ハ オヨブ コト ガ
デキス

512. *I have overtaken you at last.*
　　Wa-ta-k'-shi wa a-na-ta ni yo-o ya-ku o-i ts'-ki-ma-sh'-ta.
　　ワタクシ ハ アナタ ニ ヨウ ヤク オイ ツキ マシタ
Do.　Wa-shi wa o-ma-e ni yo-o yo-o o-i ts'-i-ta.
　　ワシ ハ オマエ ニ ヨウ ヨウ オイ ツイタ

513. *I cannot answer you now, I must take time to think.*
　　Wa-ta-k'-shi wa ta-da-i-ma go a-i sa-tsz wa i-ta-sh'-ka-ne-ma-s'
　　ワタクシ ハ タダイマ ゴ アイサツ ハ イタシ カ子 マス
　　ka-ra, to-ku to ka-n-nga-i-te, no-chi ni mo-o-shi a-nge-ma-
　　カラ トクト カンガイテ ノチ ニ マウシ アゲ マ
　　sh'-o-o.
　　シヨウ
Do.　Wa-shi wa i-ma he-n-to-o wa de-ki-na-i ka-ra, ka-n-nga-
　　ワシ ハ イマ ヘントウ ハ デキナイ カラ カンガ
　　i-te no-chi ni i-wo-o.
　　イテ ノチ ニ イヨウ

514. *I have been waiting for you two hours.*
　　Wa-ta-k'-shi wa a-na-ta wo f'-ta to-ki o ma-chi mo-o-sh'-te o-
　　ワタクシ ハ アナタ ヲ フタ トキ オ マチ マウシテ オ
　　ri-ma-sh'-ta.
　　リマシタ
Do.　Wa-shi wa o-ma-e wo f'-ta to-ki ma-t-te i-ta.
　　ワシ ハ オマエ ヲ フタ トキ マツテ イタ

515. *I cannot sit up so late.*
　　Wa-ta-k'-shi wa so-no yo-o ni na-nga-ku o-ki-te wa i-ra-re-
　　ワタクシ ハ ソノ ヨウ ニ ナガク オキテ ハ イラレ
　　ma-se-n'.
　　マセン
Do.　Wa-shi wa so-n-na-ni na-nga-ku o-ki-te i-ra-re-nu.
　　ワシ ハ ソンナニ ナガク オキテ イラレヌ

516. *I can't put up with it any longer.*
　　Wa-ta-k'-shi wa mo-o ko-no ngo wa ka-m-be-n-nga de-ki-ma-
　　ワタクシ ハ モウ コノ ゴ ハ カンベン ガ デキ マ
　　se-nu.
　　セヌ
Do.　Wa-shi wa mo-o ko-no no-chi wa ka-m-be-n nga de-ki-nu.
　　ワシ ハ モウ コノ ノチ ハ カンベン ガ デキヌ

517. *I took this coin for an ichibu by mistake.*
　　Wa'-ta-k'-shi wa ko-ko-ro e chi-nga-i de ko-no ka-ne wo i-chi
　　ワタクシ ハ ココロ エ チガイ デ コノ カ子 ヲ イチ
　　bu no ts'-mo-ri ni u-ke to-ri-ma-sh'-ta.
　　ブ ノ ツモリ ニ ウケ トリマシタ
Do.　Wa-shi wa ko-ko-ro e chi-nga-i de ko-no ka-ne wo i-chi bu
　　ワシ ハ ココロ エ チガイ デ コノ カ子 ヲ イチ ブ
　　no ts'-mo-ri ni u-ke to-t-ta.
　　ノ ツモリ ニ ウケ トツタ

518. *I went with him all the way home.*
　　Wa-ta-k'-shi wa a-no h'-to to i-s-sh'-o ni a-no h'-to no i-ye ma-
　　ワタクシ ハアノヒトトイッショニアノヒトノイエ マ
　　de ma-i-ri-ma-sh'-ta.
　　デ マイリマシタ
Do. 　Wa-shi wa a-re to i-s-sh'-o ni a-re no u-chi ma-de i-t-ta.
　　ワシ ハ アレ トイッショニ アレノウチ マデイッタ

519. *I carry this cane to keep off the dogs.*
　　Wa-ta-k'-shi wa i-nu wo o-u ta-me-ni ko-no tsz-e wo mo-chi-
　　ワタクシ ハ イヌヲオウタメニ コノツエ ヲ モ チ
　　ma-s'.
　　マス
Do. 　Wa-shi wa i-nu wo o-u ta-me-ni ko-no tsz-e wo mo-tsz.
　　ワ シ ハ イヌ ヲオウタメニ コノ ツエ ヲ モ ツ

520. *I find the material; he pays for the work.*
　　Wa-ta-k'-shi wa sh'-o-sh'-ki no i-ri yo-o wo da-shi-ma-s'; a-
　　ワタクシ ハ シヨシキ ノイリヨウ ヲ ダシマス ア
　　no o ka-ta wa te-ma wo o da-shi na-sa-re-ma-s'.
　　ノオカタ ハテマ ヲオダシ ナサレ マス
Do. 　Wa-shi wa sh'-o-sh'-ki wo da-sh'-te, a-no h'-to wa te-ma wo da-s'.
　　ワ シ ハ シヨシキ ヲダシテアノヒト ハテマ ヲダス

521. *Is this fruit wholesome?*
　　Ko-no ku-da-mo-no wa ha-ra no ta-me-ni na-ri-ma-s'-ka?
　　コノ クダモノ ハ ハラノタ メニ ナリマス カ
Do. 　Ko-no ku-da-mo-no wa ha-ra no ta-me-ni na-ru ka?
　　コノクダモノ ハ ハラノタメニ ナル カ

522. *I beg you to come quickly.*
　　Do-o-zo a-na-ta o ha-ya-ku o i-de na-sa-re-te ku-da-sa-re.
　　ドウゾ アナタ オハヤク オイデ ナサレテ クダサレ
Do. 　Do-o'-zo o-ma-e ha-ya-ku k'-te ku-re-ro.
　　ドウゾ オマエハヤク キテクレロ

523. *I cannot do two things at once.*
　　Wa-ta-k'-shi wa h'-to-ri de f-ta ya-ku wa ts'-to-ma-ri-ma-se-nu.
　　ワタクシ ハヒトリデフタヤク ハットマリマセス
Do. 　Wa-shi wa h'-to-ri de f-ta ya-ku wa ts'-to-ma-ra-nu.
　　ワ シ ハ ヒトリ テフタヤク ハットマラス

524. *I can do it as well as not.*
　　Wa-ta-k'-shi wa ko-re wo i-ta-sh'-te mo, ɪ-ta-shi-ma-se-nu de-
　　ワタクシ ハ コレ ヲイタシテ モイタシマセヌデ
　　mo o-na-ji ko-to de go za-ri-ma-s'.
　　モ オナジコト デ ゴザリマス
Do. 　Wa-shi wa ko-re wo sh'-te mo shi na-ku te mo o-na-ji
　　ワシ ハ コレ ヲシテ モ シ ナク テ モオナジ
　　ko-to da.
　　コト ダ

525. *I advise you to accept his offer.*
A-no o ka-ta no o da-n-ji na-sa-ru ko-to wo o u-ke-a-i na-
アノオ カタ ノオダンジ ナサル コト ヲオウケアイナ
sa-re-ma-sh', ko-re wa a-na-ta ni o sz-sz-me mo-o-sz.
サレマシ コレ ハ アナタニ オススメ モウス

Do. A-re no da n-ji-ru ko-to wo u-ke-a-i ko-re wa o-ma-e ni
アレ ノ ダンジル コト ヲウケアイ コレ ハ オマエ ニ
sz-sz-me-ru.
ススメル

526. *I beg your pardon.*
Ma-p-pi-ra go me-n na-sa-re-ma-sh'.
マッピラ ゴ メン ナサレマシ

Do. Go me-n na-sa-i.
ゴ メン ナサイ

527. *I go to see him now and then.*
Wa-ta-k'-shi wa ta-bi-ta-bi a-no o ka-ta wo ta-dz-ne-te ma-i-
ワタクシ ハ タビタビ アノオ カタ ヲ タズ子テ マイ
ri-ma-s'.
リマス

Do. Wa-shi wa ta-bi-ta-bi a-no h'-to wo ta-dz-ne-te yu-ku.
ワシ ハ タビタビ アノヒト ヲ タズ子ノユク

528. *I long for a little rain.*
Wa-ta-k'-shi wa s'-ko-shi o shi-me-ri nga ho-shi-u go za-ri
ワタクシ ハ スコシ オシメリ ガ ホシウ ゴ ザリ
ma-s'.
マス

Do. Wa-shi wa s'-ko-shi a-me nga ho-shi-i.
ワシ ハ スコシ アメ ガ ホシイ

529. *I leave that for you to do.*
Wa-ta-k'-shi wa so-no sz-ru ko-to wo a-na-ta ni o ta-no-mi-
ワタクシ ハ ソノ スル コト ヲ アナタ ニオ タノミ
mo-o-shi-ma-s'.
モウシマス

Do. Wa-shi wa so-no sz-ru ko-to wo o-ma-e ni ta-no-mu.
ワシ ハ ソノ スル コト ヲ オマエ ニ タノム

530. *I barely see the ship.*
Wa-ta-k'-shi wa ka-s'-ka ni fu-ne nga mi-e-ma-s'.
ワタクシ ハ カスカ ニ フ子 ガ ミエマス

Do. Wa-shi wa ha-ru-ka ni fu-ne nga mi-e-ru.
ワシ ハ ハルカ ニ フ子 ガ ミエル

531. *I will raise your wages next month.*
Wa-ta-k'-shi wa ra-i nge-tsz a-na-ta no ki-u-bu-n wo ma-sh'-te
ワタクシ ハ ライ ゲツ アナタ ノ キウブン ヲ マシテ
a-nge-ma-sh'-o-o.
アゲ マシヨウ

531. Wa-shi wa ra-i nge-tsz te-ma-i no ki-u-ki-n wo ma-sh'-to-ya ro-o.
　　ワシハライゲッテマイノキウキンヲマシノヤロウ

532. *I have made it as good as it was before.*
　　Wa-ta-k'-shi wa ko-re wo mo-to no to-o-ri ni na-o-shi-me-sh'-ta.
　　ワタクシハコレヲモトノトウリニナヲシメシタ
Do.　Wa-shi wa ko-re wo mo-to no to-o-ri ni na-o-sh'-ta.
　　ワシハコレヲモトノトウリニナヲシタ

533. *I am going to take my pick out of these.*
　　Wa-ta-k'-shi wa ko-ko-no u-chi de e-ra-n-de to-ri-ma-sh'-o-o.
　　ワタクシハココノウチデエランデトリマシヨウ
Do.　Wa-shi wa ko-no u-chi de yo-ri do-ri ni shi-yo-o.
　　ワシハコノウチデヨリドリニシヨウ

534. *I am near sighted.*
　　Wa-ta-k'-shi wa chi-ka me de go za-ri-ma-s'.
　　ワタクシハチカメデゴザリマス
Do.　Wa-shi wa chi-ka-me da.
　　ワシハチカメダ

535. *I have not suspected him in the least heretofore and* **now when** *I hear what he has done I am very much surprised.*
　　Wa-ta-k'-shi wa i-ma ma-de a-no h'-to wo s'-ko-shi mo u-ta-nga-i-ma-se-n, ta-da-i-ma so-no ko-to wo ki-ki-ma-sh'-te o-o-ki-ni o-do-ro-ki-ma-sh'-ta.
　　ワタクシハイママデアノヒトヲスコシモウタガイマセンタダイマソノコトヲキキマシテヲオキニオドロキマシタ
Do.　Wa-shi wa i-ma ma-de a-no h'-to wo s'-ko-shi mo u-ta-nga wa na-ka-t-ta, ta-da-i-ma so-no ko-to wo ki-i-te o-o-ki ni o-do-ro-i-ta.
　　ワシハイママデアノヒトヲスコシモウタガハナカッタタダイマソノコトヲキイテオヲキニオドロイタ

536. *I shall be ready by the time you are.*
　　A-na-ta sh'-ta-ku wo na-sa-ru to-ki ni, wa-ta-k'-shi mo i-s-shi-o ni i-ta-shi-ma-sh'-o-o.
　　アナタシタクヲナサルトキニワタクシモイッシウニイタシマシヨウ
Do.　O-ma-e sh'-ta-ku wo sz-ru na-ra wa-shi **mo i-s-shi-o** ni shi-yo-o.
　　オマエシタクヲスルナラハシモイッシヲニシヨウ

537. *I offered a thousand dollars for that house.*
　　Wa-ta-k'-shi wa a-no i-e wo se-n do-ra ni ne wo ts'-ke-ma-sh'-ta.
　　ワタクシハアノイエヲセントラニ子ヲツケマシタ
Do.　Wa-shi wa a-no u-chi wo se-n do-ra ni ne wo ts'-ke-ta.
　　ワシハアノウチヲセントラニ子ヲツケタ

538. *I took him up at his price.*
Wa-ta-k'-shi wa a-no o ka-ta no ne wo o ts'-ke na-sa-ru to-ko-ro de, te wo u-chi-ma-sh'-ta.
ワタクシ ハアノオカタ ノ子ヲオツケナサルトコロデテヲ ウチマシタ

Do. Wa-shi wa a-re no ne wo ts'-ke-ru to-ko-ro de te wo u-t-ta.
ワシ ハアレノ子ヲツクルトコロデテヲウツタ

539. *I have been offered $100 for my watch, but I would not take it.*
Wa-ta-k'-shi no to-ke-i wo h'-ya.ku do-ra ni ne wo ts'-ke-ra-re-ma-sh'-ta nga, so-no ka-ne wo to-ru ko-to wo ko-no-mi-ma-se-n.
ワタクシノトケイヲヒヤクドラニ子ヲツケラレマシタガ ソノカ子ヲトルコトヲコノミマセン

Do. Wa-shi no-to-ke-i wo h'-ya-ku do-ra ni ne wo ts'-ke-ra-re-ta nga so-no ka-ne wo to-ru ko-to wo s'-ka-nu.
ワシ ノトケイヲヒヤクドラニ子ヲツケラレタガ ソノカ子ヲトルコトヲツカヌ

540. *I have more than I know what to do with.*
Wa-ta-k'-shi no i-ri yo-o yo-ri yo-ke-i go za-ri-ma-s'.
ワタクシノイリヨウヨリヨケイゴザリマス

Do. Wa-shi no i-ri yo-o yo-ri yo-ke-i ni a-ru.
ワシノイリヨウヨリヨケイニアル

541. *I have less than I want.*
Wa-ta-k'-shi no i-ri yo-o yo-ri s'-ku-no-o go za-ri-ma-s'.
ワタクシノイリヨウヨリスクノウゴザリマス

Do. Wa-shi no i-ri yo-o yo-ri s'-ku-na-i.
ワシノイリヨウヨリスクナイ

542. *I have been all over town for flannel, but do not find any.*
Wa-ta-k'-shi wa ko-o-e-ki-ba wo ma-wa-t-te shi-ro-ra-sh'-a wo ta-dz-ne-ma-sh'-ta ke-re-do-mo ma-da mi-e-ma-se-nu.
ワタクシ ハコウエキバヲマワツテシロラシヤヲタズ子マシタケレドモマダ三エマセヌ

Do. Wa-shi wa ko-o-e-ki-ba wo ma-wa-t-te shi-ro-ra-sh'-a wo ta-dz-ne-ta ke-re-do-mo ma-da me ts'-ka-ra-nu.
ワシ ハコウエキバヲマワツテシロラシヤヲタズ子タケレドモマダメツカラス

543. *I have been there many a time.*
Wa-ta-k'-shi wa a-s'-ko e i-ku ta.bi mo ma-i-ri-ma-sh'-ta.
ワタクシワ アスコエイクタビモマイリマシタ

Do. Wa-shi wa a-s'-ko e i-ku do mo i-t-ta.
ワシ ハアスコエイクドモイツタ

544. *I still owe him for a day's work.*
Wa-ta-k'-shi wa a-no h'-to ni ma-da i-chi ni-chi no hi yo-o wo ya-ri-ma-se-nu.
ワタクシ ワアノヒトニマダイチ ニチノヒヨウヲ ヤリマセヌ

544. Wa-shi wa a-no h'-to ni ma-da i-chi ni-chi no hi yo-o wo ya-ra-nu.
ワシ ハ アノヒト ニ マダ イチニチ ノ ヒヨウ ヲ ヤラス

545. *I have cock's-combs growing in my garden.*
Wa-ta-k'-shi no ha-ta-ke ni ke-i to-o nga ha-ye-ma-sz-ru.
ワタクシ ノ ハタケ ニ ケイトウ ガ ハエマスル
Do. Wa-shi ha-ta-ke ni ke-i to-o nga ha-ye-ru.
ワシ ハタケ ニ ケイトウ ガ ハエル

546. *I am of the same opinion still.*
Wa-ta-k'-shi no dzo-n-ji-yo-ri wa i-ma-da ka-wa-ri-ma-se-nu.
ワタクシ ノ ゾンジヨリ ハ イマダ カワリマセヌ
Do. Wa-shi no o-mo-o ko-to wa ma-da ka-wa-ra-nu.
ワシ ノ オモウコト ハ マダ カワラス

547. *I have paid off all my carpenters.*
Wa-ta-k'-shi wa mi-na da-i-ku no te-ma wo ya-ri-ma-sh'-ta.
ワタクシ ハ ミナ ダイク ノ テマ ヲ ヤリマシタ
Do. Wa-shi wa da-i-ku no te-ma wo mi-na ya-t-ta.
ワシ ハ ダイク ノ テマ ヲ ミナ ヤッタ

548. *I have paid all my servants wages.*
Wa-ta-k'-shi wa ko-dz-ka-i no ki-u-ki-n wo mi-na ya-ri-ma-sh'-ta.
ワタクシ ハ コズカイ ノ キウキン ヲ ミナ ヤリマシタ
Do. Wa-shi wa ko-dz-ka-i no ki-u-ki-n wo mi-na-ya-t-ta.
ワシ ハ コズカイ ノ キウキン ヲ ミナ ヤッタ

549. *I have paid off all my day laborers.*
Wa-ta-k'-shi wa ya-to-i-bi-to ni hi yo-o wo mi-na-ya-ri-ma-sh'-ta.
ワタクシ ハ ヤトイビト ニ ヒヨウ ヲ ミナ ヤリマシタ
Do. Wa-shi wa ya-to-i-bi-to ni hi yo-o wo mi-na ya-t-ta.
ワシ ハ ヤトイビト ニ ヒヨウ ヲ ミナ ヤッタ

550. *I am captain of this ship.*
Wa-ta-k'-shi wa ko-no fu-ne no se-n-do-o de go za-ri-ma-s'.
ワタクシ ハ コノ フ子 ノ センドウ デゴザリマス
Do. Wa-shi wa ko-no fu-ne no se-n-do-o da.
ワシ ハ コノ フ子 ノ センドウ ダ

551. *I am looking for crimson velvet.*
Wa-ta-k'-shi wa hi bi-ro-o-do wo ta-dz-ne-te o-ri-ma-s'.
ワタクシ ハ ヒビロウド ヲ タズ子テオリマス
Do. Wa-shi wa hi bi-ro-o-do wo ta-dz-ne-te i-ru.
ワシ ハ ヒビロウド ヲ タズ子テイル

552. *I want a wide ribbon to match it.*
Do-o yo-o no sa-na-da hi-mo nga i-ri-ma-s'.
ドウヨウ ノ サナダ ヒモ ガ イリマス

J

552. Do-o-yoo no sa-na-da hi-mo nga i-ru.
ドウヨウノサナダ ヒモ ガ イル

553. *I shall sail tomorrow morning*.
Wa-ta-k'-shi wa mi-o-o a-sa sh'-p-pa-n i-ta-shi-ma-sh'-o-o.
ワタクシ ハ ミヤウアサ シツパンイタシマシヤウ

Do. Wa-shi wa mi-o-o a-sa sh'-p-pa-n shi-yo-o.
ワシ ハ ミヤウアサ シツパン シヤウ

554. *I came into port yesterday*.
Wa-ta-k'-shi wa sa-ku-ji-tsz ni-u shi-n i-ta-shi-ma-sh'-ta.
ワタクシ ハ サクジツ ニウシン イタシマシタ

Do. Wa-shi wa sa-ku ji-tsz mi-na-to ni ha-i-t-ta.
ワシ ハ サクジツ ミナト ニハイツタ

555. *I shall go out of the harbour to throw ballast over board*.
Wa-ta-k'-shi wa fu-ne no o-mo-ri wo da-shi-ma-s' ta-me ni mi-
ワタクシ ハ フ子 ノ オモリ ヲ ダシマス タメ ニ ミ
na-to no so-to ni yu-ki-ma-sh'-o-o
ナト ノ ソト ニ ユキマシヤウ

Do. Wa-shi wa fu-ne no o-mo-ri wo da-s' ta-me ni mi-na-to no
ワシ ハ フ子 ノ オモリ ヲダス タメ ニ ミナト ノ
so-to ni yu-ko-o.
ソト ニ ユコウ

556. *I have ordered a saddle from America*.
Wa-ta-k'-shi wa m'-ma no ku-ra wo i-s-sa-i A-me-ri-ka e chi-
ワタクシ ハ ムマ ノ クラ ヲイツサイ アメリカ エチ
u-mo-n i-ta-shi-ma-sh'-ta.
ウモン イタシマシタ

Do. Wa-shi wa m'-ma no ku-ra wo i-s-sa-i A-me-ri-ka e chi
ワシ ハ ムマ ノ クラ ヲイツサイ アメリカ エチ
u-mo-n sh'-ta.
ウモン シタ

557. *I have left my umbrella behind*.
Wa-ta-k'-shi no ka-ra-ka-sa wo i-p-po-n wa-sz-re-te ma-i-ri-
ワタクシ ノ カラカサ ヲイツポン ワスレテ マイリ
ma-sh'-ta.
マシタ

Do. Wa-shi wa ka-ra-ka-sa wo i-p-po-n wa-sz-re-te k'-ta.
ワシ ハ カラカサ ヲイツポン ワスレテ クタ

558. *I cannot get on without it*.
Wa-ta-k'-shi so-re nga na-ku-te wa na-ri-ma-se-nu.
ワタクシ ソレ ガ ナクテ ハ ナリマセヌ

Do. Wa-shi wa so-re nga na-ku-te wa na-ra-nu.
ワシ ハ ソレ ガ ナクテ ハ ナラヌ

559. *I am like a blind man without a cane*.
Wa-ta-k'-shi wa dza-to-o nga tsz-e ni ha-na-re-ta yo-o de go
ワタクシ ハ ザトウ ガ ツエ ニ ハナレタ ヨウデゴ

za-ri-ma-s'.
ザリマス

559. Wa-shi wa dza-to-o nga tsz-e ne ha-na-re-ta yo-o da.
ワシ ハ ザトウ ガ ツエニ ハナレタ ヨウダ

560. *I did not know that before.*
So-no ko-to wo i-dze-n wa dzo-n-ji-ma-se-n.
ソノコト ヲ イゼン ハ ゾンジマセン

Do. So-re wo ma-i ni **wa** shi-ru-nu.
ソレ ヲ マイニ ハ シラヌ

561. *I am just now going to shave.*
Wa-ta-k'-shi wa ta-da-i-ma hi-nge wo sz-ri-ma-sh'-o-o.
ワタクシ ハ タダイマ ヒゲ ヲ スリマシヨウ

Do. Wa-shi wa i-ma hi-nge wo sz-ro-o.
ワシ ハ イマ ヒゲ ヲ スロウ

562. *I can outrun you.*
Wa-ta-k'-shi wa a-na-ta yo-ri sa-ki ni ha-shi-ru ko-to nga de-ki-ma-s'.
ワタクシ ハ アナタ ヨリ サキニ ハシル コト ガ デキマス

Do. Wa-shi wa o-ma-e yo-ri sa-ki ni ha-shi-ru ko-to nga de-ki-ru.
ワシ ハ オマエヨリ サキニ ハシル コト ガ デキル

563. *I can do nothing more for you.*
Wa-ta-k'-shi wa a-na-ta wo mo-o s'-ku-u ko-to nga de-ki-ma-se-nu.
ワタクシ ハ アナタ ヲ モウ スクウ コト ガ デキマセス

Do. Wa-shi wa o-ma-i wo mo-o s'-ku-u ko-to nga de-ki-nu.
ワシ ハ オマイ ヲ モウ スクウ コト ガ デキス

564. *I never find him at home.*
Wa-ta-k'-shi wa a-no o ka-ta no u-chi e ma-i-ri-ma-sh'-ta nga, tsz-i ni o me ni ka-ka-ri-ma-se-nu.
ワタクシ ハ アノオ カタノ ウチ エ マイリマシタ ガ ツイニオ メニ カカリマセス

Do. Wa-shi wa a-no h'-to no u-chi e i-t-te mo tsz-i ni a-wa-nu.
ワシ ハ アノ ヒト ノ ウチ エ イッテモ ツイニ アワス

565. *I make nothing on it.*
Wa-ta-k'-shi wa ko-no shi-na de ri-bu-n nga **go** za-ri-ma-se-nu.
ワタクシ ハ コノ シナ デ リブン ガ ゴザリマセス

Do. Wa-shi wa ko-no shi-na de mo-o-ke nga na-i.
ワシ ハ コノ シナ デ モウケ ガ ナイ

566. *I do not know what to make of him.*
A-no o ka-ta **wa** i-ka yo-o na mo-no ka wa-ka-ri-ma-se-nu.
アノオ カタ ハ イカ ヨウナ モノ カ ワカリマセス

566. A-no h'-to wa i-ka na-ru mo-no ka wa-ka-ra-nu.
アノヒト ハイカ ナル モノ カ ワカラヌ

567. *I am out of debt.*
Wa-ta-k'-shi wa sh'-a-k' ki-n nga mo-o go za-ri-ma-se-nu.
ワタクシ ハ シャクキン ガ モウ ゴ ザリマセヌ

Do. Wa-shi wa mo-o sh'-a-k' ki-n nga na-i.
ワシ ハ モウ シャクキン ガ ナイ

568. *I cannot do it alone.*
Wa-ta-k'-shi h'-to-ri de wa de-ki-ma-se-n'.
ワタクシ ヒトリデ ハ デキマセン

Do. Wa-shi h'-to-ri de wa de-ki-nu.
ワシ ヒトリデ ハ デキヌ

569. *If I speak to a Japanese in his own language, he is so surprised that he sometimes does not answear me.*
Wa-ta-k'-shi wa a-ru to-ke Ni-p-po-n ji-n ni wa ngo de ha-
ワタクシ ハ アル トキ ニッポン ジン ニ ワ ゴ デ ハ
na-shi-ma-sh'-ta-ra-ba a-no h'-to wa he-n ni o-mo-t-te, he-n
ナシマシタラバ アノ ヒト ハ ヘン ニ オモッテ ヘン
to-o wo i-ta-shi-ma-se-nu.
トウ ヲ イタシ マセヌ

Do. Wa-shi wa a-ru to-ki Ni-p-po-n ji-n ni so-no ku-ni no ko-
ワシ ハ アル トキ ニッポン ジン ニ ソノ クニ ノ コ
to-ba de ha-na-sh'-ta-ra a-no h'-to wa he-n ni o-mo-t-te he-
トバ デ ハナシタラ アノ ヒト ハ ヘン ニ オモッテ ヘ
n-ji wo se-nu.
ンジ ヲ セヌ

570. *I have not the least objection to it.*
Wa-ta-k'-shi wa so-no ko-to ni s'-ko-shi mo sa-wa-ri go-za-ri-
ワタクシ ハ ソノ コト ニ スコシ モ サワリ ゴザリ
ma-se-nu.
マセヌ

Do. Wa-shi wa so-no ko-to ni s'-ko-shi mo sa-wa-ri-nga na-i.
ワシ ハ ソノ コト ニ スコシ モ サワリ ガ ナイ

571. *I do not see any objection to it.*
Wa-ta-k'-shi nga ka-n-nga-i-te mi-ma-s' ni so-no ko-to ni wa
ワタクシ ガ カンガイテ ミマス ニ ソノ コト ニ ハ
s'-ko-shi mo sa-sa-wa-ri nga go za-ri-ma-se-nu to o-mo-i ma-s'
スコシ モ ササワリ ガ ゴ ザリ マセス ト オモイマス

Do. Wa-shi nga o-mo-t-te mi-ru ni so-no ko-to ni wa s'-ko shi
ワシ ガ オモッテ ミル ニ ソノ コト ニ ハ スコシ
mo sa-sa-wa-ri nga na-i to o-mo-o.
モ ササワリ ガ ナイ ト オモウ

572. *I am very glad to see you.*
Wa-ta-k'-shi wa a-na-ta ni o me ni ka-ka-ri-ma-sh'-te ta-i ke-
ワタクシ ハ アナタニ オ メ ニ カカリ マシテ タイゲ

i ni dzo-n-ji-ma-s'.
イニ ゾンジマス

Do., Wa-shi wa o-ma-i wo **mi-te** ha-na-ha-da yo-ro-ko-bu.
ワシ ハ オマイ ヲ ミテ ハナハダ ヨロコブ

573. *I never heard of such a thing.*
Wa-ta-k'-shi wa ma-da so-no yo-o-na ko-to wo ki-ki-ma-se-nu.
ワタクシ ハ マダ ソノ ヨウナ コト ヲ キキマセヌ

Do. Wa-shi wa ma-da so-n-na ko-to wo ki-ka-nu.
ワシ ハ マダ ソンナ コト ヲ キカヌ

574. *I have got thro' the worst of it.* (of any difficult work.)
Wa-ta-k'-shi wa ko-no ko-to no na-n j'-o wo ko-e-ma-sh'-ta.
ワタクシ ハ コノ コト ノ ナンジヨ ヲ コエマシタ

Do. Wa-shi wa ko-no ko-to no na-n j'-o wo ko-e-ta.
ワシ ハ コノ コト ノ ナンジヨ ヲ コエタ

575. *I shall go at all events, whether you do or not.*
A-na-ta o i-de na-sa-re-te mo o i-de na-sa-ra na-ku-te mo wa-ta-k'-shi wa dze-hi ma-i-ri-ma-sh'-o-o.
アナタ オ イデ ナサレテ モ オ イデ ナサラ ナクテ モ ワタクシ ハ ゼヒ マイリマシヨウ

Do. O-ma-i i-t te mo i-ka-na-ku-te mo wa-shi wa dze-hi yu-ku.
オマイ イツテモ イカナクテ モ ワシ ハ ゼヒ ユク

576. *I can't keep up with you.*
Wa-ta-k'-shi wa a-na-ta no yo-o ni ha-ya-ku wa de-ki-ma-se-nu.
ワタクシ ハ アナタ ノ ヨウ ニ ハヤク ハ デキマセヌ

Do. Wa-shi wa o-ma-i **no** yo-o ni ha-ya-ku wa de-ki-nu.
ワシ ハ オマイ ノ ヨウ ニ ハヤク ハ デキヌ

577. *I have spoken to him about it.*
Wa-ta-k'-shi **wa** u-no o ka-ta **ni** ko-no ko-to wo o ha-na-shi mo-o-shi-ma-sh'-ta.
ワタクシ ハ アノ オ カタ ニ コノ コト ヲ ウ ハナシ モウシマシタ

Do. Wa-shi wa a-re ni ko-no ko-to-wo ha-na-sh'-ta.
ワシ ハ アレ ニ コノ コト ヲ ハナシタ

578. *I can't see how it is done.*
Ko-re wa do-o sh'-te ts'-ku-ri-ma-sh'-ta ka wa-ta-k'-shi wa wa-ka-ri-ma-se-n'.
コレ ハ ドウ シテ ツクリマシタ カ ワタクシ ハ ワカリマセン

Do. Ko-re wa do-o sh'-te ts'-ku-t-ta ka wa-shi wa wa-ka-ra-nu.
コレ ハ ドウ シテ ツクツタ カ ワシ ハ ワカラヌ

579. *I have no time* **to do** *it now.*
Wa-ta-k'-shi **wa** so-no ko-to wo sz-ru hi-ma nga go za-ri-ma-
ワタクシ ハ ソノ コト ヲ スル ヒマ ガ ゴザリマ

se-nu.
セス

579. Wa-shi wa so-no ko-to wo sz-ru hi-ma nga na-i.
ワシハソノコトヲスルヒマガナイ

580. *I feel better than I did the other day.*
Wa-ta-k'-shi wa se-n ji-tsz yo-ri ko-ko-ro yo-o go za-ri-ma-s'.
ワタクシハセンジツヨリココロヨウゴザリマス

Do. Wa-shi wa ko-no a-i-da yo-ri ko-ko-ro yo-i.
ワシハコノアイダヨリココロヨイ

581. *I do not want it just now.*
Ko-re wa ta-da-i-ma i-ri-ma-se-nu.
コレハタダイマイリマセス

Do. Ko-re wa ta-da-i-ma i-ra nu.
コレハタダイマイラヌ

582. *I dreamt of flying last night.*
Wa-ta-k'-shi wa sa-ku-ya so-ra wo hi-ngi-o-o sz-ru yu-me wo mi-ma-sh'-ta.
ワタクシハサクヤソラヲヒギャウスルユメヲミマシタ

Do. Wa-shi wa yu-u-be so-ra wo to-bu yu-me wo mi-ta.
ワシハユウベソラヲトブユメヲシタ

583. *I can do it twice to your once.*
A-na-ta ko-re wo i-chi do na-sa-re-ma-sz, u-chi ni, wa-ta-k'-shi ni do de-ki-ma-sh'-o-o.
アナタコレヲイチドナサレマスウチニワタクシニドデキマシャウ

Do. O-ma-i ko-re wo i-chi do sz-ru u-chi ni wa-shi wa ni do de-ki-yo-o.
オマイコレヲイチドスルウチニワシハニドデキヨウ

584. *If you do so what will people think.*
A-na-ta so-no yo-o ni na-sa-re-ma-s' na-ra-ba h'-to nga na-ni to ka o-mo-i-ma-sh'-o-o?
アナタソノヨウニナサレマスナラバヒトガナニトカオモイマシヨウ

Do O-ma-i so-no yo-o ni sz-ru na-ra-ba h'-to nga na-ni to ka o-mo-o da-ro-o?
オマイソノヨウニスルナラバヒトガナニトカオモウダロウ

585. *If you do not pay me soon I will enter a complaint to the Governor.*
A-na-ta ha-ya-ku o ka-i-shi na-sa-ra-ne-ba, o bu-ngi-o-o sh'-o e go u-tta-e mo-o-shi-ma-s'.
アナタハヤクオカイシナサラネバオブギヤウシヨエゴウッタエモウシマス

585. O-ma-i ha-ya-ku he-n-sa-i se-ne-ba, o bu-ngi-o-o sh'-o e go u-
オマイ ハヤク ヘンサイ セネバ オブギヤウシヨエ ゴウ
i-ta e ni sz-ru.
ツタエニスル

586. *If you will do it, I will bear the blame.*
A-na-ta-so-re wo na-sa-ru na-ra-ba, wa-ta-k'-shi no me-i wa-ku
アナタソレ ヲ ナサル ナラバ ハタクシ ノ メイワク
ni na-ri-ma-s'.
ニナリマス

Do. O-ma-i so-o sz-ru na-ra-ba wa-ta-k'-shi no me-i-wa-ku ni
オマイソウ スルナラバ ワタクシ ノ メイワクニ
na-ru.
ナル

587. *If you wish to get it done, stick to it.*
A-na-ta o shi-ma-i na-sa-re-ta-ku-ba ya-me-dz ni na-sa-re.
アナタ オ シマイ ナサレタクバ ヤメズ ニ ナサレ

Do. O-ma-i shi-ma-i-ta-ku-ba ya-me-dz ni shi-ro.
オマイ シマイタクバ ヤメ ズ ニ シロ

588. *If you lose by it, I will make it up.*
A-na-ta ko-re de so-n wo na sa-re-ta na-ra-ba, so-re-da-ke wa wa-
アナタ コレ デ ソン ヲ ナサレタ ナラバ ソレダケ ハ ワ
ta-k'-shi ts'-ku-na-i-ma-sh'-o-o.
タクシ ツクナイマシヨウ

Do. O-ma-i ko-re de so-n wo sh'-ta na-ra-ba so-re da-ke wa wa-
オマイ コレ デソン ヲ シタ ナラバ ソレダケ ハ ワ
ta-k'-shi nga ts'-ku-no-wo-o.
タクシ ガ ツクノヨウ

589. *If that servant behaves well I think I will keep him.*
A-no ko-dz-ka-i no ts'-to-me nga yo-ro sh'-ke-re-ba wa-ta-k'-shi
アノ コズカイ ノ ツトメ ガ ヨロシケレバ ワタクシ
wa na-ngu-ku ts'-ka-e-ma-sh'-o-o to o-mo-i-ma-s'.
ハ ナガク ツカエマシヨウ ト オモイマス

Do. A-no ko-dz-ka-i no ha-ta-ra-ki nga i-i na-ra-ba wa-ta-k'-shi
アノ コズカイ ノ ハタラキ ガ イイ ナラバ ワタクシ
wa na-ngu-ku ts'-ka-wo-o to o-mo-o.
ハ ナガク ツカヲウ ト オモウ

590. *If you find it bad, I will take it back at any time.*
A-na-ta so-re wo o-mo-chi-i na-sa-re-te mo-shi wa-ru-i na-ra-ba,
アナタ ソレ ヲ オモチイ ナサレテ モシ ワルイ ナラバ
wa-ta-k'-shi i-tsz-de-mo u-ke to-ri-ma-so'-o-o.
ワタクシ イツデモ ウケ トリマツヨウ

Do. O-ma-i a-re wo mo-chi-i-te mo-shi wa-ru-i na-ra-ba wa-ta-k'-
オマイ アレ ヲ モチイテ モシ ワルイ ナラバ ワタク
shi i-tsz-de-mo h'-ki-to-ro-o.
シ イツデモ ヒキトロウ

591. *If the article is only good, never mind the price; buy it and bring it here.*
Yo-ro-shi-i shi-na na-ra ne-da-n ni wa ka-ma-i-ma-se-nu ka-ra o
ヨロシイ シナ ナラ ネダン ニハ カマイマセヌ カラ オ
ka-i na-sa-re-te h'-te ku-da-sa-re.
カイ ナサレテキテクダサレ

Do. Shi-na sa-e yo-ke-re-ba ne-da-n ni wa ka-ma-wa-nu ka-ra ka-
シナ サエ ヨケレバ ネダン ニハ カマワヌ カラ カ
t-te ki na-sa-e.
ツテキ ナサエ

592. *If you do so any more, I will punish you.* (said to children.)
O-ma-e ma-ta so-no yo-o ni sz-ru na-ra-ba, wa-ta-k'-shi k'-t-to
オマエ マタ ソノ ヨウニ スル ナラバ ワタクシ キット
shi-o-o-ki wo shi-ma-s'.
シヨウキ ヲシマス

593. *If this is lost you must make it good.*
Ko-re wo mo-shi u-shi-na-i na-sa-re-ru na-ra-ba a-na-ta o ma-do-
コレ ヲ モシ ウシナイ ナサレル ナラバ アナタ オ マド
i na-sa-re.
イ ナサレ

Do. Ko-re wo mo-shi na-ku-sz na-ra-ba o-ma-e k'-t-to ka-wa-ri-wo
コレヲ モシ ナクス ナラバ オマエ キット カワ リヲ
da-se.
ダセ

594. *If the best were so bad, what must the rest be?*
I-chi ba-n yo-ro-shi-i-no nga so-no yo-o ni wa-ru-u go za-ri-ma-
イチ バン ヨロシイノ ガ ソノ ヨウニ ハル ウ ゴ ザリマ
sz na-ra-ba, ho-ka-no wa do-no yo-o de go za-ri-ma-sh'-o-o?
スナラバ ホカノハ ドノ ヨウデ ゴ ザリマシヨウ

Do. I-chi ba-n i-i nga so-n-na-ni wa-ru-i na-ra, ho-ka-no wa do-
イチ バン イイ ガ ソンナニ ハルイ ナラ ホカノ ワ ド
n-na da-ro-o?
ンナ ダロウ

595. *If you are not in a hurry, go around by the main road.*
O i-so-ngi de na-ke-re-ba ho-n do-o wo o ma-wa-ri na-sa-re.
オ イソギ デ ナケレバ ホンドウ ヲ オ マワリ ナサレ

Do. I-so-nga na-ku-ba ka-i do o wo ma-wa-re.
イソガ ナクバ カイドウ ヲ マ ワレ

596. *If I give to the beggars, there will be no end to it.*
Wa-ta-k'-shi ko-j-ji-ki ni ho-do-ko-shi wo shi-ma-s' na-ra-ba ka-
ワ タクシ コツジキニ ホドコシ ヲ シマス ナラバ カ
ngi-ri wa go za-ri-ma-s'-ma-i.
ギリ ワ ゴ ザリマスマイ

Do. Wa-shi ko-ji-ki ni ho-do-ko-shi wo sz-ru na-ra-ba ka-ngi-ri
ワ シ ゴジマニ ホドコシ ヲ スル ナラバ カギリ

wa na-ka-ro-o.
ハナカロウ

597. *If you blot out a word correct it over the erasure.*
Mo-n-ji wo ke-sh'-ta na-ra-ba, **u-e ni o** ka-ki-na-o-shi na-sa-re.
モンジ ヲ ケシタ ナラバ ウエニ オ カキ ナヲシ ナサレ

Do. Mo-n-ji **wo** ke-sh'-ta na-ra, u-e ni ka-ki na-o-se.
モンジ ヲ ケシタ ナラ ウエニ カキ ナヲセ

598. *Ignorant people are the most positive in their opinions.*
O-ro-ka no mo-no **wa** i-ta-t-te ga nga tsz-yo-o go za-ri-ma-s'
オロカ ノ モノ ハイタッテ ガ ガ ツヨウ ゴ ザリマス

Do. Gu-ni-n wa i-chi-ba-n ga nga tsz-yo-i.
グニン ハ イチバン ガ ガ ツヨイ

599. *Intelligent persons are the most gentle and yielding.*
Ha-ku-sh'-ki no h'-to wa i-ta-t-te o-n j'-yu-n de **go** za-ri-ma-s'.
ハクシキ ノ ヒト ハイタッテ オンジュン デ ゴ ザリマス

Do. Mo-no wo shi-ru h'-to wa i-ta-t-te o-n j'-yu-n da.
モノ ヲ シル ヒト ハイタッテ オンジュンダ

600. *In what street did you meet him.*
A-na-ta wa a-no o ka-ta ni do-ko no ma-chi de o a-i **na-sa-re-ma-sh'-ta**.
アナタハ アノ オカタ ニ ドコ ノ マチ デ オアイ ナサレマシタ

Do. O-ma-i wa a-no h'-to **ni do-ko no ma-chi** de a-t-ta.
オマイ ハ アノヒト ニ ドコ ノ マチ デアッタ

601. *Is it high water or low?*
Mi-chi shi-wo de go za-ri-ma-s' ka, **h'-ki** shi-wo de go za-ri-ma-s' ka?
ミチ シヲ デ ゴ ザリマス カ ヒキ シヲ デ ゴ ザリマス カ

Do. Mi-chi shi-wo ka h'-ki shi-wo ka?
ミチ シヲ カ ヒキ シヲ カ

602. *Is your new house finished?*
A-na-ta no shi-n ta-ku wa go shi-t-ta-i ni na-ri-ma-sh'-ta **ka?**
アナタ ノ シン タク ハ ゴ シッタイ ニ ナリマシタ カ

Do. O-ma-e no a-ta-ra-sh'-ki uchi wa de-ki a-nga-t-ta ka?
オマエ ノ アタラシキ ウチ ハ デキ アガッタ カ

603. *Is this for sale?*
Ko-re wa u-ra-re-ma-s' **ka?**
コレ ハ ウラレマスカ

Do. **Ko-re** wa u-ra-re-ru ka?
コレ ハ ウラレルカ

Is it true?
Ma-ko-to de go za-ri-ma-s' ka?
マコト デ ゴ ザリマス カ

Do. Mu-ko-to ka? (or) Ho-n to-o ka?
マコトカ　　ホントウカ

604. *Is it right for us to do so.*
Wa-ta-k'-shi do-mo ka-yo-o ni i-ta-shi-ma-sh'-te mo yo-ro-shi-u go za-ri-ma-s' ka?
ワタクシドモカヨウニイタシマシテモヨロシウ
ゴザリマスカ

Do. Wa-ta-shi do-mo ko-no yo-o ni sh'-te mo yo-i ka?
ワタシドモコノヨウニシテモヨイカ

605. *Is this enough?*
Ko-re de ta-k'-sa-n go za-ri-ma-s' ka?
コレデタクサンゴザリマスカ

Do. Ko-re de ta-k'-sa-n ka?
コレデタクサンカ

606. *Is this your pencil?*
Ko-no fu-de wa a-na-ta no go sh'-o-ji de go za-ri-ma-s' ka?
コノフデハアナタノゴショジデゴザリマスカ

Do. Ko-no fu-de wa o-ma-e no sh'-o-ji ka?
コノフデハオマエノショジカ

607. *Is that all?*
So-re ba-ka-ri de go za-ri-ma-s' ka?
ソレバカリデゴザリマスカ

Do. So-re ba-ka-ri ka?
ソレバカリカ

608. *Is it odd or even?*
Ta-m me-i de go za-ri-ma-s' ka ch'-o-o me-i de go za-ri-ma-s' ka?
タンメイデゴザリマスカチヨウメイデゴザリマ
スカ

Do. Ta-m me-i ka ch'-o-o me-i ka?
タンメイカチヨウメイカ

609. *Is it time for us to go?*
Wa-ta-k'-shi do-mo no ma-i-ri-ma-s' ji-ko-ku ni na-ri-ma-sh'-ta ka?
ワタクシドモノマヘリマスジユクニナリマシ
タカ

Do. Wa-ta-k'-shi do-mo no yu-ku ji-bu-n ni na-t-ta ka?
ワタクシドモノユクジブンニナッタカ

610. *Is it a good time to transplant trees?*
I-ma ki wo u-e-ka-e ma-sh'-te mo yo-ro-shi-u go za-ri-ma-s' ka?
イマキヲウエカヘマシテモヨロシウゴザリマ
スカ

Do. I-ma ki wo u-e-ka-e-te mo yo-i ka?
イマキヲウエカヘテモヨイカ

611. *Is this house to let.*
Ko-re wa ka-shi i-e de go za-ri-ma-s' ka?
コレ ハ カシ イエ デゴ ザリマスカ
Do. Ko-re wa ka-shi i-e ka?
コレ ハ カシ イエ カ

612. *Is this gun loaded?*
Ko-no te-p-po-o **wa** ta-ma-ngu-sz'-ri nga ko-me-te go za-ri-ma-s' ka?
コノ テッポウ ハ タマグスリ ガ コメテ ゴザリマ スカ

613. *Is this piece silver?*
Ko-no gi-n wa mu-ku de go za-ri-ma-s' ka?
コノ ギン ハ ムク デゴ ザリマスカ
Do. Ko-no gi-n wa mu-ku ka?
コノ ギン ハ ムク カ

614. *Is it safe to keep money here?*
Ko-ko ni ka-ne wo o-ki-ma-sh'-te mo a-n shi-n de go za-ri-ma-s' ka?
ココニ カ子 ヲ オキ マシテ モ アンシン デ ゴ ザリ マスカ
Do. Ko-ko ni ka-ne wo o-i-te mo a-n shi-n ka?
ココニ カ子 ヲ オイテ モ アン シン カ

615. *Is this child a girl or a boy?*
Ko-no o ko wa o-na-ngo de go za-ri-ma-s' ka o-to-ko de go za-ri-ma-s' ka?
コノ オコ ハ オナゴ デゴ ザリマスカ オトコ デゴ ザリマスカ
Do. Ko-no ko wa o-na-ngo ka, o-to-ko ka?
コノコ ハ オナゴ カ オトコ カ

616. *Is there a fruit called the apple?*
Ri-n-ngo to i-u ku-da-mo-no nga go za-ri-ma-s' ka?
リンゴ トイフ クダモノ ガ ゴザリマスカ
Do. Ri-n-ngo to i-u ku-da-mo-no nga a-ru ka?
リンゴ トイフ クダモノ ガ アルカ

617. *If spoils the teeth to file them.*
Ya-sz-ri de ha wo **sz-ru** to so-ko-na-i-ma-s'.
ヤスリデ ハ ヲ スルト ソコナヒマス
Do. Ya-sz-ri de ha **wo sz-ru** to so-ko-na-u.
ヤスリデ ハ ヲ スルト ソコナフ

618. *It takes two to make a row.*
F'-ta-tsz na-ke-re ba h'-to na-ra-bi ni na-ri-ma-se-nu.
フタツ ナケレバ ヒト ナラビ ニ ナリマセヌ
Do. F'-ta-tsz na-ke-re-ba h'-to na-ra-bi ni na-ra-nu.
フタツ ナケレバ ヒト ナラビ ニ ナラヌ

619. *It takes more cloth to make it in that way.*
So no yo-o ni ts'-ku-t-te wa ki-re nga o-o-ku i-ri-ma-sh'-o-o.
ソノ ヤウ ニ ツクツテ ハ キレ ガ オホク イリマシヨウ

Do. So-no yo-o ni ts'-ku-t-te wa ki-re nga o-o-ku i-ru de a-ro-o.
ソノ ヤウ ニ ツクツテ ハ キレ ガ オホクイル デ ア ラフ

620. *It makes no difference to me which you do; suit yourself.*
Do-chi-ra na-sa-re-te-mo wa-ta-k'-shi ni ka-ma-i wa go-za-ri-ma-se-nu, o-bo-shi-me-shi shi-da-i ni na-sa-ri-ma-sh'.
ドチラ ナサレテモ ワタクシ ニ カマヒ ハ ゴザ リマセス オボシメシ シダイ ニ ナサリマシ

Do. O-ma-i do-o sh'-te mo wa-ta-k'-shi ni ka-ma-i wa na-i ka-ra, no-zo-mi shi-da-i ni shi-ro.
オマイ ドウ シテ モ ワ タクシ ニ カマヒ ハ ナイカ ラ ノヅミ シダイ ニ シロ

621. *It is a long time since I bade you adieu.*
A-na-ta ni o wa-ka-re mo-o-sh'-te yo-ri hi-sa-sh'-ku o me ni ka-ka-ri-ma-se-na-n-da.
アナタ ニ オワ カレ マウシテ ヨリ ヒサシク オ メ ニ カカリマセナンダ

Do. O-ma-i ni wa-ka-re-te yo-ri. hi-sa-sh'-ku a-wa-na-n-da.
オマイ ニ ワカレテ ヨリ ヒサシク アハナンダ

622. *It is my time to go.*
Wa-ta-k'-shi nga yu ku j'-yu-m-ba-n ni a-ta-ri-ma-sh'-te go za-ri-ma-s'.
ワ タクシ ガ ユク ジユンバン ニ アタリマシテ ゴザ リマス

Do. Wa-shi nga yu-ku j'-yu-m-ba-n ni a-ta-t-ta.
ワシ ガ ユク ジユンバン ニ アタツタ

623. *It will do very well as it is; do not be too particular about it.*
So-re de mo-o yo-ro-shi-u go za-ri-ma-s', ta-i so-o ni ne-n wo i-re-te sz-ru ni wa o-yo-bi-ma-se-n.
ソレ デ モウ ヨロシウ ゴ ザリマス タイソウ ニ子ン ヲ イレテ スル ニ ハ オヨビマセス

Do. So-re de mo-o yo-ro-shi-i a-ma-ri ne-n wo i-re-te sz-ru ni wa o-yo-ba-nu.
ソレ デ モウ ヨロシイ アマリ子ン ヲ イレテ スル ニ ハ オヨバス

624. *It will not last long.* (said of the weather)
Hi-sa-sh'-ku wa tsz-dz-ki ma-s' ma-j.
ヒサシク ハ ツヅキマス マイ

Do. Na-nga-ku wa tsz-dz-ku ma-i.
ナガク ハ ツヅクマイ

625. *It won't last long.* (of any thing in use.)
Na-nga-ku wa mo-chi-ma-s' ma-i.
ナガクハモチマスマイ
Do. Na-nga-ku wa mo-tsz. ma-i.
ナガクハモツマイ

626. *It was an accident on my **part**, I beg pardon.*
Wa-ta-k'-shi wa so-so-o wo i-ta-shi-ma-sh'-ta, go me-n ku-da-sa-re-ma-sh'.
ワタクシハソソオヲイタシマシタゴメンクダサレマシ
Do. Wa-shi wa so-so-o wo sh'-ta, go me-n na-sa-i.
ワシハソソオヲシタゴメンナサイ

627. *It has been done already.*
Mo-o sa-ki ho-do sh'-te o shi-ma-i na-sa-re-ma-sh'-ta.
モウサキホドシテオシマニナサレマシタ
Do. Mo-o sa-k'-ki sh'-te shi-ma-wa-re-ta.
モウサツキシテシマワレタ

628. *It is sun set.*
Hi no i-ri de go za-ri-ma-s'.
ヒノイリデゴザリマス
Do. Hi no i-ri da.
ヒノイリダ

629. *It is as plain as can be.*
Ko-re yo-ri a-ki-ra-ka na-ru ko-to wa go za-ri-ma-se-n'.
コレヨリアキラカナルコトハゴザリマセス
Do. Ko-re yo-ri a-ki-ra-ka na-ru wa na-i.
コレヨリアキラカナルハナイ

630. *It is no such thing.*
Sa-yo-o de wa go za-ri-ma-se-n'.
サヤウデハゴザリマセス
Do. Sa-o de wa na-i.
サウデハナイ

631. *It is as light as a feather.*
To-ri no ke no yo-o ni ka-ru-u go za-ri-ma-s'.
トリノケノヤウニカルウゴザリマス
Do. To-ri no ke no yo-o ni ka-ru-i.
トリノケノヤウニカルイ

632. *It is not good without salt.*
Shi-wo ke nga na-ku-te wa a-ji-a-i nga go za-ri-ma-se-n'.
シホケガナクテハアジワイガゴザリマセス
Do. Shi-wo ke nga na-ke-re-ba a-ji-a-i nga na-i.
シホケガナケレバアジワイガナイ

633. *It has lost its savour.*
Ko-no a-ji nga nu-ke-ma-sh'-ta.
コノアジガヌケマシタ

Do. Ko-no a-ji nga nu-ke-ta.
コノアジ ガ スケタ

634. *It is exactly noon.*
I-ma ni-t-chi-u de go za-ri-ma-s'.
イマニッチウデ ゴ ザリマス
Do. I-ma-ma-hi-ru da.
イマ マヒル ダ

635. *is very useful.*
Ta-i so-o ni ya-ku ni ta-chi ma-s'.
タイソウニヤク ニタチマス
Do. Ta-i so-o ni ya-ku ni ta-tsz.
タイソウニヤクニタツ

636. *It is past 8 o'clock.* (in the Japanese way)
I-tsz-tsz do-ki sz-ngi de go za-ri-ma-s'.
イツツ ドキ スギ デ ゴ ザリマス
Do. I-tsz-tsz do-ki sz-ngi da.
イツツ ドキ スギ ダ

637. *It is easy, because we have been accustomed to it from ancient times.*
Mu-ka-shi yo-ri na-re-te o-ri-ma-s' ka-ra, ya-sa-shi-u go za-ri-ma-s'.
ムカシ ヨリ ナレテオリマス カラ ヤサシウ ゴ ザリマス
Do. Mu-ka-shi yo-ri na-re-te i-ru ka-ra ya-sa-shi-i.
ムカシ ヨリ ナレテ イル カラ ヤサシイ

638. *It is now 11 o'clock.*
I-ma yo-tsz do-ki ha-n de go za-ri-ma-s'.
イマ ヨッ ドキ ハンデ ゴ ザリマス
Do. I-ma yo-tsz do-ki ha-n da.
イマ ヨッドキ ハン ダ

639. *It is 9 o'clock.*
I-tsz-tsz do-ki ha-n de go za-ri-ma-s'.
イツツ ドキ ハンデ ゴ ザリマス
Do. I-tsz-tsz do-ki ha-n da.
イツツ ドキ ハン ダ

640. *It will do you good.* (as medicine)
Ko-re wa a-na-ta no k'-sz-ri ni na-ri-ma-sh'-o-o.
コレ ハ アナタ ノ クスリ ニ ナリマショウ
Do. Ko-re wa o-ma-i no k'-sz-ri ni na-ro-o.
コレ ハ オマイノ クスリ ニ ナラウ

641. *It must be so.*
Ta-sh'-ka ni sa-yo-o de go za-ri-ma-s'.
タシカニ サヤウ デ ゴ ザリマス
Do. Ta-sh'-ka ni sa-yo-o da.
タシカ ニサヤウ ダ

642. *It must be true.*
Ta-sh'-ka ni ma-ko-to de go za-ri-ma-s'.
タシカニマコトデゴザリマス
Do. Ta-sh'-ka ni ma-ko-to da.
タシカニマコトダ

643. *Itcannot be true.*
Ka-na-ra-dz ma-ko-to de go za-ri-ma-se-n'.
カナラズマコトデゴザリマセス
Do. Ka-na-ra-dz ho-n to-o de wa na-i.
カナラズ ホント フデハナイ

644. *It must be you that did it.*
Ki-t-to a-na-ta nga i-ta-sa-re-ma-sh'-ta.
キットアナタガ イタサレマシタ
Do. Ki-t-to o-ma-e nga shi na-sa-t-ta.
キットオマユガ シナサッタ

645. *It was bought for nine **dollars**.*
Ko-re wa do-ra ku-ma-i de ka-wa-re-ma-sh'-ta.
コレ ハ ドラ クマイデカハレマシタ
Do. Ko-re wa do-ra ku-ma-i de ka-i na-sa-t-ta.
コレ ハ ドラ クマイデカイナサッタ

646. *It is as **hard** as a stone.*
I-shi no yo-o ni ka-to-o go za-ri-ma-s'.
イシノヤウニ カタウゴ ザリマス
Do. I-shi no yo-o ni ka-ta-i.
イシノヤウニカタイ

647. *It is **hot**, let it get cold.*
A-tsz-u go za-ri-ma-s', sa-ma-sh'-te o o-ki na-sa-re-ma-sh'.
アツウゴザリマス サ マシテオキナサレマシ
Do. A-tsz-i ka-ra; sa-ma-sh'-te o-ki na-sa-i.
ナツイカラサ マシテオキナサイ

648. *It may be so, or **it may not**.*
O-o-ka-ta sa-yo-o de go za-ri-ma-sh'-o-o o-o-ka-ta sa-yo-o de
オホカタ サヤウデゴ ザリマシヨウオホカタ サヤウデ
go za-ri-ma-s' ma-i.
ゴザリマスマイ
Do. O-o-ka-ta so-o da-ro-o, o-o-ka-ta so-o de n-ru ma-i.
オホカタソウダロウオホカタソウデ アルマイ

649. *It is **running** over.*
I-p-pa-i sz-ngi-te wa, na-nga-re de-ma-s'.
イッパイスギテ ハ ナガレデマス
Do. I-p-pa-i de wa na-nga-re de-ru.
イッパイデハ ナガレデル

650. *It is impossible for **him** to recover.*
A-no o ka-ta no ya-ma-i wa na-o-ra-re-ma-s'-ma-i.
アノオカタ ノヤマヒ ハ ナオラレマスマイ

650. A-no h'-to no ya-ma-i wa na-o-ru ma-i.
アノヒトノヤマヒハナオルマイ

651. *It takes up too much time.*
So-re de wa hi ka-dz nga ka-ka-ri sz-ngi-ma-s'.
ソレデハヒカズガカカリスギマス

Do. So-re de wa hi ka-dz' nga a-ma-ri o-o-i.
ソレデハヒカズガアマリオホイ

652. *It is up hill all the way.*
Ko-no mi-chi wa tsz-ma-sa-ki a-nga-ri de go za-ri-ma-s'.
コノ三チハツマサキアガリデゴザリマス

Do. Ko-no mi-chi wa tsz-ma-sa-ki a-nga-ri da.
コノ三チハツマサキアガリダ

653. *It is down in the hold,*
Fu-ne no so-ko ni go za-ri-ma-s'.
フ子ノソコニゴザリマス

Do. Fu-ne no so-ko ni a-ri-ma-s'.
フ子ノソコニアリマス

654. *It is in the middle compartment of the ferry boat.*
Wa-ta-shi-bu-ne no do-o-no-ma ni go za-ri-ma-s'.
ワタシブ子ノドウノマニゴザリマス

Do. Wa-ta-shi-bu-ne no do-o-no-ma ni a-ru.
ワタシブ子ノドウノマニアル

655. *It is in the bow of the boat.*
He-sa-ki ni go za-ri-ma-s'.
ヘサキニゴザリマス

Do. He-sa-ki ni a-ru.
ヘザキニアル

656. *It is in the stern.*
To-mo ni go za-ri-ma-s'.
トモニゴザリマス

Do. To-mo ni a-ru
トモニアル

657. *It was a mere joke*
So-re wa jo-o-da-n ba-ka-ri de go za-ri-ma-sh'-ta.
ソレハゾウダンバカリデゴザリマシタ

Do. So-re wa jo-o-da-n ba-ka-ri de a-t-ta.
ソレハゾウダンバカリデアッタ

658. *It has all come to nothing.*
Sz-he-te na-shi ni na-ri-ma-sh'-ta.
スベテナシニナリマシタ

Do. Sz-he-te na-ku na-t-ta.
スベテナクナッタ

659. *It is a pity to lose all this trouble.*
Se-k'-ka-ku ta-n se-i wo i-ta-shi-ma-sh'-ta ka-ra, ma-ko-to ni dza-
セツカクタンセイヲイタシマシタカラ マコトニザ

n ne-n de go za-ri-ma-s'.
シチンデ ゴ ザリマス

Do. Se-k-ka-ku da-i-ji ni sh'ta ka-ra ma-ko-to ni ku-chi-o-shi-i.
セツカク ダイジニ シタ カラ マコト ニ クチオシイ

660. *It is expensive living here.*
Ko-ko ni i-ma-s' to tsz-i-ye nga o-o ku ka-ka-ri-ma-s'.
ココニイマスト ツイエ ガ オホク カカリマス

Do. Ko-ko ni i-ru to dza-p-pi nga ta-n-to i-ru.
ココニイルト ザツピ ガ タントイル

661. *It is well worth the trouble.*
Ko-re wa shi-n-ro-u wo ts'-ku-sh'ta da-ke no ko-to nga go za-ri-ma-sz-ru.
コレ ハ シンロウ ヲ ツクシタ ダケ ノコト ガ ゴザリマスル

Do. Ko-re wa ko-ko-ro wo ts'-ku-sh'ta da-ke no ko-to nga a-ru.
コレ ハ ココロ ヲ ツクシタ ダケ ノ コト ガ アル

662. *It is not worth the trouble.*
Ko-re wa shi-n-ro-u wo ts'-ku-sh'ta ho-do de mo go za-ri-ma-se-n'.
コレ ハ シンロウ ヲ ツクシタ ホド デ モ ゴ ザリマ セヌ

Do. Ko-re wa ko-ko-ro wo ts'-ku-sh'ta ho-do no ko-to ngu na-i.
コレ ハ ココロ ヲ ツクシタ ホド ノ コト ガ ナイ

663. *It is good as far as it goes.*
Na-ni ni o-yo-bo-sz ho-do ho-shi-u go za-ri-ma-s'.
ナニ ニ オヨボス ホド ホシウ ゴザリマス

Do. Na-ni ni o-yo-bo-sz da-ke ho-shi-i.
ナニ ニ オヨボス ダケ ホシイ

664. *It is enough such **as** it is.*
So-no yo-o-na no na-ra-ba ko-re-de ta-ri-ma-s'.
ソノヤウナ ノ ナラバ コレデ タリマス

Do. So-n-na no na-ra-ba ko-re de ta-ri-ru.
ソンナ ノ ナラバ コレデ タリル

665. *It is better than it looks.*
Mi-ka-ke yo-ri yo-ro-shi-u go za-ri-ma-s'.
ミカケ ヨリ ヨロシウ ゴ ザリマス

Do. Mi-ka-ke yo-ri yo-i.
ミカケ ヨリ ヨイ

666. *It looks better than it is.*
Mi-ka-ke da-o-shi de go za-ri-ma-s'.
ミカケ ダオシ デ ゴ ザリマス

Do. Mi-ka-ke da-o-shi da.
ミカケ ダオシ ダ

667 *It thundered last night.*
　　Sa-ku-ya ra-i nga i-ta-shi-ma-sh'-ta.
　　サクヤ ライ ガ イタシマシタ
Do.　Yu-u-be ka-mi-na-ri nga na-t-ta.
　　ユフベ カミナリ ガ ナッタ

668. *It is a shame to him.*
　　A-no o h'-to wa so-re ni ts'-ke-te mo o ha-ji na-sa-ru nga
　　アノオ ヒト ハ ソレ ニ ツケテ モ オハヂ ナサル ガ
　　yo-ka-ro-o.
　　ヨカロウ
Do.　A-re wa so-re ni ta'-ke-te mo ha-ji-ru nga yo-i.
　　アレ ハ ソレ ニ ツケテ モ ハヂル ガ ヨイ

669. *It is not a whit better than it was before.*
　　Mo-to no yo-ri s'-ko-shi mo yo-ro-sh'-ku go za-ri-ma-se n'.
　　モトノヨリ スコシモ ヨロシク ゴ ザリマセヌ
Do.　Mo-to no yo-ri s'-ko-shi mo yo-ro-sh'-ku na-i.
　　モトノヨリ スコシモ ヨロシク ナイ

670. *It must be done by this time.*
　　I-ma wa k'-t-to de-ki-te o-ri-ma-sh'-o-o.
　　イマ ハ キット デキテ オリマシヨウ
Do.　I-ma wa k'-t-to de-ki-te i-ru da-ro-o.
　　イマ ハ キット デキテ イル ダロウ

671. *It may be better for a short time, but not in the long run.*
　　S'-ko-shi no a-i-da wa yo-ro-shi-u go za-ri-ma-sh'-o-o nga, na-
　　スコシ ノ アイダ ハ ヨロシウ ゴ ザリマシヨウ ガ ナ
　　nga-ku wa yo-ro-shi-u go za-ri-ma-s' ma-i.
　　ガク ハ ヨロシウ ゴ ザリマスマイ
Do.　S'-ko-shi no a-i-da wa yo-ka-ro-o nga na-nga-ku wa yo-
　　スコシ ノ アイダ ハ ヨカロウ ガ ナガク ハ ヨ
　　ku na-ka-ro-o.
　　ク ナカロウ

672. *It must be done somehow or other.*
　　Do-o de-mo ko-o de-mo k'-t-to i-ta-sa-se-ma-s'.
　　ドウデモ コオデモ キット イタサセマス
Do.　Do-o de-mo ko-o de-mo k'-t-to i-ta-sa-se-ru.
　　ドウデモ コウデモ キット イタサセル

673. *It is better not to build here, for I do not know how long I may live here.*
　　Wa-ta-k'-shi wa ko-ko ni i-tsz-ma-de o-ri-ma-sh'-o-o ka shi-
　　ワタクシ ハ ココ ニ イツマデ オリマシヨウ カ シ
　　ri-ma-se-n' ka-ra sa-n-za-i wo sh'-te f-shi-n wo i-ta-shi-ma-
　　リマセン カラ サンザイ ヲ シテ フシン ヲ イタシマ
　　s' yo-ri i-ta-sa-nu ka-ta nga ma-shi de go za-ri-ma-s'.
　　ス ヨリ イタサヌ カタ ガ マシ デ ゴ ザリマス

673. Wa-shi wa ko-ko ni i-tsz-ma-de i-ru ka shi-re-nu ka-ra, sa-
ワシ ハ ココ ニ イツマデイル カ シレヌ カラ サ
n-za-i sh'te f'-shi-n wo sz-ru yo-ri shi-na-i ho o nga ma-
ンザイシテ フシン ヲ スル ヨリ シナイ ホウ ガ マ
shi-da.
シダ

674. *It will not keep more than a day or two.*
Ko-re wa i-chi ni-chi f'-ts'-ka yo-ri sa-ki ni wa o-ka-re-ma-
コレ ハ イチ ニチ フツカ ヨリ サキ ニ ハ オカレマ
se-nu.
セヌ

Do. Ko-re wa i-chi ni-chi f'-ts'-ka yo-ri sa-ki ni wa o-ka-
コレ ハ イチ ニチ フツカ ヨリ サキ ニ ハ オカ
re-nu.
レヌ

675. *It is too late to do it now, put it off till tomorrow.*
I-ma i-ta-sh'te wa o-so-o go za-ri-ma-s' ka-ra mi-o-o ni chi
イマ イタシテ ハ オソウ ゴザリマス カラ メウ ニチ
ni o no-be na-sa-re-ma-sh'.
ニ オ ノベ ナサレマシ

Do. I-ma sh'-te wa o-so-i ka-ra a-sh'-ta ni no-be-ro.
イマシテ ハ オソイ カラ アシタ ニ ノベロ

676. *It is dark we must feel our way.*
Ku-ro-o go za-ri-ma-s' ka-ra wa-ta-k'shi do-mo ka-na-ra-dz
クロウ ゴザリマス カラ ワタクシ ドモ カナラズ
sa-ngu-t-te yu-ki-ma-s'.
サグッテ ユキマス

Do. Ku-ra-i ka-ra ka-na-ra-dz sa-ngu-t-te yu-ku.
クライ カラ カナラズ サグッテ ユク

677. *It must be done some time or other.*
Sa-ki e yo-t-te ka-na-ra-dz ts'-ku-ra-se-ma-s'.
サキ エ ヨッテ カナラズ ツクラセマス

Do. Sa-ki e yo-t-te ka-na-ra-dz ts'-ku-ra-se-ru.
サキ ヘ ヨッテ カナラズ ツクラセル

678. *It is falling in price.*
Ko-re wa to-o-ji no so-o-ba wa sa-nga-t-te o-ri-ma-s'.
コレ ハ トウジ ノ ソウバ ハ サガッテ オリマス

Do. Ko-re wa to-o-ji no so-o-ba wa sa-nga-t-te i-ru.
コレ ハ トウジ ノ ソウバ ハ サガッテ イル

679. *It is well that you waited.*
A-na-ta o ma-chi na-sa-re-ta no nga sa-i-wa-i ni na-ri-ma-
アナタ オ マチ ナサレタ ノ ガ サイワイ ニ ナリマ
sh'-ta.
シタ

Do. O-ma-e ma-t-ta no nga sa-i-wa-i ni na-t-ta.
オマエ マッタ ノ ガ サイハイ ニ ナッタ

680. *It is high time for us to go.*
　　Wa-ta-k'-shi do-mo no ma-i-ru ji-ko-ku ni na-ri-ma-sh'-ta.
　　ワタクシドモノマイルジコクニナリマシタ
Do.　Wa-shi no yu-ku ji-ko-ku nga k'-ta.
　　ワシノユクジコクガキタ

681. *It will take at least four men to lift this.*
　　Ko-re wo mo-chi a-nge-ru ni wa yo-t-ta-ri nga ka-ke-nu yo-
　　コレヲモチアゲルニハヨッタリガカケヌヤ
　　o ni i-ta-sh'-to-o go za-ri-ma-s'.
　　ウニイタシトウゴザリマス
Do.　Ko-re wo mo-chi a-nge-ru ni yo-t-ta-ri nga ka-ke-nu yo-
　　コレヲモチアガルニヨッタリガカケヌヤ
　　o ni sh'-ta-i.
　　ウニシタイ

682. *It is not safe to live here.*
　　A-s'-ko ni o i-de na-sa-re-te wa a-n-do i-ta-shi-ma-se-nu.
　　アスコニオイデナサレテハアンドイタシマセヌ
Do.　A-s'-ko ni i-te wa a-n-do se-nu.
　　アスコニイテハアンドセヌ

683. *It is dangerous to live there.*
　　A-s'-ko ni o i-de na-sa-re-te wa ki-dz-ka-i de go za-ri-ma-s'.
　　アスコニオイデナサレテハキヅカイデゴザリマス
Do.　A-s'-ko ni i-te wa ki-dz-ka-i.
　　アスコニイテハキヅカイ

684. *It is a good thing to have plenty of money.*
　　Ka-ne wa o-o-i ho-do yo-ro-shi-u go za-ri-ma-s'.
　　カネハオホイホドヨロシウゴザリマス
Do.　Ka-ne wa o-o-i ho-do yo-ro-shi-i.
　　カネハオホイホドヨロシイ

685. *It has always been so and always will be so.*
　　I-ma ma-de ka-wa-ri nga na-i ka-ra, mi-ra-i mo sa-da-me-te
　　イママデカハリガナイカラミライモサダメテ
　　ka-wa-ri wa go za-ri-ma-s' ma-i.
　　カハリハゴザリマスマイ
Do.　I-ma ma-de ka-wa-ra-nu ka-ra sa-da-me-te mi-ra-i mo ka-
　　イママデカハラヌカラサダメテミライモカ
　　wa-ru ma-i.
　　ハルマイ

686. *It has not rained here for 60 days.*
　　Ro-ku ji-u ni-chi no a-i-da ma-da a-me nga fu-ri ma-se-n'.
　　ロクジウニチノアヒダマダアメガフリマセヌ
Do.　Ro-ku ji-u ni-chi no a-i-da ma-da a-me nga fu-ra-nu.
　　ロクジウニチノアヒダマダアメガフラヌ

687. *It has begun to rain to-day, and the farmers will be glad, for the rice fields are very dry.*

Ya-t-to ko-n ni-chi a-me nga fu-ri-ma-sh'-ta ta ni mi-dz nga
ヤット コンニチ アメガ フリマシタ タ ニ ミヅ ガ
na-i ka-ra, h'-ya-k'-sh'-o-o wa sa-da-me-te yo-ro-ko-bi de go
ナイカラ ヒヤクシヤウ ハ サダメテ ヨロコビ デ ゴ
za-ri-ma-sh'-o-o.
ザルマショウ.

Do. Ki-o-o ha ji-me-te a-me nga f'-t-ta ka-ra, ta ni mi-dz nga
キウ ハジメテ アメガ フッタカラ タ ニ ミヅ ガ
na-i yu-e, h'-ya-k'-sh'-o-o wa yo-ro-ko-bu da-ro-o.
ナイユヘ ヒヤクシヤウ ハ ヨロコブ ダロウ

688. *It is laughable to hear his jokes.*
A-no h'-to no j'-o-o-da-n wo ki-ku to o-ka-shi-u go za-ri-ma-s'.
アノヒト ノ ジヨウダン ヲ キクト オカシウ ゴ ザリマス

Do. A-no h'-to no j'-o-o-da-n wo ki-ke-ba o-ka-shi-i.
アノヒト ノ ジヨウダン ヲ キケバ オカシイ

689. *Jewels are not worn in Japan.*
Ni-p-po-n de wa ta-ma no ka-za-ri wo ts'-ke-ma-se-nu.
ニッポン デ ハ タマ ノ カザリ ヲ ツケマセス

Do. Ni-p-po-n de wa ta-ma no ka-za-ri wo ts'-ke na-i.
ニッポン デ ハ タマ ノ カザリ ヲ ツケナイ

690. *Jump over the ditch.*
Do-bu wo ko-e-te o-i-de na-sa-re-ma-se.
ドブ ヲ コヘテ オイデ ナサレマセ

Do. Do-bu wo ko-e-te o i-de.
ドブ ヲ コヘテ オイデ

691. *June is the 6th month.*
J'-yu-n wa ro-ku nge-tsz de go za-ri-ma-s'.
ジユン ハ ロク ガツ デ ゴ ザリマス

Do J'-yu-n wa ro-ku nga-tsz da.
ジユン ハ ロク ガツ ダ

K.

692. *Keep out of the sun, or you will be tanned.*
Hi na-ta e de-te a-ru-ki na-sa-ru-na, i-ro nga ku-ro-ku na-ri-
ヒナタ ヘ デテ アルキ ナサルナ イロ ガ クロク ナリ
ma-s'.
マス

Do. Hi na-ta e de-te a-ru-ku-na i-ro nga ku-ro-ku na-ru.
ヒナタ ヘ デテ アルクナ イロ ガ クロク ナル

693. *Keep your book clean; by handling it carelessly, the letters will be defaced.*
Ho n wo ki-re-i ni sh'-te o mo-chi na-sa-re, dza-tsz ni mo-tsz
ホン ヲ キレイ ニ シテ オ モチ ナサレ ザツ ニ モツ

to ji nga ku-sz-re-te mi-e na-ku na-ri-ma-s'.
トジガ クヅレテ ミエナク ナリマス

Do. Ho-n wo ki-re-i ni mo-te, dza-tsz ni to-ri-a-tsz-ka-u to ji nga
ホン ヲ キレイニ モテ ダ ツニ トリアツカウ トジガ
ku-sz-re-te mi-e na-i.
クヅレテ ミエナイ

694. *Keep on doing as you are now.*
I-ma no to-o-ri ni ko-re ka-ra na-sa-re-ma-sh'.
イマノトオリニ コレ カラ ナサレマシ

Do.. I-ma no to-o-ri ni ko-re ka-ra shi-ro,
イマノトオリニ コレカラ シロ

695. *Keep what I have told you to yourself; do not tell any one else of it.*
Wa-ta-k'-shi nga mo-o-shi a-nge-ta ko-to wo hi-mi-tsz ni sh'-
ワタクシガ マウシアゲタ コト ヲ ヒミツニ シ
te o-o-ki na-sa-re-ma-sh' h'-to ni wa o ha-na-shi na-sa-ru-na.
テオオキナサレマシ ヒトニハオハナシ ナサルナ

Do. O-re nga ha-na-sh'-ta ko-to wo na-i-sh'-o-o ni sh'-te o-ke, h'-
オレガ ハナシタ コト ヲ ナイシヨウニシテオケ ヒ
to ni wa ha-na-sz-na.
トニハ ハナスナ

696. *Keep out of my way, you bother me.*
So-chi-ra e o no-ki a-so-ba-sa-re, j a-ma ni na-ri-ma-s'.
ソチラヘオ ノキアソバ サレ ジヤマ ニ ナリマス

Do. So-chi-ra e no-ke j a-ma ni na-ru.
ソチラヘ ノケ ジヤマ ニ ナル

697. *Kill that dragon fly.*
So-no to-m-bo wo o ko-ro-shi na-sa-re.
ソノ トンボ ヲ オ コロシ ナサレ

Do. A-no to-m-bo wo ko-ro-se.
アノ トンボ ヲ コロセ

698. *Kind treatment, every body likes.*
Na-sa-ke wo ka-ke-ru ko-to wo da-re de-mo yo-ro-ko-bi-ma-
ナサケ ヲ カケル コト ヲ ダレデモ ヨロコビマ
sz-ru.
スル

Do. Na-sa-ke wo ka-ke-ru wo da-re de-mo yo-ro-ko-bu.
ナサケ ヲ カケル ヲ ダレデモ ヨロコブ

L.

699. *Last night I could not sleep, it was so hot & close.*
Sa-ku ya, mu-shi a-ts'-ku-te, wa-ta-k'-shi ne-mu-ra-re-ma-
サクヤ ムシ アツクテ ワタクシ ネムラレマ
se-n'.
セス

699.　Yu-u-be mu-shi a-ts'-ku-te wa-ta-k'-shi no ts'-ka-n'.
ユウベムシアツクテ ワタクシ子ッカス

700. *Lend me five dollars.*
Wa-ta-k'-shi ni do-ra wo go ma-i ka-sh'-te ku-da-sa-re-ma-sh'.
ワタクシニドラヲゴマイカシテ クダサレマシ

Do.　Wa-shi ni do-ra go ma-i ka-sh'-te ku-re-ro.
ワシニドラゴマイカシテクレロ

701. *Let it alone.*
So-re wo o yo-shi na-sa-re.
ソレヲオヨシナサレ

Do.　So-re wo yo-se.
ソレヲヨセ

702. *Let it be for the present where it is, tomorrow we will move it into the parlor.*
Ta-da-i-ma o-ku to-ko-ro wo yo-shi-ma-sh'-te, mi-o-o ni-chi
タダイマオクトコロ ヲヨシマシテ メウ ニチ
o za-sh'-ki e sa-shi da-shi-ma-sz-ru.
オザシキヘサシダシマスル

Do.　Ta-da-i-ma o-ku to-ko-ro wo yo-sh'-te, a-sh'-ta o za-sh'-ki
タダイマオクトコロ ヲヨシテ アシタオザシキ
e sa-shi da-shi-ma-s'.
ヘサシダシマス

703. *Let who will say it,* **I do not believe** *it.*
Da-re de-mo so-no yo-o ni mo-o-shi-ma-sz-ru nga wa-ta-k'-
ダレデモソノヤウニマウシマスル ガ ワタク
shi wa shi-n-ji-ma-se nu.
シハシンジマセス

Do.　Da-re de-mo so-no yo-o ni mo-o-sz nga, wa-ta-k'-shi wa
ダレデモソノヤウニモウス ガ ワタクシ ハ
shi-n-ji na-i.
シンジナイ

704. *Let him do it, he has nothing else to do.*
A-no o ka-ta wa ho-ka-no shi-ngo-to nga **go** za-ri-ma-se-
アノオカタハ ホカノシゴト ガ ゴ ザリマセ
nu ka-ra, ko-re wo o sa-se na-sa-re.
スカラ コレヲオサセナサレ

Do.　A-no h'-to wa ho-ka-no shi-ngo-to nga na-i ka-ra ko-re
アノヒトハ ホカノシゴトガ ナイカラ コレ
wo sa-se-ro.
ヲセセロ

705. *Let us see who can throw a stone the farthest; you or I.*
A-na-ta to wa-ta k'-shi to i-shi na-nge wo i-ta-shi-ma-sh'-o-o,
アナタト ワタクシトイシナゲ ヲイタシマシヨウ
do-chi-ra nga to-o-ku e yu-ki-ma-s' ka.
ドチナ ガトフクヘユキマスカ

705. O-ma-i to wa-ta-k'-shi to i-shi na-nge wo shi-yo-o do-chi nga
オマイトワタクシトイシナゲ ヲシヨウドチガ
to o-ku e yu-ku ka.
トフクヘユクカ

706. *Let us do it at a venture.*
Wa-ta-k'-shi do-mo ko-re wo dze-hi i-ta-shi-ma-sz-ru.
ワタクシドモコレヲゼヒイタシマスル
Do. Wa-ta-k'-shi do-mo ko-re wo dze-hi sz-ru.
ワタクシドモコレヲゼヒスル

707. *Let it be just as it is.*
So-o sh'-te o o-ki a-so-ba-sa-re.
ソウシテオオキアソバサレ
Do. So-o sh'-te o o-ki na-sa-re.
ソウシテオオキナサレ

708. *Let us take a pipe under this tree.*
Wa-ta k'-shi do-mo ko-no ki no sh'-ta de i-p-pu-ku ts'-ka-ma-
ワタクシドモコノキノシタデイツプクツカマ
tsz-ri-ma-sh'-o-o.
ツリマシヨウ
Do. Ko-no ki no sh'-ta de wa-shi do-mo i-p-pu-ku no-mi-ma-
コノキノシタデワシドモイツプクノミマ
sh'-o-o.
シヨウ

709. *Let us cool ourselves under this tree.*
Ko-no ki no sh'-ta de sz-dz-mi-ma-sh'-o-o.
コノキノシタデスズミマシヨウ
Do. Ko-no ki no sh'-ta de sz-dz-mo-o.
コノキノシタデスズモウ

710. *Let us take a ride together into the country to day.*
Ko-n ni-chi go do-o yo-o ni m'-ma ni no-t-te no na-ka de ka-ke-
コンニチゴドウヤウニムマニノツテノナカデカケ
ma-sh'-o-o.
マシヨウ
Do. Ki-o-o mi-n-na-sh'-te m'-ma ni no-t'te no na-ka e de-ma-sh'-
ケウミンナジテムマニノツテノナカヘデマシ
o-o.
ヨウ

711. *Let him ride the piebald horse, & I will ride the bay.*
A-no h'-to wo bu-chi no m'-ma ni o no-se na-sa-re; wa-ta-k'-
アノヒトヲブチノムマニオノセナサレワタク
shi wa a-ka-i m'-ma ni no-ru.
シハアカイムマニノル
Do. A-no h'-to wo bu-chi no m'-ma ni no-se, wa-shi wa a-ka-i
アノヒトヲブチノムマニノセ ワシハアカイ

712. *Level the ground well for the foundation of the house.*
I-ye no ji-ngi-o-o wo ta-i-ra ni o ka-ta-me a-so-ba-sa-re-ma-shi.
イエノヂギャウヲタイラニオ カタメアソバサレマシ

Do. U-chi no ji-ngi-o-o wo ta-i-ra ni ka-ta-me-ro.
ウチノヂギャウヲタイラニカタメロ

713. *Lexicons in Japanese & English are most needed by foreigners in learning the Japanese language.*
Ga-i ko-ku no h'-to nga Ni-ho-n no ko-o j'-o-o wo na-ra-u ni wa Wa ngo Ye ya-ku no ji-bi-ki nga da-i i-chi-i-ri yo-o de go za-ri-ma-s'.
ガイコクノヒトガ ニホンノコウシヨウヲ ナラフ ニハ ワゴ ヱヤクノジビキガ ダイイチイリヨ ウデ ゴザリマス

Do. Ga-i ko-ku no h'-to nga Ni-p-po-n no ko-o j'-o-o wo na-ra-u ni wa Wa ngo Ye ya-ku no ji-bi-ki nga da-i i-chi i-ri yo-o da.
ガイコクノヒトガ ニッポン ノコウジヨウヲナラ ウニハワ ゴ ヱヤクノジビキガ ダイイチイリ ヨウダ

714. *Lift this board up, and set it on end.*
Ko-no i-ta wo mo-chi a-nge-te o ta-te a-so-ba-sa-re-ma-shi.
コノイタヲ モチアゲテオタテアソバサレマシ

Do. Ko-no i-ta wo mo-chi a-nge-te ta-te-ro.
コノイタヲ モチ アゲテ タテロ

715. *Light the lamp.*
A-ka-ri wo o ts'-ke a-so-ba-sa-re-ma-sh'.
アカリヲ オツケ アソバサレマシ

Do. A-ka-ri wo ts'-ke-ro.
アカリ ヲ ツケロ

716. *Lightning is the cause of thunder.*
Ka-mi-na-ri no mo-to wa i-na-bi-ka-ri de go za-ri-ma-s'.
カミナリ ノモト ハイナビカリデ ゴザリマス

Do. Ka-mi-na-ri no mo-to wa i-na-bi-ka-ri da.
カミナリ ノモト ハイナビカリダ

717. *Lilies abound in the woods and Pinks grow wild by the road sides in Japan.*
Ha-ya-shi no na-ka ni yu-ri nga ta-k'-sa-n ha-e-te o-ri, mi-chi ba-ta ni wa na-de-sh'-ko nga ya-ta-ra-ni ha-e-te o-ri-ma-s.
ハヤシノナカ ニユリ ガ タクサンハエテオリ ミチ バタニハ ナデシコガ ヤタラニハエテ オリマス

717. Ha-ya-shi no na-ka ni yu-ri nga o-o-ku ha-e-te o-ri, mi-chi
ハヤシノナカニ ユリ ガオホク ハエテオリ メチ
ba-ta ni na-de-sh'-ko nga ya-mi-ko-mo ha-e-te o-ru.
バタニ ナデシコ ガ ヤミコモ ハエテオル

718. *Lions and tigers are not natives of Japan.*
Shi-shi to to-ra wa Ni-p-po-n ni o-ra-na-i ke-da-mo-no de go
シシ トトラ ハ ニッポン ニオラナイ ケダモノ デゴ
za-ri-ma-s'.
ザリマス

Do. Shi-shi to to-ra wa Ni-p-po-n ni i-na-i ke-da-mo-no da.
シシ トトラ ハ ニッポン ニイナイ ケダモノ ダ

719. *Lock the doors.*
Mo-n no j'-o-o wo o-ro-shi a-so-ba-sa-re.
モン ノ ジョウヲ オロシ アソバサレ

Do. Mo-n no j'-o-o wo o-ro-shi na-sa-re.
モン ノ ジョウヲ オロシ ナサレ

720. *Look them over, and pick out the bad ones, and throw them away*
Ko-re wo mi-wa-ke-te wa-ru-i no wo o to-ri s'-te na-sa-re-
コレヲ ミワケテ ワルイノヲオトリステ ナサレ
ma-sh'.
マシ

Do. Ko-re wo mi-wa-ke-te wa-ru-i no wo to-ri s'-te-ro.
コレヲ ミワケテ ワルイ ノ ヲトリ ステロ

721. *Look again; it must be about here somewhere.*
Mo-o i-chi do o ta-dz-ne na-sa-ri-ma-sh' so-ko no ki-n-j'-o
モウ イチド オ タヅ子 ナサリマシ ソコ ノ キンジョ
ni k'-t-to go za-ri-ma-sh'-o-o.
ニ キットゴ ザリマショウ

Do. Mo-o i-chi do o sa-nga-shi na-sa-re, so-ko no ma-wa-ri ni
モウ イチド オ ザガシ ナサレ ソコ ノ マワリ ニ
k'-t-to a-ri-ma-sh'-o-o.
キット アリマショウ

722. *Look out or you will get hurt.*
Ki wo ts'-ke-na ke-re-ba ke-nga wo i-ta-shi-ma-sz-ru.
キ ヲ ツケナ ケレバ ケガ ヲ イタシマスル

Do. Ki wo ts'-ke-na ke-re-ba ke-nga wo sz-ru.
キ ヲ ツケナ ケレバ ケガ ヲ スル

723. *Loosen that horse's girth a little.*
So-no m'-ma no ha-ra-o-bi wo s'-ko-shi o yu-ru-me na-sa-re.
ソノ ムマ ノ ハラオビ ヲ スコシ オ ユルメ ナサレ

Do. A-no m'-ma no ha-ra-o-bi wo s'-ko-shi yu-ru-me-ro.
アノ ムマ ノ ハラオビ ヲ スコシ ユルメロ

724. *Love your enemies, bless them that curse you; do good to them that hate you, and pray for them that despitefully use you and persecute you.*

A-na-ta wo a-da ka-ta-ki-ni sz-ru mo-no wo ba, a-na-ta ko-
アナタヲアダ カタキニ スルモノヲバアナタコ
re wo ka-wa-i-nga-re, a-na-ta wo wa-ru-ku yu-u mo-no, wo,
レヲカワイガレアナタヲワルクイフモノヲ
a-na-ta so-re wo yo-ku i-i, a-na-ta wo u-ra-mi-ru mo-no wo,
アナタソレヲ ヨクイイアナタヲウラミルモノヲ
a-na-ta so-re wo yo-ku to-ri-a-ts'-ka-i; a-na-ta wo hi-do-ku
アナタソレ ヲ ヨクトリアツカヒアナタ ヲ ヒドク
wo a-shi-ra-i, a-na-ta ni ga-i ja-ma wo sz-ru mo-no wo,
ヲアシラヒアナタ ニガイ ジャマヲ スル モノ ヲ
a-na-ta ko-re nga ta-me-ni ka-mi sa-ma ni o i-no-ri na-
アナタコレガ タメニカミ サマニオイノリ ナ
sa-re.
サレ

725. *Lunatics in Japan are taken care of by their friends if they have any; if not, they fall into beggary.*
Ni-p-po-n de wa ki-chi-nga-i mo-no wa shi-n-ru-i nga se-wa
ニッポンデ ハキチガイ モノハ シンルイ ガ セワ
wo i-ta-shi-ma-s, shi-n-ru-i nga na-ke-re-ba ko-ji-ki ni o-
ヲイタシマス シンルイ カ ナケレバ コジキニオ
chi-ma-s'.
チマス

Do. Ni-p-po-n de wa ki-chi-nga-i wa mi yo-ri nga se-wa sz-
ニッポンデ ハキチガイハ ミヨリ ガ セワ ス
ru, na-ke-re-ba ko-ji-ki ni na-ru.
ル ナケレバ コジキ ニ ナル

M.

726. *Make haste back.*
Ji-ki-ni o ka-e-ri a-so-ba-sa-re.
ジキニオ カエリアソバサレ
Do. Ji-ki-ni ka-e-re.
ジキニ カエレ

727. *Make the most of this, there is no more.*
Ko-re ngi-ri go za-ri-ma-se-n' ka-ra, da-i-ji-ni o ts'-ka-e a-so-
コレ ギリ ゴ ザリマセス カラ ダイジニオツカヒアソ
ba-sa-re.
バサレ
Do. Ko-re ki-ri na-i ka-ra da-i-ji-ni ts'ka-i na-sa-re.
コレキリナイ カラダイジニツカヒナサレ

728. *Make sure of this whatever becomes of the other.*
A-chi-ra wa do-o-de-mo yo-i nga ko-chi-ra wa dze-hi mo-to-
アチラ ハドウデモ ヨイガ コチラハ ゼヒモト

me o-ki-ta-i.
メオキタイ

728. A-chi wa do-o-do-mo yo-i nga ko-chi wa dze-hi to-me-te
アチハドウデモヨイガコチハゼヒトメテ
o-ki-ta-i.
オキタイ

729. *Make out your bill, I will pay you.*
Ku-wa-sh'-ki u-ke-to-ri nga-ki wo o da-shi na-sa-re, wa-ta-k'-
クハシキウケトリガキヲオダシナサレワタク
shi ka-ne wo ha-ra-i-ma-s'.
シカ子ヲハラヒマス

Do. U-ke-to-ri wo o da-shi, ka-ne wo ya-ri-ma-s'.
ウケトリヲオダシカ子ヲヤリマス

730. *Make him do it over and over again, till he gets it right.*
A-no h'-to nga yo-ku de-ki-ma-sz-ru ma-de na-m-be-n de-mo
アノヒトガヨクデキマスルマデナンベンデモ
o sa-se na-sa-re-ma-sh'.
オサセナサレマシ

Do. A-no h'-to nga yo-ku de-ki-ru ma-de, na-m-be-n de-mo o
アノヒトガヨクデキルマデナンベンデモオ
sa-se na-sa-i.
サセナサイ

731. *Mark my name on my handkerchief in Japanese characters.*
Wa-ta-k'-shi no ha-na-f'-ki e a-na-ta nga Ni-ho-n mo-ji de
ワタクシノハナフキヘアナタガニホンモジデ
wa-ta-k'-shi no na wo ka-i-te ku-da-sa-re-ma-se.
ワタクシノナヲカイテクダサレマセ

Do. Wa-shi nga ha-na-f'-ki e o-ma-e nga Ni-ho-n mo-ji de wa-
ワシガハナフキヘオマエガニホンモジデワ
shi nga na wo ka-i-te ku-da-sa-re.
シガナヲカイテクダサレ

732. *Masks of various descriptions are worn at the Japanese religious festivals in their pantomimes and dances*
Wa-ko-ku no ma-tsz-ri ni i-ro-i-ro-na me-n wo ka-bu-ri-te o-
ワコクノマツリニイロイロナメンヲカブリテオ
do-ri ha-ne-ma-sz-ru.
ドリハ子マスル

Do. Wa ko-ku no ma-tsz-ri ni wa i-ro-i-ro no me-n wo ka-bu-
ワコクノマツリニハイロイロノメンヲカブ
t-te o-do-ri ha-ne-ru.
ツテオドリハ子ル

733. *May I not have a pear Sir?*
Da-n-na, Wa-ta-k'-shi wa na-shi wo h'-to-tsz mo-ra-t-te yo-ro-
ダンナワタクシハナシヲヒトツモラツテヨロ

shi-u go za-ri-ma-s' ka?
シウ ゴザリマスカ

734. *May I take this?*
Wa-ta-k'-shi wa ko-re wo ka-ri-te, yo-ro-shi-u go za-ri-ma-s' ka?
ワタクシ ハ コレヲ カリテ ヨロシウ ゴ ザリマ スカ

Do.　Wa-shi wa ko-re wo ka-ri-te yo-i ka?
ワシ ハ コレヲカリテヨイカ

735. *Mend my clothes nicely.*
Wa-ta-k'-shi nga ki-mo-no wo yo-ro-sh'-ku nu-i na-o-sh'-te ku-re-ro.
ワタクシ ガ キモノ ヲ ヨロシク ヌヒ ナオシテク レロ

736. *Miners are not long lived in the island of Sado.*
Sa-do no ka-na-ho-ri wa na-nga-i-ki de go za-ri-ma-se-n'.
サド ノ カナホリ ハ ナガイキ デ ゴ ザリ マセヌ

Do.　Sa-do no ka-na-ho-ri wa na-nga-i-ki de na-i.
サド ノ カナホリ ハ ナガイキ デ ナイ

737. *Mind your own business, don't **bother me**,*
O-ma-e o-ma-e nga sz-ru ko-to wo na-sa-re wa-ta-k'-shi ngu
オマエオマエ ガ スル コト ヲ ナサレ ワタクシ ガ
j'-a-ma wo sz-ru-na.
ジャマ ヲ スルナ

Mix these two together.
Ko-no f'-ta-tsz wo o ma-ze **na-sa-re**.
コノ フタツ ヲ オ マゼ ナサレ

Do.　Ko-no f'-ta-tsz wo ma-ze-ro.
コノ フタツ ヲ マゼロ

738. *Murders are numerous in Japan of late years.*
Ni-p-po-n de h'-to-ngo-ro-shi wa chi-ka-ngo-ro ta-k'-sa-n' go za-ri-ma-s'.
ニッポン デ ヒトゴロシ ハ チカゴロ タクサンゴザ リマス

Do.　Ni-p-po-n de h'-to-ngo-ro-shi wa chi-ka-ngo-ro ta-k'-sa-n a-ru.
ニッポンデ ヒト ゴロシ ハ チカゴ ロ タクサン アル

739. *My feet are cold.*
Wa-ta-k'-shi no a-shi nga tsz-me-ta-o go za-ri-ma-s'.
ワタクシ ノアシ ガ ツメタウ ゴ ザリマス

Do.　Wa-shi nga a-shi nga hi-e-ru.
ワシ ガ アシ ガ ヒエル

740. *My house is overrun with **rats**.*
Wa ta-k'-shi no i-ye wa ne-dz-mi nga ta-i-so-o ni o-ri-ma-sz-ru.
ワタクシ ノイエハ子ヅミ ガタイソウニオリマスル

740. Wa-shi 'nga a-chi wa ne-dz-mi nga ta-i-so-o i-ru.
ワシ ガ ウチ ハ子ヅミ ガタイソウイル
741. *My finger has a felon on it, or is sore of a felon.*
Wa-ta-k'-shi no yu-bi nga hi-o-o-so de ya-me-ma-sz-ru
ワタクシノ ユビ ガ ヒヨウソデヤメマスル
Do. Wa-shi nga yu-bi nga hi-o-o-so de i-ta-mu.
ワシ ガ ユビ ガ ヒヨウソデ イタム

N.

742. *Never mind (that is, Do not be concerned about it.)*
Ki ni o ka-ke a-so-ba-sa-re-ma-s'-na.
キニオカケアソバサレマスナ
Do. Ki ni ka-ke na-sa-ru-na.
キニカケ ナサルナ
743. *No matter how you do it if you only do it.*
Do-o de-mo yo-i ka-ra ko-shi-ra-i sa-i sz-re-ba yo-ro-shi-u go za-ri-ma-s'
ドウデモ ヨイ カラ コシラヘサヘスレバ ヨロシウゴ ザリマス
Do. Do-o de-mo yo-i ka-ra ko-shi-ra-i sa-i sz-re-ba yo-i.
ドウデモ ヨイ カラ コシラヘサヘスレバ ヨイ
744. *No one knows where it came from.*
Ko-re wa do-ko ka-ra ki-ma-sh'-ta ka da-re mo shi-ri-ma-se-n'.
コレ ハ ドコカラキマシタ カダレ モ シリマセス
Do. Ko-re wa do-ko ka-ra k'-ta ka da-re mo shi-ra-n'.
コレ ハ ド コカラ キタカダレ モ シラス
745. *No, they are my brothers.*
I-i-ye, wa-ta-k'-shi ki-o-o-da-i no mo-no de go za-ri-ma-s'.
イイエ ワタクシキヤウダイノモノデゴ ザリマス
Do. I-i-ye wa-ta-k'-shi ki-o-o-da-i no mo-no da.
イイエ ワタクシキヤウダイノモノダ
746. *No, I am the taller.*
I-i-ye wa-ta-shi se-i nga ta-ko-o go za-ri-ma-s'.
イイエ ワタシ セイ ガ タコフ ゴ ザリマス
Do. I-i-ye wa-shi nga se-i nga ta-ka-i.
イイエ ワシ ガ セイ ガ タカイ
747. *Nobody thinks so but you.*
A-na-ta yo-ri ho-ka ni wa h'-to wa sa-yo-o wa o-mo-i-ma-se-nu.
アナタ ヨリ ホカ ニ ハ ヒト ハ サヤウ ハ オモイマ セス
Do. O-ma-e yo-ri ho-ka no h'-to wa so-o wa o-mo-wa-nu.
オマエ ヨリ ホカ ノ ヒト ハ ソウ ハ オモ ワス

748. *Nothing can be raised in this land without manure.*
Ko-no ts'-chi wa ko-ya-shi nga na-ku-te wa na-ni mo de-ki-
コノツチハコヤシガナクテハナニモデキ
ma-se-n'.
マセヌ

Do. Ko-no ts'-chi wa ko-ya-shi nga na-ku-te wa na-ni mo de-
コノツチハコヤシガナクテハナニモデ
ki-na-i.
キナイ

749. *Now is the time to do it.*
Ko-re wo ko-shi-ra-i-ru ni i-ma nga yo-ro-shi-u go za-ri-ma-s'.
コレヲコシラヘルニイマガヨロシウゴザリマス

Do. Ko-re wo sz-ru ni i-ma nga yo-i.
コレヲスルニイマガヨイ

750. *Now I see into it.*
Wa-ta-k'-shi wa i-ma wa-ka-ri-ma-s'.
ワタクシハイマワカリマス

Do. Wa-shi wa i-ma wa-ka-t-ta.
ワシハイマワカツタ

751. **Nutmegs** *are in great demand.*
I-ma ni-ku-dz-ku wo o-o-ku h'-to nga ho-shi-nga-ri-ma s'.
イマニクヅクヲオホクヒトガホシガリマス

Do. I-ma ni-ku-dz-ku wo o-o-ku h'-to nga ho-shi-nga-ru.
イマニクヅクヲオホクヒトガホシガル

O.

752. *Oats* **grow wild in** *this country, but the farmers pull them up and throw them away, though they are very good for horse-feed.*
Ka-ra-sz mu-ngi wa ko-no ku-ni de ma-ka-dz-ni ha-e-ma-sz-
カラスムギハコノクニデマカズニハヘマス
ru, **sa-ri** na-nga-ra h'-ya-ku-sh'-o-o wa nu-i-te s'-te-ma-sz-
ルサリナガラヒヤクシヤウハヌイテステマス
ru nga, m'-ma no ta-be-mo-no ni wa ha-na-ha-da yo-ro-shi-u
ルガムマノタベモノニハハナハダヨロシウ
go za-ri-ma-s'.
ゴザリマス

Do. Ka-ra-sz **mu-ngi wa ko-no ku-ni** de ma-ka-dz-ni ha-e-ru, sh'-
カラスムギハコノクニデマカズニハヘルシ
ka-shi-na-nga-ra h'-ya-ku-sh'-o-o wa nu-i-te s'-te-ru nga, m'-
カシナガラヒヤクシヤウハヌイテステルガム
ma no ku-i-mo-no ni wa ha-na-ha-da yo-ro-shi-u go za-ru.
マノクイモノニハハナハダヨロシウゴザル

753. *Oaths are taken in Japan by writing them out, and signing them with one's blood.*

Ni-p-po-n de wa chi-ka-i wo i-ta-shi-ma-sz-ru ni wa shi-m-
ニツポンデ ハ チカヒ ヲ イタシマスル ニ ハ シン
mo-n ka-i te ke-p-pa-n wo ts'-ka-ma-tsz-ri-ma-sz ru.
モン カイテ ケツパンヲ ツカマツリマスル

Do. Ni-p po-n de chi-ka-i ni wa shi-m-mo-n ka-i te ke p-pa-n
ニツポンデ チカニ ハ シンモン カイテ ケツパン
sz-ru.
スル

754. *Of all bad things, that is the worst.*
Mi-na wa-ru-i ko-to no u-chi de wa so-re nga i-chi-ba-n wa-
ミナ ワルイ コト ノ ウチ デ ハ ソレ ガ イチバン ワ
ru-u go za-ri-ma-s'.
ルウ ゴ ザリマス

Do. Mi-na wa-ru-i no ko-to u-chi de wa a-re nga i-chi-ba-n
ミナ ハルイ ノ コト ウチ デ ハ アレ ガ イチバン
wa-ru-i.
ワルイ

755. *Of what nation are you?*
A-na-ta wa do-ko no ku-ni de go za-ri-ma-s'.
アナタ ハ ドコ ノ クニ デ ゴ ザリマス

Do. O-ma-e wa do-ko no ku-ni de go za-ru.
オマエ ハ ドコ ノ クニ デ ゴ ザル

756. *Of what use is such a thing to you?*
Ko-no yo-o-na mo-no wo na-ni ni o mo-chi-i na-sa-ru ka?
コノ ヤウナ モノ ヲ ナニ ニ オ モチイ ナサル カ

Do. Ko-n-na mo-no wo o-ma-e wa na-ni ni ts-ka-e-ma-sz-ru ka?
コンナ モノ ヲ オマエ ハ ナニ ニ ツカヒ マスル カ

757. *Once there was a house here.*
I-ze-n ko-no to-ko-ro ni i-ye nga go za-ri-ma-sh'-ta.
イゼン コノ トコロ ニ イエ ガ ゴ ザリマシタ

Do. I-ze-n ko-no to-ko-ro ni u-chi nga a-t-ta.
イゼン コノ トコロ ニ ウチ ガ アツタ

758. *One of the spoons is missing.*
Sa-ji nga i-p-po-n mi-e na-ku na-ri-ma-sh'-ta.
サジ ガ イツポン ミエ ナク ナリマシタ

Do. Sa ji nga i-p-po-n mi-e na-ku na-t-ta.
サジ ガ イツポン ミエ ナク ナツタ

759. *One of my horses is lame in the fore shoulder, and I cannot ride him till he is well.*
Wa-ta-k'-shi m'-ma nga i-p-pi-ki ka-ta wo i-ta-me-ma-sh'-ta ka-
ワ タクシ ム マ ガ イツピキ カタ ヲ イタメ マシタ カ
ra, na-o-sz ma-de no-ru ko-to de-ki-ma-se-nu.
ラ ナオス マデ ノル コト デキマセヌ

Do, Wa-shi nga m'-ma nga i-p-pi-ki ka-ta wo i-ta-me-ta ka-ra na-
ワシ ガ ム マ ガ イツピキ カタ ヲ イタメタ カラ ナ

o-sz ma-de no-ru ko-to nga de-ki-na-i.
オスマデノルコト ガ デキナイ

760. *One and one are two; two and two are four; four and four are eight; eight and eight are sixteen.*
H'-to-tsz h'-to-tsz wo yo-se-te f'-ta-tsz; f'-ta-tsz f'-ta-tsz wo yo-
ヒトツ ヒトツ ヲ ヨセテ フタツ フタツ フタツ ヲ ヨ
se-te yo-tsz; yo-tsz yo-tsz wo yo-se-to ya-tsz; ya-tsz ya-tsz
セテ ヨツ ヨツ ヨツ ヲ ヨセテ ヤツ ヤツ ヤツ
wo yo-se-te ji-u ro-ku.
ヲ ヨセテ ジウ ロク

761. *Onions have no bulbs in Japan.*
Ni-p-po-n de wa ne-ngi ni wa ta-ma wa go za-ri-ma-se-n'.
ニツホンデハ子ギニハ タマ ハ ゴ ザリマセス

Do. Ni-p-po-n de ne-ngi ni wa ta-ma wa na-i.
ニツポン デ 子ギ ニ ハ タマ ハ ナイ

762. *Opium, being a contraband article, cannot be imported.*
A-he-n wa go ha-t-to no mo-no da go za-ri-ma-s' ka-ra, mo-
アヘン ハ ゴ ハツトノ モノ デ ゴ ザリマス カラ モ
chi-ko-mu ko-to wa na-ri-ma-se-n'.
チコム コト ハ ナリマセス

Do. A-he-n wa ha-t-to mo-no da ka-ra, u-ri-ko-mu ko-to wa na-
アヘン ハ ハツト モノ ダ カラ ウリ コム コト ハ ナ
ra-n'.
ラス

763. *Orphans who have no relatives to take care of them become beggars.*
Mi-na-shi-ngo wa shi-n-ru-i ni so-da-te-ru mo-no nga na-ke-re-
ミナシゴ ハ シンルイニ ソダテル モノ ガ ナケレ
ba ko-ji-ki ni o-chi-ma-sz-ru.
バ コジキ ニ オチマスル

Do. Mi-na-shi-ngo wa shi-n-ru-i nga ku-wa-se-n' to ko-ji-ki ni
ミナシゴ ハ シンルイガ クワセス ト コジキ ニ
na-ru.
ナル

764. *Our work is behind hand.*
Wa-ta-k'-shi do-mo no shi-ngo-to nga o-so-ku na-ri-ma-sh'-ta.
ワタクシ ドモ ノ シゴト ガ オソク ナリマシタ

Do. Wa-shi nga shi-ngo-to nga o-so-ku na-t-ta.
ウシ ガ シゴト ガ オソクナツタ

P.

765. *Paper can be made of straw.*
Wa-ra de ka-mi wo ts'-ku-ru ko-to nga de-ki-ma-sz-ru.
ワラデ カミ ヲ ツクル コト ガ デキマスル

Do. Wa-ra de ka-mi wo ts'-ku-ru ko-to nga de-ki-ru.
ワラデ カミ ヲ ツクル コト ガ デキル

P.

766. *Pass the bread to all the guests.*
　　Mi-na-mi-na o ki-a-ku sa-ma ye pa-n wo a-nge-ro.
　　ミナミナ オキヤク サマ エ パン ヲ アゲロ

767. *Pirates are numerous on the coast of China.*
　　Ka-ra no ka-i-nga-n ni wa o-o-ku ka-i-zo-ku go-za-ri-ma-s'.
　　カラノ カイガンニ ハ オウク カイゾク ゴザリマス

Do.　Ka-ra no ka-i-he-n ni wa, ta-i-so-o ka-i-zo-ku nga a-ru.
　　カラノ カイヘンニ ハ タイソウ カイゾク ガ アル

768. *Please shut the sliding papered door.*
　　Ka-ra-ka-mi wo ta-te-te ku-da-sa-re.
　　カラカミ ヲ タテテ クダサレ

Do.　Ka-ra-ka-mi wo ta-t-te ku-re-ro.
　　カラカミ ヲ タッテ クレロ

769. *Pray walk in.*
　　Ma-dz u-chi ye o a-nga-ri na-sa-re.
　　マズ ウチ エ オアガリ ナサレ

Do.　Ma-a u-chi ye ha-i-re.
　　マア ウチ エ ハイレ

770. *Pray take a chair.*
　　Ma-dz ko-shi wo o ka-ke na-sa-re.
　　マズ コシ ヲ オカケ ナサレ

Do.　Ma-a ko-shi wo ka-ke-ro.
　　マア コシ ヲ カケロ

771. *Prop up this board fence.*
　　Ko-no he-i wo o-ko-sh'-te ku-da-sa-re.
　　コノ ヘイ ヲ オコシテ クダサレ

Do.　Ko-no he-i wo o-ko-sh'-te ku-re-ro.
　　コノ ヘイ ヲ オコシテ クレロ

772. *Pull off your loose trousers, and rest yourself.*
　　Ha-ka-ma wo to-t-te, ki-u-so-ku na-sa-re-ma-sh'.
　　ハカマ ヲ トッテ キウソク ナサレマシ

Do.　Ha-ka-ma wo to-t-te ya-sz-me.
　　ハカマ ヲ トッテ ヤスメ

773. *Pull off my boots.*　　　　　　(to a servant.)
　　Wa-ta-k'-shi no na-nga-ngu-tsz wo nu-ke.
　　ワタクシ ノ ナガグツ ヲ ヌケ

774. *Put on your clothes quick; the house is on fire.*
　　Ka-ji-da ka-ra, i-so-i-de ki-mo-no wo o ki na-sa-re.
　　カジダ カライソイデ キモノ ヲ オキ ナサレ

775. *Put on your outside coat; it is very cold to-day.*
　　Ko-n-ni-chi wa ha-na-ha-da sa-mu-u go za-ri-ma-s' ka-ra, ha-
　　コンニチ ハ ハナハダ サムウ ゴザリマス カラ ハ
　　o-ri wo o ki na-sa-re.
　　ヲリ ヲ オキ ナサレ

Do.　Ko-n-ni-chi wa me-s-so-o sa-mu-i ka-ra, ha-o-ri wo ki-ro.
　　コンニチ ハ メッソウ サムイ カラ ハヲリ ヲ キロ

776. *Put out the lights.*
A-ka-ri wo o ka-shi na-sa-re.
アカリ ヲ オカシ ナサレ
A-ka-ri wo ka-se.
アカリ ヲ カセ

777. *Put these side by side, not one upon another.*
Ko-re wo i-chi i-chi na-ra-be-te o-ki na-sa-re, ka-sa-ne na-sa-ru-na.
コレ ヲ イチ イチ ナラベテ オオキ ナサレ カサネ ナサルナ

Do. Ko-re wo i-chi i-chi na-ra-be-te o-ke, ka-sa-ne-ru-na.
コレ ヲ イチ イチ ナラベテ オケ カサ子ルナ

778. *Put every thing in its place before you go to bed.*
Mi-na mo-no wo ba mo-to no to-ko-ro e ka-ta-dz-ke-te o ne na-sa-re.
ミナ モノ ヲ バ モト ノ トコロ エ カタヅケテ オ子 ナサレ

Do. Mi-na mo-no wo ba mo-to no to-ko-ro ni ka-ta-dz-ke-te ne-ro.
ミナ モノ ヲ バ モト ノ トコロ ニ カタヅケテ 子ロ

779. *Put it down here.*
Ko-ko ni o o-ki na-sa-re-ma-sh'.
ココ ニ オオキ ナサレマシ

Do. Ko-ko ni o-ke.
ココ ニ オケ

780. *Put it on the table.*
Da-i no u-e ni o o-ki na-sa-re-ma-sh'
ダイ ノ ウエ ニ オオキ ナサレ マシ

Do. Da-i no u-e ni o-ke.
ダイ ノ ウエ ニ オケ

781. *Put this in the sun to dry.*
Ko-re wo hi-na-ta ni ho-sh'-te o o-ki na-sa-re-ma-sh'.
コレ ヲ ヒナタ ニ ホシテ オオキ ナサレ マシ

Do. Ko-re wo hi-na-ta ni ho-sh'-te o-ke.
コレ ヲ ヒナタ ニ ホシテ オケ

782. *Put this away.*
Ko-re wo shi-ma-t-te o o-ki na-sa-re.
コレ ヲ シ マッテ オオキ ナサレ

Do. Ko-re wo shi-ma-t-te o-ke.
コレ ヲ シ マッテ オケ

783. *Put it down any where.*
Do-ko ni de-mo o o-ki na-sa-re-ma-sh'.
ドコ ニ デモ オオキ ナサレ マシ

Do. Do-ko ni de-mo o-ke.
ドコ ニ デモ オケ

784. *Put it back again.*
Ma-ta mo-to no to-ko-ro e o o-ki na-sa-re ma-sh'.
マタモトノトコロエオオキナサレマシ
Ma-ta mo-to no to-ko-ro ni o-ke.
マタモトノトコロニオケ

785. *Put it in writing, that you will deliver the goods tomorrow.*
K'-t-to mi-o-o ni-chi shi-na wo yo-ko-sz to yu-u, ya-ku-so-ku-
キットミヤウニチシナヲヨコストユウヤクソク
nga-ki wo shi na-sa-re.
ガキヲシナサレ

786. *Put off going till tomorrow.*
Yu-ku ko-to wo mi-o-o ni-chi ma-de o no-be na-sa-re.
ユクコトヲミヤウニチマデオノベナサレ

Do. Yu-ku ko-to wo a-sh'-ta ma-de no-be-ro.
ユクコトヲアシタマデノベロ

787. *Put both together and get the amount.*
Ri-o-o ho-o i-s-sh'-o ni sh'-te ka-n-j'-o-o shi na-sa-re.
リョウホウイッショニシテカンジョウシナサレ

Do. So-o ho-o h'-to-tsz ni sh'-te ka-n-j'-o-o shi-ro.
ソウホウヒツニシテカンジョウシロ

Q.

788. *Quack-doctors practice empiricism for the sake of getting money.*
De-mo-i-sh'-a nga ka-ne wo to-ru ta-me-ni i-i-ka-nge-n na ri-o-o-
デモイシヤガカ子ヲトルタメニイイカゲンナリョウ
ji wo sz-ru.
ジヲスル

789. *Quadrupeds are four-footed animals.*
Yo-tsz a-shi a-ru mo-no wa, shi-so-ku-de go za-ri-ma-s'.
ヨツアシアルモノハシソクデゴザリマス

790. *Quails, wild geese, ducks, pigeons, pheasants, deer and wild boars*
U-dz-ra, ga-n, ka-mo, ya-ma-ba-to, ki-ji, sh'-ka, i-no-shi-shi, fu-
ウズラガンカモヤマバトキジシカイノシシフ
yu wa ko-o-e-ki-ba ni ta-k"-sa-n go za-ri-ma-s'.
ユハコウエキバニタクサンゴザリマス

791. *Queens reign in some countries of Europe.*
Yo-ro-pa no u-chi, ni-sa-n nga ko-ku, ni-yo-te-i nga o-sa-
ヨロパノウチニサンガコクニヨテイガオサ
me-ru.
メル

792. *Queen Victoria, of England, is distinguished as a wife, a mother, and a sovereign.*
I-ngi-ri-sz ngo-ku no ni-yo-te-i Bi-k'-to-ri-a wa, tsz-ma no mi-
イギリスゴクノニヨテイビクトリアハツマノミ

chi mo, ha-ha no mi-chi mo ta-mi wo-o-sa-me-ru mi-chi mo,
子モ ハハノ三チ モ タミ ヲオサメル三チモ
ka-ku be-tsz sz-ngu-re-te o-ri-ma-s'.
カク ベッス グレテオリマス

793. *Quench that fire with water.*
So-no hi ni mi-dz wo ka-ke-te ke-sh'-te ku-da-sa-re.
ソノ ヒ ニ ミヅ ヲ カケテ ケシテ クダサレ

Do.　So-no hi-ni mi-dz wo ka-ke-te ke-se.
ソノ ヒ ニ ミヅ ヲ カケテ ケセ

794. *Question him, and see if he knows any thing about it.*
A-no h'-to wa ko-re wo shi-ru ka, shi-ra-nu ka, o ki-ki na-
アノヒト ハ コレ ヲ シル カ シラス カオ キキ ナ
sa-re.
サレ

Do.　A-no h'-to wa shi-ru ka, shi-ra-nu ka, ki-ki-na.
アノヒト ハ シルカ シラス カ キキナ

795. *Quick: bring it here.*
Ha-ya-ku, mo-t-te o-i-de na-sa-re.
ハヤク モツテオイデ ナサレ

Do.　Ha-ya-ku, mo-t-te ko-i.
ハヤク モツテコイ

796. *Quit my house, you are in the way.*
O-ma-e ja-ma ni na-ru ka-ra, wa-ta-k'-shi no i-ye wo de-ro.
オマエジャマニ ナル カラ ワタクシ ノ イエ ヲ デロ

797 *Quit claim deeds are taken when land and houses are bought.*
Gi-me-n to i-ye wo ka-u to-ki, yu-dz-ri j'-o-o-mo-n wo to-ri-ma
ジメン トイエヲカウ トキ ユヅリジョウモン ヲ トリマ
s'z-ru.
スル

R.

798. *Rabbits dig* **holes,** *and burrow in them.*
U-sa-ngi wa a-na wo ho-t-te sz-ma-i wo i-ta-shi-ma-s'.
ウサギ ハ アナ ヲ ホッテ スマ井 ヲ イタシ マス

Do.　U-sa-ngi wa a-na wo ho-t-te sz-mu.
ウサギ ハ アナ ヲ ホッテスム

799. *Rags that once were thrown away in Japan, having become an article of commerce, a ship load has gone to London.*
Mo-to s'-te-ta bo-ro nga to-o ji wa ko-u-e-ki-mo-no ni na-ri-ma-
モト ステタ ボロ ガ トウジ ハ コウエキモ ノ ニ ナリマ
sh'-ta ka-ra, fu-ne i-s-so-o ye i-p-pa-i ts-n-de Ro-n-do-n ye
シタ カラ フ子 イツソウ ヘ イッパイ ツンデ ロンドン ヘ
ma-i-ri-ma-sh'-ta.
マイリマシタ

800. *Rake up those leaves, and throw them into the gutter.*
A-no ha wo ku-ma-de de ka-ki yo-se-te do-bu ni s'-te-ro
アノ ハ ヲ クマデ デ カキ ヨセテ ドブ ニステロ

801. *Ransack the house till you find that spoon.*
Sa-ji nga de-ru ma-de, u-chi ji-u sa-nga-se.
サジ ガ デル マデ ウチジウ サガセ

802. *Rap at the door, if it is shut.*
Mo-n nga shi-me-te a-ru na-ra ka-do yo-ri o-to-dz-re-ro.
モン ガ シメテ アル ナラ カド ヨリ オトヅレロ

803. *Rape seed is largely raised in Japan for making oil.*
Ni-p-po-n de wa a-bu-ra to-ru tu-me-ni, na-ta-ne wo ta-k'-sa-n ts'-ku-ru.
ニッポンデ ハ アブラ トル タメニ ナタ子 ヲ タクサン
ツクル

804. *Rats, snakes, fleas, mosquitos, and flies, I do detest.*
Ne-dz-mi, he-bi no-mi, ka, ha-i wa, wa-ta-k'-shi wa ki-tsz-i ki-ra-i de go za-ri-ma-s'.
子ヅミ ヘビ ノミ カ ハイ ハ ワタクシ ハ キツ イキ
ラヒ デ ゴ ザリマス

Do. Ne-dz-mi, he-bi, no-mi, ka, ha-i wa, wa-shi wa ki-tsz-i ki-ra-i da.
子ズミ ヘビ ノミ カ ハヒ ハ ワシ ハ キツ イ キ
ラヒ ダ

805. *Reach up, and take down that picture.*
Se-i wo no-ba-sh'-te so-no e-dz wo to-t-te ku-da-sa-re.
セイ ヲ ノバシテ ソノ ヱヅ ヲ トッテ クダサレ

Do. So-no e-dz wo se-i wo no-ba-sh'-te, to-t-te ku-re-ro.
ソノ ヱヅ ヲ セイ ヲ ノバシテ トッテ クレロ

806. *Read louder.*
Ko-e wo a-nge-te o yo-mi na-sa-re.
コヱ ヲ アゲテ オ ヨミ ナサレ

Do. Ko-e wo a-nge-te yo-me.
コヱ ヲ アゲテ ヨメ

807. *Read in a lower voice.*
Ko-e wo sh'-ku-ku sh'-te o yo-mi na-sa-re.
コヱ ヲ ヒククシテ オ ヨミ ナサレ

Do. Ko-e wo sh'-ku-ku sh'-te yo-me.
コヱ ヲ ヒククシテ ヨメ

808. *Reindeer are called tonakai by the Ainos of Karaf'to.*
O-o-ji-ka wo ka-ra-f'-to no A-i-no wa to-na-ka-i to mo-o-shi-ma-s'.
オホジカ ヲ カラフト ノ アイノ ハ トナカイ ト マウシ
マス

Do. O-o-ji-ka wo ka-ra-f'-to no A-i-no wa to-na-ka-i to i-u.
オホジカ ヲ カラフト ノ アイノ ハ トナカイ トイフ

809. *Remember what you said yesterday, for I shall hold you to your promise.*
A-na-ta no ya-ku-so-ku no mo-do-ra-nu yo-o ni ma-mo-ri-ma-s'
アナタ ノ ヤクソク ノ モドラヌ ヤウニ マモリマス
ka-ra, sa-ku-ji-tsz ha-na-shi-ma-sh'-ta ko-to wo o-bo-ye-te
カラ サクジツ ハナシマシタ コトヲ オボエテ
o i-de na-sa-re.
オイデナサレ

Do. O-ma-e no ya-ku-so-ku no mo-do-ra-nu yo-o ni ma-mo-ru
オマエ ノ ヤクソク ノ モドラス ヤウニ マモル
ka-ra sa-ku-ji-tsz ha-na-sh'-ta ko-to wo o-bo-ye-te i-ro.
カラ サクジツ ハナシタ コトヲ オボエテイロ

810. *Remit the value to me, as soon as you have sold the goods.*
Shi-ro-mo-no wo u-ri na-sa-re-ta-ra-ba da-i-ki-n wo sa-s-so-ku
シロモノヲ ウリナサレ タラバ ダイキンヲ サッソク
wa-ta-sh'-te o ts'-ka-wa-shi na-sa-re-ma-sh',
ワタシテ オツカワシ ナサレマシ

Do. Shi-ro-mo-no wo u-re-te na-ra sz-ngu-ni da-i-ki-n wo wa-
シロモノ ヲ ウレテ ナラ スグ ニ ダイキン ヲ ワ
ta-sh'-te yo-ko-se.
タシテ ヨコセ

811. *Rents of land are paid to the Taikun in rice, and the rice is inspected and deposited in the storehouses at A-sa-k'-sa by the Collector.*
Ta-i-ku-n no ne-n-ngu wa ko-me de a-nge-ma-s' ka-ra so-no
タイクン ノ子ング ハ コメ デ アゲ マス カラ ソノ
ko-me wa da-i-ka-n nga a-ra-ta-me-te A-sa-k'-sa no ku-ra
コメ ハ ダイカン ガ アラタメテ アサクサ ノ クラ
ni o-sa-me-ma-s'.
ニオサメマス

Do. Ta-i-ku-n no ne-n-ngu wa ko-me de a-nge-ru ka-ra so-no
タイクン ノ子ング ハ コメ デ アゲル カラ ソノ
ko-me wa da-i-ka-n nga a-ra-ta-me-te A-sa-k'-sa no ku-ra ni
コメ ハ ダイカン ガ アラタメテ アサクサ ノ クラ ニ
o-sa-me-ru.
オサメル

812. *Re-write that page, for there are errors in it.*
So-no ma-i wa ma-chi-nga-t-te o-ri-ma-s' ka-ra ma-ta o ka-ki
ソノ マイ ハ マチガッテ オリマス カラ マタ オカキ
na-o-shi na-sa-re.
ナオシナサレ

Do. So-no ma-i wa ma-chi-nga-t-te i-ru ka-ra ma-ta ku-ki na-
ソノ マイ ハ マチガッテイル カラ マタ カキ ナ
o-se.
オセ

813. *Rice and salt are indispensable articles of food.*
　　Ko-me to shi-wo wa na-ku-te na-ra-nu ta-be-mo-no de go za-
　　コメトシホハナクテナラヌタベモノデゴザ
　　ri-ma-s'.
　　リマス

Do.　Ko-me to shi-wo wa na-ku-te na-ra-nu ta-be-mo-no da.
　　コメトシホハナクテナラヌタベモノダ

814. *Ring the bell for dinner.*
　　Hi-ru me-shi no sh'-ta-ku nga de-ki-ta ka-ra re-i wo fu-re.
　　ヒルメシノシタクガデキタカラレイヲフレ

815. *Rip this seam.*
　　Ko-no nu-i-me wo to-ke
　　コノヌイメヲトケ

816. *Ripe fruits are not unwholesome.*
　　Ji-ku-shi-ma-sh'-ta ku-da-mo-no wa ta-be-ma-sh'-te mo a-ta-ri-
　　ジクシマシタクダモノハタベマシテモアタリ
　　ma-se-n'.
　　マセヌ

Do,　Ji-ku-sh'-ta ku-da-mo-no wa ta-be-te mo a-ta ra-nu.
　　ジクシタクダモノハタベテモアタラヌ

817. *Roast that duck.*
　　So-no a-hi-ru wo a-bu-ri-mo-no ni shi-ro.
　　ソノアヒルヲアブリモノニシロ

818. *Roll up the sun screens.*
　　Sz-da-re wo ma-ki a-nge-ro.
　　スダレヲマキアゲロ

819. *Row with all your might; it is late.*
　　O-so-i ka-ra se-i wo da-sh'-te ro wo o-se.
　　オソイカラセイヲダシテロヲオセ

820. *Rub your hands together briskly, and they will soon become warm.*
　　Ri-o-o te wo a-wa-se-te ki-u-ni sz-ri-ma-s' na-ra-ba ji-ki-ni a-ta-
　　リャウテヲアハセテキウニスリマスナラバジキニアタ
　　ta-ma-ri-ma-s'.
　　タマリマス

Do　Ri-o-o te wo a-wa-se-te ki-u-ni sz-ru na-ra ji-ki-ni a-ta-ta-
　　リャウテヲアハセテキウニスルナラジキニアタタ
　　ma-ru.
　　マル

821. *Rust is decomposed iron.*
　　Sa-bi wa te-tsz nga ku-sa-ru no de go za-ri-ma-s'.
　　サビハテツガクサルノデゴザリマス

822. **Sales** *for ready money are the cheapest.*
Ge-n-ki-n de u-ri-ma-s' **wa** ge ji-ki de go za-ri-ma-s'.
ゲンキンデウリマス ハ ゲ ジキ デ ゴ ザリマス

Do. Ge-n-ki-n de u-ru wa ya-sz-i.
ゲンキンデウル ハ ヤスイ

823. *Sales on credit are the dearest.*
Ka-ke-u-ri wa ta-ka-o go za-ri-ma-s'.
カケウリ ハ タカウ ゴ ザリマス

Do. Ka-ke-u-ri wa ta-ka-i.
カケウリ ハ タカイ

824. *Salmon* **are brought** *in large quantities by junks from Matszmai to Yedo.*
Sh'-a-ke wa Ma-tsz-ma-i yo-ri o-o-ku Ye-do e fu-ne de tsz-mi o-ku-ri-ma-s'.
シャケ ハ マツマイ ヨリ オホク エド ヘ フ子 デ ツミ
オクリマス

Do. Sh'-a-ke wa Ma-tsz-ma-i yo-ri o-o-ku fu-ne de Ye-do e tsz-mi o-ku-ru.
シャケ ハ マツマイ ヨリ オホク フ子 デ エド ヘ ツミオクル

825. *Sailors, grooms, and chair-bearers, are regarded as degraded* **men** *in Japan.*
Ni-p-po-n de wa fu-ne no-ri, m'-ma-ka-ta, ni-n-so-ku, o-chi no h'-to to o-mo-i-ma-s'.
ニッポン デ ハ フ子ノリ ム マ カタ ニン ソク オチ ノ
ヒト ト オモイマス

826. **Sandal wood, being expensive,** *is used for burning incense, and for medicine.*
Bi-a-ku-da-n wa a-ta-e nga tu-ko-o go za-ri-ma-sh'-te ko-o ni mo ta-ki-ma-s' ya-ku-shi-u ni mo mo-chi-i-ma-s'.
ビヤクダン ハ アタヘ ガ タカウ ゴ ザリマシテ カウニ
モ タキマス ヤクシユ ニ モ モチイマス

Do. Bi-a-ku-da-n wa a-ta-e nga ta-ka-ku sh'-te ko-o ni mo **ta-ku** k' sz-ri ni mo ts'-ka-u.
ビヤクダン ハ アタヘ ガ タカク シテ カウニ モ タク
クスリ ニ モ ツカウ

827. *Save this for to-morrow.*
Mi-o-o ni-chi mo-chi-i-ma-s' **ta-me-ni** ko-re wo shi-ma-t-te o o-ki na-sa-re.
ミヤウニチ モチイマス タメニ コレ ヲ シ マツテ オオ
キ ナサレ

Do. Mi-o-o ni-chi ts'-ka-u ta-me-ni ko-re wo shi-ma-t-te o-ke.
ミヤウニチ ツカウ タメニ コレ ヲ シ マツテ オケ

828. *Say it in Japanese.*
Ni-p-po-n no ko to-ba de o ha-na-shi na-sa-re.
ニッポン ノ コトバ デ オ ハナシ ナサレ

828. Ni-p-po-n no ko-to-ba de ha-na-se.
　　ニッポン ノ コトバデ ハナセ
829. *Scare that dog away.*
　　A-no i-nu wo o-i i-da-sh'-te ku-da-sa-re.
　　アノイヌヲオイイダシテ クダサレ
Do.　A-no i-nu wo o-i i-da-se.
　　アノイヌヲオイイダセ
830. *Scour the pots and kettles bright, inside and out.*
　　Ka-ma to na-be wo u-chi so-to wo mi-nga-ke
　　カマト ナベヲウチ ソトヲ ミガケ
831. *Scrape the ink off from that desk.*
　　So-no ts'-ku-e ni tsz-i-te a-ru sz-mi wo ke-dz-ri o-to-sh'-te ku-da-sa-re.
　　ソノ ツクエニツイテアル スミ ヲケヅリオトシテク
　　ダサレ
Do.　A-no ts'-ku-e ni tsz-i-ta sz-mi wo ke-dz-ri o-to-se.
　　アノ ツクエニツイタ スミ ヲ ケヅリオトセ
832. *Scribble on scraps of paper; it is a waste to use whole sheets.*
　　Ka-ri-nga-ki wo ha nga-mi ni na-sa-re; ma-t-ta-o sh'-te i-ru ka-mi wo ts'-ka-i-ma-s' wa tsz-i-e de go za-ri-ma-s'.
　　カリガキ ヲ バガミニナサレ マツタフシテイルカ
　　ミヲ ツカヒマス ハツイエデ ゴ ザリマス
Do　Ka-ri-nga-ki wo ha nga-mi ni shi-ro; ma-t-ta-ki ka-mi wo ts'-ka-u wa tsz-i-e da.
　　カリガキ ヲ バガミニシロ マツタキ カミヲ
　　ツカフ ハ ツイエダ
833. *Scrub the floor.*
　　Yu-ka wo f'-ki-na-sa-i.
　　ユカ ヲ フキナサイ
834. *Scuds fly wheresoever the wind drives them.*
　　U-ki-ngu-mo wa ka-ze ni sh'-ta-nga-t-te yu-ku ewo sa-da-me-ma-se-n'.
　　ウキグモ ハ カゼニシタガッテ ユクエヲ サダメ
　　マセヌ
Do　U-ki-ngu-mo wa ka-ze ni sh'-ta-nga-t-te yu-ku e wo sa-da-me-nu.
　　ウキグモ ハ カゼニシタガッテ ユクヘヲ サ
　　ダメヌ
835. *Seal up that money box.*
　　A-no ka-ne-ba-ko ni fu-u-i-n wo na-sa-re-ma-sh'.
　　アノ カ子バコニ フウインヲナサレマシ
Do.　A-no ka-ne-ba-ko ni fu-u-i-n wo shi-ro.
　　アノ カ子バコニ フウインヲシロ
836. *Seat yourself in the Japanese fashion.*
　　Ni-p-po-n no yo-o ni o sz-wa-ri na-sa-re.
　　ニッポン ノヤウ ニオスハリ ナサレ

837. *See that butterfly and locust.*
A-no ch'-o-ch'-o to se-mi wo go-ra-n na-sa-re.
アノ テウテウ ト セミ ヲ ゴラン ナサレ

Do. A-no ch'-o-ch'-o to se-mi wo mi-ro
アノ テウテウト セミ ヲ ミロ

838. *See to this now and then.*
Ko-re wo o-ri-o-ri ki wo ts'-ke-te ku-da-sa-re
コレ ヲ オリオリ キ ヲ ツケテ クダサレ

Do. Ko-re wo o-ri-o-ri ki wo ts'-ke-ro.
コレ ヲ オリオリ キ ヲ ツケロ

839. *Sell the goods for what they will fetch.*
Ko-no shi-ro-mo-no wa so-o-ba ni na-ra-t-te n-t-te ku-da-sa-re.
コノ シロモノ ハ ソウバ ニ ナラッテ ウッテ クダ サレ

840. *Set the dog on that hog.*
A-no bu-ta ni i-nu wo ke-shi-ka-ke na-sa-re.
アノ ブタ ニ イヌ ヲ ケシカケ ナサレ

Do. A-no bu-ta ni i-nu wo ke-shi-ka-ke-ro.
アノ ブタ ニ イヌ ヲ ケシカケロ

841. *Send me word how it is.*
Ts'-ka-i wo o ya-ri na-sa-re-te, i-na-ya wo o ki-ka-se na-sa-re.
ツカイ ヲ オヤリ ナサレ テ イナヤ ヲ オ キカセ ナサレ

Do. Ts'-ka-i wo ya-t-te a-m-pi wo ki-ka-se-te ku-re.
ツカイ ヲ ヤッテ アンピ ヲ キカセテ クレ

842. *Several persons have told me of it.*
H'-to-bi-to nga so-no ko-to wo wa-ta-k'-shi ni ha-na-shi-ma-sh'-ta.
ヒトビト ガ ソノ コト ヲ ワタクシ ニ ハナシ マ シタ

Do. H'-to-bi-to nga so-no ko-to wo wa-shi-ni ha-na-sh'-ta.
ヒトビト ガ ソノ コト ヲ ワシニ ハナシタ

843. *Shall I help you?*
A-na-ta no o te-tsz-da-i wo i-ta-sh'-i-ma-sh'-o-o ka?
アナタ ノ オテツダイ ヲ イタシ イマシャウカ

Do. O-ma-e no te-tsz-da-i wo shi-yo-o ka?
オマエ ノ テツダイ ヲ シヤウカ

844. *Shall I feel your pulse?*
A-na-ta no mi-a-ku wo u-ka-nga-i-ma-sh'-o-o ka?
アナタ ノ ミヤク ヲ ウカ ガヒ マシャウカ

Do. O-ma-e no mi-a-ku wo mi-yo-o ka?
オマエ ノ ミヤク ヲ ミヤウ カ

845. *Shall we have fair weather to-day?*
Ko-n-ni-chi wa o te-n-ki ni na-ri-ma-sh'-o-o ka?
コンニチ ハ オテンキ ニ ナリマ シャウカ

Do Ki-o wa hi-yo-ri ni na-ro-o ka?
ケフ ハ ヒヨリ ニ ナロウ カ

746. *Shake the bottle before you take the medicine.*
K'-sz-ri wo no-mu ma-e-ni to-k'-ku-ri wo o fu-ri na-sa-re.
クスリ ヲ ノム マエニ トックリ ヲ オフリ ナサレ

Do. k'-sz-ri wo no-mu ma-e-ni to-k'-ku-ri wo fu-re.
クスリ ヲ ノム マエニ トックリ ヲ フレ

847. *She has three children.*
A-no o-na-ngo wa ko-do-mo nga sa-n ni-n go za-ri-ma-s'.
アノオナゴ ハ コドモ ガ サン ニンゴ ザリマス

Do. A-no o-n-na wa ko-do-mo nga sa-n ni-n a-ru.
アノオンナ ハ コドモ ガ サン ニンアル

848. *She must be upwards of twenty years old.*
A-no o-na-ngo wa ta-sh'-ka-ni ha-ta-chi no u-e de go za-ri-ma-sh'-o-o.
アノオナゴ ハ タシカニ ハタチ ノウエデ ゴ ザリ マシャウ

Do. A-no o-n-na wa ta-sh'-ka-ni ha-ta-chi no u-e da-ro-o.
アノ オンナ ハ タシカニ ハタチ ノウエダロウ

849. *She is a handsome woman.*
A-no o-na-ngo wa u-ts'-ku-shi-i sz-nga-ta de go za-ri-ma-s'.
アノオナゴ ハ ウツクシイス ガタ デゴ ザリマス

Do. A-no o-n-na wa u-ts'-ku-shi-i sz-nga-ta da.
アノオンナ ハ ウツクシイスガタダ

850. *She cannot walk without help.*
A-no o-na-ngo wa ka-i-ho-o shi na-ku-te wa a-yu-ma-re-ma-se-n'.
アノオナゴ ハ カイホウシ ナクテ ハ アエマレ マセス

Do. A-no o-n-na wa ka-i-ho-o shi na-ku-te wa a-ru-ka-re-ma-se-n'.
アノオンナ ハ カイホウシ ナクテ ハ アルカレ マセス

851. *Shut the windows* (sliding ones)
Ma-do wo ta-te-te ku-da-sa-re.
マド ヲ タテテ クダサレ

Do. Ma-do wo ta-te-ro
マド ヲ タテロ

852. *Sign this paper.*
Ko-no ka-ki-ts'-ke ni go se-i me-i nga-ki wo na-sa-re.
コノ カキツケ ニ ゴセイメイ ガ キ ヲ ナサレ

Do. Ko-no ka-ki-ts'-ke ni se-i me-i wo shi-ru-se.
コノ カキツケ ニ セイメイ ヲ シルセ

853. *Sit still* (i.e. do not rise)
Go-a-n-dza wo na-sa-re.
ゴアンザ ヲ ナサレ

Do. Sz-wa-t-te i-ro. (in the Japanese fashion)
スハツテイロ
Do. Go-a-n-dza wo na-sa-re. (of sitting in a chair)
ゴアンザ ヲ ナサレ
Do. Ko-shi-wo ka-ke-te i-ro.
コシ ヲ カケテ イロ

854. *Smell this rose.*
Ko-no ba-ra no ni-wo-i wo ka-i-de go ra-n na-sa-re.
コノ バラ ノ ニホヒ ヲ カイデ ゴラン ナサレ
Do. Ko-no ba-ra no ni-wo-i wo ka-i-de mi-ro.
コノ バラ ノ ニホヒ ヲ カイデ ミロ

855. *So much the better.*
So-re da-ke na-wo yo-ro-shi-i go za-ri-ma-s'.
ソレ ダケ ナヲ ヨロシイ ゴザリマス
Do. So-re da-ke na-wo yo-ro-shi-i.
ソレ ダケ ナヲ ヨロシイ

856. *Some of them are good, some bad.*
Yo-ki mo a-sh'-ki-mo go za-ri-ma-s'.
ヨキ モ アシキ モ ゴザリマス
Do. Yo-i no mo wa-ru-i no mo a-ru.
ヨイ ノ モ ワルイ ノ モ アル

857. *Speak plainly.*
Wa-ka-ru yo-o-ni o ha-na-shi na-sa-re.
ワカル ヤウニ オ ハナシ ナサレ
Do. Wa-ka-ru yo-o-ni ha-na-se.
ワカル ヤウニ ハナセ

858. *Spread this **out on the grass**.*
Ko-re wo k'-sa no **u-e-ni** hi-ro-n-ge-te o o-ki na-sa-re.
コレ ヲ クサ ノ ウエニ ヒロゲテ オオキ ナサレ
Do. Ko-re **wo** k'-sa no u-e-ni hi-ro-n-ge-te o-ke.
コレ ヲ クサ ノ ウエニ ヒロゲテ オケ

859. *Sprinkle some water on those flowers.*
So-no ha-na ni s'-ko-shi mi-dz wo o so-so-ngi na-sa-re.
ソノ ハナ ニ スコシ ミヅ ヲ オ ソソギ ナサレ
Do. So-no ha-na ni s'-ko-shi mi-dz wo fu-ri ka-ke-ro.
ソノ ハナ ニ スコシ ミヅ ヲ フリ カケロ

860. *Squalls rise suddenly.*
Ha-ya-te wa ni-wa-ka-ni o-ko-ri-ma-s'.
ハヤテ ハ ニハカニ オコリマス
Do. Ha-ya-te wa ki-u-ni o-ko-ru.
ハヤテ ハ キウニ オコル

861. *Stand.*
O ta-chi na-sa-re-ma-sh'.
オタチ ナサレ マシ
Do. Ta-te.
タテ

862. *Stay here while I am gone.*
Wa-ta-k'-shi nga i-t-te ki-ma-s' ma-de ko-ko-ni ma-t-te o i-de na-sa-re.
ワタクシ ガ イツテキマス マデ ココニ マツテオイデ ナサレ

Do. Wa-shi nga i-t-te ku-ru ma-de ko-ko-ni ma-t-te i-ro.
ワシ ガ イツテクル マデ ココ ニ マツテイロ

863. *Stay here till I come back.*
Wa-ta-k'-shi nga ka-e-ri-ma-s' ma-de ko-ko-ni ma-t-te o i-de na-sa-re.
ワタクシ ガ カエリマス マデ ココニ マツテオイデ ナサレ

Do. Wa-shi nga ka-e-ru ma-de ko-ko-ni ma-t-te i-ro.
ワシ ガ カエル マデ ココニ マツテイロ

864. *Strange that you should think so!*
A-na-ta so-no yo-o-ni o-bo-shi-me-shi ko-to wa a-ya-shi-i ko-to de go za-ri-ma-s'.
アナタ ソノ ヤウニ オボシメシ コト ハ アヤシイ コトデ ゴザリマス

Do. O-ma-e so-o o-mo-o ko-to wa a-ya-shi-i ko-to da.
オマエ ソウ オモフ コト ハ アヤシイ コトダ

865. *Stretch out this line, and hang the clothes on it to dry.*
Ki-mo-no ka-ke-te ho-sz ta-me-ni, ko-no na-wa wo ha-re.
キモノ カケテ ホス タメニ コノ ナハ ヲ ハレ

866. *String the bow.*
Yu-dz-ru wo o ka-ke na-sa-re.
ユヅル ヲ オカケ ナサレ

Do. Yu-dz-ru wo ka-ke-ro.
ユヅル ヲ カケロ

867. *String those cash.*
Ko-no ze-ni wo sa-shi ni o to-o-shi na-sa-re.
コノ ゼニ ヲ サシ ニ オ トウシ ナサレ

Do. Ko-no ze-ni wo sa-shi ni to-o-se.
コノ ゼニ ヲ サシ ニ トウセ

868. *Strive once more with all your might.*
Mo-o i-chi wo-o chi-ka-ra wo ts'-ku-sh'-te o ts'-to-me na-sa-re.
モウ イチ オフ チ カラヲ ツクシテ オツ トメ ナサレ

Do. Mo-o i-chi wo-o ho-ne wo o-t-te ts'-to-me-ro.
モウ イチ オフ ホ子 ヲ オツテ ツトメロ

869. *Study makes the ripe scholar.*
H'-to nga ma-na-te-ba se-ki nga-ku ni i-ta-ri-ma-s'.
ヒト ガ マナ子バ セキ ガク ニ イタリマス

Do. H'-to nga ma-na-n-de se-ki nga-ku ni na-ru.
ヒト ガ マナンデ セキ ガク ニ ナル

870. *Stumbling horses are dangerous to ride.*
Tsz-ma-dz-i-te hi-za-o-ru m'-ma ni no-ru wa a-bu-no-o go za-
ツマヅイテヒザオルムマニノルハアブノヲゴザ
ri-ma-s'.
リマス

Do. Tsz-ma-dz-i-te hi-za-o-ru m'-ma ni no-ru wa a-bu-na-i.
ツマヅイテヒザオルムマニノルハアブナイ

871. *Stutterers can speak like ordinary people, by counting their syllables.*
Do-mo-ri wa o-n wo ka-dzo-e-te i-wa-se-re-ba tsz-ne no h'-to ha-
ドモリハオンヲカヅエテイハセレバツ子ノヒトハ
na-s' ko-to nga de-ki-ma-s'.
ナスコトガデキマス

Do. Do-mo-ri wa o-n wo ka-dzo-e-te i-wa-se-re-ba te-da no h'-to
ドモリハオンヲカヅエテイハセレハタダノヒト
no yo-o ni i-wa-re-ru.
ノヤウニイワレル

872. *Subdue those evil passions.*
So-no a-ku j'-o-o wo go-o-f-ku na-sa-re.
ソノアクジャウヲゴウフクナサレ

Do. So-no a-ku j'-o-o wo he-i-f-ku shi-ro.
ソノアクジャウヲヘイフクシロ

873. *Suffer wrong rather than do it.*
H'-to wo ga-i sz-ru yo-ri wa, h'-to ni ga-i se-ra-ru-ru nga
ヒトヲガイスルヨリハヒトニガイセラルルガ
ma-shi to o-mo-i na-sa-re.
マシトオモヒナサレ

Do H'-to wo so-ko-na-u yo-ri, h'-to ni so-ko-na-wa-ru-ru nga
ヒトヲソコナフヨリヒトニソコナハルルガ
ma-shi to o-mo-e.
マシトオモエ

874. *Superintend my business while I am absent.*
Wa-ta-k'-shi no ru-sz no u-chi, a-na-ta wa-ta-k'-shi no ts-to-
ワタクシノルスノウチアナタワタクシノツト
me wo o o-sa-me na-sa-re.
メヲオオサメナサレ

Do. Wa-shi nga ru-sz no a-i-da, o-ma-e wa-shi nga shi-ngo-to
ワシガルスノアイダオマエワシガシゴト
wo o-sa-me-ro.
ヲオサメロ

T.

875. *Take care*
Go yo-o-ji-n na-sa-re-ma-sh'.
ゴヤウジンナサレマシ

875. Yo-o-ji-n wo shi-ro.
ヨウジンヲシロ

876. *Take this away.*
Ko-re wo mo-t-te o i-de na-sa-i.
コレヲモッテオイデナサイ
Do. Ko-re wo mo-t-te yu-ke.
コレヲモッテユケ

877. *Take all but one.*
H'-to-tsz no-ko-sh'-te no-ko-ra-dz o mo-chi na-sa-i.
ヒトツノコシテノコラズオモチナサイ
Do. H'-to-tsz no-ko-sh'-te no-ko-ra-dz mo-t-te yu-ke.
ヒトツノコシテノコラズモッテユケ

878. *Take these eggs out, one by one.*
Ko-no ta-ma-ngo wo h'-to-tsz dz tsz o to-ri na-sa-re.
コノタマゴヲヒトツヅツオトリナサレ
Do. Ko-no ta-ma-ngo wo h'-to-tsz dz-tsz to-re.
コノタマゴヲヒトツズツトレ

879. *Take good care of that.*
A-no shi-na-mo-no wo da-i-ji ni na-sa-re-ma-sh'.
アノシナモノヲダイジニナサレマシ
Do. A-no shi-na wo da-i-ji ni shi-ro.
アノシナヲダイジニシロ

880. *Take your choice.*
Go ka-t-te no wo o to-ri na-sa-re.
ゴカッテノヲオトリナサレ
Do S'-ki-na wo to-re.
スキナヲトレ

881. *Take which you please.*
A-na-ta o-bo shi-me-shi ni ka-na-i-ma-sh'-ta no wo o to-ri na-sa-re.
アナタオボシメシニカナイマシタノヲオトリナサレ
Do. O-ma-e ki ni i-t-ta no wo to-re.
オマエキニイッタノヲトレ

882. *Take as many as you please.*
A-na-ta i-ku-tsz de-mo o-bo-shi-me-shi ho-do o to-ri na-sa-re.
アナタイクツデモオボシメシホドオトリナサレ
Do. O-ma-e i-ku-tsz de-mo o-mo-o ho-do to-re.
オマエイクツデモオモフホドトレ

883. *Take three a piece.*
Ko-re wo h'-to-ri de mi-tsz dz-tsz o mo-chi na-sa-re.
コレヲヒトリデミツヅツオモチナサレ
Do. Ko-re wo h'-to-ri de mi-tsz dz-tsz mo-te.
コレヲヒトリデミツヅツモテ

884. *Take care! you will set the house on fire if you do not.*
Go yo-o-ji-n wo na-sa-re-ma-sh' ki wo ts'-ke-ma-se-nu na-ra-
ゴヨウジンヲナサレマシキヲツケマセヌナラ
ba so-so-o bi wo da-sh'-te i-ye wo ya-ki-ma-s'.
バソソウビヲダシテイエヲヤキマス

Do. Yo-o-ji-n wo shi-ro-ki wo ts'-ke-nu na-ra-so-so-o bi wo da-
ヨウジンヲシロキヲツケヌナラソソウビヲダ
sh'-te i-ye wo ya-ku-dzo.
シテイエヲヤクゾ

885. *Talk to me about that some other time; I am too busy to listen to it now.*
Wa-ta-k'-shi ta-da-i-ma a-ma-ri ko-u-za-ts' i-ta-sh'-te o-ri-ma-s'
ワタクシタダイマアマリコンザツイタシテオリマス
ka-ra, o ha-na-shi wo u-ke-ta-ma-wa-ru ko-to nga de ki-ma-
カラオハナシヲウケタマハルコトガデキマ
se-nu ta-ji-ts' o ha-na-shi-na sa-re.
セヌタジツオハナシナサレ

Do. Wa-shi wa i-ma to-ri-ko-n-de i-ru ka-ra, ha-na-shi wo ki-
ワシハイマトリコンデイルカラハナシヲキ
ku ko-to nga de-ki-nu ma-ta ho-ka-no hi ni ha-na-se.
クコトガデキヌマタホカノヒニハナセ

886. *Tallow is made from the fruit of the tallow tree, and from that of the varnish tree.*
Ro-o wa ha-ji no ki no mi de ts'-ku-ri-ma-s', u-ru-shi no ki
ロウハハジノキノミデツクリマスウルシノキ
no mi de mo ts'-ku-ri-ma-s'.
ノミデモツクリマス

887. *Teach by example as well as by precept.*
Gi-o-o-j'-o-o to o-ki-te to wo mo-t-te h'-to wo o o-shi e na-
ギャウジャウトオキテトヲモッテヒトヲオシエナ
sa-re.
サレ

Do. Gi-o-o-j'-o-o to o-ki-te to wo mo-t-te h'-to wo o-shi-e-ro.
ギャウジャウトオキテトヲモッテヒトヲオシエロ

888. *Teachers are respected for their instructions; but the military class are respected only for fear of their power and authority.*
Shi wa o-shi-e wo ta-t-to-n-de u-ya-ma-i-ma-s', bu-shi wa ke-n
シハオシエヲタットンデウヤマイマスブシハケン
i ni o-so-re-te u-ya-ma-i-ma-s'.
イニオソレテウヤマイマス

Do. Shi-sh'-o-o wa o-shi-e wo ta-t-to-n-de u-ya-ma-u, bu-shi wa
シシャウハオシエヲタットンデウヤマウブシハ
ke-n i ni o-so-re-te u-ya-ma-u.
ケンイニオソレテウヤマウ

889. *Tell your father that I will take all the shirtings he has for sale.*
So-no u-ri-mo-no no ka-na-ki-n wo i-ku-ra go za-ri-ma-sh'-te
ソノウリモノノカナキンヲイクラ ゴザリマシシテ
mo ka-i-ma-sh'-o-o to chi-chi ni o ha-na-shi na-sa-re.
モカヒマシヤウト チ チ ニオ ハナシ ナサレ

Do. So-no u-ri-ta-i ka-na-ki-n wo i-ku-ra-de-mo ka-wo-o to chi-
ソノウリタイ カナキン ヲイクラデモ カワクト チ
chi ni ha-na-se.
チ ニ ハナセ

890. *Ten brave men are better than a hundred cowards.*
O-ku-bi-o-o mo-no h'-a-ku ni-n yo-ri mo ji-u ni-n tsz-yo-ki mo-
オクヒヤウモノ ヒヤクニン ヨリ モジウニンツ ヨキモ
no nga ma-shi de go za-ri-ma-s'.
ノガ マシデ ゴ ザリマス

Do. O-ku-bi-o-o mo-no h'-a-ku ni-n yo-ri mo ji-u ni-n tsz-yo-
オクヒヤウモノ ヒヤクニン ヨリ モジウニンツ ヨ
i mo-no nga ma-shi-da.
ヒモノ ガ マシタ

891. *Thank you.*
A-ri-nga-to-o go za-ri-ma-s'.
アリガトウ ゴ ザリマス
Do. Ka-ta-ji-ke na-i.
カタジケナイ

892. *That will do.*
So-re de yo-ro-shi-u go za-ri-ma-s'.
ソレデ ヨロシウ ゴザリマス
Do. So-re de yo-i.
ソレ デ ヨイ

893. *That is right.* (not wrong)
So-re nga yo-ro-shi-u go za-ri-ma-s'.
ソレガ ヨロシウ ゴ ザリマス
Do. So-re nga yo-i.
ソレ ガ ヨイ

894. *That is right.* (correct)
So-re nga ma-ko-to de go za-ri-ma-s'.
ソレガ マコト デゴ ザリマス
Do. So-re nga ho-n-to-o da.
ソレガ ホントウダ

895. *That is wrong.* (morally)
So-re nga yo-ko-shi-ma de go za-ri-ma-s'.
ソレガ ヨコシマデ ゴ ザリマス
Do. So-re nga yo-ko-shi-ma da.
ソレ ガ ヨコシマタ

896. *That is the worst of all.*
Mi-na no u-chi de so-re wa i-chi-ba-n wa-ru-u go za-ri-ma-s'.
ミナ ノ ウチデ ソレ ハ イチバン ワルウ ゴザリマス

896. Mi-na no u-chi de so-re wa i-chi-ba-n wa-ru-i.
ミナノウチデソレハイチバンワルイ

897. *That is a Chinese custom.*
A-re 'wa Mo-ro-ko-shi ho-o-sh'-ki de go za-ri-ma-s'.
アレハモロコシホウシキデゴザリマス

Do. A-re wa ka-ra no ho-o-sh'-ki da.
アレハカラノホウシキダ

898. *That is not my fault.*
A-re wa wa-ta-k'-shi no tsz-mi de wa go za-ri-ma-se-n'.
アレハワタクシノツミデハゴザリマセヌ

Do. A-re wa wa-shi no tsz-mi de wa na-i.
アレハワシノツミデハナイ

899. *That is his look out.*
So-re wa a-no h'-to no ka-ka-ri de go za-ri-ma-s'.
ソレハアノヒトノカカリデゴザリマス

Do. A-re wa a-no h'-to no ka-ka-ri da.
アレハアノヒトノカカリダ

900. *That ship is out of sight.*
A-no fu-ne wa mo-u mi-e na-ku na-ri-ma-sh'-ta.
アノフ子ハモウミエナクナリマシタ

Do. A-no fu-ne wa mo-u mi-e na-ku na-t-ta.
アノフ子ハモウミエナクナッタ

901. *That is not for me to speak of.*
So-no ko-to ni wa wa-ta-k'-shi wa na-ni to-mo mo-o-sa-re-ma-se-n.
ソノコトニハワタクシハナニトモマウサレマセン

Do. So-re ni wa wa-shi wa na-ni to-mo i-wa-re-nu.
ソレニハクシハナニトモイワレヌ

902. *That is not true.*
So-re wa ma-ko-to de go za-ri-ma-sen
ソレハマコトデゴザリマセン

Do. So-re wa ho-n-to de wa na-i.
ソレハホントデハナイ

903. *That was not my meaning.*
A-re wa wa-ta-k'-shi no ko-ko-ro-dza-shi de go za-ri-ma-se-n'.
アレハワタクシノココロザシデゴザリマセヌ

Do. A-re wa wa-shi no ko-ko-ro-dza-shi de wa na-i.
アレハワシノココロザシデハナイ

904. *That is very useful.*
So-re wa o-o-ki-ni ya-ku-ni-ta-chi-ma-sz-ru.
ソレハオホキニヤクニタチマスル

Do. A-re wa ta-n-to ya-ku-ni-ta-tsz.
アレハタントヤクニタツ

905. *That is the custom.*
So-re wa sa-ho-o de go za-ri-ma-s'.
ソレ ハ サホウ デ ゴ ザリマス

Do.　A-re wa sa-ho-o da.
アレ ハ サホウ ダ

906. *That will not do; it is too short.*
A-ma-ri mi-ji-ko-o go za-ri-ma-s' ka-ra, a-re de wa de-ki-ma-se-n'.
アマリ ミジコウ ゴ ザリマス カラ アレ デ ハ デキマセヌ

Do.　A-ma-ri mi-ji-ka-i ka-ra a-re de wa de-ki na-i.
アマリ ミジカイ カラ アレ デ ハ デキナイ

907. *That is not half so good as this.*
A-re wa ko-no go bu do-o-ri ho-do yo-ro-sh'-ku go za-ri-ma-se-n.
アレ ハ コノ ゴブ ドウリ ホド ヨロシク ゴ ザリマセン

Do.　A-re wa ko-no go bu do-o-ri wa-ru-i.
アレ ハ コノ ゴブ ドウリ ワルイ

908. *That man is sea-sick.*
A-no h'-to wa fu-ne ni yo-i-ma-sh'-ta.
アノ ヒト ハ フ子 ニ ヨイマシタ

Do.　A-no h'-to wa fu-ne ni yo-t-ta.
アノ ヒト ハ フ子 ニ ヨッタ

909. *That is all he cares for.*
A-no h'-to wa so-re ba-ka-ri ni mi wo i-re-ma-s'.
アノ ヒト ハ ソレ バカリ ニ ミ ヲ イレマス

Do.　A-re wa so-re ba-ka-ri ni mi wo i-re-ru.
アレ ハ ソレ バカリ ニ ミ ヲ イレル

910. *That is just what he is good for.*
So-no ko-to wa a-no h'-to no mo-chi-ma-i ni ch'-o-do yo-ro-shi-u go za-ri-ma-s'
ソノ コト ハ アノ ヒト ノ モチ マイ ニ テウド ヨロシウ ゴ ザリマス

Do.　So-no ko-to wa a-re no mo-chi-ma-i ni ch'-o-do yo-i.
ソノ コト ハ アレ ノ モチ マイ ニ テウド ヨイ

911. *That man's words and actions do not differ.*
A-no o h'-to wa mo-o-shi-ma-s' ko-to to o-ko-na-i to chi-nga-i ma-se-n'.
アノ オヒト ハ モウシマス コト ト オコナヒ ト チガイ マセヌ

Do.　A-re no ku-chi to o-ko-na-i to chi-nga-wa-nu.
アレ ノ クチ ト オコナヒ ト チガワヌ

912. *That is not at all like this.*
A-re wo ko-re ni ku-ra-be-te wa s'-ko-shi mo-o-na-ji to-ko-ro
アレ ヲ コレ ニ クラベテ ハ スコシ モ オナジ トコロ

wa go za-ri-ma-se-n.
ハ ゴザリマセン

Do. A-re wo ko-re ni ku-ra-be-to s'-ko-shi mo o-na-ji to-ko-ro
アレ ヲ コレ ニ クラベテ スコシ モ オナジ トコロ
wa na-i.
ハ ナイ

913. *That was a great mistake.*
A-re wa o-o-ki-ni ma-chi-nga-i de go za-ri-ma-sh'-ta.
アレ ハ オホキニ マ チガイ デ ゴ ザリマシタ

Do. A-re wa o-o-ki-ni ma-chi-nga-i de a-t-ta.
アレ ハ オホキニ マ チガイ デ アッタ

914. *That is a great delusion.*
A-re wa o-o-ki-ni ma-yo-i de go za-ri-ma-s'.
アレ ハ オホキニ マ ヨイ デ ゴザリマス

Do. A-re wa o-o-ki-ni ma-yo-i da.
アレ ハ オホキニ マ ヨイダ

915. *That is very strange.*
A-re wa ha-na-ha-da ki-k'-wa-i no ko-to de go za-ri-ma-s'.
アレ ハ ハナハダ キクワイ ノ コト デ ゴ ザリマス

Do. A-re wa o-o-ki-ni a-ya-shi-i ko-to da.
アレ ハ オホキニ アヤ シイ コト ダ

916. *That never will be.*
A-no ko-to wa tsz-i-ni go za-ri-ma-s' ma-i.
アノ コト ハ ツイニ ゴ ザリマス マイ

Do. A-no ko-to wa ke-s'-sh'-te a-ru ma-i.
アノ コト ハ ケッシテ アルマイ

917. *That we can never do.*
So-re **wa** do-o mo wa-ta-k'-shi-do-mo ni wa de-ki-ma-se-n.
ソレ ハ ドウ モ ワタクシドモ ニ ハ デキマセン

Do. So-re wa do-o mo shi-do-mo ni wa de-ki-nu.
ソレ ハ ドウ モ ワ シド モニ ハ デキヌ

918. *That man is probably lying.*
A-no h'-to wa u-so wo i-i so-o de go za-ri-ma-s'.
アノ ヒト ハ ウソ ヲ イヒ ソウ デ ゴ ザリマス

Do. A-re wa u-so wo i-i so-o da.
アレ ハ ウソ ヲ イヒ ソウダ

919. *That looks like a fast horse.*
A-no m'-ma wa ha-ya so-o ni **mi-e-ma-s'**.
アノ ムマ ハ ハヤ ソウニ ミエマス

Do. A-no m'-ma wa ha-ya so-o ni mi-e-ru.
アノ ムマ ハ ハヤ ソウニ ミエル

920. *That man is likely to recover.*
A-no o h'-to wa na-o-ri so-o de go za-ri-ma-s'.
アノ オヒト ハ ナオリ ソウダ ゴ ザリマス

920. A-re wa na-o-ri so-o da.
アレ ハ ナオリ ソウ ダ

921. *That is none of your business.*
So-re wa a-na-ta no o ka-ma-i na-sa-ru ko-to de wa go za-
ソレ ハ アナタ ノ オカマイ ナサル コト デ ハ ゴ サ
ri-ma-se-n.
リマセン

Do. So-re wa o-ma-e no ka-ma-u ko-to de wa na-i.
ソレ ハ オマエ ノ カマウ コト デ ハ ナイ

922. *That is a pretty child.*
A-no o ko wa ki-re-i de go za-ri-ma-s'.
アノ オコ ハ キレイ デ ゴ ザリマス

Do. A-no ko wa ki-re-i da.
アノ コ ハ キレイ ダ

923. *That is no easy matter.*
A-re wa ta-ya-sz-i ko-to de wa go za-ri-ma-se-nu.
アレ ハ タヤスイ コト デ ハ ゴ ザリマセス

Do. A-re wa ya-sa-shi-i ko-to de wa na-i.
アレ ハ ヤサシイ コト デ ハ ナイ

924. *That, I cannot think of doing.*
A-no ko-to wo i-ta-so-o to o-mo-o-te mo ka-na-i-ma-se-nu.
アノ コト ヲ イタソウ ト オモウテ モ カナイマセス

Do. A-no ko-to wo shi-yo-o to o-mo-o-te mo ka-na-wa-nu.
アノ コト ヲ シヤウ ト オモウテ モ カナワス

925. *That is all wrong; begin again.*
A-re wa mi-na chi-nga-i-ma-sh'-ta ka-ra, ma-ta ha-ji-me yo-
アレ ハ ミナ チ ガイ マシタ カラ マタ ハジメ ヨ
ri o na-o-shi na-sa-re.
リ オナオシ ナサレ

Do. A-re wa mi-na chi-nga-t-ta ka-ra, ma-ta ha-ji-me yo-ri na-
アレ ハ ミナ チ ガツタ カラ マタ ハジメ ヨリ ナ
o-se.
オセ

926. *That hat is old fashioned.*
So-no ka-bu-ri mo-no wa mu-ka-shi no ka-ta-chi de go za-ri-
ソノ カブリ モノ ハ ムカシ ノ カタチ デ ゴ ザリ
ma-s'.
マス

Do. A-no ka-bu-ri mo-no wa mu-ka-shi no ka-ta da.
アノ カブリ モノ ハ ムカシ ノ カタ ダ

927. *That is not so much as its first cost.*
So-no ne-da-n de wa mo-to ne ni na-ri-ma-se-nu.
ソノ子ダン デ ハ モト子 ニ ナリマセス

Do. So-no ne de wa mo-to ne ni na-ra-nu.
ソノ子 デ ハ モト子 ニ ナラス

928. *That is all idle talk.*
So-re wa mi-na mu-e-ki no ha-na-shi de go za-ri-ma-s'.
ソレ ハ ミナ ムエキ ノ ハナシ デ ゴザリマス
Do.　A-re wa mi-na mu-da ba-na-shi da.
アレ ハ ミナ ムダ バナシ ダ

929. *That is a first rate one.*
So-re wa i-chi-ba-n yo-ro-shi-i no de go za-ri-ma-s'.
ソレ ハ イチバン ヨロシイノデ ゴザリマス
Do.　A-re wa i-chi-ba-n yo-i no da.
アレ ハ イチ バン ヨイノダ

930. *That is contrary to law.*
A-re wa ko-ku ho-o ni so-mu-i-te o-ri-ma-s'.
アレ ハ コク ホウ ニ ソムイテ オリマス
Do.　A-re wa ko-ku ho-o ni so-mu-i-te i-ru.
アレ ハ コク ホウ ニ ソムイテイル

931. *That was a great while ago.*
A-no ko-to wa o-o mu-ka-shi go za-ri-ma-sh'-ta.
アノ コト ハ オホム カシ ゴザリマシタ
Do.　A-no ko-to wa o-o mu-ka-shi a-t-ta.
アノ コト ハ オホム カシ アッタ

932. *That is a portrait of my friend.*
A-re wa wa-ta-k'-shi no ho-o-yu-u no e-sz-nga-ta de ga za-ri-ma-s'.
アレ ハ ワタクシ ノ ホウユウ ノ エスガタ デ ゴザリマス
Do.　A-re wa wa-shi nga ho-o-ba-i no e-sz nga-ta da.
アレ ハ ワシ ガ ホウバイノエス ガタダ

933. *That is my business,*
Ko-no ko-to wa wa-ta-k'-shi no mi ni ka-ka-ri-ma-s'.
コノ コト ハ ワタクシ ノ ミニ カカリマス
Do.　So-re wa wa-shi nga mi ni ka-ka-ru.
ソレ ハ ワシ ガ ミニ カカル

934. *That horse is what I say he is.*
A-no m'-ma wa wa-ta-k'-shi no mo-o-sh'-ta to-o-ri de go za-ri-ma-s'.
アノ ムマ ハ ワタクシ ノ モウシタ トオリ デ ゴザリマス
Do.　A-no m'-ma wa wa-shi nga i-t-ta to-o-ri da.
アノ ムマ ハ ワシ ガ イッタ トオリ ダ

935. *That is not the key, it does not fit.*
A-no ka-ngi wa a-i-ma-se-nu ka-ra, chi-nga-t-te o-ri-ma-s'.
アノ カギ ハ アイマセヌ カラ チ ガッテ オリマス
Do.　A-no ka-ngi wa a-wa-nu ka-ra chi-nga-t-te i-ru.
アノ カギ ハ アハヌ カラ チ ガッテイル

936. *That boy has been well brought up.*
　　A-no o ko wa yo-ku so-da-te-ra-re-ma-sh'-ta.
　　アノオコ ハ ヨク ソダテラレマシタ
Do.　A-no ko wa yo-ku so-da-te-ra-re-ta.
　　アノコ ハ ヨク ソダテラレタ

937. *That sketch was meant for a horse, but looks like a dog.*
　　A-no ga-ku wa m'-ma wo ka-i-ta ko-ko-ro de go za-ri-ma-s'
　　アノガク ハ ムマヲカイタ ココロ デゴ ザリマス
　　nga; i-nu wo ka-i-ta yo-o ni mi-e-ma-s'.
　　ガ イヌ ヲ カイタ ヤウニ ミエマス
Do.　A-no ga-ku wa m'-ma wo ka-i-ta ki da nga i-nu wo ka-i-ta yo-o ni mi-e-ru.
　　アノガク ハ ムマヲカイタ キダ ガ イヌ ヲ カイタ ヤウニ ミエル

938. *That cinnamon is not pounded fine.*
　　A-no ke-i-hi wa ma-da tsz-i-te sa-i-ma-tsz ni i-ta-shi-ma-se-nu.
　　アノ ケイヒ ハ マダ ツイテ サイマス ニ イタシ マセヌ
Do.　A-no ni-k'-ke-i wa ma-da tsz-i-te ko-ma-ka ni se-nu.
　　アノ ニッケイ ハ マダ ツイテ コマカ ニ セヌ

939. *The rich have troubles as well as the poor.*
　　To-me-ru h'-to mo ma-dz-sh'-ki h'-to mo ku-ro-o wa o-na-ji-ko-to de go za-ri-ma-s'.
　　トメル ヒト モ マヅシキ ヒト モ クロフ ハ オナジ コト デゴ ザリマス
Do.　Ka-ne-mo-chi mo bi-m-bo-o ni-n mo ku-ro-o wa o-na-ji-ko-to da.
　　カ子モチ モ ビンボウ ニン モ クロフ ハ オナジ コ トダ

940. *The lots on that street are all taken up.*
　　A-no ma-chi no ji-me-n wa mi-na mo-chi-nu-sh' nga go za-ri-ma-s'.
　　アノ マチ ノ ジメン ハ ミナ モチ ヌシ ガ ゴザ リマス
Do.　A-no ma-chi no ji-me-n wa mi-na mo-chi-nu-sh' nga a-ru.
　　アノ マチ ノ ジメン ハ ミナ モチ ヌシ ガ アル

941. *The Ainos do not improve; they are always about the same.*
　　A-i-no wa a-ra-ta-me-ru ko-to wo i-ta-shi-ma-se-nu, i-tsz-mo o-yo-so o-na-ji-ko-to de go za-ri-ma-s'.
　　アイノ ハ アラタメル コト ヲ イタシマセヌ イツモ オヨソ オナジ コト デ ゴ ザリマス

Do. **A-i-no** wa a-ra-ta-me-ru ko-to wo se-nu i-tsz-mo ta-i-nga-i
アイノハ アラタメル コト ヲ セヌ イツモ タイガイ
o-na-ji-ko-to da.
オナジコトダ

942. *The snail carries his house on his back.*
Ka-ta-tsz-mu-ri wa i-ye wo sh'-o-t-te a-ru-ki-ma-s'.
カタツムリ ハ イエ ヲ シヨツテ アルキ マス
Do. Ma-i-ma-i-tsz-bu-ri wa i-ye wo sh'-o-t-te a-ru-ku.
マイマイツブリ ハ イエ ヲ シヨツテ アルク

943. *The English are always getting up something new.*
I-ngi-ri-sz no h'-to wa i-tsz-de-mo me-dz-ra-shi-i mo-no wo
イギリス ノ ヒト ハ イツデモ メヅラシイ モノ ヲ
ka-n-nga-i i-da-shi-ma-s'.
カンガヒ イダシマス
Do. I-ngi-ri-sz no h'-to wa i-tsz-mo me-dz-ra-shi-i mo-no wo
イギリス ノ ヒト ハ イツモ メヅラシイ モノ ヲ
ka-n-nga-i da-s'.
カンガヒ ダス

944. *The price of sugar has doubled, the last month.*
Sa-to-o wa se-n nge-tsz ji-u yo-ri ne-da-n nga i-chi ba-i ni
サトウ ハ センゲツ ジウ ヨリ ネダン ガ イチ バイ ニ
na-ri-ma-sh'-ta.
ナリマシタ
Do. Sa-to-o wa se-n nge-tsz ji-u yo-ri ne nga i-chi ba-i ni na-
サトウ ハ センゲツ ジウ ヨリ ネ ガ イチ バイ ニ ナ
t-ta.
ツタ

945. *The doctor has bled him twice.*
I-sh'-a nga a-no h'-to no chi wo ni-do o to-ri na-sa-ri-ma-
イシヤ ガ アノ ヒト ノ チ ヲ ニド オ トリ ナサリ マ
sh'-ta.
シタ
Do. I-sh'-a nga a-no h'-to no chi wo ni-do to-t-ta.
イシヤ ガ アノ ヒト ノ チ ヲ ニド トツタ

946. *The lamp has gone out.*
To-mo-shi-bi nga ki-e-ma-sh'-ta.
トモシビ ガ キエマシタ
Do. To-mo-shi-bi nga ki-e-ta.
トモシビ ガ キエタ

947. *The wind has put the lamp out.*
Ka-ze nga to-mo-shi-bi wo ke-shi-ma-sh'-ta.
カゼ ガ トモシビ ヲ ケシマシタ
Do. Ka-ze nga to-mo-shi-bi wo ke-sh'-ta.
カゼ ガ トモシビ ヲ ケシタ

948. *The more you do it, the more you may.*
Sz-re-ba sz-ru ho-do ka-ngi-ri wa go za-ri-ma-se-nu.
スレバスルホドカギリハゴザリマセヌ
Do. Sh'-te mo sh'-te mo ka-ngi-ri wa na-i.
シテモシテモカギリハナイ

949. *The longer wine is kept, the better it is.*
Bu-do-o shi-u wa hi-sa-sh'-ku ka-ko-i-ma-s' ho-ko yo-ro-sh'-ku na-ri-ma-s'.
ブドウシュハヒサシクカコイマスホドヨロシクナリマス
Do. Bu-do-o shi-u wa to-shi wo ko-sz ho-do yo-ro-sh'-ku na-ru.
ブドウシュハトシヲコスホドヨロシクナル

950. *The hearts of all joyfully united to follow him.*
Ko-ko-ro wo h'-to-tsz ni sh'-te mi-na yo-ro-ko-n-de a-no h'-to ni sh'-ta-nga-i-ma-sh'-ta.
ココロヲヒトツニシテミナヨロコンデアノヒトニシタガイマシタ
Do. Ko-ko-ro wo h'-to-tsz ni sh'-te mi-na yo-ro-ko-n-de a-no h'-to ni sh'-ta-nga-t-ta.
ココロヲヒトツニシテミナヨロコンデアノヒトニシタガッタ

951. *The earth quaked.*
Ji-shi-n nga yu-ri-ma-sh'-ta.
ジシンガユリマシタ
Do. Ji-shi-n nga yu-t-ta.
ジシンガユッタ

952. *The enemy and our troops commenced the battle.*
Te-ki mi-ka-ta to ta-ta-ka-i wo ha-ji-me-ma-sh'-ta.
テキミカタトタタカイヲハジメマシタ
Do. Te-ki mi-ka-ta to ta-ta-ka-i wo ha-ji-me-ta.
テキミカタトタタカイヲハジメタ

953. *The carpenter will probably get through to-day.*
Da-i-ku wa ko-n-ni-chi shi-ma-i so-o de go za-ri-ma-s'.
ダイクハコンニチシマイソウデゴザリマス
Do. Da-i-ku nga ki-o-o wa shi-ma-i so-o da.
ダイクガキヤウハシマイソウダ

954. *The sun sets in the west.*
Hi wa ni-shi ni i-ri-ma-s'.
ヒハニシニイリマス
Do. Hi wa ni-shi ni i-ru.
ヒハニシニイル

955. *The water here is up to your chin.*
Ko-no to-ko-ro wa a-na-ta no a-ngo ma-de mi-dz nga go za-ri-ma-s'.
コノトコロハアナタノアゴマデミヅガゴザリマス

955. Ko-ko wa o-ma-e no a-ngo ma-de mi-dz nga a-ru.
ココハオマエノアゴマデミツガアル

956. *The water here is over your head.*
Ko-no to-ko-ro no mi-dz wa a-na-ta no se-i nga ta-chi-ma-se-n'.
コノトコロノミヅハアナタノセイガタチマセス

Do. Ko-ko no mi-dz wa o-ma-e no se-i nga ta-ta-nu.
ココノミヅハオマエノセイガタタヌ

957. *The mud is ankle deep.*
Nu-ka-ru-mi wa a-shi ku-bi ma-de go za-ri-ma-s'.
ヌカルミハアシクビマデゴザリマス

Do. Nu-ka-ru-mi wa a-shi ku-bi ma-de ha-e-ru.
ヌカルミハアシクビマデハエル

958. *The man has been given up by the doctor.*
Ko-no o-ka-ta wa i-sh'-a ni mi ha-na-sa-re-ma-sh'-ta.
コノオカタハイシヤニミハナサレマシタ

Do. Ko-no h'-to wa i-sh'-a ni mi ha-na-sa-re-ta.
コノヒトハイシヤニミハナサレタ

959. *The greater part are good.*
Ta-i-nga-i wa yo-ro-shi-u go za-ri-ma-s'.
タイガイハヨロシウゴザリマス

Do. Ta-i-nga-i wa yo-ro-shi-i.
タイガイハヨロシイ

960. *The salt is almost gone.*
Shi-wo nga s'-ko-shi ni na-ri-ma-sh'-ta.
シホガスコシニナリマシタ

Do. Shi-wo nga-s'-ko-shi ni na-tta.
シホガスコシニナツタ

961. *The cat has caught a rat.*
Ne-ko nga ne-dz-mi wo i-p-pi-ki to-ri-ma-sh'-ta.
ネコガネヅミヲイツピキトリマシタ

Do. Ne-ko nga ne-dz-mi wo i-p-pi-ki to-tta.
ネコガネヅミヲイツピキトツタ

962. *The other is just right.*
A-chi-ra no wa ch'-o-do yo-ro-shi-u go za-ri-ma-s'.
アチラノハチヨホドヨロシウゴザリマス

Do. A-chi no wa ch'-o-do yo-i.
アチノハチヨホドヨイ

963. *The other is better than this.*
Ko-re yo-ri a-chi-ra no nga yo-ro-shi-u go za-ri-ma-s'.
コレヨリアチラノガヨロシウゴザリマス

Do. Ko-re yo-ri-a-chi no nga yo-i.
コレヨリアチノガヨイ

964. *The bait is all used up.*
E-sa wa ts'-ka-t-te shi-ma-i-ma-sh'-ta.
エサ ハ ツカッテ シマイマシタ
Do.   E-sa wa ts'-ka-t-te shi-ma-t-ta.
エサ ハ ツカッテ シマッタ

965. *The rice is all gone.*
Ko-me nga na-ku-na-ri-ma-sh'-ta.
コメ ガ ナクナリマシタ
Do.   Ko-me nga na-ku-na-t-ta.
コメ ガ ナクナッタ

966. *The table is too high.*
Da-i nga ta-ka sz-ngi-ma-s'.
ダイ ガ タカ スギマス
Do.   Da-i nga ta-ka sz-ngi-ru.
ダイ ガ タカ スギル

967. *The clock has stopped.*
To-ke-i nga to-ma-ri-ma-sh'-ta.
トケイ ガ トマリマシタ
Do.   To-ke-i nga to-ma-t-ta.
トケイ ガ トマッタ

968. *The next may read.*
So-no tsz-ngi no h'-to o-yo-mi na-sa-re.
ソノ ツギ ノ ヒト オヨミ ナサレ
Do.   Tsz-ngi no h'-to yo-me.
ツギ ノ ヒト ヨメ

969. *The mountain flowers are scattered by the wind.*
Bo-ta-n no ha-na nga ka-ze ni chi-ri-ma-sh'-ta.
ボタン ノ ハナ ガ カゼニ チリマシタ
Do.   Bo-ta-n no ha-na nga ka-ze de chi-t-ta.
ボタン ノ ハナ ガ カゼデ チッタ

970. *The more I see of him the less I like him.*
Wa-ta-k'-shi a-no h'-to no o-ko-na-i wa mi-re-ba mi-ru ho-do
ワタクシ アノ ヒト ノ オコナヒ ハ ミレバ ミルホド
na-wo ki ni i-ri-ma-se-n.
ナヲ キ ニ イリマセン
Do.   A-re no sz-ru ko-to wa mi-re-ba, mi-ru bo-do na-wo ki
アレノ スル コト ハ ミレバ ミルホド ナヲ キ
ni i-ra-nu.
ニ イラヌ

971. *The tears fell like rain.*
A-me no yo-o ni na-mi-da nga o-chi-ma-sh'-ta.
アメ ノ ヤウニ ナミダ ガ オチマシタ
Do.   Na-mi-da nga a-me no yo-o ni o-chi-ta.
ナミダ ガ アメ ノ ヤウニ オチタ

972. There is no oil.
A-bu-ra nga mo-o go za-ri-ma-se-n'.
アブラ ガ モウ ゴ ザリマセヌ
Do. A-bu-ra nga mo-o na-i.
アブラ ガ モウ ナイ

973. There is not quite enough.
S'-ko-shi fu-so-ku de go za-ri-ma-s'.
スコシ フソク デ ゴ ザリマス
Do. S'-ko-shi ta-ra-nu.
スコシ タラヌ

974. There is nothing there.
So-ko ni wa na-ni mo go za-ri-ma-se-n.
ソコニ ハ ナニ モ ゴ ザリマセン
Do. So-ko ni wa na-ni mo na-i.
ソコニ ハ ナニ モ ナイ

975. There are thousands of them.
So-no yo-o-na mo-no wa sz ma-n go za-ri-ma-s'.
ソノヤウナ モノ ハ スマン ゴ ザリマス
Do. So-no yo-o-na mo-no wa sz-ma-n da.
ソノヤウナ モノ ハ スマンダ

976. There are but few left.
S'-ko-shi ba-ka-ri no-ko-sh'-te go za-ri-ma-s'.
スコシ バカリ ノコシテ ゴザリマス
Do. S'-ko-shi ba-ka-ri no-ko-sh'-te a-ru.
スコシ バカリ ノコシテ アル

977. There is not light enough here.
Ko-ko ni wa a-ka-ri nga fu-so-ku de go za-ri-ma-s'.
ココニ ハ アカリ ガ フソク デ ゴザリマス
Do. Ko-ko ni wa a-ka-ri nga ta-ra-nu.
ココニ ハ アカリ ガ タラヌ

978. There is no doubt of it.
Ko-re wa u-ta-nga-i wa go za-ri-ma-se-nu.
コレ ハ ウタガイ ハ ゴ ザリマセヌ
Do. Ko-re wa u-ta-nga-i wa na-i.
コレ ハ ウタガイ ハ ナイ

979. There is sickness in my family.
Wa-ta-k'-shi no ka-na-i no u-chi ni bi-o-o sh'a go za-ri-ma-s'.
ワタクシ ノ カナイ ノ ウチ ニ ビヤウシヤ ゴ ザリマス
Do. Wa-shi no ka-na-i no u-chi ni wa-dz-ra-t-te i-ru mo-no nga a-ra.
ワシ ノ カナイ ノ ウチ ニ ワヅラッテ イル モノ ガ アル

980. *There are but three words that end in mui, viz. samui, nemui, and kemui.*
Sh'-ta ni *mu-i* to ts'-ku ko-to-ba wa mi-tsz ba-ka-ri shi-ra go
シタニムイトツクコトバハ三ツバカリシラゴ
za-ri-ma se-n', sa-mu-i, ne-mu-i, ke-mu-i no-mi.
ザリマセスサムイ子ムイケムイノ三

Do. Sh'-ta ni *mu-i* to ts'-ku ko-to-ba wa mi-tsz ba-ka-ri sh'-ka
シタニムイトツクコトバハ三ツバカリシカ
na-i, sa-mu-i, ne-mu-i, ke-mu-i.
ナイサムイ子ムイケムイ

981. *There is no body to blame but yourself.*
A-na-ta h'-to-ri no tsz-mi de go za-ri-ma-s' ho-ka no h'-to
アナタヒトリノツミデゴザリマスホカノヒト
no a-dz-ka-ru ko-to de wa go za-ri-ma-se-n'.
ノアヅカルコトデハゴザリマセス

Do. O-ma-e h'-to-ri no tsz-mi de ho-ka no h'-to no to-mo-ni
オマエヒトリノツ三デホカノヒトノトモニ
sz-ru ko-to de wa na-i.
スルコトデハナイ

982. *There is two-thirds as much as there was before.*
Ta-da-i-ma wa ma-i no sa-m bu no ni bo-do go za-ri-ma-s.
タダイマハマイノサンブノニホドゴザリマス

Do. I-ma wa ma-i no sa-m bu ni bo-do a-ru.
イマハマイノサンブニホドアル

983. *There are many kinds of grapes.*
Bu-do-o no sh'-u-ru-i wa a-ma-ta go za-ri-ma-s'.
ブドウノシユルイハアマタゴザリマス

Do. Bu-do-o no ru-i wa i-ro-i-ro a-ru.
ブドウノルイハイロイロアル

984. *There are not more than 50 at most.*
Ka-dz nga o-o ke-re-ba go ji-u ho-do go za-ri-ma-sh'-o-o.
カヅガオホケレバゴジウホドゴザリマシヤウ

Do. O-o ke-re-ba go ji-u ho-do a-ru de a-ro-o.
オホケレバゴジウホドアルデアロフ

·985. *There is to be a great wedding next week.*
Ko-no tsz-ngi no na-no-ka ni wa go ko-n-re-i nga go za-
コノツギノナノカニハゴコンレイガゴザ
ri-ma-s'.
リマス

Do. Ko-no tsz-ngi no na-no-ka ni wa go ko-n-re-i nga a-ru
コノツギノナノカニハゴコンレイガアル

986. *There is no hope of his getting well.*
A-no o h'-to no ya-ma-i wa na-o-ro-o to wa o-mo-wa-re-ma-
アノオヒトノヤマイハナヲロウトハオモハレツ
se-n.
セン

986. A-re no ya-ma-i wa na-o-ro-o to wa o-mo-wa-re-nu.
アレノヤマイハナヲロウト ハオモハレヌ

987. *There is too little to be of any use.*
A-ma-ri s'-ko-shi yu-e na-ni no ya-ku ni mo ta-chi-ma-se-nu.
アマリスコシユエナニノ ヤクニモタチマセヌ

Do. A-ma-ri chi-t-to yu-e na-ni no yo-o ni mo ta-ta-nu.
アマリチツトユエナニノヤクニモタタヌ

988. *There is not a good one among them.*
Ko-no na-ka ni wa h'-to-tsz mo yo-ro-shi-i no wa go za-ri-ma-se-n'.
コノ ナカ ニハ ヒトチモ ヨロシイノハ ゴ ザリマセン

Do. Ko-no na-ka ni wa h'-to-tsz mo yo-i no wa na-i.
コノナカニハヒトツモヨイノハナイ

989. *There is to be a man executed to-day.*
Ko-n-ni-chi wa h'-to-ri shi-za-i ni o-ko-no-wa-re-ma-sh'-o-o.
コンニチハヒトリシザイニオコノハレマシヤウ

Do. Ko-n-ni-chi wa h'-to-ri shi-za-i ni a-ro-o.
コンニチハヒトリシザイニアロフ

990. *There is a picul and so much over.*
Hi-a-k' ki-n no ho-ka-ni ma-ta ko-re ho-do go za-ri-ma-s'.
ヒヤツキンノホカニマタ コレ ホド ゴザリマス

Do. Hi-a-k' ki-n no ho-ka-ni ma-ta ko-re ho-do a-ru.
ヒアツキンノホカニ マタ コレ ホド アル

991. *There is nothing to hang it on.*
Ka-ke-ru to-ko-ro nga go za-ri-ma-se-n'.
カケルトコロガ ゴ ザリマセヌ

Do. Ka-ke-ru to-ko-ro nga na-i.
カケルトコロガナイ

992. *These two look alike.*
Ko-re wa f'-ta-tsz to-mo o-na-ji yo-o ni mi-e-ma-s'.
コレハフタツトモオナジヤフニミエマス

Do. Ko-re wa f'-ta-tsz to-mo o-na-ji yo-o ni mi-e-ru.
コレハフタツトモオナジヤフニミエル

993. *These are not good to eat.*
Ko-re wo o a-ngo-ri na-sa-re-te wa yo-ro-sh'-ku go za-ri-ma-se-n'.
コレヲオアガリナサレテハヨロシクゴザリマセヌ

Do. Ko-re wo ku-u-te wa wa-ru-i.
コレヲクウテハワルイ

994. *These horses are well matched.*
Ko-no f'-ta-tsz no m'-ma wa ta-nga-i ni yo-ku ni-te o-ri-ma-s'.
コノフタツ ノムマ ハタガイニ ヨクニテオリマス

994. Ko-no f'-ta-tsz no m'-ma wa ta-nga-i ni yo-ku ni-te i-ru.
コノフタツノムマハタンガイニヨクニテイル

995. *These children look like twins.*
Ko-no ko-do-mo wa f'-ta-ngo to mi-e-ma-s'.
コノコドモハフタガ ト ミエマス

Do. Ko-no ko-do-mo wa f'-ta-ngo to mi-e-ru.
コノコドモハフタゴ ト ミエル

996. *This is hard work.*
Ko-no shi-ka-ta wa mu-dz-ka-shi-u go za-ri-ma-s'.
コノシカタハムヅカシウゴザリマス

Do. Ko-no shi-ka-ta wa mu-dz-ka-shi-i.
コノシカタハムヅカシイ

997. *This is easy work.*
Ko-no shi-ka-ta wa ya-sa-shi-u go za-ri-ma-s'.
コノシカタハヤサシウゴザリマス

Do. Ko-no shi-ka-ta wa ya-sa-shi-i.
コノシカタハヤサシイ

998. *This milk is half water.*
Ko-no chi-chi wa ha-m-bu-n mi-dz nga ma-ji-t-te o-ri-ma-s'.
コノチチハハンブン ミヅ ガ マジツテオリマス

Do. Ko-no chi-chi wa ha-m-bu-n mi-dz nga ma-ji-t-te i-ru.
コノチチハハンブンミヅ ガ マジツテイル

999. *This is too large.*
Ko-re wa o-o-ki sz-ngi-ma-s'.
コノハオホキスギマス

Do. Ko-re wa a-ma-ri o-o-ki-i.
コレハアマリオホキイ

1000. *This and that are different.*
Ko-re to so-re to wa chi-nga-i-ma-s'.
コレトソレトハチガイマス

Do. Ko-re to so-re to wa chi-nga-u.
コレトソレトハチガウ

1001. *This boy is all for play.*
Ko-no ko wa i-tsz-de-mo na-ma-ke-te o-ri-ma-s'.
コノコハイツデモナマケテオリマス

Do. Ko-no ko wa i-tsz-de-mo na-ma-ke-te i-ru.
コノコハイツデモナマケテイル

1002. *This cloth cost me seven kobangs.*
Ko-no ta-m-mo-no wa sh'-chi ri-o de ka-i-ma-sh'-ta.
コノタンモノハシ チリヤウデカイマシタ

Do. Ko-no ta-m-mo-no wa sh'-chi ri-o de ka-t-ta.
コノタンモノハシ チリヤウデカッタ

1003. *This coat does not fit me.*
Ko-no ha-o-ri wa yu-ki-ta-ke nga a-i-ma-se-nu.
コノハオリハユキタケ ガアイマセヌ

1003. Ko-no ha-o-ri wa yu-ki-ta-ke nga a-wa-nu.
コノハオリハ ユキタケ ガ アハヌ

1004. *This oil won't burn it has something in it.*
Ko-no a-bu-ra wa ma-ze-mo-no nga a-ru ka-ra ta-chi-ngi-e
コノアブラ ハ マゼモノ ガ アル カラ タチギエ
nga i-ta-shi-ma-s'.
ガ イタシマス

Do. Ko-no a-bu-ra wa ma-ze-mo-no nga a-ru ka-ra, ta-che-
コノアブラ ハ マゼモノ ガ アルカラ タチ
ngi-e nga sz-ru.
ギエ ガ スル

1005. *This tea is too weak.*
Ko-no ch'-a wa u-sz sz-ngi-ma-s'.
コノチャ ハ ウスス ギマス

Do. Ko-no ch'-a wa u-sz sz-ngi-ru.
コノチャ ハ ウスス ギル

1006. *This meat is not done.*
Ko-no ni-ku wa ma-da hi nga to-o-ri-ma-se-n'.
コノニク ハ マダ ヒ ガ トヲリマセン

Do. Ko-no ni-ku wa ma-da hi nga to-o-ra-nu.
コノニク ハ マダ ヒ ガ トヲラヌ

1007. *This meat is not boiled enough.*
Ko-no ni-ku wa na-ma ni-e de go za-ri-ma-s'.
コノニクハ ナマ ニエデ ゴ ザリマス

Do. Ko-no ni-ku wa na-ma ni-e da.
コノニクハ ナマ ニエダ

1008. *This meat is not baked enough.*
Ko-no ni-ku wa na-ma ya-ke de go za-ri-ma-s'.
コノニクハナマ ヤケデ ゴ ザリマス

Do. Ko-no ni-ku wa na-ma ya-ke-da.
コノニクハナマ ヤケダ

1009. *This is all news to me.*
Ko-re wa wa-ta-k'-shi ni wa me-dz-ra-shi-i-ko-to de go za-
コレ ハ ワタクシニ ハ メヅラシイコト デ ゴ ザ
ri-ma-s'.
リマス

Do. Ko-re wa wa-shi ni wa me-dz-ra-shi-i ko-to da.
コレ ハ ワシニ ハ メヅラシイコト ダ

1010. *This well is very deep.*
Ko-no i-do wa ta-i-so-o-ni f-ko-o go za-ri-ma-s'.
コノイド ハ タイソウニ フカウ ゴ ザリマス

Do. Ko-no i-do wa ta-i-so-o f-ka-i.
コノイド ハ タイソウ フカイ

1011. *This is still worse.*
Ko-re wa na-wo wa-ru-u go za-ri-ma-s'.
コレ ハ ナヲ ワルウ ゴ ザリマス

1011. Ko-re wa na-wo wa-ru-i.
コレハナヲワルイ

1012. *This room is too small.*
Ko-no he-ya wa se-ma sz-ngi-ma-s'.
コノヘヤハセマスギマス
Do. Ko-no he-ya wa a-ma-ri se-ma-i.
コノヘヤハアマリセマイ

1013. *This is just what I want.*
Ko-re wa wa-ta-k'-shi no ch'-o-do i-ru shi-na de go za-ri-ma-s'.
コレハワタクシノチャウドイルシナデゴザリマス
Do. Ko-re wa wa-shi no ch'-o-do i-ru shi-na da.
コレハワシノチャウドイルシナダ

1014. *This book is out of print.*
Ko-no sh'-o-mo-tsz wa dze-p-pan i-ta-shi-ma-sh'-ta.
コノシヨモツハゼッパンイタシマシタ
Do. Ko-no sh'-o-mo-tsz no ha-n wa na-ku-na-ri-ma-sh'-ta.
コノシヨモツハハンガナクナリマシタ

1015. *This is a bad dollar.*
Ko-no do-ra wa gi-n no sh'-o nga wa-ru-u go za-ri-ma-s'.
コノドラハギンノセウガワルウゴザリマス
Do. Ko-no do-ra wa gi-n no sh'-o nga wa-ru-i.
コノドラハギンノセウガワルイ

1016. *This is his favorite child.*
Ko-no ko-do-mo wa a-no o ka-ta no i-chi-ba-n a-i-shi de go za-ri-ma-s'.
コノコドモハアノオカタノイチバンアイシデゴザリマス
Do. Ko-no ko-do-mo wa a-no h'-to no i-chi-ba-n ka-wa-i-nga-ru ko da.
コノコドモハアノヒトノイチバンカワイガルコダ

1017. *This is not well done.*
Ko-re wa yo-ku ts'-ku-ri-e-ma-se-n'.
コレハヨクツクリエマセス
Do. Ko-re wa yo-ku ko-shi-ra-i-e-nu.
コレハヨクコシライエヌ

1018. *This tree has begun to bear fruit this year.*
Ko-no ki wa ko-n ne-n ha-ji-me-te mi nga na-ri-ma-sh'-ta.
コノキハコンチンハジメテミガナリマシタ

1019. *This is rather better than that.*
So-re yo-ri ko-re wa s'-ko-shi yo-ro-shi-u go za-ri-ma-s'
ソレヨリコレハスコシヨロシウゴザリマス

1019. A-re yo-ri ko-re wa s'-ko-shi yo-i.
アレヨリコレハスコシヨイ

1020. *This is the best.*
Ko-re wa i-chi-ba-n yo-ro-shi-u go za-ri-ma-s'.
コレハイチバンヨロシウゴザリマス

Do. Ko-re wa i-chi-ba-n yo-ro-shi-i.
コレハイチバンヨロシイ

1021. *This is mine.*
Ko-re wa wa-ta-k'-shi no de go za-ri-ma-s'.
コレハワタクシノデゴザリマス

Do. Ko-re wa wa-shi no da.
コレハワシノダ

1022. *This is the one.*
Ko-re de go za-ri-ma-s'.
コレデゴザリマス

Do. Ko-re da.
コレダ

1023. *This is good for nothing.*
Ko-re wa ya-ku ni ta-chi-ma-se-nu.
コレハヤクニタチマセヌ

Do. Ko-re wa ya-ku ni ta-ta-nu.
コレハヤクニタタヌ

1024. *This hoe is more handy than that.*
So-no ku-wa yo-ri ko-no ho-o nga ts'-ka-i yo-o go za-ri-ma-s'.
ソノクワヨリコノホウガ ツカヒ ヨウゴザリマス

Do. So-no ku-wa yo-ri ko-no ho-o nga ts'-ka-i i-i.
ソノクワヨリコノホウガ ツカヒイイ

1025. *This coffee is not well roasted.*
Ko-no *ka-he* wa ma-da na-ma i-ri de go za-ri-ma-s'.
コノカヘハマダナマイリデゴザリマス

Do. Ko-no *ka-he* wa ma-da i-re-nu.
コノカヘハマダイレヌ

1026. *This is made exactly to my mind.*
Ko-re wa ch'-o-do wa-ta-k'-shi no o-mo-o to-o-ri ni ts'-ku-re-ma-sh'-ta.
コレハチヤウドワタクシノ オモフトヲリニツクレマシタ

Do. Ko-re wa ch'-o-do wa-shi no o-mo-o to-o-ri ni ko-shi-ra-e-ta.
コレハチヤウドワシノオモフトヲリニコシラエタ

1027. *This must be well attended to; don't neglect it.*
Ko-re ni ko-ko-ro dz-ke-te k'-tto ma-mo-t-te o-ri-ma-s';
コレニココロヅケテキット マモッテオリマス

yu-da-n wa na-ra-dz.
ユダン ハ ナラズ

Do. Ko-re ni ki wo ts'-ke-te k'-t-to mi-te i-ru yu-da-n na-ra-nu.
コレニ キ ヲ ツケテ キット ミテ イル ユダン ナラヌ

1028. *This table is warped.*
Ko-no da-i wa so-ri-ma-sh'-ta.
コノ ダイ ハ ソリマシタ

Do. Ko-no da-i wa so-t-ta.
コノ ダイ ハ ソッタ

1029. *This is better than nothing.*
Ko-re wa na-i ni wa ma-sa-ri-ma-s'.
コレ ハ ナイ ニ ハ マサリマス

Do. Ko-re wa na-i nga ma-shi da.
コレ ハ ナイ ガ マシダ

1030. *This money does not pass here.*
Ko-no ka-ne wa ko-ko de wa tsz-yo-o i-ta-shi-ma-se-n'.
コノ カ子 ハ ココ デ ハ ツヨウ イタシマセン

Do. Ko-no ka-ne wa ko-ko de wa tsz-yo-e se-nu.
コノ カ子 ハ ココ デ ハ ツヨウ セヌ

1031. *This horse is no match for that.*
Ko-no m'-ma wa so-no m'-ma ni o-yo-bi-ma-se-nu.
コノ ムマ ハ ソノ ムマ ニ オヨビマセヌ

Do. Ko-no m'-ma wa so-no m'-ma ni o-yo-ba-nu.
コノ ムマ ハ ソノ ムマ ニ オヨバヌ

1032. *This house needs repairs.*
Ko-no i-ye wa sh'-yu-f'-ku i-ta-sh'-to-o go za-ri-ma-s'.
コノ イエ ハ シユフク イタシトウ ゴザリマス

Do. Ko-no u-chi wo sh'-yu-f'-ku sh'-ta-i.
コノ ウチ ヲ シユフク シタイ

1033. *This is a good looking one.*
Ko-no h'-to-tsz wa yo-ro-sh'ku mi-e-ma-s'.
コノ ヒトツ ハ ヨロシク ミエマス

Do. Ko-no h'-to-tsz wa yo-ku-mi-e-ru.
コノ ヒトツ ハ ヨク ミエル

1034. *This board is uneven.*
Ko-no i-ta wa u-ne-t-te o-ri-ma-s'.
コノ イタ ハ ウ子ッテ オリマス

Do. Ko-no i-ta wa u-ne-t-te i-ru.
コノ イタ ハ ウ子ッテ イル

1035. *This kind is not common.*
Ko-no yo-o-na mo-no wa tsz-ne ni go za-ri-ma-s'.
コノ ヤウナ モノ ハ ツ子ニ ゴザリマス

Do. Ko-o yu-u mo-no wa tsz-ne ni nu-i.
コオ ユウ モノ ハ ツ子ニ ナイ

1036. *This large dictionary is full of words.*
　　Ko-no o-o ji-bi-ki wa ko-to-ba nga s'-ki-ma na-ku shi-ru-sh'-te
　　コノオホジビキハコトバガスキマナクシルシテ
　　go za-ri-ma-s'.
　　ゴザリマス

Do.　Ko-no o-o ji-bi-ki wa ko-to-ba nga s'-ki-ma na-ku ka-i-
　　コノオホジビキハコトバガスキマナクカイ
　　te a-ru.
　　テアル

1037. *This money chest is left open.*
　　Ko-no ka-ne ba-ko wa f'-ta nga hi-ra-i-te go za-ri-ma-s'.
　　コノカ子バコハフタガヒライテゴザリマス

Do.　Ko-no ka-ne ba-ko wa f'-ta nga a-i-te a-ri-ma-s'.
　　コノカ子バコハフタガアイテアリマス

1038. *This tree appears to be dying.*
　　Ko-no ki wa ka-re so-o ni mi-e-ma-s'.
　　コノキハカレソウニミエマス

Do.　Ko-no ki wa ka-re so-o ni mi-e-ru.
　　コノキハカレソウニミエル

1039. *This is just like the other.*
　　Ko-re wa so-re ni ku-ra-be-ru to ch'-o-do o-na-ji-ko-to de
　　コレハソレニクラベルトチヨウトオナジコトデ
　　go za-ri-ma-s'.
　　ゴザリマス

1040. *This is the only one I have.*
　　Wa-ta-k'-shi wa ko-re h'-to-tsz ngi-ri de go za-ri-ma-s'.
　　ワタクシハコレヒトツギリデゴザリマス

Do.　Wa-shi wa mo ko-re h'-to-tsz ngi-ri da
　　ワシハモコレヒトツギリダ

1041. *This thread is very fine.*
　　Ko-no i-to wa ha-na-ha-da ho-so-o go za-ri-ma-s'.
　　コノイトハハナハダホソウゴザリマス

Do.　Ko-no i-to wa o-o-ki ni ho-so-i.
　　コノイトハオホキニホソイ

1042. *This will cure the tooth ache.*
　　Ko-re wo ts'-ke-ru to ha no i-ta-mi nga na-o-ri-ma-s'.
　　コレヲツケルトハノイタミガナオリマス

Do.　Ko-re wo ts'-ke-ru to ha no i-ta-mi nga na-o-ru.
　　コレヲツケルトハノイタミガナオル

1043. *This is not equal to that.*
　　Ko-re to a-re to wa i-chi-yo-o de wa go za-ri-ma-se-n'.
　　コレトアレトハイチヨウデハゴザリマセン

Do.　Ko-re to so-re to wa o-na-ji-ko-to de wa na-i.
　　コレトソレトハオナジコトデハナイ

1044. *This coffee is not well settled.*
Ko-no ka-he wa ma-da yo-ku o-do-mi-ma-se-n'.
コノカヘハマダヨクオドミマセン
Ko-no ka-he wa ma-da yo-ku o-do-ma-nu.
コノカヘハマダヨクオドマヌ

1045. *This is very much like the other.*
Ko-re wa a-re ni yo-ku ni-te o-ri-ma-s'.
コレハアレニヨクニテオリマス
Do.　Ko-re wa a-re ni yo-ku ni-te i-ru.
コレハアレニヨクニテイル

1046. *This is the one I had before.*
Ko-re wa wa-ta-k'-shi ko-no ma-i mo-t-te o-ri-ma-sh'-ta de go za-ri-ma-s'.
コレハワタクシコノマイモッテオリマシタデゴザリマス
Do.　Ko-re wa wa-ta-k'-shi ko-no ma-i mo-t-te i-ta no da.
コレハワタクシコノマイモッテイタノダ

1047. *This has been of great use to me.*
Ko-re wa wa-ta-k'-shi no ta-me-ni ha-na-ha-da ya-ku ni ta-chi ma-sh'-ta.
コレハワタクシノタメニハナハダヤクニタチマシタ
Do.　Ko-re wa wa-shi no ta-me-ni ta-i-so o ya-ku ni ta-t-ta.
コレハワシノタメニタイソウヤクニタッタ

1048. *This is the first time I have had the honor to see you.*
Ta-da-i-ma ha-ji-me-te o me ni ka-ka-ri-ma-sh'-ta.
タダイマハジメテオメニカカリマシタ
Do.　Ta-da-i-ma ha-ji-me-te a-t-ta.
タダイマハジメテアッタ

1049. *This is the only one I ever saw.*
Ko-re ba-ka-ri wa-ta-k'-shi ko-no ma-i mi-ma-sh'-ta no de go za-ri-ma-s'
コレバカリワタクシコノマイミマシタノデゴザリマス
Do.　Ko-re ba ka-ri wa-shi nga ma-i-ka-ta mi-ta no da.
コレバカリワシガマイカタミタノダ

1050. *This is a poor soil.*
Ko-no de-n-ji wa ya-se-te o-ri-ma-s'.
コノデンヂハヤセテオリマス
Do.　Ko-no de-n-ji wa ya-se-te i-ru.
コノデンヂハヤセテイル

1051. *This is a rich soil.*
Ko-no de-n-ji wa ko-ye-te o-ri-ma-s'.
コノデンヂハコエテオリマス
Do.　Ko-no de-n-ji wa ko-ye-te i-ru.
コノデンヂハコエテイル

1052. *This rice is not thoroughly boiled.*
　　Ko-no me-shi wa shi-n ma-de ma-da ni-e-ma-se-nu.
　　コノメシハシンマデマダニエマセヌ

Do.　Ko-no me-shi wa shi-n nga a-ru.
　　コノメシハシンガアル

1053. *This clock is out of order.*
　　Ko-no to-ke-i wa ku-ru-t-te o-ri-ma-s'.
　　コノトケイハクルッテオリマス

Do.　Ko-no to-ke-i wa ku-ru-t-te i-ru.
　　コノトケイハクルッテイル

1054. *This is not a good knife; it has a flaw in it.*
　　Ko-no ko-nga-ta-na wa yo-ro-sh'-ku go za-ri-ma-se-nu, ki-dz nga a-ri-ma-s'.
　　コノコガタナハヨロシクゴザリマセスキヅガアリマス

Do.　Ko-no ko-nga-ta-na wa yo-ku na-i, ki-dz nga a-ru.
　　コノコガタナハヨクナイキヅガアル

1055. *This is the one I told you about the other day.*
　　Ko-re wa wa-ta-k'-shi nga se-n ji-tsz a-na-ta ni o ha-na-shi mo-o-sh'-ta de go za-ri-ma-s'.
　　コレハワタクシガセンジツアナタニオハナシマウシタデゴザリマス

Do.　Ko-re wa wa-shi nga ko-no a-i-da o-ma-e ni ha-na-sh'-ta no da.
　　コレハワシガコノアイダオマエニハナシタノダ

1056. *This is not good for you; do not eat it.*
　　Ko-re wa a-na-ta ni yo-ro-sh'-ku go za-ri-ma-se-n' ka-ra, o a-nga-ri na-sa-ri-ma-s'z-na.
　　コレハアナタニヨロシクゴザリマセンカラオアガリナサリマスナ

Do.　Ko-re wa o-ma-e ni yo-ku na-i ka-ra ta-be-ru-na.
　　コレハオマエニヨクナイカラタベルナ

1057. *This house was built twenty or thirty years ago.*
　　Ko-no i-ye wa ni sa-n ji-u ne-n a-to ni ts'-ku-ra-re-ma-sh'-ta.
　　コノイエハニサンジウネンアトニツクラレマシタ

Do.　Ko-no u-chi wa ni sa-n ji-u ne-n a-to-ni ts'-ku-ra-re-ta.
　　コノウチハニサンジウネンアトニツクラレタ

1058. *This is worn out; we must have a new one.*
　　Ko-re wa mo-chi-i-te ya-ku ni ta-chi-ma-se-nu ka-ra, a-ta-ra-shi-i no wo mo-to-me-ma-sh'-o-o.
　　コレハモチイテヤクニタチマセヌカラアタラシイノヲモトメマシャウ

144   T.

1058. Ko-re wa fu-ru-k'-te mo-chi-i ni na-ra-nu ka-ra a-ta-ra-
コレハフルクテモチイニナラヌカラアタラ
shi-i no wo mo-to-me-yo-o.
シイノヲモトメヨウ

1059. *This is the last day of the month.*
Ko-n ni-chi wa mi-so-ka de go za-ri-ma-s',
コンニチハミソカデゴザリマス

Do. Ki-o-o wa mi-so-ka da.
ケフハミソカダ

1060. *This kind is apt to break.*
Ko-no yo-o-na shi-na wa ji-ki ni ko-wa-re so-o de go za-
コノヤウナシナハジキニコワレソウデゴザ
ri-ma-s'.
リマス

Do. Ko-n-na mo-no wa ji-ki ni ko-wa-re so-o-da.
コンナモノハジキニコワレソウダ

1061. *This ship has made four voyages to England.*
Ko-no fu-ne wa I-ngi-ri-s' no ku-ni e yo ta-bi yu-ki ka-c
コノフネハイギリスノクニエヨタビユキカヒ
wo i-ta-shi-ma-sh'-ta.
ヲイタシマシタ

Do. Ko-no fu-ne wa I-ngi-ri-s' no ku-ni e yo ta-bi yu-ki ki
コノフニハイギリスノクニエヨタビユキキ
wo sh'-ta.
ヲシタ

1062. *This boy makes nothing of his father.*
Ko-no ko wa chi-chi wo na-i-nga-shi-ro ni na-sa-ru.
コノコハチチヲナイガシロニナサル

Do. Ko-no ko wa chi-chi wo a-ru-nga-na-shi ni sz-ru.
コノコハチチヲアルガナシニスル

1063. *This thing is not worth much, but it cost a great deal.*
Ko-no shi-na wa yo-o ni ta-tsz ko-to wa s'-ku-na-ku-te, ne-
コノシナハヨウニタツコトハスクナクテ子
da-n nga ha-na-ha-da ta-ko-o go za-ri-ma-s'.
ダンガハナハダタカウゴザリマス

Do. Ko-re wa ts'-ka-u ko-to wa s'-ku-na-ku-te ne-da-n nga o-
コレハツカフコトハスクナクテ子ダンガオ
o-ki-ni ta-ka-i.
ホキニタカイ

1064. *This is worth more than it cost.*
Ko-re wa ne-da-n yo-ri ts'ka-i-ma-s' to-ko-ro nga o-o go za-
コレハ子ダンヨリウカヒマストコロガオホゴザ
ri-ma-s'
リマス

Do. Ko-re wa ne yo-ri ts'-ka-u to-ko-ro nga o-o-i.
コレハ子ヨリツガフトコロガオホイ

1065. *This wood is so heavy that it sinks in water.*
Ko-no ki wa o-mo-i yu-e-ni mi-dz ni shi-dz-mi-ma-s'
コノキハオモイユエニミヅニシヅミマス

Do.　Ko-no ki wa o-mo-i ka-ra mi-dz ni shi-dz-mu.
コノキハオモイカラミズニシズム

1066. *Those fowls are not full grown.*
Ko-no ni-wa-to-ri wa ma-da hi-na de go za-ri-ma-s'.
コノニハトリハマダヒナデゴザリマス

Do.　Ko-no ni-wa-to-ri wa ma-da o-o-ki-ku na-ri-ma-se-nn.
コノニハトリハマダオホキクナリマセス

1067. *Those are better made than these.*
Ko-re yo-ri so-re wa yo-ku ts'-ku-ra-re-ma-sh'-ta.
コレヨリソレハヨクツクラレマシタ

Do.　Ko-re yo-ri a-re wa yo-ku ts'-ku-ra-re-ta.
コレヨリアレハヨクツクラレタ

1068. *Those men hate each other.*
A-no o ka-ta f-ta-ri wa a-i ta-nga-i ni i-mi-ma-sz-rw.
アノオカタフタリハアイタガイニイミマスル
A-no h'-to f-ta-ri wa ta-nga-i ni ki-ra-i-ma-s.'
アノヒトフタリハタガイニキライマス

1069. *Those gentlemen do not live together.*
A-no ka-ta ta-chi wa i-s-sh'-o-ni o sz-ma-i na-sa-ri-ma-se-n'.
アノカタタチハイツジヨニオスマイナサリマセン

Do.　A-no h'-to ta-chi wa i-s-shi-o-ni sz-ma-wa-nu.
アノヒトタチハイツシヨニスマハス

1070. **Those** *people are our neighbours.*
A-no ka-ta ta-chi wa wa-ta-k'-shi do-mo no to-na-ri no ka-
アノカタタチハワタクシドモノトナリノカ
ta de go za-ri-ma-s'.
タデゴザリマス

Do.　A-no h'-to ta-chi wa wa-shi do-mo no to-na-ri no h'-to da.
アノヒトタチハワシドモノトナリノヒトダ

1071. *Those coolies have come for their pay.*
A-no ni-n-so-ku nga hi-yo-o wo mo-ra-i ni ma-i-ri-ma-sh'-ta.
アノニンソクガヒヨウヲモライニマイリマシタ

Do.　A-no ni-n-so-ku nga hi-yo-o wo to-ri ni k'-ta.
アノニンソクガヒヨウヲトリニキタ

1072. *Those are all of a size.*
So-re wa mi-na o-na-ji-ko-to ni o-o ki-u go za-ri-ma-s'.
ソレハミナオナジコトニオホキウゴザリマス

Do.　A-re wa mi-na o-na-ji-ko-to ni o-o-ki-i.
アレハミナオナジコトニオホキイ

1073. *Those women with blackened teeth are married, but unmarried women from twenty years old and upwards blacken their **teeth** and shave their **eyebrows**, though prostitutes and dancing **girls** do not.*

A-no ge-m-bu-ku wo sh'-ta o-na-ngo wa yo-me-i-ri wo i-ta-
アノゲンブクヲシタオナゴハヨメイリニイタ
shi-ma-sh'-ta, shi-ka-shi na-nga-ra o-t-to no na-i o-na-ngo
シマシタシカシナガラオットノナイオナゴ
wa ha-ta-chi no sa-ki yo-ri ka-ne wo ts'-ke-te ma-yu wo
ハハタチノサキヨリカ子ヲツケテマユヲ
so-ri-ma-s'. Ke-re-do-mo yu-u-j'-o u-ka-re-me no ta-ngu-i
ソリマス　ケレドモユウジョウカレメノタグイ
wa sa-yo-o i-ta-shi-ma-se-n'.
ハサヤウイタシマセス

1074. *Those are not very good.*
A-re wa ha-na-ha-da yo-ro-shi-u go za-ri-ma-sz-nu.
アレハハナハダヨロシウゴザリマセス
Do. A-re wa o-o-ki-ni yo-ku na-i.
アレハオホキニヨクナイ

1075. *Those men are going to kill a bullock pretty soon.*
A-no h'-to ta-chi wa mo s'-ko-shi no-chi ni o-u-shi wo ko-
アノヒトタチハモスコシノチニオウシヲコ
ro-shi-ma-s'.
ロシマス
Do. A-no h'-to ta-chi wa o-shi-t-ke o-u-shi wo ko-ro-s'.
アノヒトタチハオシツケオウシヲコロス

1076. *To-morrow is pay day.*
Mi-o-o-ni-chi wa ki-u-ki-n wo wa-ta-shi-ma-s' to-ki de go za-
メウニチハギウキンヲワタシマストキデゴザ
ri-ma-s'.
リマス
Do. A-sh'-ta wa ki-u-ki-n wo wa-ta-s' to-ki da.
アシタハキウキンヲワタストキダ

1077. *Travellers are always passing Kanagawa, on their way up to Miako.*
Mi-a-ko e no-bo-ru h'-to wa i-tsz-mo Ka-na-nga-wa wo to-o-
ミヤコエノボルヒトハイツモカナガワヲトヲ
ri-ma-s'.
リマス
Do. Mi-a-ko e no-bo-ru h'-to wa i-tsz-mo Ka-na-nga-wa wo
ミヤコエノボルヒトハイツモカナガワヲ
to-o-ru.
トヲル

1078 *Tribute is paid by the king of Corea to the Taikun.*
Ch'-o-se-n no wo-o yo-ri mi-tsz-ngi wo Ta-i-ku-n ni a-nge-
テウセンノワウヨリミツギヲタイクンニアゲ
ma-s'.
マス
Do. Ch'-o-se-n no wo-o yo-ri mi-tsz-ngi wo Ta-i-ku-n ni
テウセンノワウヨリニツギヲタイクンニ

T. U. 147

o-sa-me-ru.
オサメル

1079. *Try again once more.*
Mo-o h'-to-ta-bi ko-ko-ro mi na-sa-re.
モウヒトタビココロミナサレ

Do. Mo-o i-chi-do ko-ko-ro mi-ro.
モウイチドココロミロ

1080. *Turn it bottom upwards.*
Ka-e-sh'-te o o-ki na-sa-re.
カエシテオオキナサレ

Do. Ka-e-sh'-te o-ke.
カエシテオケ

1081. *Turn it up-side down.*
U-e wo sh'-ta-ni sh'-te o o-ki na-sa-re.
ウエヲシタニシテオオキナサレ

Do. U-e wo sh'-ta-ni sh'-te o-ke.
ウエヲシタニシテオケ

1082. *Turn it inside out.*
U-ra-nga-i sh'-te o o-ki na-sa-re.
ウラガイシテオオキナサレ

Do. U-ra-nga-i sh'-te o-ke.
ウラガイシテオケ

1083. *Turn the bread; don't let it burn.*
Pa-n wo ma-wa-sh'-te ko-nge-nu yo-o ni o ya-ki na-sa-re.
パンヲマハシテコゲヌヤウニオヤキナサレ

Do. Pa-n wo ma-wa-sh'-te ko-nge-nu yo-o ni ya-ke.
パンヲマハシテコゲヌヤウニヤケ

1084. **Turn it over and over again.**
Ta-bi-ta-bi ka-e-sh'-te o o-ki na-sa-re.
タビタビカエシテオオキナサレ

Do. Do-do ka-e-sh'-te o-ki.
ドドカエシテオケ

U

1085. *Umbrellas are covered with paper, and then smeared with a bean oil.*
Ka-ra-ka-sa wa ka-mi de ha-ri-ma-sh'-te no-chi-ni e-no-a-bu-ra wo nu-ri-ma-s'.
カラカサハカミデハリマシテノチニエノアブラヲヌリマス

Do. Ka-ra-ka-sa wa ka-mi de ha-t-te, no-chi-ni e-no-a-bu-ra wo nu-ru.
カラカサハカミデハツテノチニエノアブラヲスル

1086. *Unless you pay the cash, you cannot have this article.*
A-na-ta ka-ne wo ya-ri-ma-se-nu na-ra-ba, ko-no shi-na-mo-no wa u-ke-to-ra-re-ma-se-n'.
アナタカ子ヲヤリマセヌナラバコノシナモノハウケトラレマセン

Do. O-ma-e ka-ne wo ya-ra-nu na-ra, ko-no shi-na-mo-no wa u-ke-to-ra-re-nu.
オマエカ子ヲヤラヌナラコノシナモノハウケトラレヌ

1087. *Under the table you will find my cane.*
Da-i no sh'-ta wo ta-dz-ne-re-ba, wa-ta-k'-shi no tsz-e nga mi-e-ma-sh'-o-o.
ダイノシタヲタヅ子レバワタクシノツエガミエマシヤウ

Do. Da-i no sh'-ta wo sa-nga-se-ba, wa-shi no tsz-e nga mi e-yo-o.
ダイノシタヲサガセバワシノツエガミエヤウ

1088. *Unfortunately the ship being wrecked, all hands were drowned.*
F'-ko-o-ni sh'-te ha-se-n i-ta-shi-ma-sh'-te no-ri-a-i no mo-no wa no-ko-ra-dz de-ki shi shi-ma-sh'-ta.
フカウニシテハセンイタシマシテノリアイノモノハノコラズデキシシマシタ

Do. F'-ka-o-ni sh'-te fu-ne wo ya-bu-t-te no-ri-a-i wa no-ko-ra-dz sz-i-shi sh'-ta.
フカウニシテフ子ヲヤブツテノリアイハノコラズスイシシタ

V

1089. *Vaccination was introduced into Japan about 30 years ago, by the Dutch.*
I-re-bo-o-so-o wa sa-n ji-u ne-n i-zen O-ra-n-da ji-n nga Ni-p-po-n ye mo-chi-wa-ta-ri-ma-sh'-ta.
イレボウソウハサンジウ子ンイゼンオランダジンガニツポンニモチワタリマシタ

Do. I-re-bo-o-so-o wa sa-n ji-u ne-n ma-i O-ra-n-da ji-n nga Ni-p-po-n ye mo-chi-wa-ta-t-ta.
イレボウソウハサンジウ子ンマイオランダジンガニツポンエモチワタツタ

1090. *Vinegar can be made of rice.*
Sz wa ko-me de mo ts'-ku-ra-re-ma-s'.
スハコメデモツクラレマス

Do. Sz wa ko-me de mo ts'-ku-ra-re-ru.
スハコメデモツクラレル

1091. *Wait a little, I am busy.*
Wa-ta-k'-shi yo-o ngu go za-ri-ma-s' ka-ra shi-ba-ra-ku o ma-
ワタクシ ヨウ ガ ゴザリマス カラ シバラク オマ
chi na-sa-i.
チナサイ

Do. Wa-ta-k'-shi i-so-nga shi-i ka-ra s'-ko-shi ma-t-te i-ro.
ワタクシ イソガシイ カラ スコシ マツテイロ

1092. *Wash your hands.*
Te wo o a-ra-i na-sa-re.
テ ヲ オアライナサレ

Do. Te wo a-ra-e.
テ ヲ アラエ

1093. *We beat into the harbour because the wind was ahead.*
Ka-ze ni mu-ka-i-ma-sh'-ta ka-ra wa-ta-k'-shi-do-mo mi-na-to
カゼニ ムカヒマシタ カラ ワタクシドモ ミナト
e ma-ngi ri ko-mi-ma-sh'-ta.
エマギリ コミマシタ

Do. Ka-ze ni mu-ka-t-ta ka-ra wa-shi-do-mo mi-na-to e ma-ngi-
カゼニ ムカッタ カラ ワシドモ ミナト エマギ
ri ko-n-da.
リコンダ

[a pupil]
1094. *We never shall make anything of him, he is so stupid* (said of
O-shi-e-ma-sh'-te mo, ts-i-ni mo-no-ni-wa-na-ri-ma-s' ma-i.
オシエマシテ モ ツイニ モノニハナリマス マイ

Do. A-re wa ni-bu-i ka-ra, o-shi-e-te-mo-tz-i-ni-wa-h'-to ni na-
アレ ハ ニブイカラ オシエテモツイニハヒト ニナ
ru ma-i.
ルマイ

1095. *We are going to touch at Shimoda.*
Wa-ta-k'-shi do-mo Shi-mo-da ni a-nga-ri-ma-sh'-te, s'-ko-shi
ワタクシドモ シモダニ アガリマシテ スコシ
to-ma-ri-ma-sh'-o-o.
トマリマシヤウ

Do. Wa-shi do-mo Shi-mo-da ni a-nga-t-te s'-ko-shi to-ma-ro-o.
ワシドモ シモダニ アガッテ スコシ トマロウ

1096. *We are out of rice.*
Wa-ta-k'-shi do-mo ko-me nga na-ku na-ri-ma-sh'-ta
ワタクシドモ コメ ガ ナク ナリマシタ

Do. Wa-shi do-mo ko-me nga na-ku na-t-ta.
ワシドモ コメ ガ ナカナッタ

1097. *We have only enough for ourselves.*
Wa-ta-k'-shi do-mo no da-ke go za-ri-ma-s'.
ワタクシドモ ノ ダケ ゴザリマス

Do. Wa-shi do-mo no da-ke a-ri-ma-s'.
ワシドモ ノ ダケ アリマス

1098. *We cannot get off under a month.*
Wa-ta-k'-shi do-mo h'-to ts'-ki no a-i-da ma-i-ru ko-to nga de-ki-ma-se-n'.
ワタクシドモヒトツキノアイダマイルコトガデキマセン

Do. Wa-shi do-mo h'-to ts'-ki no a-i-da yu-ku-ko-to nga de ki nu.
ワシドモヒトツキノアイダユクコトガデキヌ

1099. *We must do as well as we can.*
Wa-ta-k'-shi do-mo chi-ka-ra no o-yo-bu da-ke ka-na-ra-dz i-ta-shi-ma-s'.
ワタクシドモチカラノオヨブダケカナラズイタシマス

Do. Wa-shi do-mo chi-ka-ra no o-yo-bu da-ke k'-t-to sz-ru.
ワシドモチカラノオヨブダケキットスル

1100. *We have warm weather here all the year round.*
Ko-no to-ko-ro no ji-ko-o wa ne-n ji-u a-ta-ta-ka de go za-ri-ma-s'.
コノトコロノジコウハネンジウアタタカデゴザリマス

Do. Ko-no to-ko-ro ji-ko-o wa ne-n ji-u a-ta-ta-ka da.
コノトコロジコウハネンジウアタタカダ

1101. *We have it still on hand.*
Wa-ta-k'-shi do-mo ma-da mo-t-te o-ri-ma-s'.
ワタクシドモマダモッテオリマス

Do. Wa-shi do-mo ma-da mo-t-te i-ru.
ワシドモマダモッテイル

1102. *We move to-morrow.*
Wa-ta-k'-shi do-mo mi-o-o ni-chi h'-ki-u-tsz-ri wo i-ta-shi-ma s'
ワタクシドモメウニチヒキウツリヲイタシマス

Do. Wa-shi do-mo a-sh'-ta h'-ki-ko-sz.
ワシドモアシタヒキコス

1103. *We have been separated for a long time.*
Wa-ta-k'-shi do-mo to-o-ku he-da-t-te o-ri-ma-s'.
ワタクシドモトヲクヘヅッテオリマス

Do. Wa-ta-k'-shi do-mo to-o-ku he-da-t-te i-ru.
ワタクシドモトヲクヘダッテイル

1104. *Well then, how much will you give for it?*
Sa-yo-o na-ra i-ku-ra ni o ka-i-na-sa-ru ka.
サヤウナライクラニオカイナサルカ

Do. So-n na-ra i-ku-ra ni ka-u ka.
サウナライクラニカウカ

1105. *We must take up with what we can get.*
　Wa-ta-k'-shi do-mo na-ni de mo te ni i-ri-ma-sz-ru na-ra-ba,
　ワタクシドモナニデモテニイリマスルナラバ
　ka-na-ra-dz yo-o ni ta-te-ma-sz-ru.
　カナラズヨウニタテマスル

Do.　Wa-ta-k'-shi do-mo na-ni de mo te ni i-ru na-ra-ba k'-t-to
　ワタクシドモナニデモテニイルナラバキット
　yo-o ni ta-te-ru.
　ヨウニタテル

1106. *We must take turns in* watching to-night.
　Wa-ta-k'-shi do-mo ko-n ya ka-wa-ri-nga-wa-ri ni k'-t-to
　ワタクシドモコンヤカハリガハナニキット
　ba-n wo i-ta-shi-ma-sh'-o-o.
　バンヲイタシマシヤウ

Do.　Wa-ta-shi do-mo ko-n ya ka-wa-ri a-t-te k'-t-to-ba-n wo
　ワタシドモ コンヤカハリアッテキットバンヲ
　shi-yo-o.
　シヤウ

1107. *Were you* at the auction to-day.
　A-na-ta ko-n-ni-chi se-ri u-ri no ba-e o i-de na-sa-ri-ma-sh'-
　アナタコンニチセリウリノバエオイデナサリマシ
　ta ka.
　タカ

Do.　O-ma-e ko-n-ni-chi se-ri u-ri no ba-e i-t-ta ka?
　オマエ コンニチ セリウリ ノバエイッタカ

1108. *What is the matter* with this gun ? *It will not* go off.
　Ko-no te-p-po-o wa do-o i-ta-shi-ma-sh'-ta ka, ha-s-shi-ma-
　コノテツポウハドウイタシマシタカ ハツシマ
　se nu.
　セヌ

Do.　Ko-no te-p-po-o wa do-o sh'-ta ka ha-s-se-nu.
　コノテツポフハドフシタカハツセス

1109. *What interest do you get for your money ?*
　A-na-ta ka-ne wo ka-e-sz ni wa ri-ki-m wo na-n-bu o to-
　アナタカ子ヲカエスニハリキンヲナンブオト
　ri na-sa-ru ka ?
　リナサルカ

Do.　O-ma-e ka-ne wo ka-e-sz ni wa ri wo na-m-bu to-ru ka.
　オマエカ子ヲカエスニハリヲナンブトルカ

1110. *Whatever you do, I shall go at* all events.
　A-na-ta wa do-o-de-mo na-sa-ri-ma-s-k' wa-ta-k'-shi wa dze-
　アナタハドウデモナサリマスカワタクシハゼ
　hi ma-i-ri-ma-s'.
　ヒマイリマス

Do　O-ma-e wa do-o-de-mo na-sa-i wa-ta-k'-shi wa ze-hi yu-ku.
　オマエハドウデモナサイワタクシハゼヒユク

1111. *What are shooting stars a sign of?*
Ri-u se-i wa na-ni no ze-m-pi-o de go za-ri-ma-s' ka?
リウセイ ハナニ ノゼンピヤウデゴザリマスカ

Do. Ri-u se-i wa na-ni no ze-m-pi-o da ka?
リウセイ ハナニ ノゼンピヤウダカ

1112. *What is the difference between this and that?*
Ko-re to a-re to wa do-ko nga chi-nga-i-ma-s' ka?
コレ トアレト ハドコガ チガイマスカ

Do. Ko-re to a-re to wa do-ko nga chi-nga-u ka?
コレ トアレト ハドコガ チガウカ

1113. *What have you been about all this time?*
A-na-ta hi-sa-sh'-ku na-ni wo na-sa-re-te o i-de na-sa-ri-ma-sh'-ta ka?
アナタ ヒサシク ナニヲ ナサレテ オイデナサリマ シタカ

Do. O-ma-e hi-sa-sh'-ku na-ni wo sh'-te i-ta ka?
オマエ ヒサシク ナニヲ シテイタカ

1114. *What shall I do with this.*
Ko-re wo i-ka-nga i-ta-shi-ma-sh'-o-o ka?
コレ ヲ イカガ イタシマシヤウカ

Do. Ko-re wo do-o shi-yo-o ka?
コレヲ トウシヨウカ

1115. *What is the market price of beef?*
Ko-no se-tsz u-shi ni-ku no so-o-ba wa na-ni ho-do i-ta-shi-ma-s' ka?
コノセツ ウシニクノ ソウバ ハナニホド イタシ マスカ

Do. Ko-no se-tsz u-shi ni-ku no so-o-ba wa i-ku-ta sz-ru ka?
コノセツ ウシニクノ ソウバ ハ イクタスルカ

1116. *What is that fellow skulking about here for?*
A-no h'-to wa na-ze so-ko ko-ko ni ka-ku-re-te o-ri-ma-s' ka?
アノヒト ハナゼ ソココ ニカクレテ オリマスカ

Do. A-re wa na-ze a-chi ko-chi ni ka-ku-re-te o-ru ka?
アレ ハナゼ アチコチ ニカクレテ オルカ

1117. *What have you done with it?*
A-na-ta so-re wo mo-t-te o i-de na-sa-re-te na-ni ni na-sa-ri-ma-sh'-ta ka?
アナタ ソレヲ モツテオイデナサレテ ナニニ ナサリ マシタカ

Do. O-ma-e so-re wo mo-t-te i-t-te na-ni ni sh'-ta ka?
オマエ ソレヲ モツテイツテナニニ シタカ

1118. *What makes this horse act so?*
Ko-no m'-ma-wa na-ze ka-yo-o-ni i-ta shi-ma-s' ka?
コノムマ ハナゼ カヤウニ イタシマスカ

Do. Ko-no m'-ma wa na-ze ko-o sz-ru ka?
コノムマ ハナゼ カウスルカ

1119. *What are you doing now a days?*
A-na-ta ko-no ngo-ro na-ni wo na-sa-ri-ma-s' ka?
アナタコノゴロナニヲナサリマスカ
Do.　O-ma-e ko-no se-tsz wa na-ni wo sz-ru ka?
オマエコノセツハナニヲスルカ

1120. *What use do you make of this?*
A-na-ta ko-re wo na-ni ni o mo-chi-i na-sa-ru ka?
アナタコレヲナニニオモチイナサルカ
Do.　O-ma-e ko-re wo na-ni ni mo-chi-i-ru ka?
オマエコレヲナニニモチイルカ

1121. *What are you waiting for?*
A-na-ta na-ni wo o me-chi na-sa-ru ka?
アナタナニヲオマチナサルカ
Do.　O-ma-e na-ni wo ma-tsz ka?
オマエナニヲマツカ

1122. *What else can it be for?*
Na-n-zo ho-ka ni ts'-ka-i mi-chi de go za-ri-ma-s' ka?
ナンゾホカニツカイミチデゴザリマスカ
Do.　Na-n-zo ho-ka ni mo-chi-i-ru ko-ta nga a-ru ka?
ナンゾホカニモチイルコトガアルカ

1123. *What objection is there to Foreigners coming to Japan?*
Ga-i ko-ku no h'-to nga Ni-p-po-n e ki-te wa na-ni nga ki ni i-ri-ma-se-n' ka?
ガイコクノヒトガニッポンヱキテハナニガキニイリマセヌカ
Do.　Ga-i ko-ku no h'-to nga Ni-p-po-n e ki-te wa na-ni nga ki ni i-ra-nu ka?
ガイコクノヒトガニッポンヱキテハナニガキニイラヌカ

1124. *What is that?*
Se-re wa na-ni de go za-ri-ma-s' ka?
ソレハナニデゴザリマスカ
Do.　A-re wa na-ni ka?
アレハナニカ

1125. *What for?*
Na-ni yu-e de go za-ri-ma-s' ka?
ナニユヱデゴザリマスカ
Do.　Do-o i-u wa-ke da?
ドウイウワケダ

1126. *What is the news?*
Na-n-zo me-dz-ra-sh'-ki ko-to nga go za-ri-ma-s' ka?
ナンゾメヅラシキコトガゴザリマスカ
Do.　Na-n-zo me-dz-ra-shi-i ko-to nga a-ru ka?
ナンゾメヅラシイコトガアルカ

1127. *What do you want?*
A-na-ta na-ni nga ho-shi-u go za-ri-ma-s' ka?
アナタナニガ ホシウ ゴ ザリマスカ
Do. Te-ma-e na-ni nga ho-shi-i ka?
テマエナニガ ホシイカ

1128. *What are you doing?*
A-na-ta na-ni wo na-sa-ri-ma-s' ka?
アナタナニヲ ナサリマスカ
Do. O-ma-e na-ni wo sz-ru ka?
オマエナニヲ スルカ

1129. *What is the matter with you?*
A-na-ta do-o ka na-sa-ri-ma-sh'-ta ka?
アナタドウカナサリマシタカ
Do. O-ma-e do-o ka sh'-ta ka?
オマエドウカシタカ

1130. *What is your name?*
A-na-ta no o na wa na-ni to o-s-sh'-a-ri-ma-s' ka?
アナタノオナハナニトオッシャリマスカ
Do. O-ma-e no na wa na-ni to i-u ka?
オマエノナ ハナニトイウカ

1131. *What do you think of that affair?*
A-na-ta so-no ko-to wa na-ni to o-bo-shi-me-shi-ma-s' ka?
アナタソノコト ハ ナニ トオボシメシマスカ
Do. O-ma-e so-no ko-to wa na-ni to o-mo-o ka?
オマエソノコト ハ ナニト オモフカ

1132. *What boy is that?*
So-re wa ta-re no o ko de go za-ri-ma-s' ka?
ソレハタレノオコデゴ サリマスカ
Do. A-re wa da-re no ko da ka?
アレ ハダレ ノコダカ

1133. *What tree is that?*
So-re wa na-ni no ki de go za-ri-ma-s' ka?
ソレ ハ ナニノキデゴ ザリマスカ
Do. A-re wa na-ni no ki da ka?
アレ ハ ナニノキダカ

1134. *What are you looking for?*
A-na-ta na-ni wo o ta-dz-ne na-sa-ri-ma-s' ka?
アナタ ナニヲ オタヅ子ナサリマスカ
Do. O-ma-e na-ni wo sa-nga-s' ka?
オマエナニヲ サガスカ

1135. *What does he say?*
A-no h'-to wa na-ni wo ha-na-shi-ma-s' ka?
アノヒト ハナニヲ ハナシマスカ
Do. A-re wa na-ni wo ha-na-s' ka?
アレ ハナニヲ ハナスカ

1136. *What did you do that for?*
　A-na-ta na-ni no ta-me ni so-re wo na-sa-re-ma-sh'-ta **ka**?
　アナタナニノタメニソレヲナサレマシタカ
Do.　O-ma-e na-ni no ta-me ni so-re wo sh'-ta ka?
　オマエナニノタメニソレヲシタカ

1137. *What did you strike him for?*
　A-na-ta wa a-no h'-to wo na-ze o bu-chi na-sa-re-ma-sh'-ta ka?
　アナタハアノヒトヲナゼオブチナサレマシタカ
Do.　O-ma-e a-no h'-to wo na-ze bu-t-ta ka?
　オマエアノヒトヲナゼブツタカ

1138. *What is that musical instrument called?*
　A-no na-ri-mo-no wa na-ni to i-u mo-no de go za-ri-ma-s' ka?
　アノナリモノハナニトイウモノデゴザリマスカ
Do.　A-no na-ri-mo-no wa na-ni to i-u ka?
　アノナリモノハナニトイウカ

1139. *What day of the month is it?*
　Ko-n ni-chi wa i-ku ka de go za-ri-ma-s' ka?
　コンニチハイクカデゴザリマスカ
Do.　Ki-o-o wa i-ku ka da ka?
　キヤフハイクカダカ

1140. *What are you laughing at?*
　A-na-ta na-ni wo o wa-ra-i na-sa-re-ma-s' ka?
　アナタナニヲオワライナサレマスカ
Do.　O-ma-e na-ni wo wa-ra-u ka?
　オマエナニヲワラフカ

1141. *What are you going to do?*
　A-na-ta no-chi ni wa na-ni wo na-sa-re-ma-sh'-o-o ka?
　アナタノチニハナニヲナサレマシヤウカ
Do.　O-ma-e no-chi ni wa na-ni wo sz-ru ka?
　オマエノチニハナニヲスルカ

1142. *What is the meaning of this word?*
　Ko-no ko-to-ba no gi-ri wa na-ni de go za-ri-ma-s' ka?
　コノコトバノギリハナニデゴザリマスカ
Do.　Ko-no ko-to-ba no wa-ke wa na-ni da ka?
　コノコトバノワケハナニダカ

1143. *What sort of a man is he?*
　A-no h'-to wa do-no yo-o-na h'-to de go za-ri-ma-s' ka?
　アノヒトハドノヤフナヒトデゴザリマスカ
Do.　A-re wa do-no yo-o-na h'-to da ka?
　アレハドノヤフナヒトダカ

1144. *What gentleman is that?*
　A-no o ka-ta wa do-na-ta de go za-ri-ma-s' ka?
　アノオカタハドナタデゴザリマスカ
Do.　A-no h'-to wa da-re da ka?
　アノヒトハダレダカ

1145. *What is his occupation?*
A-no h'-to wa na-ni no ka-ngi-o-o wo i-ta-shi-ma-s' ka?
アノヒト ハ ナニ ノ カギヤフ ヲ イタシマス カ
Do. A-re wa na-ni no to-se-i wo sz-ru ka?
アレ ハ ナニ ノ トセイ ヲ スル カ

1146. *What is the reason of it?*
So-no wa-ke wa na-ni de go za-ri-ma-s' ka?
ソノ ワケ ハ ナニ デ ゴザリマス カ
Do. A-no wa-ke wa na-n da ka?
アノ ワケ ハ ナンダ カ

1147. *What have you been about all day?*
A-na-ta ko-n ni-chi wa i-chi ni-chi na-ni wo na-s'-te o i-de na-sa-ri-ma-sh'-ta ka?
アナタ コンニチ ハ イチ ニチ ナニ ヲ ナステ オイデ ナサレマシタ カ
Do. O-ma-e ki-o-o wa i-chi ni-chi na-ni wo sh'-te i-ta ka?
オマエ キヤフ ハ イチ ニチ ナニ ヲ シテ イタ カ

1148. *What o'clock do you think it is?*
A-na-ta i-ma na-n do-ki to o-bo-shi-me shi-ma-s' ka?
アナタ イマ ナンドキ ト オボシメシマス カ
Do. O-ma-e i-ma na-n do-ki to o-mo-o ka?
オマエ イマ ナンドキ ト オモフ カ

1149. *What do you want of me?*
A-na-ta wa-ta-k'-shi ni na-ni no go yo-o nga go za-ri-ma-s' ka?
アナタ ワタクシ ニ ナニ ノ ゴヤフ ガ ゴザリマス カ
Do.. O-ma-e wa-ta-k'-shi ni na-ni no yo-o nga a-ru ka?
オマエ ワタクシ ニ ナニ ノ ヤウ ガ アル カ

1150. *What noise is that?*
A-re wa na-ni no o-to de go za-ri-ma-s' ka?
アレ ハ ナニ ノ オト デ ゴザリマス カ
Do. A-re wa na-ni no o-to da ka?
アレ ハ ナニ ノ オト タ カ

1151. *What had we better do?*
Wa-ta-k'-shi do-mo do-o i-ta-sh'-ta-ra yo-ro-shi-u go za-ri-ma-sh'-o-o ka?
ワタクシ ドモ ドウ イタシタラ ヨロシウ ゴザリマ シヤフ カ
Do. Wa-shi do-mo do-o sh'-ta-ra yo-ka-ro-o ka?
ワシ ドモ ドウ シタラ ヨカロウ カ

1152. *What makes you think so?*
A-na-ta na-ze sa-yo-o ni c-bo-shi-me-shi-ma-s' ka?
アナタ ナゼ サヤウ ニ オホシメシマス カ
Do. O-ma-e na-ze so-o o-mo-o ka?
オマエ ナゼ ソウ オモウ カ

1153. *What shall I do next?*
　　　Ko no tsz-ngi wa na-ni wo i-ta-shi-ma-sh'-o-o ka?
　　　コノツギ ハ ナニ ヲ イタシ マシヤウカ
Do.　Ko-no tsz-ngi wa na-ni wo shi-yo-o ka?
　　　コノツギ ハ ナニ ヲ シヤウカ

1154. *What did you say?*
　　　A-na-ta na-ni wo o-s-shi-a-ri-ma-sh'-ta ka?
　　　アナタ ナニ ヲ オッシヤリマシタカ
Do.　O-ma-e na-ni wo i-ta ka?
　　　オマエ ナニ ヲ イッタカ

1155. *What is that to you?*
　　　So-re wa a-na-ta nga do-o i-u wa-ke de ka-ma-i na-sa-ru ka?
　　　ソレ ハ アナタ ガ ドウイウ ワケ デ カマヒ ナサルカ
Do.　So-re wa o-ma-e nga do-o i-u wa-ke de ka-ma-u ka?
　　　ソレ ハ オマエ ガ ドウイウ ワケ デ カマフカ

1156. *What do you call this?*
　　　Ko-re wa a-na-ta na-ni to na-dz-ke-ma-s' ka?
　　　コレ ハ アナタ ナニ ト ナヅケマスカ
Do.　Ko-re wa o-ma-e na-n to na-dz-ke-ru ka?
　　　コレ ハ オマエ ナント ナヅケルカ

1157. *What more can I do?*
　　　Wa-ta-k'-shi wa ko-no u-e wa na-ni wo i-ta-sa-re-ma-sh'-o ka?
　　　ワタクシ ハ コノ ウエ ハ ナニ ヲ イタサレ マシヤフカ
Do.　Wa-shi wa ko-no u-e wa na-ni nga shi-ra-re-yo-o ka?
　　　ワシ ハ コノウエ ハ ナニ ガ シラレヤフカ

1158. *What more do you want?*
　　　A-na-ta ma-da na-ni nga o i-ri-yo-o de go za-ri-ma-s' ka?
　　　アナタ マダ ナニ ガ オイリヤフデ ゴ ザリマスカ
Do.　O-ma-e ma-da na-ni nga i-ru ka?
　　　オマエ マダ ナニ ガ イルカ

1159. *What is this good for?*
　　　Ko-re wa na-ni ni mo-chi-i-ru ko-to nga go za-ri-ma-s' ka?
　　　コレ ハ ナニニ モチイル コト ガ ゴ ザリマスカ
Do.　Ko-re wa na-ni ni ts'-ka-u ko-to nga a-ru ka?
　　　コレ ハ ナニニ ツカフ コト ガ アルカ

1160. *What do you want this for?*
　　　A-na-ta ko-re wa na-ni no ta-me ni o i-ri na-sa-ru ka?
　　　アナタ コレ ハ ナニ ノ タメ ニ オイリナサルカ
Do.　O-ma-e ko-re wa na-ni no ta-me ni i-ru ka?
　　　オマエ コレ ハ ナニ ノ タメ ニ イルカ

1161. *What made you so late?*
　　　A-na-ta na-ni wo sh'-te o i-de na-sa-re-te ka-yo-o ni o-so-o
　　　アナタ ナニ ヲ シテ オイデ ナサレテ カヨウニ オソウ

go za-ri-ma-s' ka?
ゴザリマスカ

Do. O-ma-e na-ni wo sh'-te i-te ko-no yo-o ni o-so-i ka?
オマエナニヲシテイテコノヨウニオソイカ

1162. *What have you for me to do?*
A-na-ta wa-ta-k'-shi ni na-ni no go yo-o nga go za-ri-ma-s' ka?
アナタ ワタクシニ ナニノゴ ヨウガ ゴザリマスカ

Do. O-ma-e wa-ta-shi ni na-ni no yo-o nga a-ru ka?
オマエワタシニ ナニ ノ ヨウ ガ アル カ

1163. *What have you come for?*
A-na-ta na-n-zo go yo-o nga a-t-te o i-de na-sa-ri-ma-sh'-ta ka?
アナタナンゾ ゴヨウ ガ アツテオイデナサリマシタカ

Do. O-ma-e na-n-zo yo-o nga a-t-te k'-ta ka?
オマエナンゾ ヨウ ガ アツテキタカ

1164. *What is the matter with this?*
Ko-re wa do-o sh'-te ka-yo-o ni na-ri-ma-sh'-ta ka?
コレ ハ ドウシテ カヤウニナリマシタカ

Do Ko-re wa do-o sh'-te so-o na-t-ta ka?
コレ ハ ドウ シテソウナッタカ

1165. *What is your name?*
A-na-ta no go se-i me-i wa na-ni to o-s-shi-a-ri-ma-s' ka?
アナタノゴセイメイハ ナニトオッシャリマスカ

Do. O-ma-e no se-i me-i wa na-ni to i-u ka?
オマエノセイメイ ハ ナニトイフカ

1166. *What is the date of his letter?*
A-no o ka-ta no te-nga-mi wa i-tsz ngo-ro o ka-ka-se na-sa-ri-ma-sh'-ta ka?
アノオカタノテガミ ハ イツ ゴロオカカセナサレマシタカ

A-no h'-to no te-nga mi wa i-tsz ngo-ro ka-i-ta ka?
アノヒトノテガ ミ ハ イツ ゴロカイタカ

1167. *What right have you to this land?*
A-na-ta na-ni no gi ni tsz-i-te ko-no gi-me-n wo o ts'-ka-i na-sa-ru ka?
アナタ ナニ ノギ ニツイテコノジメン ヲ オツカイ ナサルカ

Do. O-ma-e do-o i-u wa-ke de ko-no gi-me-n wo ts'-ka-u ka?
オマエドウイフワケデコノジメン ヲ ツカウカ

1168. *When does he sail?*
A-no o ka-ta wa i-tsz fu-ne ni no-t-te o i-de na-sa-ru ka?
アノオカタ ハ イツ フ子 ニ ノッテオイデナサルカ

1168. A-no h'-to wa i-tsz fu-ne ni no-t-te i-ku da-ro-o ka?
アノヒト ハイツフ子ニノッテイクダロウカ

1169. When you are ready, let me know it.
A-na-ta sh'-ta-ku nga de-ki-ma-sh'-ta-ra-ba wa-ta-k'-shi ni sa-
アナタ シタクガ デキマジタラバ ワタクシニサ
yo-o o-s-shi-a-ri-ma-sh'.
ヤウオッシャリマシ

Do. O-ma-e sh'-ta-ku nga de-ki-ta-ra-ba wa-shi ni so-o i-e.
オマエ シタクガ デキタラバ ワシ ニソウイエ

1170. When are you going?
A-na-ta wa i-tsz o i-de na-sa-ru ka?
アナタ ハイツオイデナサル カ

Do. O-ma-e i-tsz yu-ku ka?
オマエイツ ユク カ

1171. When shall you return?
A-na-ta i-tsz ngo-ro ma-de ni o ka-e-ri na-sa-ru ka?
アナタイツゴロ マデニオ カエリナサル カ

Do. O-ma-e i-tsz ngo-ro ka-e-ru ka?
オマエイツ ゴロカエル カ

1172. When shall you get it done?
A-na-ta i-tsz ma-de ni de-ki a-nga-ri-ma-s' ka?
アナタイツマ デニデキ アガリマスカ

Do. O-ma-e i-tsz ma-de ni shi a-nga-ru ka?
オマエイツマデ ニシ アガル カ

1173. When do you go on board?
A-na-ta i-tsz fu-ne ni o no-ri na-sa-ru ka?
アナタ イツ フ子ニオ ノリ ナサル カ

Do. O-ma-e i-tsz fu-ne ni no-ru ka?
オマエイツ フ子ニノル カ

1174. When comets make their appearance, the Japanese say they are signs of changes in the world.
He-o-ki-bo-shi de-ma-s' to-k, wa, Ni-p-po-n no h'-to nga se-
ハウキボシ デマストキ ハニッポンノヒト ガセ
ka-i ni he-n no a-ru shi-ru-shi da to mo-o-shi-ma-s'.
カイニヘンノ アルシルシダト マウシマス

Do. Ho-o-ki-bo-shi nga de-ru to-ki wa Ni-p-po-n ji-n nga yo
ハウキボシ ガ デルトキ ハニッポンジン ガ ヨ
ni ka-wa-ru ko-to no a-ru shi-ru-shi da to i-n.
ニカワル コトノ アルシルシ ダトイフ

1175. When you called to see me, unfortunately I was out.
A-na-ta nga wa-ta-k'-shi wo o mi-ma-i ku-da-sa-ri-ma-sh'-
アナタガ ワタクシヲオ ミマイ クダサリマシ
ta to-ki wa, o-ri-a-sh'-ku ru-sz de go za-ri-ma-sh'-ta.
タトキ ハオリアシク ルスデゴ ザリマシタ

1175. O-ma-e nga wa-ta-shi wo mi-ma-t-te ku-re-ta to-ki wa, a-
オマエ ガ ワタシ ヲ ミマッテ クレタ トキ ハ ア
i-ni-ku ru-sz de a-t-ta.
イニクルス デアッタ

1176. *When you have done with it, bring it back.*
A-na-ta o ts'-ka-i na-sa-re-ta no-chi-ni o ka-e-shi na-sa-re.
アナタ オ ツカイ ナサレタ ノチニ オカエシ ナサレ
Do. O-ma-e ts'-ka-t-te shi-ma-t-ta-ra a-to de ka-e-se.
オマエ ツカッテ シマッタラ アト デ カエセ

1177. *When did he promise to bring it back?*
A-no o ka-ta wa i-tsz-ma-de ni mo-t-te ka-e-ri-ma-s' ya-ku-
アノオカタ ハ イツ マデニ モッテ カエリマス ヤク
so-ku wo i-ta-shi-ma-sh'-ta ka?
ソク ヲ イタシマシタ カ
Do. A-no h'-to wa i-tsz-ma-de ni mo-t-te ka-e-ru ya-ku-so-ku
アノヒト ハ イツ マデ ニ モッテ カエル ヤクソク
wo sh'-ta ka?
ヲ シタ カ

1178. *When it is done I will let you know.*
Ko-re wo ts'-ku-t-te shi-ma-i-ma-sh'-ta to-ki wa-ta-k'-shi nga
コレ ヲ ツクッテ シマイマシタ トキ ワタクシ ガ
a-na-ta ni mo-o-shi a-nge-ma-sh'-o-o.
アナタニ マウシ アゲマシャウ
Do. Ko-re wo ko-shi-ra-e-te shi-ma-t-ta-ra wa-shi nga o-ma-e ni
コレ ヲ コシラエテ シマッタラ ワシ ガ オマエニ
i-wo-o.
イハウ

1179. *When you see him, put him in mind of it.*
A-na-ta a-no h'-to wo go ra-n na-sa-re-ta to-ki o shi-ra-se
アナタ アノ ヒト ヲ ゴラン ナサレタ トキ オ シラセ
ku-da-sa-re.
クダサレ
Do. O-ma-e a-no h'-to wo mi-ta to-ki, shi-ra-sh'-te ku-re-ro.
オマエ アノ ヒト ヲ ミタ トキ シラシテ クレロ

1180. *When do you begin?*
A-na-ta i-tsz ka-ra o ha-ji-me na-sa-ru ka?
アナタ イツ カラ オ ハジメ ナサル カ
Do. O-ma-e i-tsz ka-ra ha-ji-me-ru ka?
オマエ イツ カラ ハジメル カ

1181. *When does that note of hand become payable.*
A-no sh'-o-mo-n wa i-tsz ka-i-sz yo-o ni na-ri-ma-sh'-o-o ka?
アノ シャウモン ハ イツ カイス ヤフ ニ ナリマシャフ カ
Do. A-no sh'-o-mo-n wa i-tsz ka-i-sz yo-o ni na-ru ka?
アノ シャウモン ハ イツ カイス ヤフ ニ ナル カ

1182. *When do you expect him, to come?*
A-na-ta a no o ka-ta no o i-de na-sa-ru wo i-tsz ma-de o-ma-chi na-sa-ru ka?
アナタアノオカタノオイデナサルヲイツマデオマチナサルカ

Do O-ma-e wa a-no h'-to no ku-ru no wo i-tsz ma-de ma-ts' ka?
オマエハアノヒトノクルノヲイツマデマツカ

1183. *When will you come?*
A-na-ta wa ko-no no-chi i-tsz o i-de na-sa-re-ma-s' ka?
アナタハコノノチイツオイデナサレマスカ

Do. O-ma-e ko-no ngo i-tsz ku-ru ka?
オマエコノゴイツクルカ

1184. *When shall we settle our accounts?*
Wa-ta-k'-shi do-mo no ka-n-j'-o-o wa i-tsz o ta-te na-sa-re-te ku-da-sa-ri-ma-s' ka?
ワタクシドモノカンジヤウハイツオタテナサレテクダサリマスカ

Do. Wa-shi do-mo no ka-n-j'-o-o wa i-tsz ta-t-te ku-re-ru ka?
ワシドモノカンジヤウハイツタッテクレルカ

1185. *Where were you born?*
A-na-ta wa do-chi-ra no o m'-ma-re de go za-ri-ma-sh'-ta ka?
アナタハドチラノオムマレデゴザリマシタカ

Do. O-ma-e wa do-chi-ra no m'-ma-re-ta ka?
オマエハドチラノムマレタカ

1186. *Where was he brought up?*
A-no o ka-ta wa do-chi-ra de o so-da-te-ra-re na-sa-re-ta ka?
アノオカタハドチラデオソダテラレナサレタカ

Do. A-re wa do-ko de so-da-te-ra-re-ta ka?
アレハドコデソダテラレタカ

1187. *Where has he gone?*
A-no o ka-ta wa do-ko e o i-de na-sa-re-ma-sh'-ta ka?
アノオカタハドコヱオイデナサレマシタカ

Do A-no h'-to wa do-ko e ma-i-ri-ma-sh'-ta ka?
アノヒトハドコヱマイリマシタカ

1188. *Where was this book printed?*
Ko-no ho-n wa do-chi-ra de ka-i-ha-n ni na-ri-ma-sh'-ta ka?
コノホンハドチラデカイハンニナリマシタカ

Do. Ko-no ho-n wa do-ko de ha-n ni na-t-ta ka?
コノホンハドコデハンニナッタカ

1189. *Where does he board?*
A-no o-ka-ta wa do-chi-ra de sh'-o-ku-ji wo i-ta-shi-ma-s' ka?
アノオカタハドシラデショクジヲイタシマスカ

Do. A-re wa do-ko de me-shi wo ku-u ka?
アレハドコデメシヲクウカ

1190. *Where shall we go.*
Wa-ta-k'-shi do-mo do-ko e ma-i-t-te yo-ro-shi-u go za-ri-ma-sh'-o-o ka?
ワタクシドモ ドコエマイッテ ヨロシウ ゴ ザリマシヤウカ

Do. Wa-shi do-mo do-ko e i-t-te yo-ka-ro-o ka?
ワシドモ ドコエイッテヨカロウカ

1191. *Where shall I find him?*
Wa-ta-k'-shi wa do-chi-ra wo ta-dz-ne-ma-sh'-ta-ra a-no h'-to ni a-wa-re-ma-sh'-o-o ka?
ワタクシ ハ ドチラヲ タヅ子マシタラ アノヒトニアハレ マシヤウカ

Do. Wa-shi wa do-ko wo ta-dz-ne-ta-ra a-re ni a-wa-re-yo-o ka?
ワシ ハ ドコ ヲ タヅ子タラ アレニアハレヤフ カ

1192. *Where does opium come from?*
A-he-n wa i-dz-ku yo-ri wa-ta-ri-ma-s' ka?
アヘン ハ イヅク ヨリ ワタリマス カ

Do. A-he-n wa do-ko ka-ra wa-ta-ru ka?
アヘン ハ ドコ カラ ワタル カ

1193. *Where are you going?*
A-na-ta do-chi-ra e o i-de na-sa-ri-ma-s' ka?
アナタ ドチラ エ オイデ ナサリマスカ

Do. O-ma-e do-ko e yu-ku ka?
オマエ ドコエ ユク カ

1194. *Where is the money which I paid you the day before yesterday when you came from Yedo?*
A-na-ta i-s-sa-ku-ji-tsz Ye-do yo-ri o i-de na-sa-re-ta to-ki ni, wa-ta-k'-shi nga a-na-ta e a-nge-ma-sh'-ta ka-ne wa ta-da-i-ma do-chi-ra ni go za-ri-ma-s' ka?
アナタ イッサクジツ エド ヨリ オ イデ ナサレタ トキ ニ ワタクシ ガ アナタ エ アゲ マシタ カ子 ハ タダ イマ ドチラ ニ ゴ ザリマス カ

Do. O-ma-e i-s-sa-ku ji-tsz Ye-do ka-ra k'-ta to-ki ni, o-re nga o-ma-e ni ya-t-ta ka-ne wa i-ma do-ko ni a-ru ka?
オマエ イッサクジツ エド カラ キタ トキ ニ オレ ガ オマエ ニ ヤッタ カ子 ハ イマ ドコ ニ アル カ

1195 *Where shall I put this?*
Wa-ta-k'-shi wa ko-re wo do-ko ni o-ki-ma-sh'-o-o ka?
ウタクシ ハ コレ ヲ ドコ ニ オキ マシヤフカ

Do. Wa-shi wa ko-re wo do-ko ni o-ko-o ka?
ワシ ハ コレ ヲ ドコ ニ オコフ カ

1196. *Where have you been.*
A-na-ta do-ko e o i-de na-sa-re-ta o ka-e-ri de go za-ri-ma-s' ka?
アナタ ドコ エ オイデ ナサレタ オ カエリ デ ゴ ザリ マス カ

1197. *Where did you get that.*
So-re wo do-ko ka-ra mo-to-me-te o i-de na-sa-ra-ri-ma-sh'-
ソレヲドコカラモトメテオイデナサラレマシ
ta ka?
タカ

Do. So-re wo do-ko ka-ra mo-to-me-te k'-ta ka?
ソレヲドコカラモトメテキタカ

1198. *Where do you live?*
A-na-ta wa do-ko ni o-sz-ma-i na-sa-ri-ma s' ka?
アナタハドコニオスマイナサリマスカ

Do. O-ma-e ga do-ko ni sz-ma-t-te i-ru ka?
オマエハドコニスマツテイルカ

1199. *Which is the best; this or that?*
Ko-re to so-re de wa do-chi-ra nga yo-ro-shi-u go za-ri-ma-
コレトソレデハドチラガヨロシウゴザリマ
s' ka?
スカ

Do. Ko-re to so-re de wa do-chi-ra nga yo-i ka?
コソトソレデハドチラガヨイカ

1200. *Which do you prefer?*
Do-chi-ra nga o ki ni i-ri-ma-s' ka?
ドチラガオキニイリマスカ

Do. Do-chi-ra nga ki ni i-ru ka?
ドチラガキニイルカ

1201. *Which of these will wear longest?*
Ko-re wa do-chi-ra nga na-nga-ku mo-chi-i-ra-re-ma-s' ka?
コレハドチラガナガクモチイラレマスカ

Do. Ko-re wa do-chi-ra nga na-nga-ku ts'-ka-e-ru ka?
コレハドチラガナガクツカヘルカ

1202. *Which shall I take?*
Wa-ta-k'-shi do-chi-ra wo to-ri-ma-sh'-o-o ka?
ワタクシドチラヲトリマシヤウカ

Do. We-shi wa do-chi-ra wo to-ro-o ka?
ワシハドチラヲトロウカ

1203. *Where did you leave your penknife?*
A-na-ta no ko-nga-ta-na wa do-ko e o-i-te o i-de na-sa-re-
アナタノコガタナハドコエオイテオイデナサレ
ma-sh'-ta ka?
マシタカ

Do. O-ma-e no ko-nga-ta-na wa do-ko e o i-te i-t-ta ka?
オマエノコガタナハドコエオイテイツタカ

1204. *Which of them is most to blame?*
Do-chi-ra no tsz-mi nga o-mo-o go za-ri-ma-s' ka?
ドチラノツミガオモウゴザリマスカ

Do. Do-chi no tsz-mi nga o-mo-i ka?
ドチノツミガオモヒカ

1205. *Which of them is it best to take?*
　　　Do-chi-ra no ho-o wo to-ri-ma-sh'-te yo-ro-shi-u go za-ri-ma-s' ka?
　　　ドチラノホウヲトリマシテヨロシウゴザリマスカ

Do. Do-chi no ho-o wo to-t-te yo-i ka?
　　　ドチノホウヲトッテヨイカ

1206. *Who set the clock a going?*
　　　Da-re nga to-ke-i wo u-ngo-ka-shi-ma-sh'-ta ka?
　　　ダレガトケイヲウゴカシマシタカ

Do. Da-re nga to-ke-i wo u-ngo-ka-sh'-ta ka?
　　　ダレガトケイヲウゴカシタカ

1207. *Who wound up the clock?*
　　　Da-re nga to-ke-i wo ka-ke ma-sh'-ta ka?
　　　ダレガトケイヲカケマシタカ

Do. Da-re nga to-ke-i wo ka-ke-ta ka?
　　　ダレガトケイヲカケタカ

1208. *Who has iron for sale?*
　　　Do-na-ta nga te-tsz wo u-ru ta-me-ni mo-t-te o-ri-ma-s' ka?
　　　ドナタガテツヲウルタメニモッテオリマスカ

Do. Da-re nga te-tsz wo u-ru ta-me-ni mo-t-te i-ru ka?
　　　ダレガテツヲウルタメニモッテイルカ

1209. *Who is to blame for that?*
　　　A-re wa da-re nga tsz-mi ni na-ri-ma-s' ka?
　　　アレハダレガツミニナリマスカ

Do. A-re wa da-re nga tsz-mi ni na-ru ka?
　　　アレハダレガツミニナルカ

1210. *Who did this?*
　　　Ko-re wo do-na-ta nga na-sa-re-ma-sh'-ta ka?
　　　コレヲドナタガナサレマシタカ

Do. Ko-re wo da-re nga sh'-ta ka?
　　　コレヲダレガシタカ

1211. *Who made this?*
　　　Ko-re wo do-na-ta nga o ts'-ku-ri na-sa-re-ma-sh'-ta ka?
　　　コレヲドナタガオツクリナサレマシタカ

Do. Ko-re wo da-re nga ko-shi-ra-e-ta ka?
　　　コレヲダレガコシラヘタカ

1212. *Who knows?*
　　　Do-na-ta nga sh'-t-te i na-sa-ru ka?
　　　ドナタガシツテイナサルカ

Do. Da-re nga sh'-t-te i-ru ka?
　　　ダレカシツテイルカ

1213. *Who can tell why the tide rises and falls?*
　　　Shi-o no mi-chi hi no do-o-ri wo da-re nga to-i-te ki-ka-sa-
　　　シホノミチヒノドウリヲダレタトヒテキカサ

re-ma-s' ka?
レマスカ

Do. Shi-wo no mi-chi hi no ri wo da-re nga ha-na-sh'-te ki-ka-sa-re-ru ka?
シホノミチ ヒノリヲ ダレガ ハナシテキ カサレルカ

1214. *Who is to go next?*
Ko-no tsz-ngi wa da-re nga yu-ku ba-n do go za-ri-ma-s' ka?
コノツギ ハ ダレガ ユクバン デゴザリマ スカ

Do. Ko-no tsz-ngi wa da-re nga yu-ku ba-n da ka?
コノツギ ハ ダレガ ユクバンダカ

1215. *Who will go next?*
Do-na-ta nga ko-no tsz-ngi wa yu-ki-ma-sh'-o-o ka?
ドナタガ コノツギ ハ ユキマシヤウカ

Do. Ko-no tsz-ngi wa da-re nga yu-ku da-ro-o ka?
コノツギ ハ ダレガ ユクダロウカ

1216. *Who taught you this?*
Do-na-ta nga a-na-ta ni ko-re wo o-shi-e-ma-sh'-ta ka?
ドナタガ アナタニ コレ ヲ オシヘマシタカ

Do. Da-re nga o-ma-e ni ko-re wo o-shi-e-ta ka?
ダレガ オマエニ コレ ヲ オシヘタカ

1217. *Who sent you here?*
Do-na-ta nga a-na-ta wo ko-ko e ts'-ka-wa-shi-ma-sh'-ta ka?
ドナタガ アナタヲ ココヘ ツカハシマシタ カ

Do. Da-re nga te-ma-i wo ko-ko e ts'-ka-wa-sh'-ta ka?
ダレガ テマイ ヲ ココヘ ツカハシタカ

1218. *Who has money to lend?*
Do-na-ta nga ka-sz ta-me ni ka-ne wo mo-tte o i-de na-sa-re-ma-s' ka?
ドナタガ カスタメニ カネヲ モツテオイデナ サレマスカ

Do. Da-re nga ka-ne wo ka-so-o to i-tte mo-tte i-ru ka?
ダレガ カネヲ カソウトイツテモツテイルカ

1219. *Who is there?*
Do-na-ta nga a-s'-ko ni o i-de na-sa-re-ma-s' ka?
ドナタガ アスコニ オイデナサレマス カ

Do. Da-re nga a-s'-ko ni i-ru ka?
ダレガ アスコニ イルカ

1220. *Who is that?*
A-no h'-to wa da-re de go za-ri-ma-s' ka?
アノヒト ハ ダレデゴ ザリマスカ

Do. A-re wa da-re da ka?
アレ ハ ダレダカ

1221. *Who says so?*
　Do-na-ta nga sa-yo-o o-s'-shi-a-ri-ma-s' ka？
　ドナタガ サヤウオッシャリマスカ
Do.　Da-re nga so-o i-u ka？
　ダレガ ソウイウカ

1222. *Whom shall I call?*
　Wa-ta-k'-shi wa do-na-ta wo yo-n-de ma-i-ri-ma-sh'-te yo-ro-
　ワタクシ ハドナタヲ ヨンデマイリマシテ ヨロ
shi-u go za-ri-ma-sh'-o-o ka？
　シウゴ ザリマシヤウカ
Do.　Wa-shi wa da-re wo yo-n-de ki-te yo-ka-ro-o ka？
　ワシ ハダレ ヲヨンデ キテ ヨカロウ カ

1223. *Whom do the Chinese worship?*
　To-o ji-n wa na-ni wo o-nga-mi-ma-s' ka？
　トウジンハ ナニヲ オガミマスカ
Do.　To-o ji-n wa na-ni wo o-nga-mu ka？
　トウジンハ ナニ ヲオガムカ

1224. *Whose business is it to see to this?*
　Ko-no ko-to wo ma-mo-ru wa da-re nga ya-ku de go za-
　コノコトヲ マモルハダレガ ヤクデゴザ
ri-ma-s' ka？
　リマスカ
Do.　Ko-no ko-to wo ma-mo-ru wa da-re no ya-ku da ka？
　コノコトヲ マモルハダレノヤクダカ

1225. *Whose loss is it?*
　Ko-re wa do-na-ta no so-n ni na-ri-ma-s' ka？
　コレハ ドナタノ ソンニナリマスカ
Do.　Ko-re wa da-re no so-n ni na-ru ka？
　コレ ハダレノソンニナルカ

1226. *Whose fault is it?*
　Ko-re wa do-na-ta no o-chi-do de go za-ri-ma-s' ka？
　コレハドナタノオチドデ ゴザリマスカ
Do.　Ko-re wa da-re no o-chi-do da ka？
　コレハダレノオチドダカ

1227. *Whose book is this?*
　Ko-re wa do-na-ta no ho-n de go za-ri-ma-s' ka？
　コレハドナタノホンデゴザリマスカ
Do.　Ko-re wa da-re no ho-n da ka？
　コレハダレノホンダカ

1228. *Whose turn is it to read?*
　Do-na-ta no yo-mu j'-u-m-ba-n de go za-ri-ma-s' ka？
　ドナタノヨム ジユンバンデ ゴザリマスカ
Do.　Da-re nga yo-mu j'-u-m-ba-n da ka？
　ダレガ ヨム ジユンバンダカ

1229. *Whose land is this?*
Ko-no ji-me-n wa do-na-ta no de go za-ri-ma-s' ka?
コノジメン ハ ドナタ ノ デ ゴ ザリマス カ
Do. Ko-no ji-me-n wa da-re no da ka?
コノジメン ハ ダレ ノ ダ カ

1230. *Whose son are you?*
A-na-ta wa do-na-ta no go shi-so-ku de go za-ri-ma-s' ka?
アナタ ハ ドナタ ノ ゴ シソク デ ゴ ザリマス カ
Do. O-ma-e wa da-re no mu-s'-ko da ka?
オマエ ハ ダレ ノ ムスコ ダ カ

1231. *Why do you stop? go on.*
A-na-ta wa na-ni yu-e ni ta-chi-do-ma-t-te o i-de na-sa-ru ka? A-chi-ra e o i-de na-sa-ru nga yo-ro-shi-u go za-ri-ma-s'.
アナタ ハ ナニユエニ タチドマツテ オイデ ナサル カ アチラエ オイデ ナサル ガ ヨロシウ ゴ ザリマス
Do. O-ma-e wa na-ze ta-chi-do-ma-t-te i-ru ka? A-chi-ra e yu-ku nga yo-i.
オマエ ハ ナゼ タチドマツテ イル カ アチラエ ユク ガ ヨイ

1232. *Why not?*
Na-ze ni go za-ri-ma-se-mu ka?
ナゼニ ゴ ザリマセス カ
Do. Na-ze na-i ka?
ナゼ ナイ カ

1233. *Why did you not come earlier?*
Na-ze ni ha-ya-ku o i-de na-sa-ri-ma-se-na-n-da ka?
ナゼニ ハヤク オイデ ナサレマセナンダ カ
Do. Na-ze ha-ya-ku ku-na-ka-t-ta ka?
ナゼ ハヤク コナカツタ カ

1234. *Why put it off to another day?*
Na-ze ni ma-ta hi-no-be wo na-sa-ru ka?
ナゼニ マタ ヒノベ ヲ ナサル カ
Do. Na-ze ni ma-ta hi-no-be wo sz-ru ka?
ナゼニ マタ ヒノベ ヲ スル カ

1235. *Will this do?*
Ko-re de yo-ro-shi-u go za-ri-ma-s' ka?
コレ デ ヨロシウ ゴ ザリマス カ
Do. Ko-re de yo-i ka?
コレ デ ヨイ カ

1236. *Will this kind suit you?*
Ko-no yo-o-na shi-na nga o ki ni i-ri-ma-sh'-o-o ka?
コノ ヨウナ シナ ガ オ キニ イリマシヤウ カ
Do. Ko-n-na shi-na nga ki ni i-ro-o ka?
コンナ シナ ガ キニ イロフ カ

W.

1237. *Will you have some more?*
A-na-ta ma-da ko-re wa i-ri-ma-s' ka?
アナタ マダ コレ ハイリマスカ
Do. O-ma-e ma-da ko-re wa i-ru ka?
オマエ マダ コレ ハ アルカ

1238. *Will you not take a little less for it?*
Ko-re wa s'-ko-shi ma-ka-ri-ma-se-nu ka?
コレ ハ スコシ マカリマセヌカ
Do. Ko-re wa s'-ko-shi ma-ka-ra-nu ka?
コレ ハ スコシ マカラヌカ

1239. *Will there be a typhoon this year, think you?*
Ko to-shi wa ta-i-fu-u nga a-ro-o to o-bo-shi-me-s' ka?
コトシ ハ タイフウガ アロフト オボシメスカ
Do. Ko to-shi wa o-o ka-ze nga a-ro-o to o-mo-o ka?
コトシ ハ オホカゼ ガ アロフト オモフカ

Y

1240. *You ought not to do so.*
A-na-ta so-no yo-o-na mi-mo-chi wo na-sa-re-ma-s'-na.
アナタ ソノ ヨウナ ミモチ ヲ ナサレマスナ
Do. So-no yo-o-na mi-mo-chi wo na-sa-ru-na.
ソノ ヨウナ ミモチ ヲ ナサルナ

1241. *You read too loud.*
A-na-ta wa o-o-ki sz-ngi-ru ko-e wo sh'-te o yo-mi na-sa-ru.
アナタ ハ オホキ スギル コエ ヲ シテ オ ヨミ ナサル
Do. O-ma-e wa o-o-ki sz-ngi-ru ko-e wo sh'-te yo-mu.
オマエ ハ オホキ スギル コエ ヲ シテ ヨム

1242. *You talk too much.*
A-na-ta wa ku-chi nga o-o sz-ngi-ma-s'.
アナタ ハ クチ ガ オオスギマス
Do. Te-ma-e wa sh'-a-be-ri sz-ngi-ru.
テマエ ハ シャベリ スギル

1243. *You must not do so.*
A-na-ta k'-t-to ka-yo-o-na ko-to wo na-sa-re-ma-s'-na.
アナタ キット カ ヨウナ コト ヲ ナサレマスナ
Do. O-ma-e k'-t-to ko-o i-u ko-to wo sz-ru-na.
オマエ キット コウイフ コト ヲ スルナ

1244. *You must stay at home to-day.*
A-na-ta ko-n ni-chi wa k'-t-to u-chi ni o i-de na-sa-re-ma-sh'.
アナタ コンニチ ハ キット ウチ ニ オイデ ナサレ マシ
Do. O-ma-e ki-o-o wa k'-t-to u-chi ni i-ro
オマエ ケフ ハ キット ウチ ニ イロ

1245. *You may go home once a week.*
A-na-ta wa na-no-ka no a-i-da ni i-chi-do dz-tsz u chi e
アナタ ハ ナヌカ ノ アイダニ イチド ヅツ ウチエ
ka-i-ru ko-to nga yo-ro-shi-u go za-ri-ma-s'.
カエル コト ガ ヨロシウ ゴ ザリマス

Do. O-ma-e na-no-ka no a-i-da ni i-chi-do dz-tsz u-chi e ka-
オマエ ナヌカ ノ アイダニ イチド ヅツ ウチ エ カ
i-ru nga yo-i.
エル ガ ヨイ

1246. *You gave too much for it.*
A-na-ta wa da-i-bu-n ta-ka-ku o ka-i na-sa-re-ma-sh'-ta.
アナタ ハ ダイブン タカク オカイ ナサレマシタ

Do. O-ma-e ko-re wo ta-i-so-o ta-ka-ku ka-t-ta.
オマエ コレ ヲ タイソウ タカク カッタ

1247. *You are very welcome here.*
A-na-ta yo-o ko-so o i-de na-sa-re-te ku-da-sa-re-ma-sh'-ta.
アナタ ヨヲ コソ オイデ ナサレテ クダサレマシタ

Do. O-ma-e yo-o ko-so k'-te ku-re-ta.
オマヘ ヨヲ コソ キテ クレタ

1248. *You have spoiled it.*
A-na-ta nga ko-re wo o ko-wa-shi na-sa-re-ma-sh'-ta.
アナタ ガ コレヲ オコハシ ナサレマシタ

Do. O-ma-e nga ko-re wo ko-wa-sh'-ta.
オマエ ガ コレ ヲ コハシタ

1249. *You to ought to have done this before.*
A-na-ta wa mo-t-to ha-ya-ku i-ta-sz nga yo-ro-shi-u go za-
アナタ ハ モット ハヤク イタスガ ヨロシウ ゴ ザ
ri-ma-s'.
リマス

Do. O-ma-e wa mo-t-to ha-ya-ku sz-ru nga i-i.
オマエ ハ モット ハヤク スル ガ イイ

1250. *You do not come to the point.*
A-na-ta wa sa-shi a-ta-t-te i-ri-yo-o no ko-to wo o ha-na-
アナタ ハ サシ アタッテ イリヤウ ノ コト ヲ オ ハナ
shi na-sa-re-ma-se-nu.
シ ナサレマセス

Do. O-ma-e wa sa-shi a-ta-t-te i-ru ko-to wo ha-na-sa-nu.
オマヘ ハ サシ アタッテ イル コト ヲ ハナサヌ

1251. *You must leave off doing this*
A-na-ta sa-yo-o-na ko-to wo k'-t-to o ya-me na-sa-i-ma-sh'.
アナタ サヨウナ コト ヲ キット オ ヤメ ナサイマシ

Do. O-ma-e so-o i-u ko-to wo k'-t-to ya-me-ro.
オマエ ソウ イフ コト ヲ キット ヤメロ

1252. *You are mistaken.*
A-na-ta nga o-bo-shi-me-shi chi-nga-i de go za-ri-ma-s'.
アナタ ガ オボシメシ チガイ デ ゴ ザリマス

1252. O-ma-e nga o-mo-i chi-nga-i da.
オマエガ オモヒチガイダ

1253. *Your conduct has been bad.*
A-na-ta no o mi-mo-chi wa yo-ro-shi-u go za-ri-ma-se-na-n-da.
アナタノオミモチ ハ ヨロシウゴ ザリマセナンダ

Do. O-ma-e no o-ko-na-i wa yo-ku na-ka-t-ta.
オマエノオコナイ ハ ヨクナカツタ

1254. *You may take either of them.*
Do-re-de-mo h'-to-tsz o to-ri na-sa-ru nga yo-ro-shi-u go za-ri-ma-s'.
ドレデモヒトツオトリナサル ガ ヨロシウゴ ザリマス

Do Do-re-de-mo h'-to-tsz to-ru nga yo-i.
ドレデモヒトツットルガ ヨイ

1255. *You owe me a dollar.*
Wa-ta-k'-shi ni a-na-ta nga do-ra i-chi ma-i ka-ri-te o-ri ma-s'.
ワタクシニ アナタ ガ トライチマイ カリテオリマス

Do. Wa-ta-k'-shi ni o-ma-e nga do-ra i-chi ma-i ka-ri-te i-ru.
ワタクシニオマエガ ドライチ マイカリテイル

1256. *You can get them for nothing.*
A-na-ta ko-re wa ta-da mo-to-me-ra-re-ma-s'.
アナタ コレハ タダ モトメラレマス

Do. O-ma-e ko-re wa ta-da e-ra-re-ru.
オマヘコレハ タダ エラレル

1257 *You ride too fast.*
A-na-ta wa m'-ma wo ha-shi-ra-se-ru ko-to nga ha-ya sz-ngi-ma-s'.
アナタハ ム マ ヲ ハシラセルコト ガ ハヤ スギマス

Do. O-ma-e wa m'-ma wo ha-shi-ra-se-ru ko-to nga ha-ya sz-ngi-ru.
オマヘ ハ ム マ ヲ ハシラセル コト ガ ハヤ スギル

1258. *You have out-done me.*
A-na-ta wa-ta-k'-shi yo-ri ma-sa-t-te o-ri-ma-sh'-ta.
アナタ ワタクシ ヨリ マサッテオリマシタ

Do. O-ma-e wa wa-shi yo-ri ma-sa-t-te i-ta.
オマエハ ワシ ヨリ マサッテイタ

1259. *You flatter me.*
A-na-ta wa wa-ta-k'-shi ni he-tsz-ra-i-ma-s'.
アナタ ハ ワタクシ ニ ヘツライマス

1259. O-ma-e wa-ta-k'-shi ni he-tsz-ra-u.
オマエ ワタクシ ニ ヘツラウ

1260. *You may send the money by a messenger, and if any thing happens the risk is mine.*
So-no ka-ne wo ts'-ka-i no mo-no ni o wa-ta-shi na sa-ru
ソノカ子ヲツカイノモノニオワタシ ナサル
nga yo-i, mo-shi mo no ko-to nga a-ri-ma-sh'-te wa wa-
ガ ヨイ モシ モ ノ コト ガ アリマシテ ハ ワ
ta-k'-shi no so-n de go za-ri-ma-s'
タクシ ノ ソン デ ゴ ザリマス

Do. So-no ka-ne wo ts'-ka-i no mo-no ni wa-ta-sz nga yo-i;
ソノカ子ヲツカイノモノニワタスガ ヨイ
mo-shi mo no ko-to nga a-ru to wa-shi nga so-n da.
モシ モ ノ コト ガ アルト ワシ ガ ソンダ

1261. *You cannot trust him with so much money.*
A-na-ta wa so-no yo-o ni o-o-ku ka-ne wo a-no h'-to ni ma
アナタ ハ ソノ ヤウ ニ オオク カ子 ヲ アノヒト ニ マ
ka-se-te o-ka-re-mu-se-n'.
カセテ オカレマセヌ

Do. O-ma-e wa so-n-na ni ta-n-to ka-ne wo a-no h'-to ni ma-
オマエ ハ ソンナ ニ タントカ子 ヲ アノヒトニ マ
ka-se-te o-ka-re-nu.
カセテ オカレヌ

1262. *You should have anchored further out.*
A-na-ta mo-tto o-ki e i-ka-ri wo o-ro-sh'-ta nga yo-ro-shi-u
アナタ モット オキヘ イカリ ヲ オロシタ ガ ヨロシウ
go za-ri-ma-s'
ゴ ザリマス

Do. O-ma-e mo-tto o-ki e i-ka-ri wo o-ro sh'-ta nga yo-i.
オマエ モット オキヘ イカリ ヲ オロシタ ガ ヨイ

1263. *You must learn this by heart.*
Ko-re wa so-ra de yo-mu yo-o ni sh'-u-ngi-o-o na-sa-i.
コレ ハ ソラ デ ヨム ヨウ ニ シユギャウ ナサイ

Do. Ko-re wo so-ra de yo-mu yo-o ni ke-i-ko shi-ro.
コレ ヲ ソラ デ ヨム ヨ ニ ケイコ シロ

1264. *You may do it any how.*
Do-no yo-o ni de-mo na-sa-re-ma-sh'.
ドノ ヨウニデ モ ナサレ マシ

Do. Do-o de-mo shi-ro.
ドウ デ モ シロ

1265. *You never will get it done at this rate.*
So-no yo-o ni o-so-ku na-s'-tte wa i-tsz-ma-de mo shi-ma-i
ソノ ヨウ ニ オソク ナスッテ ハ イツマデ モ シマイ
ni wa na-re-ma-s' ma-i.
ニ ハ ナレマス マイ

1265. So-n-na ni o-so-ku sh'-te wa i-tsz-ma-de mo shi-ma-i ni
ソンナ ニ オソク シテ ハ イツマデ モ シマイ ニ
wa na-ru ma-i.
ハ ナル マイ

1266. *Your servant has arrived from Yedo.*
A-na-ta no go ke-ra-i nga Ye-do ka-ra ch'-a-ku i-ta-shi-
アナタ ノ ゴ ケライ ガ ヱド カラ チャク イタシ
ma-sh'-ta.
マシタ

Do. O-ma-e no ke-ra-i nga Ye-do ka-ra tsz-i-ta.
オマヱ ノ ケライ ガ ヱド カラ ツイタ

1267. *You have over-paid me one rio.*
A-na-ta i-chi ri-o-o yo-ke-i ni wa-ta-k'-shi e o wa-ta-shi
アナタ イチ リヤウ ヨケイ ニ ワタクシ エ オ ワタシ
na-sa-re-ma-sh'-ta.
ナサレマスタ

Do. O-ma-e i-chi ri-o-o o-o-ku wa-shi ni wa-ta-sh'-ta.
オマエ イチ リヤウ オオク ワシ ニ ワタシタ

1268. *You ought to take better care of your health.*
A-na-ta wa se-n yo-ri na-wo go yo-o-j-o-o wo na-sa-ru nga
アナタ ハ センヨリ ナヲ ゴヨウジャウヲ ナサル ガ
yo-ro-shi-u go za-ri-ma-s'.
ヨロシウ ゴ ザリマス

Do. O-ma-e wa se-n yo-ri na-wo yo-o-j'-o-o wo sz-ru nga yo-i.
オマヱ ハ センヨリ ナヲヨウジャウヲ スル カヨイ

1269. *You beat me in reading, but I possibly beat you a little in writing.*
A-na-ta yo-mu ko-to wa wa-ta-k'-shi yo-ri sz-ngu-re-te o
アナタ ヨム コト ハ ワタクシ ヨリ スグレテ オ
i-de na-sa-ru nga ka-ku ko-to wa wa-ta-k'-shi nga s'-ko-
イデナサル ガ カク コト ハ ワタクシ ガ スコ
shi ma-sa-t-te o-ri-ma-sh'-o-o.
シ マサッテ オリマシャウ

Do. O-ma-e yo-mu ko-to wa wa-shi yo-ri ma-sa-t-te i-ru nga
オマヱ ヨム コト ハ ワシ ヨリ マサッテ イル ガ
ka-ku ko-to wa wa-shi nga s'-ko-shi ma-sa-t-te i-ru de a-
カク コト ハ ワシ ガ スコシ マサッテイル テア
ro-o.
ロウ

1270. *You have put your coat on inside out.*
A-na-ta wa ha-o-ri wo u-ra-nga-e-shi ni k'-te o i-de na-sa-
アナタ ハ ハヲリ ヲ ウラガヘシ ニ キテ オイデ ナサ
re-ma-sh'-ta.
レマシタ

Do. O-ma-e wa ha-o-ri wo u-ra-nga-e shi ni k'-te-i-ta.
オマヱ ハ ハヲリ ヲ ウラガヘ シ ニ キテイタ

DIALOGUES.

DIALOGUE I.

On Buying Tea.

For. 1.—*Look here! I wish to speak with you a moment.*
Moshi, moshi, s'koshi ohanashi mooshitai koto nga aru.
モシ モシ スコシ オハナシ モウシタイ コトガ アル

Nat. 2.—*Ah? What do you want?*
Hai, nani no goyoō nga gozarimas' ka?
ハイ ナニ ノ ゴヨウ ガ ゴザリマス カ

For. 3.—*Nothing, but to ask if you have any tea.*
Hokano koto de mo nai nga, omai chawo motte iru
ホカノ コト デ モ ナイ ガ オマイ チヤ ハ モツテイル
ka, okiki mooshitai.
カ オキキ モウシタイ

Nat. 4.—*Yes, I have, but what kind do you want?*
Dzibun motte orimas' nga, donna no irimas' ka?
ズイブン モツテ オリマス ガ ドンナ ノ イリマス カ

For. 5.—*Well, I want some Uji, some Ise, and some Enshiu.*
Sayoōsa, Uji ka, Ise, Enshiu no tangui nga irimas'.
サヨウサウ ヂカ イセ エンシウ ノ タクイ ガ イリマス

Nat. 6.—*I have about 30 peculs of Uji in my godown, and about 70 peculs each of Ise, Enshiu and Shimoosa at Yedo, but I have musters here.*
Ujinga go sen ngin hodo watak'shi no kura ni goza-
ウヂガ ゴ センギン ホド ワタクシ ノ クラ ニ ゴザ
rimas', Ise, Enshiu, Shimoosa no tangui, sh'chi sen
イマス イセ エンシウ シモウサ ノ タクイ シチ セン
ngin hodo dztsz, Yedo ni gozarimas' nga, shikashi mi-
ギン ホド ヅツ エド ニ ゴザリマス ガ シカシ 三
hon wa kokoni gozarimas'.
ホン ハ ココニ ゴザリマス

For. 7.—*Well, let me look at the musters.*
Sayoo nara, mihonwo omise nasai.
サヨウナラ 三ホンヲオ三セナサイ

Not. 8.—*Wait a moment: I will bring them presently.*
S'koshi omachi nasai; tadaima jikini motte mairi-
スコシ オマチ ナサイタダイマシキニモツテマイリ
mas'.
マス

For. 9.—*The muster of Uji suits me. The leaf is good, and when drawn the flavor is good. What is the price of it?*
Uji no mihon nga ki ni irimas. Ha mo yoroshii, sen-
ウヂノ 三ホン ガ キニイリマス ハ モ ヨロシイ セン
jite kooki mo yoroshii. Nedan wa nani hodo itashima-
ジテ コウキ モ ヨロシイ子ダン ハ ナニホド イタシマ
shoō ka?
セウ カ

N. 10.—*Twenty seven dollars.*
Ni jiu sh'chi dora de gozarimas'.
ニジウシチ ドラ デゴザリマス

F. 11.—*I have no money now. What do you say to taking camlets in exchange?*
Watak'shi wa tadaima kanenga nai kara, goro to ko-
ワタクシ ハタダイマ カ子 ガナイ カラゴロウト コウ
eki ni sh'te wa ikanga de gozaimas' ka?
エキニシテ ハイカガ テゴサイマスカ

N. 12.—*If you have a lot of B. B. B., I will make the exchange for them.*
B. B. B. no kuchi nga arimas' nara, kore to koëki
ビ ビ ビ ノ クチ ガアリマスナラ コレトカウエキ
ni itashimash'oō.
ニイタシマシヤウ

F. 13.—*Yes, I have them, but I will not give $27, for this tea. If you will come down on the tea to $25, I will let you have the camlets in exchange for $23, Will that suit you?*
Hai, go zarimas' nga, kono chawa ni jiu sh'chi dora
ハイ ゴザリマス ガ コノチヤハ ニヂウ シチ ドラ
de watak'shi wa kaimasen'. Omai no chawo ni jiu go
テ ワタクシ ハ カイマセンオマイノチヤヲニ チウゴ
dora ni makete, watak'shi no goroōwo ni jiu san dora
ドラニ マケテ ワタクシ ノゴロウヲニジウサンドラ
ni sh'te, koëki ni itashimash'oō. Sore de ki ni iri-
ニシテ コウエキニイタシマシヤウソレ デ キ ニイリ
mas' ka?
マス カ

N. 14.—*The tea is very cheap, but as you are a good customer, I will trade with you at that rate.*
Cha no ne wa hanahada yaszu go zarimas' nga, ma-
チヤ ノ子 ハ ハナハダ ヤスウ ゴ ザリマス ガ マ
i do yoku katte kudasaru kara, sore de koéki ni
イドヨク カッテ クダサル カラ ソレ デコウエキニ
itashimash'oŏ.
イタシマシヤウ

F. 15.—*Well then, I will take 50 peculs. When will you bring the other tea that is in Yedo?*
Sayoŏ nara, go sen ngin kaimash'oŏ, Yedo ni arimas'
サヨウナラ ゴセンギン カイマセウ エドニアリマス
cha wa, itszngoro ko chira e motte mairimash'oŏ
チヤ ヲ イツゴロ コチラ エモッテマイリマセウ
ka?
カ

N. 16.—*In four days, positively.*
Yokka me ni wa, kitto motte mair:mash'oŏ.
ヨツカ メニハ キットモッテマイリマセウ

F. 17.—*Very well. I want, besides, that, to buy about* 20 *peculs of Szrunga tea. Will you not get it for me?*
Sore de yoroshii. Sono hokani, Szrunga no cha-
ソレ デ ヨロシイ ソノ ホカニ スルガ ノチヤ
wa ni sen ngin ngurai, kaitai omai kattewa kure-
ヲニセンギン グライ カイタイ オマイ カッテハクレ
mai ka?
マイカ

N. 18.—*At your service. I will bring all together.*
Kash'komarimash'ta. Mina isshioni motte mairima-
カシコマリマシタ ミナイッシヨニモッテ マイリマ
sh'oŏ.
セウ

F. 19.—*I wish you to put this lot into jars, and send it.*
Kono kuchi wa tszbo ni irete yokosh'te kurero.
コノ クチ ハ ツボニイレテ ヨコシテ クレロ

N. 20.—*Certainly. I will do so.*
Kash'komarimash'ta. S'a yoŏ itashimash'oŏ
カシコマリマシタ サ ヨウイタシマセウ

[*After the four days have expired*]

N. 21.—*The tea has arrived to-day.*
Konnichi cha nga ts'kimash'ta.
コンニチ チヤガ ツキマシタ

F. 22.—*I wish to see the musters.*
Mihon nga mitai.
ミホンガ ミタイ

N. 23.—*Here they are.*
   Kokoni gozarimas'.
   ココニ ゴザリマス

F. 24.—*This lot of Ise I do not like, for it is full of sticks and dirt. As to this lot of Enshiu, the leaf is uniform and has a good appearance, but it does not draw well.*
   Ise no kuchi wa, eda to gomi nga ooi kara, ki ni
   イセノ クチ ハ エダト ゴミ ガ オオイ カラ キニ
   irimasen. Kono Enshiu no kuchi wa, ha nga ichi
   イリマセン コノ エンシウノ クチ ハ ハ ガ イチ
   yooni sorotte arimash'te mingoto de gozarimas' nga,
   ヨウニ ソロウテ アリマシテ ミゴト デ ゴザイマス ガ
   senjite kooki nga waruu gozarimas'.
   センジテ コウキ ガ ワルウ ゴザリマス

N. 25.—*This lot of Szrunga is mixed. It has a great deal of old leaf, and stems in it. The lot of Shimoösa I like very much. It is very clear and free from dead leaves, and draws well. I must have 40 peculs more of it.*
   Szrunga no kuchi wa iro iro majitte orimas'.
   スルガ ノ クチ ハ イロ イロ マジッテ オリマス
   Ooku hine to eda nga mazatte orimas'. Kono Shimo-
   オオクヒネ ト エダ ガ マジッチ オリマス コノ シマ
   ösa no kuchi wa hanahada ki ni irimas'. Ita-
   ウサノ クチ ハ ハナハダ キ ニ イリマス イタ
   tte kiyoi, kore eda nga nakute, senjite kooki nga
   ッテ キヨイ カラ エダ ガ ナクテ センジテ コウキ ガ
   yoi. watak'shi wa korewo moö shi sen ngin hoshiu
   ヨイ ワタクシ ハ コレヲ モウ シ セン ギン ホシウ
   gozarimas'
   ゴザリマス

N. 25.—*All right. I will bring it immediately.*
   Sh'oöchi itashimash'ta. Sassoku motte mairimash'-
   シヨウチ イタシマシタ サッソク モッテ マイリマセ
   oö.
   ウ

F. 26.—*I wish to know the prices of the different lots.*
   Kuchi nguchi no nedan dszke nga kikitai.
   クチ グチ ノ ネダン ヅケ ガ キキタイ

N. 27.—*Well, I will state them. The Ise is $24.; the Szrunga is $21.; the Ensh'iu is $19, and the Shimoösa is $17.*
   Sayoö nara, mooshimash'oö. Ise nga ni jiu yo dora,
   サヨウ ナラ マウシマセウ イセ ガ ニジウ ヨ ドラ
   Szrunga nga ni jiu ichi dora, Enshiu nga jiu ku dora
   スルガ ガ ニシウ イチ トラ エンシウ ガ シウ ク トラ
   Shimoösa nga jiu sh'chi dora de gozarimas'.
   シマウサ ガ シウ シチ トラ デ ゴザリマス

F. 28.—*Will you barter?*
Kooēki ni itashimash'oō ka?
コウエキニイタシマセウカ

N. 29.—*What do you wish to barter?*
Anata nani to kooēki ni shitai ka?
アナタナニト コウエキニシタイカ

F. 30.—*I have grey shirtings, colored shirtings, velvets &c.*
Kinganakin ayanganakin, biroōdo nado no tangui nga arimas'
キガナキン アヤガナキン ビロウト ナド ノ タクイ
ガ アリマス

N. 31.—*What is the price of your colored shirtings?*
Aya nganakin no sooba wa nani hodo de gozarimas' ka?
アヤガナキン ノソウバ ハナニ ホド デ ゴザリマ
スカ

F. 32.—*I will sell for $3. per piece.*
Ip'piki dora sam mai de urimash'oō.
イツピキドラサンマイデ ウリマセウ

N. 33.—*How much are the 6½ catty grey shirtings?*
Mekata rok kin han no ki nganakin nani hodo de, aru ka?
メカタ ロクキン ハンノ キガナキン ナニホトデ
アルカ

F. 34.—*They are $2.40 per piece, but I cannot buy the teas at the prices you name.*
Are wa ni dora shi bu de gozarimas' nga, cha wa omai no ii ne de wa kawaremasen.
アレ ハ ニトラシブ デ ゴザリマス ガ チャ ハ
オマイノイイ子デ ハ カワレマセン

N. 35.—*What price will you give then?*
Suyoō nara, nani hodo de kai nasaru ka?
サヨウナラナニ ホドデカイ ナサルカ

F. 36.—*You must take off one dollar from each kind.*
Ii ne yori, ichi dora dztsz oh'ki nasare.
イイ子ヨリ イチ ドラヅツ オヒキ ナサレ

N. 37.—*Will you pay in dollars?*
Dora de haraimash'oō ka?
ドラデ ハライマセウカ

F. 38.—*I would rather barter.*
Kooēki ni sh'te morau hoō nga katte de gozarimas'.
コウエキ ニ シテモラフ ホウ ガ カツテ デ ゴザリ
マス

N. 39.—*I will take half in colored shirtings & half in dollars.*
Hambun wa mon nganakin wo kooeki ni sh'te, ham-
ハンブン ハモン ガネキン ヲコウエキニシテ ハン
bun wa dora de moraimash'oō.
ブン ハ ドナ デ モライマセウ

F. 40.—*Well, I will do that; you must bring the tea some time to-day.*
Sayoōnara, soō itashimash'oō. Konnichi jiu ni cha
サヨウナラサウイタシマセウ コンニチ ヂウニチヤ
wa motte oide nasai.
ヲモッテオイデナサイ

N. 41.—*Yes, I will bring it immediately.*
Hai. szngu sama motte mairimash'oō.
ハイ スグ サマ モッテ マイリマセウ

F. 42.—*When will the new tea arrive?*
Shin cha wa itszngoro ts'kimash'oō ka?
シン チヤ ハ イツ ゴロ ツキマセウ カ

N. 43.—*In about 40 days.*
Shi jiu nichi mo tachimash'tara. mairimash'oō.
シ ジウ ニチ モ タチマシタラ マイリマセウ

F. 44.—*Bring me musters as soon as possible for I intend to buy a large quantity of teas.*
Naru take hayaku mihon wo o mise nasai. Watak'-
ナル タケ ハヤク ミホン ヲ オ ミセナサイ ワタク
shiwa oōku shiire yoō to omoimas', kara.
シガ ヤウク シイレ ヨウトウモイマスカラ

N. 45.—*I will do so, and if you will buy all your teas of me I will bring you the best, and sell them as cheap as possible.*
Sayoō itashimash'oō. Mina cha wa watak'shi no te
サヨウイタシマシヨウ ミナ チヤ ハ ハタクシ ノ テ
yori okai nasaru naraba, goku yorosh'ki no wo mo-
ヨリ オカイ ナサル ナラバ ゴク ヨロシキ ノ ヲ モ
tte maitte, naru take yas'ku angemash'oo
ッテマイッテ ナル タケ ヤスク アゲマセウ

DIALOGUE II.

BETWEEN A FOREIGNER AND A JAPANESE SILK-DEALER

N. 1.—*I beg pardon (for interrupting you).*
   Gomen nasai.
   ゴメンナサイ

F. 2.—*You are welcome here.*
   Kore wa yoku oide nasaimash'ta.
   コレ ハ ヨク オイデナサイマシタ

N. 3.—*I am a silk-dealer. Do you wish to buy?*
   Watak'shi wa ito akindo de gozarimas' nga, kiitowo
   ワタクシ ハ イトアキンドデゴザリマスガキイトヲ
   okai nasaru ka?
   オカイナサルカ

F. 4.—*I do not want any now.*
   Ima irimasen.
   イマイリマセン

N. 5.—*I will sell very cheap.*
   Oō yasz uri ni itashimash'oō.
   オオヤスウリニ イタシマシヤウ

F. 6.—*I do not want any just at present.*
   Ima sashiatatte irimasen.
   イマサシアテッテ イリマセン

N. 7.—*I really do not know what to do, for if I do not immediately send some money to my friends the wholesale dealers, my credit will be injured.*
   Watak'shi wa kiu ni toiya e kanewo yarimasene-
   ワタクシ ハ キウニトイヤ エカ子ヲ ヤリマセ子
   ba, namai ni kidz nga ts'kimas' kara, makoto ni toō
   バ ナマイニ キヅ ガ ツキマスカラ マコト ニトウ
   waku itashimas'.
   ワク イタシマス

F. 8.—*I am sorry for you. How much silk and what sort have you?*
   Sorewa o ki no doku ni omoimas'. Dono yoōna ki-
   ソレハ オキ ノ ドクニ オモイマス ドノ ヨウナキ
   ito de nani hodo arimas' ka?
   イトデナニ ホド アリマスカ

N. 9.—*I have 10 peculs of Aida Nos. 1 and 2.*
   Aida no kiito de sen ngin hodo arimash'te koō o-
   アイダノキイトデ セン ガン ホドアリマシテコウオ
   tsz nga gozarimas'.
   ツ ガ ゴザリマス

F. 10.—*If there is any No. 1, let me see the muster.*
　　　Joŏ　no kuchi nga aru nara, mihonwo mise nasai.
　　　ジヤウノ クチ ガアルナラ ミホンヲ ミセナサイ

N. 11.—*Yes, here it is.*
　　　Hai, kore de gozarimas.
　　　ハイ コレ デ ゴザリマス

F. 12.—*It is worth about $440.*
　　　Kore wa shi h'yaku shi jiu dora ngurai no soŏba de gozarimas'.
　　　コレ ハ シ ヒヤク シヂウ ドラ グライ ノ ソウバ デ
　　　ゴザリマス

N. 13.—*Will you buy it at that price?*
　　　Anata sono nedan de kaemash'oŏ ka?
　　　アナタ ソノ子ダン デ カエマシヤウ カ

F. 14.—*As I do not want it just now, you had better sell it to some one else.*
　　　Ima sashiatatte irimasen kara, hoka e uru nga yoroshii.
　　　イマ サシアタッテ イリマセン カラ ホカ エ ウル ガ
　　　ヨロシイ

N. 15.—*No, there are no buyers at present, and the price has gone down very much.*
　　　Iiye, kono setsz kau h'to nga nai de, oŏki ni soŏba nga daremash'ta.
　　　イイヘ コノ セツ カウ ヒト ガ ナイ デ オオキニ ソウバ
　　　ガ ダレマシタ

F. 16.—*I expect a vessel to arrive soon, and then perhaps you may be able to sell.*
　　　Moŏ s'koshi tatsz to irifune nga aroŏ to omoimas' kara, sono toki ni ookata uraremash'oŏ
　　　モウ スコシ タツ ト イリフ子 ガ アル ト オモイマス
　　　カラ ソノ トキ ニ オヲカタ ウラレマシヤウ

N. 17.—*Yes, but I must have the money for it to-day or to-morrow.*
　　　Sayoŏ de gozarimash'oŏ nga, kom mioŏ nichi no uchi ni kane wo saikaku itash'tai.
　　　サヨウデ ゴザリマセウ ガ コン メウ ニチ ノ ウチ
　　　ニ カ子 ヲ サイカク イタシタイ

F. 18.—*How much money do you want.*
　　　Kane wa nani hodo hoshiika?
　　　カ子 ハ ナニ ホド ホシイ カ

N. 19.—*Well, I want $3000.*
　　　Sayoŏ de gozarimas', san zen dora hodo irimas'
　　　サヨウデ ゴザリマス サンゼン ドラ ホド イリマス

F. 20.—*If I take the 10 peculs of silk as security, I will lend you $3000, and you must pay me two per cent a month, interest for the money.*

Sono k'ito no sen nginwo sh'chi ni totta naraba, san
ソノキイトノセンギンヲシチニトツアナラバサン
zen dora kashimash'oö kara, mai ts'ki, ni bu no riwo
ゼンドラカシマシヤウカラ マイツキ ニ ブ ノ リヲ
o harai nasai.
オハライナサイ

N. 21.—*If you will do so, I shall be* **much obliged.**
Soö nas'te kudasareba aringatoö gozarimas'.
サウナスツテ クダサレバ アリガトウ ゴザリマス

F. 22.—*But* **if** *you overrun a month, I shall not keep the security, and unless you take it up, I shall sell it to reimburse myself.*
Naredomo, h'to ts'ki ni amareba, **sh'chiwa toma** oki-
ナレドモ ヒトツキ ニ アマレバ シ チ ハ ト メ オキ
masen; dashimasen naraba uri haraimas'.
マセン タシマセンナラバ ウリ ハライマス

N. 23. *That is* **too soon.** *If the price advances this* **month,** *I will return the money, but if it declines, I must beg you to allow me two months.*
Sore wa amari hayoö gozarimas'. Kon ngetsz no uchi
ソノ ハアマリ ハヨウゴザリマス、コンゲツノウチ
ni soöba nga angarimaszreba, kanewo kaish'te da-
ニソウバ ガ アガリマスレバ カ子ヲ カイシテ ダ
shimash'oö; szwari naraba, ni ngetsz go kamben
シマシヤウ スワリ ナラバ ニ ゲツ ゴ カンベン
nas'te kudasare.
ナスツテクダサレ

F. 24 *Very well; I agree to that. But if you take the silk before half a month is up, you must pay half a month's interest, and after half a month is past, you must pay a month's interest.*
Sh'oochi itashimash'ta. **Naredomo,** han ts'ki mai ni
シヨウチイタシマシタ ナレドモ ハンツキマイニ
dash'ta naraba, han ts'ki no ri bunwo o harai nasai;
ダシタナラバ ハンツキ ノ リブンヲオハライナサイ
han ts'ki szngite dash'ta naraba, ichi ngetsz no ri
ハンツキスギテ タシタナラバ イチ ゲツ ノ リ
bunwo o harai nasai.
ブンヲオハライナサイ

N, 25. *It is a very high rate of* **interest,** *but as I am in a tight place and have no other resource, I will do so.*
Makoto ni koö ri de gozarimas' nga, sashits'kaete,
マコト ニ コウ リ デ ゴザリマス ガ サシツカエテ
yondokoro gozarimasen kara, s'oö itashimash'oö.
ヨンドコロゴザリマセンカラ ソウイタシマシヤウ

F. 26. *When you or your friends want money, I will advance it at any time upon silk, or tea, or other merchandize as security.*

Omai mata Omai no hoöyuu ni kane no iriyoö nga
オマイマタオマイノホウユウニカ子ノイリヨウガ
areba, kiito aruwa cha, sono hoka urimonowo
アレバキイトアルイハチヤソノホカウリモノヲ
sh'chi ni totte, itszdemo kanewo kashimash'oö.
シチニトツテイツデモカ子ヲカシマシヤウ

N. 27. *Thank you. I will tell my friends what you say. I think they will be glad to get money on those terms.*
Sore wa aringatoö. Sono omomukiwo hoöyuu ni mo
ソレハアリガトウソノオモムキヲホウユウニモ
hanashimash'oö. Ima sadameta toöri de karirarenas'
ハナシマシヤウイマサダメタトウリデカリラレマス
nara, hoöyuu mo yerokobimash'oö to dzonjimas'.
ナラホウユウモヨロコビマシヤウトゾンジマス

F. 28. *When you have brought the silk here, I will weigh it, and after having ascertained the weight, I will give you a receipt for it, and take a receipt from you for the money.*
Omai kiitowo motte kita toki ni, hakari ni kakete,
オマイキイトヲモツテキタトキニハカリニカケテ
mekatawo aratameta uëde, omai ni adzkari no kaki-
メカタヲアラタメタウエデオマイニアヅカリノカキ
ts'kewo yarimash'oö; omai yori watak'shi ni kashikin
ツケヲヤリマシヤウオマイヨリワタクシニカシキン
no sh'oömonwo moraimash'oö.
ノシヤウモンヲモライマシヤウ

N. 29. *Pardon me; I wish to ask you one more question. If the silk should have been accidentally changed while deposited in your godowns, how shall I know it? I have no idea that you would do such a thing, but as it is a matter of business between merchants, I mention it so as to have it remembered.*
Gomen nasai; mata okiki moösh'te okitai koto nga
ゴメンナサイマタオキキモウシテオキタイコトガ
gozarimas'. Anata no kura ni kiitowo adzkete oki-
ゴザリマスアナタノクラニキイトヲアヅケテオキ
mas' uchi ni, f'to szrikairaruru yoöna koto nga
マスウチニフトスリカイラルルヨウナコトガ
attara, doösh'te shirimash'oö ka? Anata no hoö ni
アツタラドウシテシリマシヤウカアナタノホウニ
wa sayoöna koto wa arimas'mai to omoimaszredo-
ハサヨウナコトハアリマスマイトオモイマスレド
mo, o tangai ni akindo no koto de gozarimas' kara, nen
モオタンガイニアキンドノコトデゴザリマスカラ子ン
no tameni o kotowari moösh'te okimas'.
ノタメニオコトワリモウシテオキマス

E. 30—*What you say is quite right. Well than, have your silk nicely put up in bales, and then placed in boxes, and sealed so that they cannot be opened. Should any seal be broken, and the silk within be changed, I will pay you the value of it.*
Omai no iu tokoro wa mottomo de gozarimas'. Sayoō
オマイノイウトコロハ モツトモデゴザリマス サヨウ
naraba, h'to koōri dztsz ni irete, akerarenuyoō ni
ナラバ ヒト コウリ ヅツ ニイレテ アケラレヌヨウニ
yoku fuuinwo sh'te o oki nasai. Moshi sono fuuin
ヨクフウインヲシテ オヲキナサイ モシ ソノフウイン
nga yaburete, naka no ito nga szrikatte, attara, so-
ガ ヤブレテ ナカ ノイト ガスリカイテ アッタラ ソ
re dake no daikinwo dashimash'oō.
レダケ ノダイキンヲダシマシヤウ

F 33—*That will be fair. I have been very troublesome to you. Good bye, Sir*
Sore de yoroshiu gozarimash'oō. Oōki ni o yakama-
ソレデ ヨロシウ ゴザリマシヤウ オヲキニオ ヤカマ
shiu gozarimash'ta. Sayoō nara. Go kingen yoroshiu.
シウ ゴザリマシタ サヨウナラ ゴ キゲン ヨロシウ

DIALOGUE III.

On Shipping Goods to Foreign Countries.

N. 1.—*I wish to consult you about the state of foreign markets. If you will attend to the business for me, I will make some shipments.*
Watak'shi wa gai koku no ichiba no yoōszwo okiki
ワタクシ ハ ガイコク ノ イチバ ノ ヨウスヲオキキ
moōshitoō gozarimas'. Anata watak'shi ni nari kawat-
モウシドウゴザリマス アナタ ワタクシ ニナリ カワッ
te sewawo szru naraba shiromonowo fune ni tsznde
テ セワヲ スル ナラバ シロモノヲ フ子ニツンデ
okurimash'oō.
オクリマシヤウ

F. 2.—*What articles have you to ship?*
Nan no shiromonwo tszmi okuru ka?
ナン ノ シロモノヲツ ミオクルカ

N. 3.—*I have tea and silk to ship.*
Cha to kiitowo tszmi watashimash'oō.
チヤトキイトヲツミ ワタシマシヤウ

F. 4.—*I would not advise you to ship silk at present. If you have good tea, well prepared, it will do for the English or American market.*
Tadaima kiitowo tszmi nasaru koto wa o szszme
タダイマキイトヲツミナサルコトハオススメ
moöshimasen. Ii cha no seihoö sh'ta no nga aru nara
モウシマセン イイチヤノセイホウシタノガ アルナラ
Ingirisz, aruiwa Amerika no ichiba ni mukima-
イギリス アルイハアメリカ ノ イチバニ ムキマ
sh'oö.
シヤウ

N. 5.—*If that is the case, I will let you have tea. I have 300 peculs of the best Uji.*
Son naraba, ochawo angemash'oö. Uji no itatte
ソンナラバ オチヤヲアゲマシヤウ ウヂ ノ イタツテ
ii chawo sam man ngin motte orimasz.
イイチヤヲサン マン ギンモツテオリマス

F. 6.—*After I have seen the tea, we will talk about it. But if the tea is not well fired, and the boxes are not lined with lead, it will not stand a long voyage.*
Sono chawo mimash'ta uëde soödan itashimash'oö.
ソノチヤヲ ミマシタウヘデソウダン イタシマシヤウ
Naredomo, yoku hoiro ni kakete, hako no uchiwo nama-
ナレドモ ヨクホイロニ カケテハコ ノウチヲ ナマ
ri de harimaseneba' nangai kaish'oö wa mochima-
リデ ハリマセ子バ ナガイカイシヤウハ モチマ
sen.
セン

N. 7.—*Will you prepare the tea for me?*
Watak'shi ni kawatte cha no niwo ts'kutte kudasa-
ワタクシニカワツテチヤ ノ ニヲ ツクツテクダサ
ru ka?
ル カ

F. 8.—*I will, if you wish it.*
O tanomi nara, ts'kutte angemash'oö.
オタノミナラ ツクツテアゲマシヤウ

N. 9.—*I think I will prepare the tea myself, and bring it to you. What will the other charges come to?*
Watak'shi no hoö de niwo ts'kutte angeyoo to omoi
ワタクシ ノ ホウ デ ニヲツクツテ アゲヨウトオモイ
mas'. Sono hoka ni dzappi nga nani hodo kakarima-
マス ソノ ホカニ ザツピガ ナニホド カカリマ
sh'oö ka?
シヤウカ

F. 10.—*To what port **will** you ship it?*
Doko no minato e watashimash'oō ka?
ドコ ノ ミナト ヘ ワタシマシヤウカ

N. 11.—*If the market price is good at San Francisco, please send it there.*
San F'ranshis'ko nga soōba **nga** yoroshii naraba, soko e
サンフランシスコガ ソウバガ ヨロシイナラバ ソコヘ
yatte kudasare.
ヤツテ クダサレ

F. 12.—*Well, Japan teas are selling well at San Francisco now. The charges will be, first, the export duty of five per cent, next, my commission of five per cent, and storage, coolie and boat hire &c. The freight will amount to about 2 cents per pound, and the **import** duty in America is 20 cents per pound, and the commission of the consignee there, and the expense arising from difference of exchange will be charged to your **account**.*
Sayoōsa, Nippon no cha nga San F'ranshis'ko de
サヨウサ ニツポン ノ チヤ ガ サンフランシスコデ
tadaima ne nga yoroshiu gozarimas'. Sono hajime no
タダイマ子 ガ ヨロシウゴサリマス ソノ ハジメ ノ
dzappi nga tszmi dasz no unjoō de gozarimas'.
ザツピ ガ ツミ ダス ノ ウンジヤウデゴザリマス
Sore kara watak'shi no koōsen go bu to, kurash'ki,
ソレ カラ ワタクシ ノ コウセン ゴ ブ ト クラシキ
karukochin, funachin nado de gozarimas'. Unchin wa
カルコチン フナチンナド デ ゴザリマス ウンチン ハ
Amerika ik kin ni tszite ni rin dtsz ngurai kakari-
アメリカイツキンニツイテ ニ リンツツ クライ カカリ
mash'oō. Sore kara, kano kuni no akindo no te ni
マシヨウ ソレ カラ カノ クニ ノ アキンド ノ テニ
watashimas' **kara**, sono koōsen to kare kore no do-
ワタシマス カラ ソノ カウセン ト カレ コレ ノ ト
ra no soōba **ni** sh'tangatte dzappiwo kanj'oō
ロ ノ ソウバ ニ シタガツテ ザツピヲカンジヤウ
itashimash'oō.
イタシマシヨウ

N. 13.—*With such charges, I think **there** will be no profit for me.*
Sayoō ni dzappi nga kakattewa watak'shi no moōke
サヨウニ ザツピ ガ カカツテハ ワタクシ ノ モウケ
nga gozarimas'mai to omoō.
ガ ゴサリマスマイトオモウ

F. 14.—*At what do you value your tea?*
Omai no cha wa ikura ni tszite orimas' ka?
オマイノチヤハ イクラニツイテ オリマスカ

N. 15.—*It cost me $20 per pecul.*
H'yak' kin ni tszite ni jiu dora de kaimash'ta.
ヒヤクキンニツイテニジウドラ デカイマシタ

F. 16.—*Then it will cost you about 39 cents per pound, laid down in San Francisco.*
Son nara San F'ranshis'ko ni okimash'te ik kin
ソンナラサンフランシスカウニオキマシテイツ キン
ni tszite san jiu ku rin ni narimas'.
ニツイテサンジウク リンニナリマス

N. 17.—*And what will it sell for there by the pound?*
Achira de ik kin ni tszite dono kurai de utte
アチラ デ イツキン ニツイテドノクライデウッテ
kuremash'oŏ ka?
クレマシヤウカ

F. 18.—*It will certainly sell for 50 cents per pound.*
Kitto go jiu rin ni uremash'oŏ.
キツトゴシウリンニウレマシヤウ

N. 19.—*How long will it be before I get my money back?*
Kane wa itszngoro tedori ni narimash'oŏ ka?
カ子ハイツゴロ テドリ ニナリマシヨウカ

F. 29.—*Probably in about five or six months.*
Oŏkata go roku ngetsz nochi ni toremash'oŏ.
オオカタゴロク ゲツ ノチ ニトレマシヤウ

N. 21.—*It is a long time to be out of one's money for so small a profit but I will make one shipment for an experiment.*
Sh'oŏ ri no akinaiwo sh'te sayoŏ ni nangaku kash'te
シヤウリノアキナイヲシテ サヨウニナガク カシテ
oitewa, aimasen nga, kokoro mino tameni h'to tabi
オイテハアイマセンガココロ ミ ノ タメニ ヒトクビ
okutte mimash'oŏ.
オクツテミマシヤウ

DIALOGUE IV.

ON BUYING SILK.

Native. 1.—*Do you not wish to buy silk.*
　　Kiitowo o kai nasarimasen **ka**?
　　キイトヲオカイナサリマセンカ

Foreigner 2.—*Yes what sort have you?*
　　Hai, donnanowo motte **o** ide nasaru **ka**?
　　ハイドンナノヲモツテオイデナサルカ

N. 3.—*I have Maibashi.*
　　Maibashiwo motte **imas'**.
　　マイバシヲモツテイマス

F. 4.—*It is No.* 1. *Maibashi?*
　　Goku j'oŏ no Maibashi de arimas' ka?
　　ゴクジヤウノマイバシデアリマスカ

N. 5.—*It is No.* 1. *and* 2.
　　Ichi ban **no** mo, **ni ban no** mo de gozarimas'.
　　イチバンノモニバンノモデゴザリマス

N. 6.—*Have you a muster of it?*
　　Sono mihon nga arimas' **ka**?
　　ソノミホンガアリマスカ

N. 7.—*Yes, here it is.*
　　Hai, kokoni arimas'.
　　ハイココニアリマス

F. 8.—*How much of the No.* 1. *have you?*
　　Ichi ban no kuchi wa dono kurai arimas' ka?
　　イチバンノクチハドノクライアリマスカ

N. 9.—*I have 4 peculs of No.* 1. *and 2 peculs of No.* 2.
　　Goku j'oŏ no kuchi wa shi h'yak' kin, tszngi no
　　ゴクジヤウノクチハシヒヤクキンツギノ
　　nga ni h'yak' kin arimas'.
　　ガニヒヤクキンアリマス

F. 10.—*I will buy the No.* 1., **but do not want the other**.
　　Goku j'oŏ **wa**, kaimash'oŏ nga, tszngino wa yoshima-
　　ゴクジヤウハカイマシヤウガツギノハヨシマ
　　sh'oŏ.
　　シヤウ

N. 11.—*I would rather* **sell** *both together if possible.*
　　Naru koto nara, rioŏheŏ isshioni uritoŏ gozari-
　　ナルコトナラリヤウホウイツシヨニウリタウゴザリ
　　mas'.
　　マス

F. 12.—*What is the price of it all together?*
　　Mina de nedan **wa** ikura de gozarimas' ka?
　　ミナデネダンハイクラデゴザリマスカ

N. 13.—*Do you wish to know the true price?*
　　　　Sh'oömi no nedanwo okiki nasaritai ka?
　　　　シヤウミノ子ダンヲオキキナサリタイカ

F. 14.—*Yes, give me the lowest possible price.*
　　　　Hai, naru take yas'ku hataraite kudasai.
　　　　ハイナル タケヤスクハタライテクダサイ

N. 15.—*The very lowest price is $450.*
　　　　Ketch'aku no tokoro wa, shi h'yaku go jiu dora de
　　　　ケッチヤクノトコロハ シ ヒヤク ゴ ジウドラ デ
　　　　arimas'.
　　　　アリマス

F. 16.—*I think that is too much.*
　　　　Sore wa omoi no hoka takai yoö da.
　　　　ソレ ハオモイノホカタカイヤウダ

N. 17.—*No, it is cheap I think, but how much will you give?*
　　　　Iiye, sore wa yas'karoö to omoimas' nga, oboshimeshi
　　　　イイエソレハヤスカロウトオモイマスガ オボシメシ
　　　　wa dono kurai ka?
　　　　ハドノクライカ

F. 18.—*If it is all like the muster, I will give $430.*
　　　　Minna mihon no toöri naraba, shi h'yaku san jiu dora
　　　　ミンナミホンノトヲリナラバ シ ヒヤクサンジウドラ
　　　　de kaimash'oö.
　　　　デカイマシヤウ

N. 19.—*I cannot sell so cheap; I shall lose money.*
　　　　Soö wa yas'ku wa dekimasen; watak'shi ni son nga
　　　　ソウハ ヤスク ハ デキマセン ワタクシ ニ ソン ガ
　　　　tachimas'.
　　　　タチマス

F. 20.—*Well, I will go to your house and see the lot, and then I will see if I can give you any more.*
　　　　Son nara, watak'shi wa omai no uchi e itte, kuchiwo
　　　　ソンナラ ワタクシ ハオマイノウチエイッテ クチヲ
　　　　mite, sono uëde moö chitto yoku kaimash'oö ka kan-
　　　　ミテ ソノウヘデ モウチットヨクカイマシセウカカン
　　　　ngaite mimash'oö.
　　　　ガイテミマセウ

N. 21.—*When will you come?*
　　　　Itsz o ide nasaru ka?
　　　　イツオイデナサルカ

F. 22.—*In the course of an hour.*
　　　　Han toki no uchi ni.
　　　　ハントキノウチニ

N. 23.—*Will you certainly come?*
　　　　Kitto o ide nasaru ka?
　　　　キットオイデナサルカ

E. 24.—*Yes, where is your house?*
　　Hai, o uchi wa doko de gozarimas' ka?
　　ハイ オウチ ハ ドコ デ ゴザリマス カ

N. 25.—*It is in "Ben-ten-doori" street, the first division. Inquire for the shop called Takaszya.*
　　Ben-ten-doóri, itchoó me do gozarimas'. Takaszya
　　ベンテンドヲリ イッテウメ デゴザリマス タカスヤ
　　to o tadzne nasai
　　トウ タヅ子 ナサイ
　　　　　(*after going to the shop.*)

F. 26.—*I have come to see the silk.*
　　Watak'shi wa kiitowo mi ni mairimash'ta.
　　ワタクシ ワ キイトヲ ミ ニ マイリマシタ

N. 27.—*Ah? Walk in.*
　　Sayoó de gozarimas'ka? O angari nasarimash'
　　サヨウデ ゴザリマスカ オ アガリ ナサリマシ

F. 28.—*Thank you.*
　　Aringatoó gozarimas'
　　アリガトウ ゴザリマス

N. 29.—*This is the silk we talked about just now.*
　　Sen koku o hanashi moósh'ta kiito wa, kore da gozari-
　　センコク オハナシ モウシタ キイト ハ コレ デ ゴザリ
　　mas'.
　　マス

F. 30.—*This does not correspond with the muster.*
　　K'ore wa mihon to soo-oo itashimasen'
　　コレ ハ ミホン ト ソウ オウ イタシマセン

N. 31.—*In what respect does it differ?*
　　Dono yoó ni chingainas' ka?
　　ドノ ヨウ ニ チガイマス カ

F. 32.—*In the first place, the colour is not as good as the muster, and the thread is not as even.*
　　Dai ichi ni wa, mihon hodo, iro nga yoroshiu na-
　　ダイ イチ ニ ハ ミホン ホド イロ ガ ヨロシウ ナ
　　kute, ito ni mura nga arimas'.
　　クテ イト ニ ムラ ガ アリマス

N. 33.—*I do not think there is any difference.*
　　Watak'shi wa chingawanu hadz da to omoimas'.
　　ワタクシ ハ チガワヌ ハヅ ダト オモイマス

F. 34.—*There is a great deal of inferior silk mixed with it.*
　　Taisoó waruino nga mazatte orimas'.
　　タイソウ ワルイノ ガ マザッテオリマス

N. 35.—*Well what will you give for it?*
　　Sayoo nara, ikura de o kai nasaru ka?
　　サヨウ ナラ イクラ デ オ カイ ナサロウ カ

DIALOGUE IV.

F. 36.—*I do not think I will buy such an article.*
Kono shina de wa, kawoŏ to omoimasen.
コノシナデハ カワウト オモイマセン

N. 37.—*I will come down in the price a little.*
S'koshi ii ne yori sangemash'oŏ.
スコシイイ子ヨリ サゲマシヨウ

F. 38.—*How much?*
Dono kurai sangeru ka?
ドノクライ サゲル カ

N. 39.—*I will take off $5. a pecul.*
H'yak' kin ni tszite go dora dztsz h'kimash'oŏ.
ヒヤクキンニツイテ ゴ ドラ ヅツ ヒキマシヨウ

F. 40.—*That will not do.*
Sore de wa ikemasen.
ソレデハ イリマセン

N. 41.—*Please tell me the highest price you will give.*
Anata giringiri no tokorowo oshiatte kudasare.
アナタ キリギリ ノトコロヲ オシヤツテクダサレ

F. 42.—*Well, I will give you $420.*
Sayoŏ nara, shi h'yaku ni jiu dora de kaimash'oŏ.
サヨウナラ シ ヒヤク ニジウドラデカイマシヨウ

N. 43.—*I shall lose money, at that rate.*
Sore de wa watak'shi ni son nga yukimas'.
ソレデハ ワタクシニソン ガユキマス

F. 44.—*It is your misfortune, but I cannot give you any more.*
O ki no doku de gozarimas' nga, moŏ sore yori de-
オキノトクデゴサリマス ガ モウソレ ヨリ テ
kimasen.
キマセン

N. 45.—*Will you not give $440?*
Shi h'yaku shi jiu dora o kun nasarimasen ka?
シ ヒヤク シジウ ドラ オ クンナサリマセンカ

F. 46.—*No. I cannot give you any more.*
Iiye, s'koshi mo kai angeru koto wa dekimasen.
イイエスコシ モ カイ アゲル コト ハデキマセス

N. 47.—*You are a hard man to deal with.*
Omai akinaiwo szru ni kataku kurushii h'to da.
オマイ アキナイヲスルニ カタク クルシイヒトダ

F. 48.—*No. I am not. If I pay $440, I cannot sell (the silk) to any profit.*
Iiye, watak'shi son de wa arimasen. Shi h'yoku
イイエ ワタクシ ソウデハ アリマセン シ ヒヤク
shi jiu dora de kattewa, saki yuki nga shimasen.
シ シウ ドラデカツテハサキ ユキ ガ シマセン

N. 49.—*Then I will take* $435.
　　　Sore nara, shi h'yaku san jiu go dora moraima-
　　　ソレナラ シ ヒヤク サン ジウ ゴ ドラ モライマ
　　　sh'oŏ.
　　　シヨウ

F. 50.—*I cannot go above* $420.
　　　Shi h'yaku ni jiu dora no uēwa angeraremasen.
　　　シ ヒヤク ニ シウ ドラ ノウヘハ アゲラレマセン

N. 51.—*I cannot sell for that.*
　　　Sore de wa doō mo uraremasen.
　　　ソレ デ ハ ドウ モ ウラレマセン

F. 52.—*Well, I hope you will have some thing to sell (at another time).*
　　　Sayoŏ nara mata nanzo o nengai mooshimash'oŏ
　　　サヨウ ナラ マタ ナニゾ オ子ガイ モウシマシヨウ
　　　(*The foreigner turns to go away*).

N. 53.—*Stop a moment.*
　　　Chitto o machi nasai.
　　　チツト オ マチ ナサイ

F. 54.—*What (further) business is there?*
　　　Nani yoŏ de gozarimas' ka?
　　　ナニ ヨウ デ ゴザリマスカ

N. 55.—*What say you to* $430.
　　　Shi h'yaku san jiu dora de wa ikanga de gozarima-
　　　シ ヒヤク サン ジウ ドラ デ ハ イカガ デ ゴザリマ
　　　s' ka?
　　　スカ

F. 56.—*No, that will not do. But since I have taken the trouble to examine the article, I will add* $5. *more, and give you* $425.
　　　Iiye, dekimas'-mai. Shikashi sek'kaku mita mono
　　　イイエ デキマスマイ シカシ セツカク ミタ モノ
　　　da kara, moŏ go dora mash'te, shi h'yaku ni jiu do-
　　　ダ カラ モウ ゴ ドラ マシテ シ ヒヤク ニ ジウ ド
　　　ra angemash'oŏ.
　　　ラ アゲマシヤウ

N. 57.—*Well, I shall lose by it, but as I must have the money, I will let you have (the silk).*
　　　Sayoŏ nara, son nga mairimas' keredomo, kane nga
　　　サヨウ ナラ ソン ガ マイリマス ケレドモ カ子 ガ
　　　isongashii kara, sashi angemash'oŏ.
　　　イソガシイ カラ サシ アゲマシヤウ

F. 58.—*When will you weigh it?*
　　　Itsz mekatawo aratame nasaru ka?
　　　イツ メカタヲ アラタメ ナサル カ

N. 59.—*To-morrow if it is a fair day, but I will bring the goods to your godown.*
Mioō nichi tenki naraba, aratamemash'oō. Shikashi
ミヤウニチテンキナラバ アラタメマシヤウ シカシ
nimotsz wa kom ban anata no kara e motte mairima-
ニモツ ハ コンバンアナタノカラエモッテマイリマ
sh'oō.
シヤウ

F. 60.—*Very well. Good bye.*
Yoroshiu gozarimas'. Sayoō nara.
ヨロシウ ゴザリマス サヨウナラ

N. 61. *Good bye.*
Sayoō nara.
サヨウナラ

DIALOGUE V.

Between a Master and Servant

Master 1.—*Take this money to Ejiro's shop, in Shimoda street, and pay him for the goods I bought yesterday.*
Watak'shi sakujitsz, Shimoda no machi no Eijiroō no
ワタクシ サクジツ シモダノ マチノエイジロウノ
mise de kaimonowo sh'ta kara, kono kanewo motte
ミセ デ カイモノヲシタカラ コノ カ子ヲモッテ
itte haraiwo sh'te koi.
イッテハライヲシテコイ

Servant 2.—*Aye, at your service, Sir. How much is there here?*
Hei kash'komarimash'ta. Kono kane wa ikura gozari-
ヘイカシユ マリマシタ コノ カナ ハイクラゴザリ
mas' ka?
マスカ

M. 3.—*A hundred dollars.*
Dora nga ipp'iaku mai.
ドラ ガ イッピヤクマイ
(*Servant counts them.*)

S. 4.—*Here are $105. Is it not a mistake.*
Kore wa ipp'iaku go dora arimas' nga, machingai de
コレ ハイッピヤクゴドラアリマスガ マチガイデ
wa gozarimasen ka?
ハゴザリマセンカ

M. 5.—*Take it in order to change (any bad dollars). When you pay the money, be sure to take a receipt for it.*
Sore wa kaikin no tameni motte yuke. Kono kanewo
ソレ ハ カイキン ノ タメニ モツテ ユケ　コノ カネヲ
watasz toki ni, kitto uketoriwo tore.
ワタス トキニ キツト ウケトリヲトレ

S. 6.—*Yes, I understand your orders.*
Hei, sh'oōchi itashimash'ta.
ヘイ シヨウチ イタシマシタ

DIALOGUE VI.

On Buying Bills of Exchange.

1.—*I wish to send 500 rioō to Oōzaka, for merchandize bought there.*
Watak'shi wa Oōzaka de kaimonowo itashimash'ta
ワタクシ ハ オオサカ デ カイモノヲ イタシマシタ
kara, go h'yaku rioō nobosetai.
カラ ゴ ヒヤク リヤウ ノ ホセタイ

2.—*You can get a Bill on Oōzaka, from some bank at Yedo.*
Yedo no rioō-ngaiya kara, Oōzaka no kawasetenga-
エド ノ リヤウガイヤ カラ オオザカ ノ カハセテガ
tawo motomeraremas'.
タヲ モトメラレマス

3.—*What rate is charged for Bills on Oōzaka?*
Oōzaka no kawase tengata ni nam bu risoku nga ka-
オオザカ ノ カワセテガタ ニ ナンブ リソク ガ カ
karimash'oō ka?
カリマセウ カ

4.—*There is no fixed rate. It varies according to the amount of the Bill, & the time of payment.*
Sadamatta koto wa gozarimasen. Tengata wa kane
サダマタ コト ハ ゴザリマセン テガタ ノ カネ
hodo ni sh'tangatte, risoku no koo nge nga gozarima-
ホド ニ シタガツテ リソク ノ コウ ザ ガ ゴザリマ
s', mata dasz no osoi to hayai ni yotte chingai nga
ス マタ ダス ノ オソイ ト ハヤイ ニ ヨツテ チガイ ガ
arimas'.
アリマス

5.—*Well, what will be the rate of a Bill of 500 rios. at sight?*
   Sayoönara, tengata nga ts'ki shidai sngu ni kanewo
   サヨウナラ テガタ ガ ツキ シダイ スグ ニ カネヲ
   daseba, nam bu hodo kakarimash'oŏ ka?
   ダセバ ナンブ ホド カカリマシャウカ

6.—*I think it will be about one per cent.*
   Ichi bu ngurai to omoimas'.
   イチブ グライト オモイマス

7.—*What will it be if payable at one month's sight?*
   Tengata wa tszite kara h'to ts'ki szngite kanewo da-
   テガタ ハ ツイテ カラ ヒトツキ スギテ カネヲ ダ
   seba, nam bu hodo kakarimash'oŏ ka?
   セバ ナンブ ホド カカリマセウ カ

8.—*I think it will be about seven-tenths per cent.*
   Sh'chi rin ngurai to omoimas'.
   シチ リン グライト オモイマス

9.—*Will you do me the favor to buy a Bill for me?*
   Watak'shi ni kawatte sewawo sh'te, tengatawo tanon-
   ワタクシ ニ カワッテ セワヲ シテ テガタヲ タノン
   de kudasare.
   デ クダサレ

10.—*Certainly. I will do so at once.*
   Sh'oŏchi itashimashta, Sassoku tanomimash'oŏ.
   シャウチ イタシマシタ サッソク タノミマシャウ

DIALOGUE VII.

On Buying Lackered Ware.

Buyer, 1.—*Pardon a little* [*interruption*.]
   Chitto gomen nasare.
   チイトゴメンナサレ

Seller. 2.—*Come in.*
   O ide nasarimash'
   オイデナサリマシ

B. 3.—*I have come to make some purchases*
   Watak'shi wa kaimono ni kimash'ta.
   ワタクシ ハ カイモノニ キマシタ

S. 4.—*Yes? What do you want?*
   Hai. nani nga o iriyoŏ de gozarimas' ka?
   ハイ ナニ ガ オイリヨウデゴザリマスカ

B. 5.—*I want to look at your lackered ware, such as, cabinets, travelling trunks, chow chow boxes, stands, cups, dressing-cases, work-boxes, bath-tubs, wash-bowls, picnic-boxes, &c. &c.*

Makie no tans', mangmochi, kashidansz, zen, wan kio-
マキエノ タンス ナガ モチ カ シダンス ゼン ワンキヤ
odai, haribako, tarai, hanzo, hentoōbako no
ウダイ ハリバコ タライ ハンゾウ ベントウバコ ノ
tangui nga mitai.
タグイガ ミタイ

S. 6.— *All right, I will show you some, but first walk up here (i. e. on the elevated matted floor.)*
Sh'oōchi itashimash'ta. Madz kochira e o angari
ショウチ イタシマシタ マヅ コチラ エ オ アガリ
nasaremash'.
ナサレマシ

(certain articles being selected.)

B. 7.— *How much do all these come to?*
Kore wa nokoradz nani hodo ni naru ka?
コレ ハ ノコラヅ ナニ ホド ニ ナルカ

N. 8.— *Yes, I will add them up and see (Reckons.) All together they come to $100.*
Sayoō de gozariems. Yosete mimash'oō. Shimete
サヨウデ ゴザリマス ヨセテ ミマシヤウ シメテ
ippiaku dora ni narimas'.
イツピヤク ドラ ニ ナリマス

B. 9.— *Does it amount to that? As it is higher than my estimate, make it $75.*
Sayoō ni narimas' ka? Watak'shi no omojiri yori
サヨウニ ナリマス カ ワタクシ ノ オモイイリ ヨリ
takai kara, sh'chi jiu go dora ni o make nasai.
タカイ カラ シチジウゴ ドラ ニ オ マケ ナサイ

S. 10.— *You cannot have them for that price by any means. I did not name an extravagant price at first.*
Doō itash'te sayoō ni wa mairimasen. Hajime yori
ドウ イタシテ サヨウニ ハ マイリマセン ハジメ ヨリ
kakene wa mooshimasen.
カケネ ハ モウシマセン

B. 11.— *I cannot buy them at that rate.*
Sono nedan de wa kawaremasen.
ソノ子ダンデ ハ カハレマセン

S. 12.— *Well than I will take off $5.*
Sayoō nara go dora h'kimash'oō.
サヨウナラ ゴ ドラ ヒキマシヤウ

B. 13.— *I cannot buy at all at that price. You must come down a good deal more.*
Sore de wa doōmo kaimasen motto dzto o make
ソレ デ ハ ドウモ カエマセン モツト ヅウト オ マケ
nasai.
ナサイ

S. 14.—*Then make an estimate how much you will give.*
　　　Sayoŏ nara, go kamben nasarete, nani hodo ni o kai
　　　サヨウナラ ゴカンベンナサレテナニ ホド ニオカイ
　　　nasaru ka?
　　　ナサルカ

B. 15.—*I will give $5 more.*
　　　Moŏ go dora naosh'te kaimash'oŏ.
　　　モウ ゴドラナヲシテカイマシヤウ

S. 16.—*That will not do. I cannot let you have these articles for less than $90.*
　　　Sore de wa dekimasen. Kono shinawa ku jiu dora
　　　ソレデハ デキマセン コノ シナハ クジウドラ
　　　no uchi de wa angeraremasen.
　　　ノウチデ ハアゲラレマセン

B. 17.—*Well, I will meet you half way and take them at $85.*
　　　Sayoŏ nara, ayubi ai ni sh'te, hachi jiu go dora de
　　　サヨウナラ アユビアイニシテ ハチジウゴドラデ
　　　kaimash'oŏ.
　　　カイマシヤウ

S. 18.—*Well, if I let you have them (for that price), I beg you will make it up at another time.*
　　　Sayoŏ naraba, sashi angemas' kara, mata o iriawa-
　　　サヨウナラバ サシ アゲマス カラ マタオイレアハ
　　　sewo o nengai mooshimas'.
　　　セヲオネガイ モウシマス

B. 19.—*Very well.*
　　　Yoroshiu gozarimas'.
　　　ヨロシウ ゴザリマス

S. 20.—*Will you take these articles now, or shall I send them to your house?*
　　　Kono shinawo tadaima o mochi nasaru ka, anata no
　　　コノ シナハ タダイマオ モチ ナサル カアナタ ノ
　　　o taku e motasete angemashoŏ ka?
　　　オタク エモタセテ アゲマシヨウカ

B. 21.—*Never mind, I will send for them to-morrow.*
　　　Sore ni wa o yobimasen. Mioŏ nichi tori ni ange-
　　　ソレニハ オヨビマセン ミヤウニチ トリニ アゲ
　　　mash'oŏ.
　　　マシヤウ

WEIGHTS AND MEASURES.

Long or Timber Measure.

The unit of **Timber measure** is the sh'aku, which is equal to the English foot, and is divided into 10ths, 100ths, and 1000ths, or szu bu, and rin. This foot is called the Kane J'aku, or metallic foot.

Thus 1 Sh'aku or Is sh'aku 　　一尺＝ 12　Inches English.
     1 Szn or Is szn 　　　　　一寸＝ 1.2　do.　　do.
     1 Bu or Ichi bu 　　　　　一分＝ .12 do.　　do.
     1 Rin or Ichi rin 　　　　一厘＝ .012 do.　　do.
     3 Sh'aku or San J'aku 　　三尺＝ 1　Yard　　do.
     6 Sh'aku or Rok' sh'aku 　六尺＝ 1 Fathom or Ik ken ―間
    60 Ken or Roku jik' ken 　六十間＝ 360 Ft. or It Ch'oŏ ―町
    36 Ch'oŏ or Sanjiu rok' ch'oŏ 三十六町＝ 1296 Ft. or Ichi ri ―里

The Ri or Japanese mile = 2.45 miles English.

Cloth Measure.

The **unit** of this measure **is** also called a Sh'aku, or foot, but it is 3 inches longer than the foot of Timber measure, and is called the Kujira j'aku, or Whale foot. It is also decimally divided.

Thus, 1 Sh'aku or Is sh'aku ―尺＝ 15　Inches English.
     1 Szn or Is szn 　　　　　一寸＝ 1.5　do.　　do.
     1 Bu or Ichi bu 　　　　　一分＝ .15 do.　　do.
     1 Rin or Ichi rin 　　　　一厘＝ .015 **do.**　　do.

Square or Superficial Measure.

The unit of this is the square Ken of Long measure, or 36 square **feet**, which is denominated a Po **or** Tszbo.

Thus, 1 Po ―歩 or H'to tszbo ―坪＝ 36 square feet.
     1 Se or Is se 　　　　　　一畝＝ 30 po＝ 1080 square feet.
     1 **Tan** or It tan 　　　　一段＝ 300 po＝ 10,800 do. do.
     1 C'hoo or It ch'oŏ 　　　一町＝ 3000 po＝ 108,000　do.

An acre is equal to 1210 Tszbo 千二百十坪

WEIGHTS AND MEASURES.   198

Measure of Capacity.

Its unit is the Mas', or Sh'oŏ 升, a box $3\tfrac{2}{15}$ English inches deep, and $5\tfrac{9}{15}$ inches square, and contains $111\tfrac{393}{1000}$ cubic inches. It is used for measuring oil, sake, soy, vinegar, grain, seeds, salt, rice &c. and is decimally divided into ngoŏ, sh'aku, sai, satsz, ke, and dzoku.

Thus; 10 Dzoku or Jiu dzoku 十粟 =1 Ke or Ik ke   一圭
       10 ke or Jik' ke   十圭=1 Satsz or Is satsz   一撮
       10 Satsz or Jis satsz   十撮=1 Sai or Is sai   一抄
       10 Sai or Jis sai   十抄=1 Sh'aku or Is Sh'aku   一勺
       10 Sh'aku or Jis Sh'aku 十勺=1 ngoŏ or Ichi ngoŏ 一合
       10 ngoŏ or Jiu ngoŏ   十合=1 Sh'oo or Is Sh'oŏ   一升

AND

10 Sh'oŏ or Jis sh'oŏ 十分=1 To or It to, or tomas, 一斗 or 斗升
10 to or Jit to   十斗=1 Koku or Ichi koku 一石

A koku contains 6,446 cubic feet English, or 5.13 bushels.

Measures of Weight.

The division of weights, with the exception of the kin 斤 or catty, is also based upon a decimal scale.

1 momme or Ichi momme 一匁=2.133 drams avoirdupois or 58.33 grains Troy.

       10 fun, or Jip pun 十分=1 momme or Ichi momme 一匁
       10 rin, or Jiu rin 十厘=1 fun or Ip pun   一分
       10 mo, or Jiu mo 十毫=1 rin or Ichi rin   一厘

The precious metals are weighed by this scale.

       10 Momme, or Jiu momme is written 十匁
       100   ,,   or H'yaku me   ,,   ,,   百匁
       1,000   ,,   or Ik kam me   ,,   ,,   一貫匁
       10,000   ,,   or Jik kam me   ,,   ,,   十貫匁
       100,000   ,,   or H'yak' kam me ,,   ,,   百貫匁
       1,000,000   ,,   or Sen ngam me ,,   ,,   千貫匁
       10,000,000   ,,   or Man ngam me ,,   ,,   萬貫匁
       100,000,000   ,,   or Ok' kam me ,,   ,,   億貫匁

Apothecaries Weight.

Medicines are bought and sold by the same standard of weight as above. The smallest denomination is the rin, the next the fun, and the next the momme. 2 momme, however are called Han rioŏ me, or Half rioŏ weight, written. 4 momme are called Ichi rioo me or 1 rioŏ weight, written. One and a quarter rioŏ of medicine is denominated, **Ichi rioo** to ichi momme, or Go (five) momme. **Every** multiple of **4** momme is called so many rioŏ. Thus 12 momme **are** called S'an rioŏ, or three rioŏ, and 16 momme are called yo (4) rioŏ, and so on, until 160 me are called **1k** kin or 1 catty, which **is** 1.33¼lbs. Avoirdupois.

In speaking of weights, the word momme is used after all numbers, except the multiples of 10, when it is shortened into me.

MONEY.

COPPER AND IRON COINS.

The smallest coin in value is the Mon 文 or Zeni cash of **iron.** The next larger iron coin is equivalent to 4 zeni. Besides these there **are** no iron coins in circulation, though it is not difficult to find others that have been used in former times, and Japanese books descriptive of them. The smallest copper coin is also called a Mon or Zeni, and is likewise equal to 4 small iron Zeni in value, and hence it is frequently called the Shi-mon zeni, i. e. 4 Mon zeni. It is somewhat remarkable that the iron coin of the same dimensions, viz: **the** larger one above mentioned has **the same** value **as the copper** Shi-mon zeni.

There is **a** much larger copper **coin, in** circulation, called Tempo, from the period at which it was first issued, or Toŏ h'yaku, *i. e. worth a hundred*, because it is equal to 100 of the smaller iron zeni.

It is also sometimes denominated H'yaku Mon zeni, or the Hundred Mon zeni. In ordinary business transactions among the Japanese, the Tempo is reckoned at 96 small iron cash, or 24 copper cash, or 24 of the larger iron cash.

SILVER COINS.

The smallest silver coin in circulation **is** the quarter **bu, or** isshiu. The next larger is the half bu, or Nishiu, **and the next** the bu, **or** ichibu, which signifies **one** bu. It is **therefore** quite wrong to speak of 10 or 100 ichibus, inasmuch as it would when interpreted be equivalent to saying, 10 or 100 *one-bus*. The bu is a fourth of a rioŏ, which again used to be equal to a gold koban. Formerly there was a silver rioŏ, it is said, but it is not known to be in existence now.

The bu, (ichibu) does not represent a fixed value, but is a fourth of a rioó or koban, be the value of the latter more or less. In the times of the Dutch Monopoly, the gold koban was valued at 4 bu, or 1\frac{31}{100}$, while its value to the Dutch trader was 12½ florins. So widely different were the relative values of gold and silver in Japan and Europe. This continued till 1859, when the new treaties with Japan went into operation.

The foreigners who first came here, after the opening of the ports, very naturally bought up all the gold kobans they could, at a large profit to themselves. The Yedo government, discovered that gold was rapidly leaving the country, and to prevent it, at the suggestion, it is said, of one or more of the foreign Ministers at Yedo, offered to holders of gold a higher price than foreigners could afford to pay. The price of kobans thus rapidly rose from 4 bus to 14, or even more, and this put an effectual stop to the further exportation of gold.

The tide then set towards Japan, and kobans came back to be paid to the custom house at the enhanced government value. In 1860 a new koban was coined, which was made to correspond to the intrinsic value of silver, being equal to 4 bu, thus bringing the relative values of gold and silver to the foreign standard

Gold Coins.

Of the Koban we have already spoken. The only subdivisions of this are the half and the quarter koban. Formerly there were also eighths and sixteenths, but all have disappeared except those above named : and the eighth of a koban, in consequence of the reduction in the weight of the koban, is so light a coin, that the Japanese say of it. "It is blown away by a breath of wind".

Mixed Coins.

Besides the before-mentioned coins, half-bus and bus, and 2 bu pieces, made of a mixture of gold and silver, are in circulation.

REFERENCES AND ABBREVIATIONS
IN THE INDEX.

The figures refer to the sentences in the Alphabetical part, where the words or phrases named occur.

The Abbreviations are used as follows; viz:

Acc.	for	Accusative, or the direct object.
Adj.	,,	Adjective.
Adv.	,,	Adverb.
Conj.	,,	Conjunction.
Conj. Adv	,,	Conjunctive Adverb.
Dat.	,,	Dative, or Indirect Object.
Fut.	,,	Future.
Ger.	,,	Gerundive.
Indic,	,,	Indicative.
N.	,,	Noun.
Neg.	,,	Negative.
Pass.	,,	Passive.
Pron.	,,	Pronoun.
V.	,,	Verb.
V. Trans.	,,	Transitive Verb.

N. B.—These abbreviations refer only to the words which stand before them. The difference of idiom forbids, very often, that what is expressed by one part of speech in English, should be expressed by the same in Japanese.

INDEX AND VOCABULARY

OF THE

ENGLISH WORDS AND PHRASES

IN THE

ALPHABETICALLY ARRANGED SENTENCES,

WITH THEIR

CORRESPONDING EXPRESSIONS IN JAPANESE.

A

Abound. Tak'san orite orimas', 78.
About. Wa, following Koto, 232.
About. *i. e.* doing, Nas'te, 1147.
Absent Rusz, 874.
Accept. Uke-ai, 525.
Accident. Sosoó, 626.
Account. Ch'omen, 197.
Accounts Kanj'oó, 1144.
Accustomed. Narete, 637.
Ache. n. Itami, 1042.
Acquainted with. Dzonjimash'ta, Sh'tta, 233.
Act. Jtashimas', Szru, 1118.
Actions. Okonai, 911.
Adieu (Bade). Wakare moŏ sh'te. Wakarete, 621.
Advise. Szszme moŏsz, Szozmeru, 525.
Affair. Koto, 1131.
Afford (Cannot). Dasz koto wade kimai. or Dekimasenu. 417.

Afraid (To be). Osoremaszru, 182. Habakarimas', Habakaru, 450. Omoinas', Omoŏ, 431.
Afterwards. Atode, 91.
Again. Mata, 70. 784. 925. F"tatabi', 132. 422. Moŏ, 131. 1079. Kasanete, 132.
Age (Of). Otona ni', 296. Toshi
Ago. Mukashi, 931.
Agreat while. H.sash'ku, **338**
Ahead. *i. e.* as a wind. **Mukaimash'ta, Mukatta, 931.**
Ainos. Aino, 808. 941.
Alike. Onaji yoŏ ni, 992.
All. Mina, 896. 211. 284. 754, 928. 940. 950. 1072. Szbete, 659. Nok'oradz, 274. 398. 377.
All about it. Yoku, 22. Kuwash'ku Nokoradz, 74.
All alone H'toride, 267.
All countries. Ban koku, Se-kai, 406.

All day. Ichi nichi. 260. 1147.
All directions. Yo-hoö, Lit. 4 quarters, 407.
All I can. Dekimas' hodo, Dekiru hodo, 483.
All hands. Nori-ainomono wa nokoradz, 1088.
All the way home. Iye made, Uchi made 518.
All things. Bammotsz, 180.
Alone. H'tori de. 267.
Although. Keredomo, 420.
America. Amerika, 556.
American. Amerika no h'to, 219.
Among. Naka ni, 988.
Amount. Kanj'oö, 787.
Amount to. Narimas', Naru, 398.
Amusement. Tanoshimi, 480.
Ancient. Mukashi, 637, Ikari wo orosh'ta, 1262.
And. To, 718. 911.
Ankle. Ashi kubi, 286. 957.
Another. Hokano, 6.
Answer. Aisatsz, Hentoö, 513. Henji. 569.
Any. Nani no, 987.
Any body. Donatademo, Daredemo, 5.
Any how. Dono yoö ni demo, 1264.
Any longer. Mo haya. Mo, 418. Mo. 469. Moö. 497. Moö. Kono ngo wa, Moö kono nochi, 516.
Any more. Mada, 192. Mata 592.
Any other. Hokano wa, 416.
Any thing. Nani demo, 8. Skoshi wa, 99. Koto wa. 239, Nanzo, 53. Moshi mono koto nga, 1260.
Any thing else. Hoka no koto, 314.
Any where. Doko ni demo, 783.
A piece. Dz tsz, 883
Appears. Miemas'. 1038.
Appearance (make their.) Demas', 1174.

Apple, Rinngo, 616.
Are. Gozarimas'. and Aru. 9. and passim.
Are. (continuative.) Iru. 14. and passim following the gerundive form of a verb. e. g. 99. Sh'tte iru ka? Do you know? Also 311. Sz matte iru. He lives or dwells &c.
Are you at work? Shi ngoto wo szru ka? 16
Are you coming? O i de nagarimash'oo ka? Ki nasaru ka? 15.
Arm. Ude, 216.
Arrested. Meshitorareimash'ta, Shi barareta, 269.
Arrive, Ts'ki, Ts'kimas'. 6.
Arrived. Ts'ki nasarimash'ta 325. Ch'aku itashimash'ta. 1266. Tszita, 325.
Article. Shina 365. 591. Shina mono, 1086.
Article of commerce. Kooe ki mono, 799.
Article of food. Tabemono. 813.
Asak'sa. (A district in Yedo.) 811.
Ashamed. Hajikashiu. 18. Haji wo shiou, 18. 218.
Ashore. Oka ni, 290.
Ask. Kik'e, O kiki nasare, 22.
Assure. Makoto wo hanashi, Hon toö wo hanas'. 414.
As long as. Uchi wa, 21.
As well as you can. Kirioö no oyobu dahe, Sei ippai ni, 94.
As well as we can. Chikara no oyobu dake, 1099.
As you please. Anata no oboshimeshi ni, 93. 882.
At. Ni, 11. 732. De, 11.
At all events. Dzehi, 575. 1110.
At last. Yoö yaku, Yoö yoö, 512.
At a loss. Shiremasenu, Shirenu, 482.
At a venture. Dzehi, 706.
At once. H'tori de, 523

At pleasure. Katte shidai ni, 141.
At present Ima, 499.
Attendants. Tomo, 160.
Attended to. Kokoro dzketemamotte, 1027.
At the least. Kakenn yoòni, 49. 681.
At this rate Kono yuō ni, 1265.
At auction. Seri de, 501.
Aunt. Oba, 357.

Authority. I. 588.
Averaging. Narashte, 25.
Avoid. Hedate nasare, 26.
Awake. Okoshi nasarete kudasare, Okose, 27.
Away with it Hoka e yare, 128.
Away (Put) Shimatteo oki nasare, Shimatte, oke, 782.
Axehelves. Yoki no e, 28.
Aye Hai, or He, 29.

B

Baby. Sh'oòni, Ko, 125.
Back again, Mata, 15.
Back i. e. to the original place Meto no tokoro ni, 784.
Back. v Modose, 30.
Back (Come) Kaerimas', Kaeru, 863.
Bad. Warui, Warui, 226. 354. 491. 590. 594. 720. 754. 1015. Omoō, Omoi, Lit. heavy, 228.
Bade Adieu. Wakare, moōsh'te, Wakarete, 621.
Baggage. Ni. 428.
Bait. Esa, 964.
Baked. Yake, 1008.
Ballast Omori, 555.
Bankrupt. Jimetsz itashimas', T'sz bureru, 303.
Barely. Lit. in the dim distance. Kas'kani, Harukini, 530.
Bargain. Ts wo atta, 270.
Basket. Kango, 76.
Bathe. Yu wo ts'kaimas', Yu wo ts'kau, 471.
Battle. Tatakai. 952.
Bay. (Color.) Akai, 711.
Be there. Achira ni matte oide nasare, Achira ni matte iro, 36.
Be not long. Hisash'ku o kakari nasaruna. Hisash'ku nasaru

na, 120.
Bear. i. e. suffer. Kannin, 413.
Bear the blame. Lit the bad consequences. Meiwaku ni narimas, or naru, 586.
Beat. i e. excel. Masatte orimas', Masatte iru, Szngarete oide nasaru, 1269.
Beat into (Nautical phrase) Mangiri komimash'ta, Mangiri konda, 1093.
Because. Kara, 637. 1093.
Become. Ochimasz:u, Naru, 763. Narimash'oō, Naru, 1181. Narimash'ta, Natta, 279. 793.
Become used to (Has.) Narete o shimai nasaremash'ta, Narete shimatta, 299.
Become warm. Atatamarimes', Atatamaru, 820.
Beef. Ushi-niku, **1115.**
Been (Not.) Oide **nasaremasenu,** 266.
Been (Have.) **Mairimash'ta, Itta,** 543. Oide **nasareta koto wa** gozarimas', **Itta koto wa aru,** 194.
Before. Maini, 161. 560. 423. Izen, 560. Mai, 982. Konomai, **1046.**
Beg. Doōzo kudasare, or Kurero, 522.

Beggars. Kojjiki, or Kojiki, 596. 763.
Beggary. Kojiki ni, 725.
Beg pardon. Go men kudasarema sh', Go men nasai, 626. 526.
Begin. Hajime nasare, Hajimero, 35. 1180
Begin again. Mata hajime yori o naōshi nasare, Mata hajime yori, naose, 925.
Begun to rain. Yattoame nga furimash't:, Hajimete ame nga f'tta, 687
Behaves well (If he.) Ts'tome nga yorosh'kereba, Hataraki ngaji naraba, 589.
Behindhand. Osoku, 764.
Being Gozarimas'kara, Da kara, 762. Gozarimash'te, Sh'te, 826.
Being wrecked. Ita sen itashimash'te, Fune wo yabutte, 1088.
Believe (not.) Shinjimasenu, Makoto to senu, 466. Shinji nai, 703.
Bell Kane. 85. Rei, 814.
Besides. Hokani. 37.
Best. Ichiban yoroshü no, Ichi banü nga, 594. Ichiban yoro shiu, Ichiban yoroshii, 1020 Yoroshiu, Yoi. 1205. 1199
Better. Yoroshiu, Yorosh'ku, 184 949. 671. Yori—yoroshiu, Yori—yoi, 953. 1268 665. 669. 1019. Masarimas, Mashi, Lit surpasses, 1029. 890. 763. Yori—yoku, 1067. Yoō, Yoi, 580. Nawo yoroshii, 855.
Bill. Uketori-ngaki, Uketori, 729.
Bird-seed. Kibi, 112.
Bit. *i. e.* the least mite, S'koshi mo, 113.
Blackened teeth (with) Gembuku wo sh'ta, 1073.
Blacken their teeth. Kane wo ts'ke, 1073
Blame (To.) Adzkaru kolo, T'sz-

mi niszru koto, 981. Tszmi ni narimas', 1209.
Bless. Yoku ii, 724.
Blind of one eye. Mek'kachi, Katame, 282
Blind man. Dzatoō, 539.
Blot (If you.) Kesh'ta naraba, or Nara, 597.
Blue. Ai iro, 258.
Boar (Wild.) Inoshishi, 790.
Board. Ita, 714. 1034.
Boardfence. Hei, 771.
Board. v. Sh'okuji wo itashimas', Meshi wo kun, 1189.
Boast (Not). Hokorimasenu, Hokoranu, 408.
Body. Karada, Mi, 145.
Boil. Ni nasare, Ni nasai, 154.
Boiled (Not) Niemasenu shinngaaru, 1052.
Book. Hon, 415. 1188. Sh'omotsz, 1014.
Boots. Nangangutsz, 773.
Born. M'mare, 265. 1185.
Both. Rioōh-ō, 787.
Bother. J'ama ni narimas', or Naru, 696.
Bother (Do not. J'ama wo szruna, 737.
Bottle. Tok'kuri, 846.
Bought. Kaimash ta, Katta, 501.
Bow (of a boat.) Hesaki, 6 55.
Bow-knot. Hi'a ori ni muszbi, 1
Bow string. Yudzru, 866.
Box. Hako, 58. 77. Bako, 835.
Boy, Otoko kokodomo, 171. Kodomo, 273 Ko. 1132.
Brave. Tszyoi, Tszyoki, Lit. strong. 890.
Bread. Pan, 766. 1083.
Break (not) *i. e.* Violate. Chingaimasenu, Chinger:enu, 461
Break (Apt to). Koware soō, 1060.
Bridge. Hashi, 40. Bashi, 4 07.
Bring Tszmi okurimas', Tszmiokuru, 824. Motte oide nasare.

Motte koi, 38. 39. 41, 152
795. K'te kudasare, 152.
Bring (Do not). Motte o ide nasa-
runs, Motte kuruma, 128.
Bring back. Kaeshi nasare, Kae-
se, 1176.
Briskly. Kiuni, 820.
Broke to pieces. Kuda kemash'ta,
Kowash'ta, 312.
Broke (violated.) Yabarimash'ta,
Yabutta, 320.
Brother (Elder) Ani, Ani sama,
292
Brothers. Kioodai, 745.
Brought up. Sodaterare nasareta.
Sodaterareta, 1186.
Brush. v. Harae, 42.
Brush. i. e. to polish. Mingake,
43
Build. F'shin wo itashimas
Built (Was). Tskuraremash'ta,
Ts'kurareta, 1057
Built. (are). Ts'kuraremas', 40.
Bulbs. Tama, 761.
Burn (Not) i, e. blacken with fire,
Kongenu, 116.
Burn up. Yaite o shimai nasare,
Yaite shimae, 44. Taite shim-
ae, 45.
Burning. Yaku koto, 47.
Burrow. Szmai wo itashimas',
Szmu, 798.

Business. (Family affairs). Kan-
gioo, 235.
Do. (Mechanical). Sh'yoku, **268**.
Do (Mercantile). Akinui, 359.
Do (Doings). Szru koto, 737.
Do (Work). Ts'tome, shingoto.
874.
Do. (One's concern). Kamai nasaru koto, 921. Mi ni kakari-
mas', Mi ni kakaru, 933.
Do (Office). Yaku, 1224.
Busy Isongashiu, Isongashi, 428.
1091. Konzatsz itash'te, To-
rikonde, 885. Yoo nga goza-
rimas', 1091.
But. conj. Nga, 313. 344. 539.
671. 37. Keredomo, Conces-
sive form of the verb Keri, to
be past. 542. Sari nangara,
Shikashi nangara, 752.
But. i. e. except. Yori, Nokosh'te,
877.
But. adv. Bakari, 976, **980**.
Buy. Katte k'te kudasare. **Katte**
koi, 46. Kau, 797.
Buy & bring. Kai nasarete k'te ku
dasare, Katteki nasai, 591.
By. Ni, 10. 717. 958. 969. De,
196.
By the day. Iri ni, 16.
By the job. Uke ai ni, 16.
By this time. Ima wa, 670.
By mistake. Chingai de, 517.

C

Call. **Yonde ku** dasare, Yonde
koi, **48.** 49. 1222.
Call. (To name.) Nadzkeru, Na-
dzkemas', 1156.
Called (Is) To mooshimas', **Toiu,**
2.134. 808. 1138.
Called. (Came to see.) Mimai kudasaremash'ta, Mimatte kure
ta, 1175.

Came. Mairimash'te, K'te, 139.
382.
Came across it. Yuki awasete
427.
Came into port. Niu shin itashimash'ta, Minato ni haitta, 554.
Can. Dekimas', Dekiru, 5.50.
55. 301. 765.
Can be made. Ts'kuraremas', Ts'-
kurara, **ru,** 1090.

Can tell why. Toite kikasaremas', Hanash'te kikaseru, 1213.
Can do. Itasarema&h'oŏ, Shirare-yoŏ, 1157.
Cane. Tszye, 1087. 519.
Can get. Motomeraremas', Erareru, 1256.
Cannot. Dekimasenu, Dekinai, or Dekinu, 417. 475. 474. 516. 511. 513. 563. 568. 759. Narimasenu, Naranu, 418. Itash'-kanemasenu, 513.
Cannot tell. Hanasaremasenu, 440.
,, lift. Motaremasenu, Motarenu, 479.
,, stay. Oraremasenu, Orarenu, 469.
,, tell apart. Wakeraremasenu, Wakerarenu, 481.
,, keep out of mind. Waszraremasenu, 498.
,, do. Ts'tomaremasenu, Ts'tomaranu, 523.
,, get on without. Nakute wa narimasenu, 558.
,, see *i. e.* perceive. Wakarimasenu, 578.
,, have. Uketoraremasenu, Uketorarenu, 1086.
Cannot help. *i. e.* prevent. F'sengu koto nga dekimasenu, or Dekinu, 474.
,, help. *i. e.* remedy. Naosz koto ngu dekimasenu, or Dekinu, 475.
,, trust. Nakasete okaremasen', or okarenu, 1261.
Captain (of a vessel.) Sen-doŏ, 550.
Care. Yoŏ-jin. 875. 884. Yoŏ-j'oŏ, 1268.
Care (Not.) Kamaimasen', Kamawanu, 246. 250. 321. 437. 467. O kamai Nasaremasenu, 321. Tonj'aku itas himasenu, 467
Careful (Is.) Yoŏ-jin nasaremas', Yoŏ-jin wo szru, 300.

Carelessly (Without forethought). En-rio nashi ni, 281.
Cares. Mi wo iremas', or Ireru, 909.
Carpenters. Daiku, 547. 953.
Carries on his back. Sh'otte arukimas, or Aruku, 942.
Carry. Mochimas', Motsz, 519.
Carry back. Mochi nasarete. o kaeri nasare, Motte kaere, 56.
Carry to. -E motte oide nasarete kudasare, E motte yuke, 57. 59.
Carry in. Uchi e irero, 58.
Cart. Kur'ma, 30.
Cash. Zeni, 448. 867. Kane, 1086.
Cat. Neko, 961.
Catch. Toru koto, 78
Caught. Torimash'ta, Totta, 961.
Cause. Moto, 716.
Chair. Isz. Kiyokuroku. 39.
Chair-bearers. Ninsoku, 825.
Charcoal. Szmi, 183.
Charge (Have a.) Ch'omen ni shirush'tearu, 432.
Change. Kikaeru, 493.
Cheap. Yaszu, Yaszi, 156.
Cheaper. Yas'ku, with yori before it, 60.
Cheapest. Ge-jiki, Yaszi, 822.
Cheat. Damashi, Dam'sz, 234.
Chest. Bako, 1027
Child. Kodomo, 4. 123. 1016. Ko, 615. 922.
Children. Kodomo shiu, 11. 364. 847. 995.
Chin. Ango, 955.
Chinese. (people). Poŏ jin, 208. 1223.
Chinese. (adj). Morokoshi, 897.
Choice (the thing chosen). Katte no wo, S'kina, wo, 880.
Cinnamon. Keihi, Nókkei, 938.
Clean. Kirei, 693.
Clever. Hatszme, Rikoŏ, 229.
Clock. Tokei, 86. 478. 967. 1053. 1206. 1207.

Close. (of the air) Mushi, 699.
Cloth. Kire, 619. Tammono, 1002.
Clothes. Kimono. 343. 493. 735. 774. 865.
Cloths. Tammons, 60.
Clownish. Inaka, 356.
Club. Boō, 202.
Coat. Haori, 775. 1003.
Cobwebs. Kumo no sz, 42.
Cock's combs. Kaitoō, 545.
Coffe Coppee. Kahe, 1025. 1044.
Coin. Kane, 517.
Cold. (Disease) S'kikaze, 100, Sh'oōkan, 227.
Cold. (adj.) Sr mun, samui, 775. Tszmetoō, and. to be cold, Hieru, 755. Samash'te, lit, cooling, 647.
Collector. Daikun, 811.
Comb. v. Kushi de nade tske na- **sare, or**— nade tskero, 62.
Comb. n Kushi, 62.
Come. **O ide** nasare, Ki nasai, 61 63. **64**. 65. 66. 68. 69. 70. Koi. 64 70.
Come. (Have). Kimash'ta, K'ta, 1071. 1163. O ide nasarema- sh'ta, 1168.
Come. (By ship) Watarimas', Wa- taru, 1192.
Come. (Did not). O ide nasarema senanda, Konakatta, 1233.
Come. (Will). O ide nasaru, Kuru daroō, 500. O ide nasaremas', Kuru, 1183.
Come (to). lit coming. O ide na saruwo. Kuru no wo, 1182 Kurukoto, 203.
Come. (I beg you to). O ide nasa- rete kudasare, K'te kurero. 522.
Come to. *i. e.* Become. Narimash'- ta, natta, 658.
Come back. Kaeru, **161**. Kaeri- mas', 863
Come to the **point**. (in speaking). Sashi atatte iri yoō no koto

wo o hanashi—, or, Sashi atatte iru koto wo, 1250.
Comets. Hoōkiboshi, 1174.
Coming. K'te 1,23.
Coming (Is) Oide nasaremash'oō Kuru de aroō, 333.
Commenced. Hajimemash'ta, Ha- jimeta, 952.
Committed Hara kin' sep'puku wo itasare mash'ta, Hara **wo** K'tta, 345.
Common Tszne ni, 1035.
Compartment (Middle). Doāno ma, 654.
Complaint. (legal). Uttae, 585.
Conduct n. Mimochi, Okonai, 1253.
Confesses. Arawa ni mooshimas', Akiraka ni itta, 255.
Consider. Kanugaetego **ran** nasare, Kanngaete Miro, **75**.
Considered (are). Omowaremai, O- mowareru, 81.
Contrary. Somuiti. 930.
Cool (Let us.) Szdzmimash'oō, Sz- dzmoō, 709.
Coolies. Ninsoku.. **49**. 199. 1071.
Copper-mine. Doōzan, Akangane no deru tokoro, 2.
Corea. Ch'osen, 1078.
Corect (by writing.) kakenaoshi nasare, Kake naose. 597.
Cough. Seki, 228.
Count. Kadzoete go ran **nasare,** Kadzoete miro. 76.
Counting. Kadzoete. **871.**
Country. Kuni,96. 135. **752. as dis- **tinguished from **the town, No,** 710.
Countries (Some.) Ni san koku. **791.**
Cover. Kakete oke, **77.**
Covered. Mabure **ni** nari nasareta, Mabure ni natta, 237. Hari- **mash'te,** Hatte, 1085.
Coward. **Okubioō** Okubioō mono, 336.
Cowards. Okubioō **mono, 890.**
Cranes. Szru, 78.

Crape. Chirimen, 79.
Credit (To sell on). Kakeuri, 495.
Credit (Sales on). Kakeuri, 823.
Cross. (To step over.) Matangi. 132.
Crimson. Hi, 551.
Cure. Naorimas', Naoru, 1042.
Curse. Waruku in. 724.

Cut in two. K'tte f'tatsz ni nasare. mash', K'tte f'tatsz ni Shiro, 80.
Cut [Have]. Kiri-kidz wo koshiracmash'ta, or koshiraeta, 46.
Cuttlefish. Tako. 81,

D

Dances. lit. the verb dance. Hanemaszru, Hanera, 732.
Dancing-girls. Ukareme, 1073.
Dangerous. Kidzkai, 683. Abunoö, Abunai. 870.
Dark. Kuroö, Kurai, 676.
Day. Hi, 329. Jitsz. 1055. Nichi, 1059.
Day before yesterday, Issaku jitsz, 1194.
Day-break. Yoäke, 241. 423.
Day laborers. Yatoibito, 549.
Days' work. Ichi nichi no hi-yo, 544.
Dead. Shinimash'ta, Shinda, 47. Nakunari nasaremash'ta, Shinareta, Sh'kio, Goö kio asobasaremash'ta, Go seiki nasaremashta, 201.
Deaf. Mimi to-oö or to-oi, 412.
Deaf and dumb. Oshi. 265.
Deal (trade.) with. Uri-kai szru koto, 259.
Dearest. (in price.) Takoö, Takai, 823.
Debt. Sh'yak' kin, 278. 567.
Decomposed. Kusaru no. 821.
Deed. Ji. 142.
Deeds [of conveyance]. J'oömon, or Yudzri J'oömon, 797.
Deep. F'koö, F'kai. 1010.
Deeply [Very much]. Taiso ni, 278.
Deer. Sh'ka. 790.
Defaced [Will be]. Szrete mie naku narimas', Szrete mie nai, 693.
Degraded. Ochi no, 825.

Delicacy. (as an eatable.) Koöbutsz, 81.
Deliver. (as goods). Yokosz, 785.
Delusion. Mayoi. 914.
Denies that he did it. Itashimasenu to osshiyarimas', Shimasenu to iimas', 254.
Deposite. Osamemas', Osameru, 811.
Desk. Tskue, 831.
Despitefully. Hidoku, 724.
Detest. Kirai de gozarimas', Kirai dr 804.
Dictionary. Jibiki, 1036.
Did. (used as a principal verb.) Itashimash'ta, Shi nasatta, 644. Nasaremash'ta, Sh'ta, 1210.
Differ. Chingaimaszru, Chingaimas' 232. Chingau, chingaimas, 1000
Differ [Does not.]. Chingaimasenu, Chingawanu. 911.
Difference. Chingaimas', Chingau, 1112. Kamai, 620.
Dig. Lit. Digging. Hotte, 798.
Dinner. Hiru gohan, Hiru meshi, 88. 166. 190.
Directions. Hoö, 407.
Distinguished. Kaku betsz szngurete 792.
Ditch. Dobu, 690.
Divide. Wari nasare, Wari nasae, 89.
Do. [Principal verb] Nasaremash', Shiro, 20. 93. 94. Nasaremash'oö, Szru, 72. 586, 579. 592, Nasarete, Sh'te, Lit. Doing, 91. Nasai, 93, Nasaremase,

Shiro, 102. Itashimas, 1199.
and passim.
Do not. Negative imperative. Nasaremaszna, Nasaruna, or Na affixed to the attributive form of any verb, thereby forming a negative imperative. e. g. See 106-115. 117-125. and 127-132. Naradz, Naranu, 1027.
Do [Cannot]. Ts'tomarimasenu, Ts'tomaranu, 523.
Do [Can]. Itasaremash'oō, Shirareyoō, 1157.
Do [To be suitable]. Yoroshiu gozarimash'oō, Yoi, 892. 1235. 8.
Do [Going to]. Nasaremash'oō, Szru, 1141.
Do [good as a medicine.] K'szri ni narimash'oō, or-naroō, 640.
Do good to. [Treat well]. Yoku toriatskai, 724.
Doctor, Ish'a. 945. 958.
Dog. Inu, 840. 937.
Dogs. Inu, 549.
Doing. Nas'aremas', Szru, 1119. 1128.
Doing [of]. Lit. That I will do. Itasoō to, Shiyoo to. 924.
Dollar. Dora, 3. 1015. 1255.
Dollars. Dora, 700.
Done. [passive v.] Ts'keraremash'ta, Ts'kuraseta, 24. Shimai nasaremash'**ta**, Shimawareta, 627.
Done with. [Done **using**]. Ts'katte o shimai nasaremash'ta, Ts'katte shimatta, 193. Tskainasareta, Ts'katte shimattara. **1176.**
Done. [get it]. Deki angarimas', Deki angaru. 1172.
Done [with it]. Ts'kurase toō, **Ts'**kurasetai, 503.
Done. [made]. Ts'kurimash'ta, **Ts'**kutta. 578.

Done with, *i. e.* Disposed of. Motte **oide** nasarete... nasaremash'ta—, Motte itte....sh'ta—. 1117.
Done [Not]. Ts'kuriemasenu, [passive form] and Koshiraenu, 1017.
Done [not; **in** cooking]. Hinga toōrimasenu, Hi uga toōranu, 1007.
Done [Must be]. *i. e.* certainly is done. K'tto dekite orimash'oō, K'tto dekite iru daroō, **670.**
Done [Must be]. *i. e* It is necessary that it should be done. K'tto itasasemas', K'tto itasaseru, causative form of the verb. 672.
Done my best. Itatte mi wo irete, 502.
Done [Will not get it]. Shimai ni wa narimas' mai. Shimai in wa naru mai. negative future. 1265.
Door. Kado-nguchi, **30.** To, 115.
Doors. *i. e.* houses. Ngen, 309. and Ken, 310.
Doors. Mon, 719. 802.
Doubt. Utangai. 978.
Doubled [Has]. Ichi bai ni narimash'ta, Ichi bai ni natta, 944.
Down. Sh'ta ni. 1081.
Down in. Ni. 653.
Dragonfly. Tombo, 697.
Dress. n. Irui no koto. Kimono. 250.
Dress. v. Kimono wo kimas', 251.
Drinking. Nomi nasarete, Nonde, 305.
Drowned. Deki shishimash'ta, Szi**shi** shimash'ta, 1088.
Drunk. Sake niyotte 252. Sake **ni** yoimas', Sake niyoo, 257.
Dry. [**V**ery]. Midz nga nai, 687.
Dry [In order to]. Hosh'te, 781. Hosz Tameni. 865.

Ducks [a species of wild ones]. Kamo, 790. Tame ones. Akiru, 817.
Dumb. Oshi, 133.
Dutch [men]. Oranda jin, 1089.

Dyers. Koōya Sh'yoku nin, Somo mono szru h'to, 134.
Dying. [Withering as a tree]. Kare, 1038.

E

Each. Ono ono no. 135. Dztsz, 171.
Each kind. Iro iro—dztsz, 411.
Each other. Aitangai ni, Tangaini, 1068.
Early. Hayaku, 63.
Earlier. Hayaku, 1233,
Earthquakes. Jishin, 136.
Easy. Yaszu, Yaszi. 1. Yasashiu, Yasashii, 637. 923. 997. Tayaszi. 923.
Eat. Tabe. 610. and in neg. form, 1056. also, angari 1056. Angari nasarete, Kunte, 993.
Eating. Tabemas' koto Taberukoto, 314.
Eggs. Tamango. 76. 367. 878.
Either. Doredemo, 1254.
Elephant. Dzoō. 84.
Else. Hoka no, 704. Hoka, 1122. Hoka no koto. Lit. other thing, 321.
Empty. v. Akete kudasare, Akero. 137.
Empyricism. Jiikangennarioōji, 788.
End. n. Kangiri, 596. Lit. Limit.
End of the month. i e. the last day, Misoka, 434.
End. v. Lit. to affix to the end. Sh'ta ni ts'ku, 980.
Enemy. [in war]. Teki, 952.
Enemies. [Personal]. Ada kataki ni szru mono, 724.
England. Ingiran, 138. Ingiisz Ngoku, 792. Ingirisz no kuni, 1061.
English [language]. Ingirisz no kotoba, 95. Ye, 713.
English [people]. Ingirisz no hito. 943.
Enough. [Tobe]. Tarimas', Tariru, 664. Neg. form. Taranu, Fusoku, 973. 977. Dake, Lit. sufficient quantity. 1097.
Enter a complaint. Uttae moōshimas', Uttae ni szru, 585.
Entrance [Front]. Manguchi, 376.
Envelope [Letter]. Jioōbukuro. 185.
Equal. Ichi yoō, anaji koto. 1043.
Erasure. Kesh'ta tokoro, Understood before Ue ni. 597.
Errors. [Since there are]. Machingatte orimas' kara, Machingatte iru kara, 812.
Europe. Yoropa, 791.
Even. [of numbers]. Ch'oōme. 608.
Evening. Ban, 333. 459.
Events [At all]. Dzchi, 575. 1110.
Eventually. Shi jiu wa, Tsziniwa. 421.
Ever. [Hitherto]. Ima made, 184. 194. Kono mai, Maikata, 1049.
Ever since. Yori, 139.
Every. Mina mina, 144.
Every body. Donata mo, Daremo, 140.
Every thing. Mina mono, 778.
Evil. Ash'ki, 143. Aku, 142. 872.
Exactly. Tangawadz, Chingai naku, 36. Ch'odo, 1026.
Exactly noon. Mahiru, Nitchiu, 634.
Example. Gioōj'oō. 827.

Executed (Is to be). Shizai ni okonawaremash'oŏ, Shizai ni aroŏ, 989.
Exercise. v. Used as a noun. Ungokasz wa, 145.
Expect. Machi nasaru, Matsz, 1182
Expenditures. **Kin** ngin no de nga, 197.
Expense. Kane **wo** dashi'te, Lit. Spending money, 24.
Expensive. Tsziye nga ooku, Dzappi.

nga tanto. 660.
Explain. Toite kikasete kudasaraba, Toite kikaseru nara, Lit. If you will confer the favor of explaining, 506.
Expressed. Iimash'tara, Ittara, 369.
Extortion. Musaboritoru koto, 144.
Eye. Me. 258. Me, also, in Katame, and Mek'kachi 282, or Me-kachi.
Eyebrows. Mayu, **1073**.

F

Fade. Samemas', **Sameru**. 103.
Fail (in business). Bunsan woitashimas', Bunsan wo szru, 278.
Fair weather. Tenki, Hiyori, 845.
Fall. Ochimas, 725.
Fall (Let it). O otoshi nasareta, Otosh'ta, 312.
Falling (in price). Sangate orimas', Sangatte iru, 678.
Family. Ka-nai, 979.
Far (How?) Iku ri hodo, Nani hodo, 400.
Farmers. H'yak'sh'oŏ, 687. 752.
Farthest. Tooku, 705.
Fashioned (Old.) Mukashi nokatachi de, Mukashi no kata de, 926.
Fast. Haya, 919. 1257. Jikini, 206.
Father. Chichi, 188. 353. 359. 889. 1062.
Fault. Tszmi, 898. Ochi do, 1226. Ayamachi, 322.
Favorite. adj. Ichitan aishi, Ichi**ban** kawaingaru, 1016.
Feather. Tori no ke, 631.
Feed. Kuwasero, 146.
Feel better. Kokoro yoŏ gozarimas', Kokoro yoi, 580.
Feel (the pulse). Shall I. Ukangaimash'oŏ. Miyoŏ, 844.
Feel (one's way). Sangutte yukimas', **Sangutte** yukee, 676.

Fell. Ochimash'ta, Ochita, 971. Korobimash'ta, Koronda, 262.
Follow. H'to, ariwa, 1116. There appears to be no exact equivalent in Japanese.
Festival. [Religious]. Matszri, 732.
Fever and ague. Okori no yamai, 212.
Few. S'kunoŏ, **147**. S'koshi, **976**.
Field [Rice]. Ta, 78. 687.
Fifty. Go jiu, 984.
File. v. Yaszri de szru, 617.
Fill. Ippai o ire nasare, Ippai irero, 149. Half-full. Hambun ire nasare, Hambun irero, 150. Ire, 151.
Finally. Tszi ni, Shimai ni, 303.
Fine. *i. e.* Minute. Saimatsz ni, Komaka ni, 938.
Fine. *i. e.* handsome. Kirei, **343**.
Fine. *i. e.* slender. Hosoŏ, Hosoi, 1041.
Fined. Karioŏ kin toraremash'ta, Karioŏ kin torareta, 287.
Find. *i. e.* by searching. Tadznete kuda sare—. Tadznete kure—. 54.
Find out. Goran **nasare**, Mi nasai, 175.
Find. *i. e.* **furnish**. Dashimas', **Da**sh'te, 520.
Find [Will]. Miemash'oŏ, Mieyoŏ, 1087.

Find [Shall] *i. e.* shall meet with. Awaremash'oŏ, Awareyoŏ, 1191.
Find [Not]. Miemasenu, Mits'keranu, 542.
Find out [can]. Kanngaite nasarete shiremas', Kanngaite shireru, 52.
Find Do [not]. *i. e.* do not see, or meet with. Me ni kakarimascru, Awanu, 564.
Find it bad. Lit. if it is bad, on using it. Mochi nasarete, Moshi warui naraba. Mochitemoshi warui naraba, 590.
Finger. Yubi, 460. 741.
Finished. Shittai ni narimash'ta, Deki angatta, 602.
Fire. a conflagration. Kaji, 774.
Fire. Hi, 793.
First cost. Moto ne, 927.
First rate. Ichiban yoroshii, Ichiban yoi, 929.
First. adv. Hajimete, 1048.
Fish. Sakana, 490.
Fit [Does not.] Chingatte orimas', Chingatte iru, 93 . Aimasenu. Awanu, 1003.
Five. Go. 700.
Fix. Oki nasare, Oke 153.
Fixed. Iioŏ. 3.
Flannel. Shirorash'a, 542.
Flatter. Hetszraimas', Hetszrau, 1259.
Flaw. Kidz. 1054.
Fleas. Nomi, 804.
Flogging. Tatakare nasarete. Tatakarete, 247.
Flowers. Hana, 859. 969.
Fly. *i. e.* To go without any certain direction. Yuku e wo Sa damemasenu, Yuku e wo sadamenu, 834.
Flying. Hingioŏ szru. Tobu, 582.
Follow. Lit. followed. S'h'tangaimash'ta, Sh'tangatta. 950.
Fond of. Tszite.210. S'ki. 343.

Foot. Ashi, 237.
Foolishly. Mudani, 243.
For. prep. Ni, 129. 246. 250. 155 826. 1056 1122 1159. 1162. Yue 287. Tszmori ni. *i. e.* for the value of, 517. Tame ni, 827. De, 645. 822.
For. conj. Kara, 25. 26. 673.
For fear of. Osorote, 888.
For [a purpose]. Tame.ni, 1160.
For the sake of. Tame ni, 788.
For nothing. [Gratuitously]. Tada, 1256.
For sale. Uru tame ni, 1208.
For what they will fetch. Soŏba ni naratte, 839.
Forbidden. Kin zei de, Naranu, 407.
Fore shoulder. Kata, 759.
Foreign. Gai, 60.
Foreigner. Gai koku noh'to, 713. 1123.
Forgot. Waszreta, 478.
Forgotten [Have]. Shitsz nen itashimash'ta, Waszreta, 451.
Found. Yuki awasete mimash'ta, or mita. *i. e.* incidentally 430. Tadzne idasaremash'ta, Sangashi dash'ta, *i. e.* found, by searching. 195.
Found out. Kanngai idashimash'ta, Kanngai dash'ta, 473.
Foundation, [of a house]. Jingioŏ, 712.
Fourfooted. Yotsz ashi aru, 789.
Four. [persons]. Yottari, 681.
Four. Yotsz, 760.
Four voyages. Yo tabi yuki-kae, Yo tabi yuki-ki, 1061.
Fowls. [Domestic.] Niwatori, 1066.
Frequent. Ori ori, 136.
Friend. Hoŏyuu, Hoŏbai, 932.
From. Yori, 637.1192. Kara, 407. 1192. Instrumental, De. 886.
From—and upwards. Saki yori, 1073.
Front entrance. Manguchi, 376.

Front to rear (From). Okuyuki, 377.
Fruit Kudamono, 521. 616 Mi. 886. 1018.
Fruits. Kudamono 816.
Fry. Yaitenasare, Yaite nasai, 154.
Fuel. Szuai takingi, 156.
Fujiyama, Fujisan, 490.

Full. *i. e.* without a blank space. S'kima naku, 1036.
Full grown (not) Hina, **Ookiku** narimasenu, 1066. Hina **is a** chicken.
Furl. Lit. Let down. Orose, 157.
Furniture. Doōngu, 158.

G

Gained. Toku wo nasaremash'ta, Toku wo sh'ta, 196.
Garden. Hatake, 480.
Geese. Gan. 78. **790.**
Gentle. On, 599.
Gentleman. Okatawa, H'to wa, 1144.
Gentlemen. Okata tachi, H'ts tachi, 1069.
Get. Torinasaru, Toru, 1109. 394. Morau, 394.
Get well. Naorimas', Neg. form. Naorimasenu, Naoranu, 21.
Get wet. (So as not to). Nurenu yoō ni, 77.
Get wet (Let it not). Nurashi nasaremaszna, Nuraszna. 109.
Get [Can.] Motomeraremas', Erareru, 1256.
Get (Did.) Motomete o ide nasaremash'ta, Motomete k'ta, 1197.
Get it done. Sh'te shimai nasare, Sh'te shimai, 161. Deki angarimas', Shi angaru, 1172. Shimai ni narimas', Shimai ni naru, 1265.
Get a living. Kurashi nasaremas', Kurasz, Lit. pass one's time. 372.
Get hurt. Kenga wo itashimaszru, Kenga wo szru, 722.
Get through. *i. e.* finish. Shimai, 953.
Get out of my way. Waki e yore, Lit. (Put yourself) to one side, 162.

Get ready. Sh'taku woshiro, 159. 160.
Get up. Ooki-**nasare**, Oki **nasai,** 163. 141.
Get the amount. Kanj'oō shi nasare Kanj'oō shiro, 787.
Getting. Toru, 788.
Getting up *i. e.* Inventing. Kanngae idashimas', Kanngaedasz, 943.
Getting well. Naoru to wa, Lit. that he will get well. 986.
Girl. Onango, 615.
Girth. Haraobi, 723.
Give. imperative. Kudasaremash'. Kudasai, 167. 170. Angenasare, Yari nasai, 168. 169. Yari nasare, Yare, 171. Ange nasai, 172.
Given up (Has been). Mi hanasaremash'ta, Mi hanasareta, 958.
Glad (To be). Tai kei ni dzonjimas', Yorokobu, 572. Yorokobi, 687.
Go (**Do** not). **Oide** nasaruna, Yukuna, 124.
Go. Imperative. Yuki nasare, Yuke, 173. Itte, Lit. going. 175.
Go (Shall). Mairimash'oō, Yukoō 468. 575. Yuku 609. 622. 680, 1214. 575. 1110. Mairimas', 1110. 609. Mairu, 680. Maitte yoroshiu gozarimas', Itte yokaroō, 1190.
Go around. Mawari nasare, Mawari, 575.

Go home (May). Uchi e kaeru koto nga yoroshiu gozarimas'. Uchi e kaeru koto nga yoi, 1245.

Go off. as a gun, neg. verb. Hasshimasenu, Hassenu, 1108. Positive form. Hasshiru.

Go on. Achira e oide' nasaru nga yoroshiu gozarimas', or Yoi, 1231.

Go to bed. O ne nasare, Nero, 778.

God. Kami, 180.

Going. Yuku koto, 786.

Going to—. Expression of the immediate future. Tadaima, with the fut. verb ending sh'oŏ or oŏ, e g. 561. The verb ending alone is often sufficient. See the next word.

Going to do. Nasaremash'oŏ, Szru, 1141. The phrase *nochini*, in the sentence referred to, aids the expression of futurity.

Gone. Absent from the house, Rusz, 260.

Gone. *i. e* Has become nothing. Naku narimash'ta, Naku natta, 965.

Gone (Am). Itte kimas'. Itte kuru, 862.

Gone (Has). Oide nasaremash'ta, 331. 332. 1187. Mairimash'ta, 1187. Itta, 331. 332.

Gone out. as a lamp does, Kiemash'ta, Kieta, 946.

Good. Koŏ, 142. Yorosh'ki, 307. Yoki, 307. 856. Yoroshii, 591. 684. 988. Yo, in the word yokereba, 591. Yoroshiu, 610. 684. 752. 910. Yorosh' ku, 907. 993. 1033. 1054. 1056. Yohu, 1033. 1054. 1056. Yoi, 856. 610. 910. 988. Hoshiu, Hoshii, 663. Hoshiu, Lit. Desirable.

Good as it was before. Moto no toori ni. In the original manner, 522.

Good boy. Sznawo ni, Lit. rightly. Otonash'ku Lit. like a man. 32.

Good for nothing. Yaku ni tachimasenu, Yaku ni tatanu, 1023.

Good hand- *i. e.* shilful. J'oodz, 306.

Good looking. Yorosh'ku miemas', Yoku mieru, 1033.

Good natured. Ninwa ni, 337.

Goods. Shiromono, 323. 810. Shina, 785.

Got through (Have). Lit. have passed the summit of. Koemash'ta, Koeta. 574.

Governor. Bungioŏ. 585.

Governs. Osameraremaszru, 180.

Grapes. Budoŏ, 389. 983.

Grass. K's'a, 888.

Great. Ooki ni, Lit. greatly, 913. 914.

Great deal. Dai ji ni. Lit. (He takes it) for a great affair, 276.

Great wedding. Go konrei, 985.

Great while ago. Oŏ mukashi, 931.

Greater part. Taingaiwa, 959.

Grind. Hiite ko ni shiro, 181.

Grooms. M'makata. 825. The common term is Bettoŏ, or Kuchitori.

Grow. Lit. spring up. Heemaszru, Haeru, 545. 752. Haete orimas', Haete oru, 717.

Grows thin *i. e.* lean. Yaseru, 146.

Grows worse and worse. Tsnorimaszru, Tsznoru, Lit. increases, 143.

Guest. Okiaku sama, 776.

Guilty. Tszmi aru, 182.

Gun. Teppoŏ, 612. 1108.

Gunpowder. Enshioŏ, 183.

Gutter. Dobu, 800.

Hair Kami, 62.
Half Hambun, 150. 151. 998. Gōbu doōri, 907.
Hand v. Kudasare, Kurero, Lit. Give. 185.
Handle. v. Motsz, Toriats'kau, 693.
Handles. n. E. 28.
Hands. n. Ts. 820.
Handy. Ts'kai-yoō, Ts'kai ii, 1024.
Hang. Kakete, Lit. hanging. 865. Kakeru, 991.
Happens (If any thing). Moshi mo no koto nga arimash'te wa, Moshi mo no koto nga aru to, Moshi mo no ko to nga, signifies any accident or casualty and Aremash'te wa, and aru to, both signify, if there be. 1260.
Harbor. Minato, 1093.
Hard. (in substance). Katoō, Katai, 646.
Hard. [Difficult]. Mudzkashiu, Nikui, 259. 996. Mudzkashii, 996.
Hark! O kiki nasare, Kike, 186. 187.
Hat. Kamurimono, 152. Kaburi mono, 926.
Hate. Uramiru, 724. Imimaszru, Kiraimas', 1068.
Have. Gozarimas', 189. 192. 540. 432. **491**. 541. This word is really the verb *to be*, but by difference of idiom between English and Japanese, it is often used where we use *have*. The same is true of aru. Aru 192. 540. 432. For the neg. forms of Gozarimas, and aru, viz.; Gozarimasenu, and Nai. See 448. 507. 570. 579.
Have an eye to. O mi mawari kudasare, Mi mawari nasai, 199.
Have been, *i. e.* gone. Mairimash'ta Itta, 543. Interrog. Oide

nasareta koto **wa** gozarimas', ka? Itta koto wa aru ka? 194.
Have been ill. Wadzraimash'ta, Wadzratta, 496.
Have done with. O ts'kai nasareta, Ts'katte shi mattara, 1176.
Have. (cannot) Uketoraremasenu, Uketorarenu, 1086.
Have not had. Gozarimasenanda, Nakatta, 416.
Have seen. Hai **ken** itashimash'ta, Mita, 462.
Have not seen. Me ni kakarimasenu, Minu, 449. Hai ken itashimasenanda, Minakatta, 455.
Having become. Narimash'ta kara, 799.
Had the honor to see. O me ni kakarimash'ta. 1048. Atta. Lit. have met. 1048.
He. Ano h'to 201. Ano okata, 204. Are wa, 203. and passim.
Head. Atama, 237.
Healed. pass. **v.** Iemash'ta, **Ieta,** or Naōtta, 362.
Health. Yoō-j'oō, **1268**. Lit. care of one's life.
Hear (Did). Kiki nasaremash'ta, Kiita, 85. **86**. 87.
Hear (To). Kiku to, Kikeba, 688.
Heard. Kikimash'ta,'Kiita, 420.
Heard (Never). Kikimasenu, Kikanu, 573.
Heart (By). Sora de. Lit. **in the** air, *i. e.* with the face turned up. 1263.
Hearts. Kokoro, 950.
Heaven. Ten. 180.
Heavy. Omoi, 1065.
Help. (Can?) S'ke **moōshima-sh'oō,** Tetszdawoō, **52.**
Help [Shall I?] Tetszdaiwo Itashimash'oō, Tetszdai wo Shiyoō. 483. 843.
Help. Imperative. Tetszdai wo Shiro, 178. Tewo kashi nasarete

kudasaremash'. Te wo kash'te kurero. Lit. by lending a hand confer a favor. 346. Tetszdai nasarete kudasare. Tetszdatte kurero. 347.
Help (Pass food at the table). Ange nasarete kudasare, Kuwash'te kurero. 348.
Help it. *i. e.* prevent it. F'sengu koto, 474.
Help it. *i. e.* remedy it. Naosz koto, 475.
Helping off with baggage. Ni-ngoshirai no teszdai de, Ni wo ts'kutte yaru node, 428.
Here. Kokoni, 139. 225. 230. 263. 266. 350. 351. 367. 381. 779. 862. 863. and Koko ni instead of As'koni in 682. Koko e, 203. Koko. 349. Kochira e 382. Kokode wa, 1030.
Here and there. Achi kochi, 430.
High. Taka, 966.
High time. Jikoku nga, 680.
High water. Michi shiwo, 601.
Him. Ano o katani, Ano h'to ni, Dat. 169. Ano okata wo, Ano h'towo, acc. 527. and passim.
His. Ano h'to no. 359. Ano o katano, 357. Are no 357. and passim.
Himself. Karada, (*i. e.* body). 305. Jibun, Temai, 318. H'toride *i. e.* alone, 289.
Hoe. Kuwa, 1024.
Hog. Buta, 840.
Hold. (Contain). Hairimas', Hairu, Lit. enter. 396.
Hold. v. Mamorimas', Mamoru, Lit Guard. Keep one to a thing, 809
Hold. (of a ship). Soko, 653.
Holes. Ana, 798.
Home. adv. O taku e, 224. Uchi e, 327. 364. Iye made, Uchi made, 518.
Honest. Sh'oójiki, 330.

Horse. M'ma. 723. 146. 316. 360. 919. 934. 937. 1031. 1118.
Horses. M'ma, 205. 759. 994.
Horsefeed. M'ma no tabemono, M'ma no kuimono, 752.
Hot. Atszu, Atszi, 647. Atszkute, 699.
House. Taku, 602. Uchi 602. 740. 757. 801. 1032. 1057. Iye, 740 757. 796. 1032. 611. 884. 942. 1057. 361.
Houses. Iye. 797.
How. Nani. Lit. what. 366.
How. (In what way). Dono yoö ni 383. Doö, 383. 369. 390. 743. Ikanga, 390. Nani to. 369.
How. For what reason. Nani go yoö nga arimashte Lit. Having what business? Nani nga atte, 385.
How. Nani wo sh'te. Nani wo to sei ni sh'te. Lit. Doing what? 399.
How. Nani wo kangioö ni sh'te. Lit. Doing what for a business, 372.
How. (What condition). Inaya, Ampi, 841.
How far? Iku ri hodo, Nani hodo, 400.
How long? (hereafter). Itsz made, 370. 373. 401. 405. Itszngoro, Itsz no koro, 381. Itsz ngoro mada, 401.
How long? (of length). Nangasa Nani hodo, 371. 386. Nangasa dore hodo, 386 Nan ngen, 374. 375.
How long? (of time past) Nani hodo. 381. 382.
How many? Iku tsz. 367. 395. Ikuhodo, Ikura ni, 402.
How many days? Ika hodu, 403.
How many kinds? Iku shina hodo, 388.
How much? Ikura. 37. 368. 387. 391. 394. 398. Nani hodo de,

i. e. At what price, 365. 379.
Dono kurai, 379. Dore hodo,
396. Ika hodo, 398. Ikura
ngurai, 393.
How thick! *i. e.* numerous and troublesome, Ookute uttoshiu.
Ookute Urusai, 397.
How wide? Nan ngen hodo, 376.

Human. H'tono, 406.
Humble. Ken sonno, Herikudaru, 408.
Hundred H'yaku 890.
Hungry. Kunfku, Hara nga Szita, 443.
Hunting. **Kari, 407.**
Hurry (In a). **Isongi,** Isonga, 595.

I

I. Watah'shi, 25. Washi, **415.** and passim. Ore. 1194
Ichibu. Ichibu. **517.** Lit. **one** bu
Ichibus. Bu, **504.**
Idea. Omoö koto **wa,** 369.
Idle *i. e.* vain, useless, Mueki no, Muda, 928
If. Nara, 591. 594. 597. N raba, 584. 586. 588. 589. 590. 592. 593 594. 596. 597.
If not. Nakereba, 725. 595. Nakuba, 595.
Ignorant. Oroka no, Gu, 598.
Ill (Have been). Wadzraimash'ta. Wadzratta, 496.
Illness. Biooki. 429.
Immediately. Szngu **ni,** 176.
Imported, Watarimas', 60. Mochi **komu,** [Better Szmi komu] **762**
Impossible **to** recover. Naoraremas' mai, 650. The idea of impossibility, is expressedly the fut. potential neg. verb.
Improve. aratameru koto, 591.
Impudent. Haji wo shiranu, **221**
In. Ni. 78. 80. 96 114. 158. 342 **427.** 503. 653 **to** 656 781. 836 954. 1174 Naka ni, Lit **in** the midst of, 717. De, 81 156. 395. 560. 569. 600. 725 731. 738. 752. 751. 803. **811.** 823. 824.
In. adv. **Uchi e. 58.**
In all. **Hokoradz de, 895.**

Income. Rioöbun no **angaridaka,** 363.
Indian corn. Too Morokoshi, **92.** Morokoshi, 181.
In Japan. Nippon de, 761. 725. 689.
In Japanese. Wa ngo de. **Sono** kuni no kotoba de, 569. Nippon de wa, 366. 369. Nippon no kotoba de, 828.
Injures. Itama. Itamimas', 305.
Ink. Szmi, 831.
Ink-stone. Szdzri ishi, 164.
In large quantities, Ooku, **824.**
Inn. Hatangoya, 209.
Inside and out. Uchi Soto. **830.**
Inside out. Urangae, 1082. **1270.**
Instructions. Oshie, 888.
In strument (Musical). Narimono, 1138.
Intelligent. Hakush'ki, Mono wo shiru, 599.
Interest. Ri kin, Ri, 1109.
In the least. S'koshi **mo,** 535.
In the long run. Nangaku wa, 671.
In this way. Kono toöri **ni, 503.**
Iron. Tetsz. 21. 1208.
Is. Imas', Iru. 64. Gozarimas', 1. **and** passim. I final in the word yawarakai, 148. is the root form **of the** continuative verb *iru* to be, and is the equivalent to *is,* in the English sentence. This is a usual mo-

de of expressing the copula, when it is followed by a predicate adjective in English. The *i* is appended to the root form of the adjective in Japanese.
It. Are wa, 97. Kore wu, 101.

Sore wa, 198. Ano koto wa 390. There is no exact equivalent to *it* in Japanese. The above references are to Demonstrative pronouns.
Its own [Said of a country]. Jikoku no, Lit. own country's, 135.

J

Jacket. Haori. 222.
Japan. Nippon. 60. 78. 81. 718. 725. 7. 8. 753. 761. 803. 825.
Japanese [people]. Nippon no h'to 98. 1174. Wa jin, 141. Nippon jin, 569.
Japanese [pertaining to Japan]. Nippon no, 158. 836. Wakokuno, 732.
Japanese [Language]. Nippon 366. 369. Nippon no kotoba, 828. 713. Wa ngo, 713.
Japanese characters, *i. e.* letters. Nippon Moji. 731.
Japanese fashion. Nippon no yoö, 836.

Japanese religious festivals. Wa Koku no Matszri, 732.
Jest. Joōdun, 494.
Jewels. Tamar no kazari, 689.
Job [By the]. Uke ai ni, 16.
Joke. Joōdan. 637.
Jokes. J'oōdan, 688.
Joyfully. Yorokonde, Lit. rejoicing, gerund. ive, 950.
Jump. Koe te oide nasaremase, Koe te oide, 690.
June. J'yun. 691.
Just. adv. Ch'odo. 910. 962. 1013. 1039.
Just now. Sahi hodo, S'ak'ki, 225.

K

Kanagawa, Kanangawa, 1077.
Keep. (Deposite.) Okimash'te, Oite. gerundive, s, from verb. oki, 614.
Keep (Employ). Ts'kaimash oō, Ts'kawoo. Fut. of Ts̩kae. 589.
Keep clean. Kirei nish'te o mochi nasare, Kirei ni motte, 693.
Keep house. Kanai no koto wo nasaremas', Kanui no koto wo szru. 289.
Keep on. Kore kara nasaremash', Kore kara shiro, 694.
Keep out of. Dete aruki nasaruna, Dete arukuna. 692.
Keep out of mind (Cannot). Wa-

szrarenu, Lit. cannot forget. 498.
Keep out of my way. Sochira e o noke asobasare, Sochira e noke, 696. more properly, Get out of my way.
Keep (time). Aimas', Au, 104.
Keep to yourself. Himitsz nish'te o oki nasaremash'. Naish'oō ni sh'te oke, 695. Lit. Put it in a secret place.
Kernel. Tszbu, 112.
Kill. Koroshimas', Korosz, 1075. Koroshi nasare, Korose, 697.
Kind (This) Kono yoöna shina, Konna shina, 1236.
Kinds, Rui. 388. Iroiro. 411.

K 221

Kind treatment. Nasake wo Kakeru koto, 698.
King. Woo, 1078.
Knew. Dzonjimash'ta. Sh'tta, 272
Knife. Kongatana, 1054.
Know. Zonji de gozarimas', Sh't te iru, 99. 140. Sh'tte o ide nasaremas', Sh'tte iru, 100.
Know [let me]. *i. e.* tell me. Osshiarimash', Ie. 1169.
Know [will let you]. Mooshi an-gemash'oo. Iwoo. Lit. will tell. 1178.
Know not. Wakarimasenu, Wakaranu, 566. Shirimasen', Shiremu, 673. 744. Shiran', 744. Dzonjimasen, shiranu, 560.
Knows. Sh'tte i nasaru, Sh'tte iru 1212.
Knows not. Shirimasenu, 214. 439. Dzonjimasen' 439. 500. Shiranu, 214. 439 500.
Koban. Rioo 287. 324. 363. **1002.**

L

Lame. Itamemash'ta, Itameta, **759.**
Lamp. Tomoshibi, 946. 947.
Land. Ts'chi. 748. Jimen, 797. 1229.
Land rents. Lit. revenue, Nen ngu, 811.
Large. Oohina. 64. Ooki, 999. Oo, 1036.
Largely. Tak'san, 803.
Last. Sen. 434.
Last. v. [Continue.] Tszdzkimas', Tszdzku, 624.
Last. v. Said of a thing in use. Mochimas'. Motsz. 625.
Last day of the month. Misoka, 1059.
Last month. **Sen ngetsz, 944.** 434.
Last night. Sakuban, 478. Sakuya, 667 699. Yuube 478. 667. 699.
Late. Adv. Osoku, **325.** Nangaku, 515.
Late. Adj. Osoo, Osoi, 1161.
Late riser. Asane, Asanebo, 240.
Laughable. Okashiu, Okashii. 688.
Laughing. **Warai** nasaremas'. **Warau, 1140.**
Law. **Hatto, 7. 320.** Hoo, **930.**
Laws. **Hatto, 135.**
Learn. **Oboeru, 234.** Sh'ungioo
nasai, Keiko shiro, **1263.**
Learned. adj. Haku ngaku, **280.**
Least. S'koshi, 535. 570.
Leave. v. Set aside. Nokosh'te ooki, nasare, Nokosh'te oke, 129.
Leave. n. Permission. Yurushimasenu, Yurusanu, *i. e.* not to give leave, 132.
Leave [Did]. Oite Oide nasaremash'ta, Oide itta, 1203.
Leaves [Of plants]. Ha, 800.
Leave off. Yame nasaimash', Yamero. 1251.
Leave-open. Ake hanash'te, Lit. Leaving open. 1115.
Leave-for [Entrust to]. Tanomi mooshimas', Tanomu, 529.
Left. participle. Nokosh'te, 976.
Left. behind [by mistake]. Waszrete mairimash'ta, Waszrete k'ta, 557.
Left handed. **Hidari kiki, 335.**
Left off. **Yame nasareta, Yameta,** 35.
Left open [Is]. Hiraite gozarimas', Aite arimas, 1037.
Left to itself. **S'tete** okimas' to, **S'tete** oki to, **143.**
Leisure, Tetszngoo. 23.
Lend. Kash'te kudasare, Kash'te kurero, 700. Kasztameni **Ka**sooto, Lit. to lend 1218.

Let him do. Sase nasare, Sasero, 704.
Let him ride. Nose nasare, Nose, 711.
Let it alone. Yoshi nasaru, Yose, 701.
Let it be. Yoshimash'te, Yosh'te, 702. Oki asobasure, Oki nasai 707.
Let it fall. Otosh' nasareta, Otosh'ta, 312.
Let me know. Osshiarimas', Je, 1169.
Letter. Tengami 57. 1166.
Letters. Ji, 693.
Let us cool. Szdzmimash'oö, Szdzmoö, 709.
Let us do. Itashimaszru, Szru, 706.
Let us see. Go ran nasare, mi nasai, 67.
Let us take a pipe. Lit a whiff. Ip'puku tszkamatszrimashoö, Ip'puku nomimash'oö, 708.
Let us take a ride. M'ma ni notte Kakemash'oö, M'ma ni notte demash'oö, 710.
Let who will say it. Dare demo sono yoö ni mooshimaszru, Dare demo sono you ni moösz. 703.
Let you know [Will]. Mooshi angemash'oo, Iwoö, 1178.
Level. v. Taira ni katamero, 712.
Lexicons. Jibiki. 713.
Lies. n. Itszwari, 26.
Lift. Mochi angete. Lit. Lifting. 714.
Lift [Cannot]. Motaremasenu, Motarenu, 479.
Lift [To]. Mochiangemas, Mochianguru, 681.
Light. n. Akari, 38.
Light. v. Akari wo ts'ke asobasaremash', Akari wo ts'kero. 715.

Light. adj. Karuu, Karui, 631.
Lightning. Inabikari, 716.
Lights. Akari, 776.
Like. adj. Yoö ni, 871. Soöni, 919. Nite. 292. 1045. Onajikoto, 1039. Onaji tokoro, 912.
Like. v. Ki ni irimas', Ki ni iru, 464. Yorokobimas', Yorokobu, 698. S'ki ni narimas'. S'ki ni naru 510.
Likely. Soö, 920.
Lilies. Yuri, 717.
Lions. Shishi.
Listen. Ohanashi wo uketamawaru, Hanashi wo kiku koto, 885.
Little. S'koshi, 151. 346. 429. 528. 987. 1091. 1238. Shibaraku, [of time]. 1091. Chitto, 937.
Little less. Moö chitto herash'te, Moö s'koshi herash'te, 485. Herash'te, Lit. Diminishing.
Little (time). Shibaraku, S'koshi, 1091.
Live. i. e. Reside. Oide nasaremas, Iru, 295. Szmatte oide nasaremas'. 353. Szmatte oraremas'. 309. 310. Szmatte oru, 308. 309. Oraremas', 308. Szmatte iru, 310. 311. 353. 1198. O szmai nasaremas', 1198.
Live [Does not]. Oszmai nasaremasenu, Szmawann, 1069.
Living. Imas'to. Iru to, 660. Oide nasarete wa, Ite wa, 682.
Loaded. (as a gun). Tamangnszri komete. 612.
Lock v. J'oö wo oroshi asobasare. J'oö wo nasare, 719.
Locust. Semi, 837.
London. Rondon, 799.
Long [in time]. Hisash'ku, 120. 621. Nangaku, 120. 236.
Nanga, 236.
Long [in distance]. Tooku, 1103. Error in rendering it long time.

M 228

Longer. adv. Meta, 117. Mo haya, 418. Mo, 418. 469. Moŏ, 516.

Longer (The). Hisash'ku kakoimas', hodo, Toshi wo kosz hodo, 949.

Longest. Nangaku, 1201.

Long for. Hoshiu gozarimas', Hoshii, Lit. is desirable 528.

Long lived. Nangniki, 786.

Long run [In the] Nangaku wa, 671.

Look again. Moŏ ichi do o tadzne nasaremash', Moŏ ichi do o sangashi nasare, 721.

Looking. Miemas', Mieru, 1033.

Looking for. O tadzne nasaremas', Sangasz, 1134.

Lookout (Be on the). O ki wo ts'kete mite oide nasare, Ki wo ts'kete mite iro, 34.

Look out. Ki wo ts'ke, 722.

Look out. n. (i. e. concern). Kakari, 899.

Looks. n. Mikake, 665, 666.

Looks like. Yoŏ ni Miemas', Yoŏ ni mieru, 937.

Look like. To miemas', To mieru, 995.

Look them over. Mi wakete nasaremas', Mi wakete, 720.

Loosen. Yurume nasare, Yurumero, 723.

Lose. Son wo itashimas, Son wo Shimas', 349. Neg. fut. of the same, 249.

Lose. i. e. forget. Neg, inperative, Waszre nasaruna, Waszreruna, 121.

Lose. (If you) Son wo nasarete naraba Son wo sh'ta naraba, 588.

Losing. Nakusaremas', Nakusz, 291.

Loss. Son. 1225.

Lost. (Have). Son wo nasaremash'ta, Son wo sh'ta, 196. Nakusaremash'ta, Nakush'ta, 284. Naku narimash'ta, Funjusz itashimash'ta, 446. Nukemash'ta, Nuketa, Lit. has passed off, 633.

Lost [If it is]. Moshi ushinai nasareru naraba, Moshi. Nakusz naraba, 593.

Lots. Jimen, 940.

Louder. Koe wo angete, 806.

Love. v. Kawaingare, 724.

Low water. H'ki shiwo, 601.

Lunatics. Kichingaimono, Kichingai wa 795.

Lying. Uso wŏ ii, 918.

M

Made. Tskuremas', pass.v.60. Ts'kurimas', Ts'kuru, 79 Ts'kuremash'ta, Kozhiraeta, pass. v. 1026. Itashimash'ta, Sh'ta, 1061. Ts'kuraremash'ta, Ts'kurareta, pass. v. 1067. Ts'kuri nasaremash'ta, Koshiraeta, 1211.

Made (Can be). Ts'kuraremas', Ts'kurareru, 1090. Ts kuru koto dekimaszru, or dekiru, 765.

Made it good. i. e. repaired. Naoshimash'ta, Naŏsh'ta, 532.

Main road. Hon doŏ, Kai doŏ, 595. Kai signifies the sea.

Make. Koshiraemas', Ts'kuru, 98. Ts'kurimash'oŏ, Ts'kuroo. fut. 386. Root of Ts'kutte, 619.

Make him do it. Sase nasaremash', Sase nasai, 730.

Make it good. Madoi nasare, Kawarieoo dase, 593.

Make it up. Ts'kunaimash'oŏ, T's'kunoŏ, 588.

Make out your Bill. Uketori ngaki wo o d'ashi nasare, Uketori wo o dashi, 729.
Make sure of. Dzehi motome oki tai, Dzehi tome te okitai, 728.
Makes nothing of. Naingashiro ni nasaru, Arunganashi ni szru, 1062.
Make the most of. Dai ji ni o ts'-kai asobasare, Da iji ni ts'kai nasare, 727.
Make up your mind. O kime na sare, Kimero. 72.
Making. Ts'kuri nasaremas', Ts'-kuru, 155.
Man. H'to, 130·908. 911. 1143. H'tori, 989.
Manners. Fuudzoku, 356.
Manure. Koyashi, 748.
Many (as). Ikutszdemo, 19. 882.
Many. *i. e.* A great number. Amata, Iroiro. of many sorts, 983.
Many (How)? Ikutsz, 367.
Many a time. Ikutabimo, Ikudomo, 543.
Mark. *i. e.* write. Kaite kudasaremase, Kaite kudasare, 731.
Market. Ichi, 427
Market price. Sooba, 1115.
Married. Lit. have a wife. Go shinzo wa gozarimas', Kamisan wa arimas'. Nioobou wa aru, 12.
Married. Said of women. Yome iri wo itashimash'ta, 1073.
Masks. Men, 732.
Master. Danna, 172.
Matched. Nite orimas', Lit. are alike. 994.
Match (Is no). Oyobimasenu, Oyobanu, 1031.
Material. n. Sh'osh'ki, 520.
Matter. Koto, 75. 923.
May. auxil v. This is expressed by ookata, signifying, probably, together with the fut. verb, ending Sh'oᵘ or oᵘ, See. 648.

Also by the fut. verb. ending with the interrogative Ka. See. 673.
May I? *i. e.* Is it well to do so & so. Yoroshiu gozarimas'ka? 733. 734. Yoi ka? 734.
Me. Watak'shi, 51. 54. 74 and passim.
Meal (a). Meshi', Go zen, 173.
Meaning. *i. e.* intention, Kokorodzashi, 903.
Meaning. *i. e.* sense. Giri, Wake, 1142.
Meant. (was). *i. e.* The intended idea was, Kaita kokoro gozarimas', Kaita ki da, 937.
Meant well. Kokorodzashi wa yoroshiu gozarimash'ta, Kokorodzashi wa yoroshii, 313.
Meat Niku, 1006.—1008.
Medicine. K'szri, 145 350. 454. 826 846 Yakushiu, 826.
Meet. [Did]. O ai nasaremash'ta, Atta, 600.
Memory. Oboe, 491.
Men. H'to. 825. Okata f'tari, 1068, H'to tachi, 1075.
Mend. Naoshi nasaru, Naosz koto wa, 55.
Mended. [Get it] Naosase, 179.
Mend. (with the needle). Nui naosh'te kurero, 735.
Mere. Bakari. Lit. only, 657·
Merits. Koō, 408.
Messenger. Ts'kaino mono, Ts'kai, 472. 1260.
Middle aged. Chiu nen, 302.
Middle compartment. Doonoma, 654.
Might. n. Sei. 819.
Military class. Bushi wa, 888.
Milk. Chichi, 998.
Mind. v. *i. e.* care for. Kamai, Kaman, 110.
Mind. *i. e.* attend to. Lit. do. Nasare. 737.
Mine. pron. Watak'shi no, Ore no, 355, Washi no, 361.

Miners. Kanebori, 736.
Mischief. Itadzra, 238.
Missing. Mie naku, 758.
Mistake n. Machingai, 913.
Mistake [By]. Chingai de, 517.
Mistaken [Was] Machingaimash'ta, Machingoöta, 313.
Mistaken (Are) Chingai de gezarimas', Chingai da, 1252.
Mix. Maze nasare, Mazero' between, No. 637. and 638.
Money. Kane. 170. 206. 211. 243 321. 614. 788, 1109, 1194. 1218 1261.
Money-box. Kane-bako, 835.
Money-chest, Kane-bako, 1261.
Month. Ts'ki 363. 468. 496. 1098. Ngetsz, 394. 434. 531. Ngatsz. 691.
More. Mada, *i. e.* yet, still, 192. 1237 Kono ne wa. *i. e.* Besides this, or over and above this, 1157. Mo. 1079.
More. adj. O-ku 619. Lit. Much.
More than, *i. e.* a greater quantity, number, amount than, Yori- yokei, 303. 540. Yori—oö or oöi, 1064.
More than (a certain time). Yori saki ni, wa. 674. *i. e.* Beyond.
More and more, the more. Shidai ni, Lit. according as, 509. 510. Here the meaning is, according as I become accustomed [Narete]. to using and eating &c. Dandan. Lit. step by step. or by degrees, 509. 510.
Morning. Asa. 63. 553.

Morning (This). Kesa, 423.
Morrow [To]. Mioö. 553. 1102.
Mosquitoes. Ka, 397. 804.
Most. Superl. rel. Ichiban, 233. Daiichi, 713. Ichi, 713.
Most. Superl. abs. Itatte, 598. 599.
Mother. Haha, 792.
Moutan (Flower) Botan, 969.
Move. v. trans Sashi dashimaszru, Sashi dashimas', 702.
Move. *i. e.* To move from one house to another. H'kiutszri wo itashimas', H'k ikosz, 1102.
Much. Hodo, *i. e.* quantity. Nani hodo. Lit. what quantity or amount ? 368. 378. 379. 384. 387. 391. 392. 393. 396. 398. 982.
Much [So]. Sono Yoö ni tak'san, Konna ni, 484.
Mud. Doro, 237. Nukarumi, 957.
Murders. H'tongoroshi. 938.
Musical instrument. Narimono, 1138.
Must. [Of necessity]. **Kanaradz,** 676. 677.
Must [Of obligation]. K'tto, 621. 672. 1027. 1243. 1244.
Must. [Of certainty]: Tash'kani, 642. K'tto, 670.
My. Watak'shi no, Ore no, 355. Washi no, 446. Washi nga. 740. and passim.
Mind. (To my). Watak'shi no omoö toöri ni, washi no omoö toöri ni, 1026.
Myself. Watak'shi **nga** ji shin, 452.

N

Name. Na, 731. 1130. Sei-mei, 1165.
Nation. Kuni, Lit. country. 755.
Nearsighted. Kin-ngan, Chika me, 271.
Needs. Toö, the termination of I-tash'toö, and Tai that of Itash'-tai. These are the desiderative forms of the verb. Itasz, to make or do. 1032.
Needed. Iriyoö, 713.
Neglect. n. Yudan, 1027.
Neglected. S'tete okimas'to, or oku to, 4.

Neighbors. Tonari no kata, Tonari no h'to, 1070.
Never. Tszi ni, 234. 564. 916. 1094. Kesh'te arumai, There never will be. Kesh'te significes, *positively*, 916. Mada, with a neg. following, 449. 476. 573. Doö mo, with a neg. following. 917. So also Itaszmademo, 1265.
Never mind. *i. e.* do not be concerned. Kinikakenasaruna. Kinikakeusobasaremaszna, 742.
New. Shin-ki ni, Lit. newly, or anew. 7. Atarashii, 222. 602. Medzrashii, 943.
New-comer. Hajimete o ide nasareta o kiyaku, Hajimete k'ta kiyaku jin, 257.
News. Medzrashii koto, 1009. 1126.
Next. Rai. Lit, the coming. 531.
Next (The) person. Tszngi no h'to, 968.
Next. *i. e,* after this. Kono tszngi no, 1153. 1214.
Next week. Kono tszngi no nano ka. 985.
Night (Last). Saku ban, Yuube, 478. Saku ya, Yuube, 582. 667. 699.
Night (to). Kon ya, 1106.
Nine. Ku, 645.
Nine o'clock. Itsztsz doki han, Lit. half past 5. 639.
No. Iiye 745. 746.
Nobody. H'to with the following neg. 747.

Noise. Hibiki. 186. Oto, 1150.
No match (Is). Oyobimasenu, Oyobanu, 1031.
Noon. Nitchiu, Mahion. 634.
No one. Dare mo with a neg. after it. 744.
Not. Na. the neg. imper. ending. and Nu the neg. indic. ending. See Samaszna, and nasaruna 125. Also, Shiri masenu, and Shiranu, 214. and the same passim. Also Mai the ending of neg. fut. verbs. *e. g.* Gozarimas' mai, Arumai, 916. and passim.
Not at all. S'koshi mo, with a neg. following, 912.
Not enough. Fusoku, Taranu, 977.
Note of hand. Sh'oömon, 1181.
Nothing. Nani mo, with neg. following. 748. S'koshi mo, with neg. following. 507. Nashi, 658. Nai, 1029.
Not natives. Oranai, Inai, 718.
Not quite enough. S'koshi fusoku, S'koshi taranu, 974.
Now. Ima, 74. 263. 425. 561. 638. 694. 749. 750-885.
Now [Just]. Tadaima, 531. 561. 581. 885.
Now a days Konongoro, Kono setsz, 1119.
Now and then. Tabitabi, 527. Lit. once and again. Oriori, 838.
Numerous. Tak'san, 738. Oöku 767.
Nutmegs. Nikudzku, 751.

O

Oaths. Chikai, 753.
Oats. Karasz mungi, 752.
Objection. Sawari, 570. Sasawari, 571.
O'clock. Doki, 638. 639.
Odd. (number). Tammei, 608.

Of. (Among). Uchi de. 754.
Of a size Onajikoto ni oökiu.—, Onajikoto ni oökii, 1072.
Oil. Abura, 803. 972. 1004. 1085.
Oiled paper. Toöyun, 77.
Old. (Twenty years). Hatachi 848. 1073.

Old fashioned. Mukashi no Kata chi de, 926.
On. p. Ni- 358. 767. 780.
On. adv. Achira e. Lit. in that direction, 1231.
On board. Fune ni, 1173.
Once. Ichido. 583. Lit. one time.
O..ce (Formerly). Saru koro, 279. Izen, 757. Moto 799.
Once more. Moō h'to tabi, Moō ichi do, 1079.
One. Ichi. 1267. H'totsz, 54. 760. 877. 988. 1033.
Ippon, used of things long and slender, 51. 758. Ippiki, of animals, 759.
One by one. H'totsz dztsz. 878.
One upon another. Kasane, 777.
Only adv. Sae. 743. Bakari, 1049.
Only enough for ourselves. Watak'shi domo no dake, 1097.
Only one (The). H'totsz ngiri, 1040.
Onions. Nenzi, 761.
Open. adj. Hiraite, Aite, 1037.
Opinion. Dzonji, Omoō koto, 546. Ga. 598. Omoō, 232. 253.
Opium. Ahen. 762. 210.
Opposite. Mukoō, 361.
Or. Ookrta, repeated, 648. Also Ka, repeated, 601. 608. and passim.
Ordered. i. e. Sent an order for &c. Chiumon itashimash'ta, Chiumon Sh'ta, 556.
Ordinary. Tszne no, 871. Tada no, 871.
Orphans. Minashingo. 763.
Other. Sen. i. e. former. 580. Ta. 69. Hoka no, 416.

Other (The). Achira wa. achi wa 728. Achira no. Achi no. 962. 953. Are- 1045. Sore. 1039.
Ought. Yoroshiu gozarimas,-Yoi, 892. 1269. 1249. Ii, 1249.
Our. Watak'shi domo no, Washinga, 764.
Out. adv. Rus*, 1175.
Outdone (Have). Masatte orimash'ta, Masatte ita, 1258.
Out of order. Kurutte, 1053.
Out of print. Dzeppan itashimash'ta Hanwa naku narim..sh'ta 1014.
Out of sight. Mie naku narimash'ta. Mie naku natta, 900.
Out of these. Kono uchide, 733.
Outrun. Yori saki ni hashiru Koto, 562.
Over. p. Ue ni- 597.
Over. i. e. Across. Mukoō ni 295.
Over. (In excess). Mata, 990.
Over and over again. Namben demo, 730. Tabi tabi, Do-do, 1084.
Over paid. Yokei ni watashi nasaremash'te. Ooku watash'ta. 1207.
Over run with Taisoō ni orimaszru, Taisoō iru, 740.
Overtaken. Oi ts' kimash'ta. Oi tozita. 512.
Owe. Sh'ak'yoō nga gozarimas' Kari nga aru, 387. Hiyoō wo yarimasenu, Hiyoō wo yaranu, Lit. have not paid him &c. 544. Karite orimas', Karite iru, 1255.
Own. Go ji bun no, Jishinno, 18. Jikoku no, 135.

P

Page. Mai. 812.
Paid for. Yarimash'ta, Yatta, 548. Kai nasaremash'ta, Yatta, 362.

Paid off. Tema wo yarimash'ta or Yatta, 547. Hiyoō wo mina yarimash'tu, or Yatta, 549.
Pail. Oke. 179.

Patience. Kan-nin, 470.
Pantomimes. (Lit. to act them.) Odori. 732.
Paper. Kami. 765. 832. 1085.
Paper. (A writing.) Kahits'ke, 852.
Papered door, or moveable partition. Karakami, 768.
Pardon. Go-men. 526. 626.
Parlor. Ozash'ki. 702.
Parlors. Zash'ki, 158.
Particular (To be). Nen wo irete, 623.
Pass. [To hand]. Angero, 766.
Pass. (as current coin.) Tszyoö itashimas', neg. form, 1030.
Passing. (Going by.) Toörimas'. Toöru. 1077.
Passions. J'oö, 872.
Past. Szngi, 636.
Pay. v. Hairimas', Yarimas' 729.
Pay. (If you do not). Kaishi nasareneba, Hersai seneba, 585. Yarimasenu naraba, Yaranu nara, 1086.
Pay. n. Hiyoö, 1071.
Payable. Kaisz yoö ni, 1181.
Pay-day. Watasz toki. i. e. paying time. 1076.
Pays. (for). Dashi nasaremas', Dasz. 520.
Pear. Nashi. 733.
Pencils. Fude. 51.
Penknife. Kougatana. 1203.
People H'to, 133. 584. 599. 871. Ano katatachi, or H'to tachi, 1087. Mono, Nin, 598.
Persecute. Gai j'ama wo szru, 724.
Persons. Mono. 182.
Pick (Will take my). Erande torimash'oö, Yoridon ni shiyoö. 533.
Pick out. Tori s'te nasarimash'. Tori s'tero, 720.
Picture. Edz, 805.
Picul. Hiak'kin, 990.
Piebald. Buchi no, 711.
Piece (of money). Gin, 613.

Pigeons. (wild.) Yamabato, 790
Pinks. Nadesh'ko, 717.
Pipe. (Lit. a whiff.) Ippuku, 708.
Pirates. Kai-dzoku, 767.
Pistols. Tanengashima, 98.
Pits. Tane, 119.
Pity (a). Dzannen, Kuchioshii. 659.
Place. no. T'okoro. 121. 349.
Plain. adj. Akiraka, 629.
Plainly. (clearly, o: intelligibly.) Wakaru yöö ni. 857.
Play (Wishes to). Asobi nasaretangaru, Asobi tangaru. 264.
Play (Do not). Asobuna, Asobi nasaruna, 107.
Play things. Mochiasobi, 123.
Pleasure (At). Katte shidai ni, 141.
Plenty. Oöi hodo, 684.
Pocket-book. Kamiire. 291.
Polite. Rei ngi tadashiu, Rei ngi nga tadashii 233.
Poor. adj. Hinkiu, Bimboö, 293. 939. Madzsh'ki, 939. Yasete. said of the soil. 1050.
Poor (The). n. Hin-min, 41.
Port. Shin. [a Chinese word. The Jap. equivalent is Minato.] 554.
Portrait. E-szngata, 932.
Positive. (in opinion). Ga nga tszyoö, Ga nga tszyoi, 598.
Potatoes. J'angatara imo, 17.
Pots. Kama, 830.
Pounded. Tszite. Lit. pounding. 938.
Power. Ken. 888.
Practice. v. Szru. 788.
Precept. n. Okite. 887.
Prefer. Ki ni irimas' Ki ni iru. 1200.
Present [For the]. Tadaima. 702.
Pretending. Toboketa koto. 231.
Pretty. Kirei, 922.
Price. Nedan. 3. 591. 944. Ne. 538. 944.
Price [Market]. S'oöba, 1115.
Printed. Kaihan ni narimash'ta. Han ni natta, 1188. Kai sig-

mings corrected, as for a new edition
Print (the of). Dzeppan itashimash'te, Hon wa naku narimash'ta, 1014.
Probably Soō de. Soō, 918. 953.
Profit (At a) Moōke, nasaremas', Moōkeru. Lit. makes a profit, by selling. 298.
Promise, n. Yakusoku, 809 461
Promised Yakusoku wo itashimash'ta, Yakusoku Shimash'ta, or sh'ta, 880 1177.
Pronunciation Go on. Lit. the five sounds or vowels. 354.
Property Kazai. 274. 284.
Property (stolen) Nuszbitono mono, Dorobo no mono, 287.
Prostitute. n. Yuujoō, i. e. Licensed ones, 1073.
Published. (as laws are by setting them up on boards in public places. Tateraremash'ta, Terareta. 7.
Pull off. Totte. 772. Nuke, 773.
Pull up. Nuite, ger. from Nuki. 752.
Pulse. (of the wrist). **Miaku, 844.**

mirs... wo sh...is, 594.
Purpose (On). Kokoro etc. Wazato, 315.
Put. Ooki nasaremash', or nasare, and Oke, 779. 780 **781.** 783. 784
Put (Shall). Okimash'oō, Okos, 1195.
Put away. Shimatte o oki nasare, Shimatte oke. 782.
Put aside. Katadz kete ger. **of Ka**tadz ke, 782.
Put in mind. Shirase kudasare Shirash'te kurero, 1179.
Put in writing. Yakusoku ngaki wo shi nasare, 785. Lit. make a written promise.
Put off Nobe nasaremash', Nobero. 675. 786. Onobe nasare. 786. Nobe wo naseru, Nobe wo szru, 1234.
Put on. O ki nasare, **Kiro** 774, 775.
Put out. (as a light) Kashi **nnsa**re. Kase 776 Keshimash'**ta,** Kesh'ta 947.
Put together Issh'o nish'te **H'to**tsz ni sh'te, 787.

Q

Quack doctors. Demoish'a, 788.
Quadrupeds Shi soku 789.
Quails. Udzra, 790.
Quaked Yurimash'ta, Yutta, 951.
Quality (not of the same). Fudoō 25
Queen. Niyotei 792.
Queens. Niyotei, 794.
Quench. Kesh'te kudasare, **793.**

Question. v. O ki ki nasare, Kihina, 794.
Quick. Hayaku 33. 163. 795. Isoide, 774.
Quickly. Hayaku, 522.
Quit. Dero. Lit. Go out of. 796.
Quit claim deeds. Kokenjoō. This is preferable to the term Yudzri j'oōmon, 797. The latter signifies, a will or testament.

R

Rabbits Usangi. **798.**
Rags. Boro. 799.
Rain n Shimeri, i. e. a sprinkling. 528. Ame. 971.

Rained. Ame nga furimash'ta, Ame nga f'tta, 687.
Rained [Has not] Ame nga furimasen', or furanu, 686.

R   230

Raise [Will]. Mash'te angemash'-
oŏ, Mash'te yaroŏ. 531.
Raise [To produce]. Dehimasen',
Dekinai, neg. v. 748.
Rake up. Kumade de kaki yosete,
800.
Ran away with. Hashiraremash'ta,
Hashirareta. pass. v. The text
is wrongly printed. Hashirase-
mash'ta is a causative verb.
360. The sense is, He was run
away with by the horse &c.
Ransack. Sangase. 801.
Rap. Otodzrero. 802.
Rapeseed. Na-tane, 803.
Rate [First]. Ichiban yoroshii, no,
Ichiban yoi no, 929.
Rate [at this rate]. Sono yoŏ ni,
Sonna ni. 1265.
Rather. Yori—yoroshii, yori—yoi,
419.
Rather [a little, or slightly]. S'-
ko shi, 1019.
Rather than. Yori—mashi, 873.
Rationale. Ri, 456.
Rats. Nedzmi, 740. 804. 961.
Reach. v. Todoku, Oyobu, 511.
Nobash'te, 805.
Read. Oyomi nasare, Yome, 806.
807. O yomi nasaru, Yomu,
1241.
Read through [Have]. Yomi owari-
mash'ta, Yonde shimatta, 415.
Read [To]. Yomu, 1228.
Reading. Yomu koto, 1269.
Ready. Sh'taku, 88. 160. 159.
190. 536. 1169.
Ready money. Gen kin, 822.
Really. Makoto ni, Tash'ka ni, 101.
Receipt. Uketori ngaki, Uketori,
170.
Recover. [Get well]. Naori, 920.
Recover. [Cannot]. Naoraremas'-
mai. Naoru mai, 650.
Regarded (Are.) To Omoimas', 825.
Reign. v Osameru, 791.
Reindeer Oojika, 808.
Relatives. Shin-rui, 763.

Remember. Oboëte oide nasare-
mas', Oboëte iru, 97. Oboëte
o ide nasare, Oboëte iru, im-
per. 809..
Remit. Ts'kawashi nasaremash'.
Yokose. 810
Rents Nen-ngu, 811.
Repairs. Sh'uf'ku, 1032.
Respectable. Tattomu beki, 317.
Respected. [are]. Uyamaimas', U-
yamau, 888.
Rest n. (Remainder). Ato wa, 154.
Hokano wa, 954.
Rest. v. Kiusoku nasaremash', Ya-
szme, 772.
Return. (Shall). Kaeri nasaru,
Kaeru, 1171.
Ribbon. Sanada himo, 552.
Rice. Kome, 811. 813. 1090. 1096.
Rice. (Boiled). Gohan, 348. Meshi
348. 1052.
Ricefield. Ta. 687.
Rich. (said of soil). Koete, or Ko-
yete, 1051.
Ride. (Let us take a). M'ma ni
notte,——kakemash'oŏ, or——
demashoŏ, 710. M'ma ni notte
——oide nasare, M'má ni notte
yuki nasae. 66.
Ride. (Let him). O nose nasare,
Nose. 711.
Ride. (To). Noru. 870.
Ride too fast. M'ma wo hasiraseru
koto nga haya szngimas', or
szngiru, 1257
Ride too fast (Do not). M'ma nga
haya szngiru hashirase nasa-
runa, or hashiraseruna, 123.
Right. n. Gi. Doŏ in wake, 1167.
Michi, 304.
Right. adj. Yorosh'ku, 220. Yoro-
shiu, Yoi, 604. 893. Makoto,
Hontoŏ, 894.
Right. (In the). Yoroshiu, Yoi, 275.
Ring. v. Fure, 814.
Rioŏ. Rioŏ, 432. 1267. 4 bu.
Rip. Toke. 815.

231 S

Ripe (Are). Jik'shimas', Jik sz. 389
Ripe. adj. Jik'shimash'ta, Jiku sh'ta, 816.
Ripe. scholar. Seki ngaku, 869.
Rise. v. Okorimas', Okoru, 860.
Risk (Lit Loss) Son, 1260.
Road. Michi, 340.
Road [on the]. Michi de, 340.
Road sides. Michibata, 717.
Roast. Aburi mono ni Shiro, 817.
Roasted. [as coffee]. Iri. Not roasted, irenu. 1025.
Roll up. Maki angero, 818.

Room i, e space. Haba. Lit breadth. 111.
Rose. Bara, 854.
Row. n. Narabi, 648.
Row. v. Ro wo ose. 819.
Rub. v. Szrimas szru. 820.
Ruler. J'oōngi. 165
Running over. Nangare demas', Nangare deru, 649.
Run through. [Has] i. e. Spent. Tskai ts'kushimash'ta, Ts'katte shimoōta, 274.
Rust. Sebi, 821.

S

Saddle. M'ma no kura, 556.
Safe. Ando, 682.
Said [Never]. Moōshimasen', Iwanu, 476.
Said [Is]. Iwaremas', Iwareru, 293.
Sail. n. Ho, 157.
Sail. v. Fune ni Notte oide nasaru, Fune ni notte iku. 1168.
Sailors. Fune-nori, 825.
Sake. [a liquor]. Sake. 305.
Sale [For]. Uru tameni, 1208.
Sales. Urimas' wa, Uru wa, 822.
Sales on credit. Kakeuri wa, 823.
Salmon. Sh'aka, 824.
Salt. Shiwo, 632, 960.
Saltpetre. Sh'ooseki, 183.
Same. Doō, 25. Onajikoto, 406. 941.
Sandalwood. Biakudan, 826.
Save. [Set aside]. Shimatte o oki nasare, Shimatte oke, 827.
Savor. Aji. 633.
Saw. Mimash'ta, Mita, 1049.
Say. Moōshimas', 366, 1174. Moōshimaszru, Moōsz, 703. Iu, 366. 1174. Hanashimas', Hanas', 1135. Hanashi nasare, Hanase, 828. Itta. Moōsh'ta, Lit. have said. 934.
Say (did). Oōseraremash'ta, Itta. 82. 1154.
Says. Osshiarimas', Iu, 245. 281.

1221.
Says (What he—). Moosareru koto, Iu koto, 110.
Scare away. Oi idash'te kudasare, Oi idase, 829.
Scattered. Chirimash'ta, Chitta, 969.
Scour. Mingake. 830.
Scrape. Kedzri otosh'te kudasare, Kedzri otose, 831.
Scraps of paper. Haugami, 832.
Scribble. Karingaki wo nasare, Karingaki wo shiro, 832.
Scrub. F'ki nasai. 833.
Scuds. Ukingumo, 834.
Skulking. Kakurete orimas', Kakurete oru. 1116.
Seal in blood. Keppan, 461.
Seal up. Fuu-in wo nasare, mash', Fuu-in wo shiro, 835.
Seam. Nuime. 815.
Sea-sick. Fune ni Yotta, Fune ni oimash'ta, 908.
Seat yourself. O szwari nasare, 836.
See (Let us). Go ran nasare, Mi nasae, 67. 837. Miro 837.
See (To). Lit. in seeing, or when I see. Me ni kakarimash'te, Mite, 572. Mireba, 970. Go ran nasareta, Mita, Lit. when you have seen. Toki—when. 1179.
Had the honor to see. O me ni

kakarimash'ta, 1048. Atta.
Lit. have met. 1048.
See. Pres. indic. Miemas', Mieru,
530.
See (To think). Omoimas', Omoŏ,
571. Lit. I think, nai to, that
there is no—&c.
See into, i. e. understand, Wakari-
mas', Wakatta, 750. Neg. form
of the same, 126
See. (To visit). Mimai Mimatte,
1175.
See to. i. e. Attend to. Ki wo ts'ke-
te Kudasare, Ki wo ts'kero,
838. Mamoru, 1224.
See(to Will). Sashidz wo itashima-
sh'oŏ, Sashidz wo shiyoŏ, 452.
Mimash'oo, Miyoŏ, 488.
Seeds. Tane. 200.
Seen (Is not). Miemasenu, Mienu.
pass v. 158.
Seen (Have not). O me ni kakari-
masen', Minu, 449. Hai ken
itashimasenanda, Mi nakatta.
455.
Seen (Have). Hai ken itashimash'-
ta, Mita, 462.
Seldom. Tamani, 230.
Selfish. Wangamamano, or simply
Wangamama, 319.
Sell. Utte kudasare, 839.
Sell. Pres. indic. O uri nasaremas',
Uru, 365.
Sell on credit (Do not). Kakeuri
wa Itashimasenu, or Senu, 495.
Send. Watashi nasaru, Watasz.
1260.
Send for (Will). Tori ni ts'kawase-
mash'oŏ, Tori ni yaroŏ, 489.
Send (me) word. Ts'kai wo o ya-
ri nasarete,—O ki kase nasare. Ts'kai wo yatte kikasete
kure. Lit. By sending a
messenger, cause me to hear,
or inform me &c. 841.
Sent [have]. Ts'kawashimash'ta,

Yatta, 472. 1217. Ts'kawa-
sh'ta, 1217.
Separated. Hedatte 1103.
Servant. Kodzkai, 48. 1266. 589
Servants. Kodzkai, 548.
Service [At your]. The language
of an inferior to his superior,
when receiving an order. Ka-
sh'komarimash'ta, 29.
Service [divine]. Ongami, 190.
Set a going. Ungokashimash'ta.
Ungokash'ta, 1206.
Set—on. Keshikaki nasare, Ke-
shikake, 840.
Set on end. O tate asobasamash',
Tatero, 714.
Set on fire [Will]. Yakimas', Ya-
kudzo, 884.
Settle accounts. Kanj'oŏ wa o tate
nasarete, Kanj'oŏ wa tatte,
1184
Settled (not) [Become clear]. Odo-
mimasen', Odomanu. 1044.
Set up in business. Akinai wo ha-
jime sasemash'ta, Akinai wo
hajime saseta, 359.
Seven. Sh'chi. 1002.
Several persons. H'tobito, 842.
Several times. Iku tabi mo, Nan
do mo, 329.
Shake. Furi nasare, 846.
Shame. (It is a). Haji nasaru, nga
yokaroŏ, Hajiru nga yoi. Lit.
it were well for him to be as-
hamed.
Shave (Going to). Szrimash'oŏ,
Szr oo, 561.
Shave. Indic. pres. Sorimas', 1073
She. Ano onango. 847, 848.
Sheets [whole]. Mattoɔ sh'te iru
kami. Mattaki kami, 832.
Shimoda, name of a place on cape.
Idz. 1095.
Ship. Fune. 331. 530. 550. 900
1061. 1088, and Sen in Ha-
sen 1088.
Shirtings. Kanakin, 889.

Shoes. Kutsz, 43.
Shop. Mise, 355.
Short. Mijikoō, Mijikai, 906.
Short sword. Wakizashi, 141.
Short time. S'koshi no aida, 671.
Shut. Imperative. Tatete kudasare. Tatero, 851. **Tate** kudasare, Tatte kurero, **768.**
Shut. *i. e.* in that state. Shimete, 802.
Sick. Bioōshin 236, Bioǵki, 340. 436.
Sickness. Bioōsh'a Lit. sick person or persons. 969.
Sick of. Tabe akimash'ta, Kui akita, *i. e.* tired of eating. Koō-k'wai, *i. e.* sorry, repentant of. 270.
Sick (Was taken), Wadzrai nasaremash'ta, Wadzratta, 340.
Side. Hoō, 59.
Side by side. Narabete, 777.
Side (This). Temai ni, 308. 309.
Side [The other]. Saki ni, 310. 311.
Sign, v. Sei-mei-ngaki wo nasare, Sei-mei wo shiru se, 852.
Sign *i. e.* an omen. Zempio, 1111.
Signing with one's blood. Keppan tskamatszrimaszru, Keppan szru, 753.
Signs. (manual). Temane. 133.
Silk. Kinu. (manufactured).
Silken threads. Kinu ito, 79.
Since. **Y**ori, 382.
Single. H'totsz, 112.
Sinks. v. Shidzmimas, shidzmu, 1065.
Sir. Danna, 733.
Sit up. (Cannot). Okite wa iraremasen', Okite irarenu, 515.
Sit still. Go an dza wo nasare, 853.
Sixteen. **Jiu roku, 760.**
Sixth. Roku, 691.
Sixty. Roku jiu, 686.
Sketch. n. Gaku, 927.

Sleepy. Nemuu, Nemui, 445.
Sliding papered door, Karakami, 768.
Small. Sema, Lit. narrow, Semai, 1012. Chiisa, Chiisai, 273.
Small pox. Hoōsoō, 283.
Smeared. Nurimas', Nuru, 1085.
Smell. Kaide miro. Kaide go ran nasare. 854.
Smoke. v. Tabakowo **o** nomi nasaremas', or Nomu, 90.
Snail. Katatszmuri, Maimaitszbori, 943.
Snake. Hebi, 64.
Snakes. Hebi, 804.
So. Sono yoō ni, Lit. in that manner, or way, 147. 484. 511. 584. 592. 594. Konna ni, 484. Sonna ni, 594. Kono yoō ni, 385. 604. 1161. Kayoō ni, 385. 604. 1118. 1161. Koō, 1118. Sayoō 414. 421. 441. 463. 465. 487. 494. 641. 648. 747. 1152. **Soō**, 414. **421.** 441. 463. 465. **648.** 747. **1152.** Sono toō-ri ni, 422. Sono yoōna **koto,** 476 Sonna koto, 476. Kayoōna koto, 1243. Koō iu koto, 1243.
Soft. Yawaraka, Yawarakai, 148.
Soil (Do not). Oyongoshi nasaruna, Yongoszna, 122.
Soil. n. Denji 1050. 1051.
Sold (Can be). Uraremas', 60.
Some. S'koshi, 154. 411. 859. Ni san. Lit. two or three, 791.
Some more. Mada kore **wa,** 1237.
Some other time. **Ta jitsz, Mata** konda, **69.**
Something. Mono. 943.
Something in (or mixed **with**) it. Mazemono. 1004.
Sometimes. Toki doki, 480.
Some time or other, *i. e.* after **this. Saki** e yotte, 677.
So much. Sono yoo ni, Soō, **111.**

234　S

Sore dake, 855. Kore hodo, 990. Sonna ni tanto, Sono yoö ni oöku, 1261.
Son. Go shisoku, Mus'ko. 1230.
Soon. Kin jitsz, Sono uchi ni, 70. Jiki ni, 820. Hayaku, 585.
Soon (Pretty). Mo s'koshi nochi ni, Oshits'ke, 1075.
Sort of a. Yoöna, 1143.
So that. Yoö ni. Lit. in such a way that &c. 77.
Sovereign (As a). Tami wo osameru michi, Lit. [In] the way of governing [the] people. 792.
Spare. Idzri nasarete, Idztte, 402. Note. Idzn', is a corruption of Yudzri, which signifies to bequeath, or to give for a consideration, either money or some thing in exchange. The sentence were better rendered by Kash'te kudasaremash'oö, or Kash'te Kurero.
Spare [Can you not]. Kudasaremasenu ka? Kurenu ka, 51.
Speak. Hanashi **nasare**, Hanase, 857.
Speak of [Cannot]. Moösaremasen', Iwarenu, 901.
Spends. Ts'kai nasaru, Ts'kau, 243.
Spend—thrift. Fu shimatsz, 209. Lit. not an economist.
Spent (Has). Ts'kai hatashimash'ta, Ts'kai ts'kush'ta, 211.
Spoiled. Kowashi nasaremash'ta, Kowash'ta, 1248.
Spoken [Have]. O hanashi moöshi mash'ta, Hanash'ta, 577.
Spoon. Saji, 195. 801.
Spoons. Saji, 758.
Squalls. Hayate, 860.
Stand. O tachi nasaremash'. Tate, 861.
Stay. Matte o ide nasare, Matte iro, 862. 863. Oide nasaremash', Iro, 1244.

Stay (Cannot). Oraremasen, Orarenu, 469.
Stern. n. Tomo. **655**.
Stick to. Yamedz ni **nasare**, Yamedz ni shiro, **587**.
Still, *i. e.* quiet. Shidzka ni, 31.
Still, *i. e.* yet. Mada, 105. 1101.
Still, *i. e.* even. Nawo, 1011.
Still (Be). *i. e.* Do not **speak**. Odamari **nasare**, Damare, 31.
Stingy. Shiwoö, Shiwai, 285.
Stir. v. Kaki mawashi nasare, Kaki mawase, 116.
Stone. Ishi, 646.
Stop. Tomeru, 360.
Stopped [Has]. Tomarimash'ta, Tomatta, 967.
Storehouses. Kura, 811.
Strange. Ayashii, 864. **915**. **Kik'wai no**, 915.
Stranger. **Riosh'ku wo** sh'te, Lit. **performing the** part **of** a **traveller, or one** who is not at home. 492.
Straw. Wara. 765.
Street. Machi, 940.
Stretch. Hare. 865.
Strike [Did]. O buchi nasaremash'ta, Butta, 1137.
String the bow. Yudzruwo o Kake nasare, or kakero, 866.
String. To put on a string, as cash. Sashi ni otoöshi nasare, Sashi ni toöse, 867.
Strive with all your might. Chikara wo ts'kush'te o ts'tome **nasare**. Hone wo otte ts'tomero, 868. Sei d'ash'te, would be **preferable to chikara** wo ts'kush'te.
Strong. Ts'yoö, 244.
Struck. Tatakimash'ta, Butta, 202.
Study. Manabeba, Manande, Lit. if he study, and By studying, 869.
Stumbling. Ts'madzite hizaoru,

T   235

Lit. By hitting his toes bends his knees, 870.
Stupid. Gudon, 234. Nibni, 1094. This word should be in the first form of the Japanese sentence.
Stutterers, Domori, 871.
Subdue. Goōf'ku nasare, Heif'ku shiro.
Such. Sono yoō ni, 114. Sono yoō na, Sonna, 573. Sayoō de wa, Soō de wa, 630. Kono yoō na, Konna, 756.
Suddenly. Niwaka ni, Kiu ni, 860.
Suffer wrong. Gai seraruru, Soko-nawaruru, 873.
Sugar. Satoō, 178. 944.
Suit (Will). Ki ni irimash'oō, Ki ni iroō, 1236.
Sulphur. Iwoō, 183.
Sun. Hinata. Lit. sunshine, 692. 781. Hi 954.
Sunrise [By]. Hi no de ni, 242.
Sun-screens. Szdare. 818.
Sunset. Hi no iri, 628.
Sun sets. Hi wa irimas', Hi wa iru, 954.
Suppose. Omoimas', Omou, 441.
Sure. Tash'ka ni sh'tte, 14. Tash'ka ni, 130-458.
Surprised. Hen ni omoimas', Hen ni omoō, 477. Hen ni omotte, 569. Odorokimash'ta, Odoroita, 535.
Suspect [Did not]. Utangaimasen, Utangawa nakatta, 535.
Swallow. v. Nomikomi, Nomikomu, 119.
Syllables. On. Lit. sounds, 871.

T

Table. Dai, 780. 966. **1028. 1087.** Taikun. 811.
Take. O ts'kai nasaremash', Ts'kae, 352. Omochinasare, 877. Motte, 877, Otori nasare, Tore, 878. 880. 881.882. 1254.
Take (Do not). O tori nasaruna, Toruna, 129.
Take [may I]? Karite yoroshiu gozarimas', Karite yoi, 734.
Take a chair. Koshi wo o kake nasare, Koshi wo kakero, 770.
Take a pipe (Let us). Ippuku ts'kamatszrimash'oō, Ip'puku nominash'oō, 708.
Take a ride (Let us). M'ma ni o nori nasarete o ide nasare, M'ma ni notte Yuki nasai, 66. M'ma ni notte kakemash'oō, M'ma ni notte demash'oō, 710.
Take a walk. Oasobi ni o ide nasare, Asobi ni yuki nasai, 68.
Take away. Motte oide nasare. Motte yuke, 876.
Take back (Will). Uketorimash'oō, H'kitoroō, 590.
Take care. Go yōjin nasaremash'. Yoōjin wo shiro. 875. 884.
Take care of. Sodateru, Kuwasen, 673. The latter is the neg. form of Kuwaseru, to take care of by feeding.
Take down. Totte kudasare, Totte kurero, 805.
Take good care **of. Dai ji ni** nasaremash', **Dai ji ni Shiro,** 879.
Take (It will). Itash'too gozarimas', Sh'tai, 681.
Take my pick (Will). Erande torimash'oō, Yori dori ni shiyoō, 533.
Taken. Torimaszru. Lit. they take. The verb here is active, the Japanese often avoiding the use of the passive in this way. It is also impersonal, no subject being expressed.
Taken up. Mochi nushi nga goza-

rimas', Mochi-nushi nga aru, Lit. there are owners &c. 940.
Take up ..room (Do not). Haba wo nasaremaszua, Haba wo szruna, 111.
Taking (Have been). Nomimash'ta, Nonda, Lit. have been drinking. 454.
Takes more (It). Ooku irimash'oo, Ooku iru de aroo, 619.
Takes up too much time. Hi kadznga Kakari szngimas', Hi kadz nga amari obi, 651.
Take time to think. Toku to kanngaite, Kanngaite, 513.
Take turns. Kawari-ngawari, Kawari atte, 1106.
Take up with. Yoo ni tatemaszru, Yoo ni tateru, 1105. Lit. put to use.
Talk. Oshiemas', Oshiero, 133. Ohanashi nasare, Hanase, 885.
Tanned. Kuroku narimas', Kuroku naru, 692.
Taller. Sei nga takoö, Sei nga takai, 746.
Tallow. Roō. 886.
Tallow-tree. Haji no ki, 886.
Taught. Oshiemash'ta. Oshieta, 1216.
Tea. Ch'a, 388.
Teach. Oshiemas', Oshieru, 502. The past tense of this verb is used in the text. because it is the only finite verb there. Oshie nasare, Oshiero, 887.
Teachers. Shi wa, Shi sh'oö, 888.
Tears. Namida, 971.
Tell. O hanashi nasare, Hanase, 74. 889
Tell. (Did you?). Ossh'iyarimash'ta. ka, Hanash'ta ka. 83.
Tell them apart (Cannot). Mi wakeraremasenu, Mi wakerarenu, 481.
Tell (Can). Toite kikasaremas', Hanash'te kikasareru, 1213.

Tell [Cannot]. Hanasaremasenu Hanasarenu, 440.
Tell (To). Iu koto, 450.
Ten. Jiu, 407. 432. 890. Jik, 310.
Ten thousand. Ichi man, 324.
Than. Yori, 60. 156. 314.
Thank (Would) Aring ato³ dzonjimas', Aringatoo, 506
Thank you. Aringatoō gozarimas', Katajike nai, 891.
That. pron. Sore wa, 5, and passim. Are wa, 175, and passim.
That. adj. Sono, 75, 76. and passim. Ano, 76. 123 and passim.
Theft. Nuszmi, Doroboö, 269.
Them. Sore wo, Kore wo, Lit. these, and those, 298, and passim.
The other side of. Saki ni, i. e. beyond, 311.
There. As'ko e. 124. As'ko ni, As oko ni, 267. Mukooe, 325.
These. Kore 1067 and passim.
They. Ano okata ngata, Ano h'to tachi, 275.
Thick. i. e. Numerous and troublesome, Ookute uttoshiu' Ookute urusai, 397.
Thing. Koto, 573. Shina, 1063. Mono, 756.
Things. Koto, 754.
Think. Oboshimesz, Omou, 393. 1239. Omoimas', Omoö, 421. 463. 589. Dzonjimas', 463. 485. Oboshimesz koto, Omou koto, 864. Oboshimeshimas', Omou, 1131. 1148.
Think (Cannot). Omowaremasenu, Omowarenu, 487,
Think (Not). Dzonjimasenu, Omowanu, 468. 747. Omoimasenu, 747.
Thinks a great deal of. Chinch'oö, itasaremas', Dai ji ni szru, 276.
Thinks nothing of. Nani mo kamaimasenu, Nani mo kamawaru, 277.

T   237

Think [Will] Omoimash'oō, Omo-o daroō, 584.
Thirty. San jiu, 1057.
This pron. Kore wa, 52, Kore wo, 55. and passim.
This. adj. Kono, 57. 58, and passim.
This evening. Komban, 333.
This side of. Temai ni, 308. 309.
Thoroughly. Shim-made, Lit. to the heart, or centre. 1052.
Thousand. Sen. 142. 363. 537.
Thousands. Sz man. Lit. Several ten thousands. 975.
Thread. Ito. 1041.
Threads. Ito. 79.
Three. San, 138. Mitsz, 980.
Three hundred. Sam biaku, 25.
Through. *i. e.* to the end of his work, Shimai, 953.
Throw. Nange. 705.
Throw away. S'te nasaremash', S'-tero, 720. S'temaszru, S'teru, 752. S'tero, 800.
Thrown away. S'teta, past tense of the verb S'te, **used** attributively. 799.
Throw overboard. Dashimas', Das', 555.
Thunder. Kami-nari. Lit. the noise **or** voice of the gods. 716.
Thundered. Rai nga itashimash'ta, Kami-nari nga, natta. 667.
Tide. Shiwo no michi hi, 1213.
Tigers. Tora. 718.
Tightly [or much] twisting. Ooku yori wo kakete. Tanto yori wo kakete, **79.**
Till. Made. 730. 759. 801. 863.
Time. Toki. 536. Jikoku. Jibun, 609.
Time. Lit. **day, Jitsz. 69.**
Time. Lit. **Leisure. Hima, 579.**
Time *i. e.* turn. **J'yumban, 622.**
Times, Tabi, Do, **138. 329.** 543.
To. [Denoting direction.] E or Ye, 194. The y is not heard at

Yedo, 204. 1061. 1077. 1089, and passim.
To [Denoting the Dative relation], Ni, 172. and passim. Sometimes e is used for the same purpose.
To. (Signifying) *for the purpose* of, or *for.* Tame ni, 1047.
To. (denoting *up to*). Made, or E, 400.
To be had. *i. e.* To be bought. Kawaremas', Kawareru, pass. form of the verb Kai, to buy, 17.
To-day. Kon nichi, 339. 404. 444. 687. 710. 775. 845. 953. 989. 1244, Kio. 339. 687. 710. 845. 953. 1244.
Together. Go doō-yoō, Minnash'te, 710. Issh'o ni H'totsz ni, 787.
Told. Mooshi angeta, Hanash'ta, 695. Hanashimash'ta, Hanash'ta, 842. 1055. Hanashi moōsh'ta, 1055.
Tomorrow. Mioō, nichi, **61. 63.** 675. 702. 785. 786. **1076.** 1102. Ash'ta, 63. 675. 702. 786. 1076. 1102. Mioō, alone, signifies to-morrow, in the expressions, Mioō ban, Mioō asa, To-morrow evening, To-morrow morning. Mioō nichi, Lit. signifies to-morrow's day.
Tonakai. The Ainos' name for a reindeer, 808.
To-night. Kon ya. 1106.
Too. Amari, 107. 999. 1012. Sz **ngiru,** 127. 1005 .Szngimas', **999. 1005.** 1012.
Too **fast.** Haya szngiru, 127. 1257. Haya szngimas, 1257.
Took. Uke torimash'ta, Uke totta, 517.
Took him up. (Struck a bargain) **Te wo** uchimash'ta, Te wo utta, **538.**

T

Too loud. Ooki szugiru koe wo 'sh'te, 1241.
Too much. Oŏ szugimas', Szugiru, 1242.
Too much. (in price). Dai bun takaku, Taisoŏ takakii, 1246.
Tooth. Ha. 424. 617.
Tooth ache. Ha nga itamimas', Ha nga itamu, 413 Ha no itami, 1042.
Touch at. Angarimash'te, s'koshi tomarimash'oŏ, Angatte s'koshi tomaroŏ, 1095.
Touch (Do not). Ts'ke nasaruna, Ijiruna, 106.
Town. i. e. the business part of it. Koŏekiba, 542.
Trade [Do not]. Kaueki wo nasaruna, Kaueki wo shi nasaruna, 130.
Travellers. Noboru h'to Lit. people that are going up. 1077 Tabibito, is the common term for a traveller. In the sentence, 294, the idea of *A great traveller*, is expressed thus. Sh'o koku wo hiroku o menguri nasareta. h'to, or Kuninguni wo hiroku mawatta h'to. i. e. a man who has extensively gone about various countries.
Tree. Ki, 708. 709. 1018. 1038. 1133.
Tribute. Mitszngi. 1078.
Trick. Tawamure. J'oŏdan. Lit. a joke, or jest. 297.
Trial. [Judicial]. Gim—mi, 207.
Troops (Our). Mi-kata, Lit. Our side. 952.
Trouble (Pains). Sekkaku tan sei, 659 Shinroŏ wo ts'kush'ta. Kokoro wo ts'kush'ta, 661. 662.
Troubles. Kuroŏ. 939.
Trowsers. [Loose]. Hakama, 772.
True Makoto, 603. 642. 643. 902. Hontoŏ, 643. 902.
Trust [Cannot]. Makasete okare masen', Makasete okaranu, 1261.
Try. Kokoro mi nasare, Kokoro miro, 1079.
Turn. Mawash'te. Lit. turning around. 1083.
Turn bottom upwards. Kaësh'te. o oki nasare, Kaësh'te oke 1080.
Turn in side out. Urangai sh'te, o oki nasare, Urangai sh'te oke, 1082.
Turn out, i. e. eventuate. Natta, Narimash'ta, 890.
Turn over. Kaësh'te o oki nasare, Kaësh'te oke, 1084.
Turn upside down. Ue wo sh'tani sh'te o oki nasare, Ue wo sh'ta ni sh'te oke, 1081.
Turn out [Will not] i. e. result. Narimas'mai, Naru mai, 431.
Twenty or thirty. Ni san jiu, 1057.
Twenty years old. Hatachi, 848. 1073.
Twice. Ni do, 471. 583. 945.
Twins. F'tango, 995.
Twist. Yorimas', Yoru, 347.
Two .F'ta, 514. F'tatsz, 618. 737 760. 992. Ni h'ki, 205. H'ki is the classative for animals.
Two things. F'ta yaku, Lit. two offices. 523.
Two thirds. Sam bu no ni, Sam bu ni, 982.
Typhoon. Taifun, Oŏ kaze, 1239.

U

Umbrella. Karakasa, 557.
Umbrellas. Karakasa, 1085.
Undersell. Yas'ku uru koto, 301.
Understand (Cannot). Wakarimasen, Wakaranu, 456.
Understand. (Did not). Wakarima-

senanda, Wakaranakatta, 120.
Understand (Does not). Wakimae-
te oraremasenn, Shiranu, 235.
Uneven. Unette, 1034.
Unfortunately. F'koŏnish'te, 1088.
A book phrase. F'shi awase de
is more colloquial, Oriash'ku,
Ainiku, 1175.
United. H'totsz ni sh'te. 950.
Unless. This is expressed not by one
word, but by the neg. v. ter-
mination nu with naraba fol-
lowing, meaning, Is not, or If
it be not, 1086, and passim.
Untie. Toke, 1.
Unwell. Jibun nga ashiu, Jibun
nga waruku. 139.
Unwholesome (Are not). Tabema-
sh'te mo atarimasenu, Tabete
mo ataranu, Lit. By eating, or
being eaten, do no harm. 816
Unwilling (Is). Konomanu, Iranai,
245.
Up. Ue ni. 59.

Up. i. e. entirely. Shimai, not
shimae, as in the text, 44, 45.
Up (Has gone). Angatte nasare-
mash'ta, Angatte itta, 332.
Up (Have come). i. e. out of the
ground. Demash'ta, Deta, 200.
Upside. Ue wa sh'ta ni, 1081.
Up to. Ni, 30. E or Ye, 1077.
Upwards. i. e. Over and above. A-
mari, Yo. 433. Ue, 848, Saki
yori, 1073.
Up with it. i. e. Raise it up. Oshi
angero, 73.
Us. Watak'shi domo, 66.67. 68.
and passim.
Use. i. e. Make use of. Omochii
nasaru, Mochiiru, 1120. 756.
Ts'kaimaszru, 756.
Use. i. e. Treat. Ashirai, 724.
Used up. Ts'katte shimaimash'ta,
Ts'katte shimatta, 964.
Useful (Is). Yaku ni tachimas', Ya-
ku ni tatsz. 904.
Use (Of). Yaku ni, Yoŏni, 987.

V

Vaccination. Ire-boŏsoŏ, 1089.
Value. Dai-kin, 810.
Varnish. Urushi, 886.
Velvet. Biroŏdo, 551.
Venture (Ata). Lit. right or wrong.
Dzehi, 706.
Very. Hanahada, 144. 215. 574.
752. 915. 1041. 1074. Tai
574. Tanto, 904. Oŏkini, 535.

904. 915. 1041. 1074. Taisoŏ
ni, 635. 1010
Very glad. Taikei ni, 574.
Very much. Yoku, 1045.
Vessel. Fune, 6.
Victoria, Bik'toria, 792.
Vinegar. Sz, 1090.
Voice. Koë, 807.
Voyages. Yuki-kae, Yuki-ki, 1061.

W

Wages. Kiubun, 531. Kiukin, 531.
548.
Wait. O machi nasai, Matte iro.
1091.
Waiting. Machi moŏsh'te Matte,
514. Machi nasaru, Matsz,
1121.
Wake up (Do not.) Samashi nasa-

runa, Samaszna, 125.
Walk (Let's take a). Asobi ni o ide
nasare, Asobi ni yuki nasai, 68.
Walk (Cannot). Ayumaremasenu,
Arukaremasen, 850.
Walk in. Oangari, nasare, Haire,
769

Want. v. Oiri nasaremas', Iru, 37. 371. Oiri-yoŏ de gozarimas', 384. Hosshii 504. Iri-yoŏ, 541. Iru, 1013.
Want [Do not]. Irimasen, Iranu, 453. 499. 581.
Wants. Tangaru, 264.
Warm. Atataka, 1100.
Warped. Sorimash'ta' Sotta, 1028.
Wash. Arai nasare, Arae, 1032.
Waste [Do not]. Tsziyashi nasaruna, Tsziyaszna, 113.
Watch. n. Tokei, 104, 539.
Watching. Ban. 1106
Water. Midz, 793. 859. 998. 1065.
Way. i. e. Manner. Toŏri, 503. Yoŏ, 619.
Way (You are in my). J'ama ni naru, 796.
Way (Their own). Wanga mama, Lit. my way. 364.
Wear, (as a sword). Sashimas', Sasz, 141.
Weather. Hiyori, Tenki, 845.
Wedding. Konrei, 985.
Weigh. Hakari ni kakeru, 178.
Weight. Mekata, 391.
Well. n. Ido. 1010.
Well. adj. i. e. in good health. Go ki ngen yoroshiu, Kawaru koto wa nai, 9. Kibun nga yoroshiu, 409.
Well. adv. Yoroshiu, Yoroshii, 623. 313. Yorosh'ku, Yoku, 410. Yoku, 273. 316.
Well. i. e. abundantly. Tak'san, 146.
Well. i. e. cured. Naosz. 759.
Well as we can. Chikara no oyoba dake, 1099.
Well-bred. Rei ngi nga tadashiu, Rei ngi nga yoku sh'tte, 213.
Well brought up. (Has been). Yoku sodateraremash'ta, Yoku sodateraru, 936.
Well done (Not). Yoku ts'kurie-masen, Yoku koshiraienu, 1017.
Well dressed. Yoroshii if'ku wo o ki nasaremas', Ii kimono wo kimas'. 251.
Well matched. Yoku nite orimas', Yoku nite iru, Lit. look very much alike, 994.
Well roasted (Not). viz· as coffee. Mada nama iri, Lit. still raw roasted., 1025.
Well settled [Not]. as coffee. Mada yoku odomimasen, Mada yoku odomanu, 1044.
Well then. Sayoŏ nara, Son nara, An eliptical expression, for, if it be so, or since things are so—then something follows. 1104.
Went. Mairimash'ta, Itta, 518. Mairu signifies, to go, or come.
Wet [Let it not get]. O nurashi nasaruna, Nuraszna, 109.
What? Nani, 72. 175. 186. and passim. Doko no, Lit. which, 600. Nanzo, 1126· 1163. Doŏ, Lit. how?, 1151. Naze, Lit. Why? 1152.
What else? Nanzo hoka ni, 1122.
Whatever. Doŏ-demo. Lit, however. 1110.
What for? Naze, 1116. 1137. Nani yue, Doŏ iu wake, 1125. Nani no tame ni, i. e. for what purpose? 1160.
What interest? Ri kim wo nambu, 1109.
What is the matter with—? Doŏ ka nasaremash'ta ka, Doŏ ka sh'ta ka, 1129. Doŏ sh'te ka-yoŏ ni nusaremash'ta ka, Do ŏ sh'te soŏ natta ka, 1108.
What is that to—? Doŏ iu wake de kamai nasaru ka, Doŏ iu wake de kamau ka, 1155. Doŏ iu wake. signifies, why,

or, on what account, and ka-mau, to concern one.
What o' clock? Nan doki, 1148.
What right? Nani no gi, Doŏ iu wake, 1167.
What sort of? Dono yoŏna, 1143.
What they will fetch (For). Soŏ-ba ni **naratte,** 839.
What to do. Doŏ sh'te yokarooka, 482.
What we can get. *i. e.* what comes to hand. Manndemo te ni iri-maszru, or Te ni iru, 1105.
When? Itsz, 1168, 1170, 1173, 1181, 1183, 1184, Itsz ngoro made ni, or simply Itsz ngoro, 1171. Itsz made ni, 1172. 1177. Itsz made, 1182. Itsz kara, 1180.
When. conj. adv. Toki. Lit. time, 1174. 1175 1178. 1179. 1194. Nochi ni, Lit. after-wards. also. A to de, 1176. In 1169, this idea is expressed by the conjunctive form or mode of the verb Dekimas', viz; Dekimash'taraba. *i. e.* when [you] have finished sh'-taku nga, **your** preparations. So also in **810,** Uri nasareta-raba, means, **When,** or as soon as you **have** sold &c. In 725, Nakereba signifies, When they **have** not any—[relativ-es]. **In** 569 also, Hanashima-sh'taraba, and Hanash'tara, mean If, or when I speak.
Whenever. Itsz **nite mo,** 65 By contraction, **this** becomes Itsz-**demo.**
Where? Dochira no, 1185. Dochi-ra de, 1186. 1188. 1189. Do-chira, 1191. Dochira ni, 1194. Dochira e, 1193. Doko. 1191. Doko e, 1187. 1190. 1193. 1196. 1203. Doko de, 1189. **1186.** Doko ni, 1194. 1195. **1198.** Doko **kara,** Lit.

Whence? 1197.
Where from? Idzku **yori, Doko kara,** 1192.
Whether or no. Dzehitomo, 333. Dzehi, 575.
Which? Dochira, 620. 1199. **1200.** 1201. 1202. 1204. **1205.** Dochi 1205. Doo, 620.
Which you please. Oboshimashi ni kanaimash'ta **no,** Ki ni it-ta no, Lit. that **which has sui-**ted and does **suit your taste.** 881.
While. Uchi, 874, Aida, 874.
While [A great]. Hisash'ku, 338.
While ago [A great]. Oōmu ka-shi, 931.
Whit [A]. S'koshi mo, 669.
Who? Dare, 1206. 1207. 1208. 1209. 1210. 1211. 1212. 1213. 1214. and passim. Do-nata, 1209. 1210. 1211. 1215. 1216. 1217. 1218. 1219. &c. Dochira, Dochi, Lit. **which,** 705.
Wholesome. **Hara no** tame ni narimas', **Hara** no tame ni naru, 521.
Whom? Donata wo, Dara wo, 1222, and passim. Nani wo, Lit. what? 1223.
Whose? Dare nga, Dare no, 1224. and passim. Donata no, 1225, and passim. Tare no, 1132.
Why? Nani yue, 1231, Naze 1231. 1232. 1233. **1234.** Naze ni, 1232, 1233. **1234.**
Wide. Haba. Lit. Width, **375.**
Wide **(How)? Nan ngen-ken. 376.** Lit. **How many measures (ken) of 6 feet?**
Wife. Tszma, **357,** 792. **Note,** Different terms are used for a wife according to the rank of the persons addressed, **or** spoken of, whose wives are referred to. The **following** is

a list of terms used as aforesaid. Thus—The emperor's is called Koöngo. His second in rank viz: K'ampak'us is called Mandokoro. The Taikun's—Midai. The 6 highest Daimios—Gorenchiu, The other Daimios', Okusama. Wives of the Hatamoto, or Taikun's retainers-Okusama. Wives of the Samurai, Go shinzo. Wives of Commoners, o kamisan. The Daimio calls his own wife when speaking of her, Saij'o and Tszma, or when speaking to his servants, Oku, The Taikun speaks of his wife as Midai. The common people call their own wives, Nioöboö.

Wild. Yatara ni, i. e. in no regular order, scattered here and there. Yamikumo, i. e in no certain place, but just as it may happen, 717.

Wild. i. e. without planting. Makadz ni. 752.

Will, aux. v. Made by the fut. ending oŏ or sh'oŏ. See the last words in the 2 sentences, 483, and futures passim.

Will do. i. e. is well. Yoroshiu gozarimas', Yoi, 8.

Will not do. Dekimasen, dehinai, 906.

Wind. Kaze. 380. 947. 1093.

Windows. Mado, 851.

Wind up [a clock]. Kakeru koto, 478.

Wink. n. Mebataki, 20.

Wish to get it done [If you]. Na saretakuba. Conditional, and desiderative form of the verb Nasaru, So also Shimai taku ba. 587.

With. De. i. e. by means of, 40. 202. The latter is De instrumental.

With. i. e. in company with. To to mo ni, 71.

With all [one's] might. Chikara wo Ts'kush'te. Hone wo otte, 868.

Without. Nakute wa, Nakereba, 632. Both signify lit. If there be not.

Woman. Onango, Onna, 849.

Women, Onango.

Wood. Ki. 1065.

Word. i. e. a written one. Monji. 597.

Word. Yakusoku, i.e. promise. 505.

Words. Mooshimas' koto, Kuchi, 911. Kotoba, 1036.

Work. n. Shingoto. 189. 764. Nasaru koto, Szru koto, 358. Shikata, 996. 997.

Work [a day's]. Ichi nichi no hiyoö, 544.

Work [The pay for]. Tema, 520.

Work in the garden. Hatakewo ts'kurimas', Hatakewo ts'kuru, 480.

Worn [Not]. Ts'kemasenu, Ts'kenai, Lit. do not wear. 689. Kaburite, Lit. putting on the head, 732.

Worse. Nawo waruu, Nawo warui, 1011.

Worse and worse. Shidai ni Waruku, 4.

Worst. Itatte warui, Ichiban warui, 272. 754. 896.

Worst. [The most difficult part]. Nan j'o. 574.

Worth [Is]. Ts'kaimas' tokoro nga—gozarimas', Ts'kau tokoro nga—i, Its utility is— &c. 1064.

Worth much [Is not]. Yoöni tatsz koto wa s'kunakute, Ts'kau koto nga s'kunakute, 1164.

Worth the trouble. Shinroö wo ts'kush'ta dake no koto nga

zo/zarimas', *i. e.* It is a thing [koto] of the value [Dake] of the trouble [shinroō] expended upon it (ts'kush'ta). 661. 662 is only the negative of 661.
Wound. Kidz. 362.
Wrecked. Ha—sen itashimash'te, Fune wo Yabutte, 1088.

Wrist. Te—kubi, 217.
Writes. Kaku, 288. Noō j'o, 288. Lit. Can write, or Able to write.
Writing. Kaite. 753. Kaku koto wa, 1269.
Wrong. Mudos no, 144. Soō—i, 275. Yokoshima, 895. Chingaimash'ta, Chingatta, 925.

Y.

Year. Nen. 433. 1018. 1100.
Years. Nen. 1057.
Years old [Twenty]. Hatachi. 848. 1073.
Yedo. Yedo. 204. 353. 407. 824.
Yesterday. Sakujitsz, 554. 809.
Yet. Mada, 126. 191.
Yielding. J'yun. 599.
You. Anata, 10 and passim. Omai or Omae, 10 and passim. Temai or Temae, 12. The first of these is the most respectful, and the others less so, in the order in which they succeed each other. The honorific prefix o, before a verb, or Go before a noun, often takes the place of the pronoun of the second person, and frequently it is altogether omitted, being easily inferred from the use of the above prefixes, or the circumstances of the speaker, or some thing already said.
Your. Anata no, Omai no. 11 and passim.
Your own. Anata go jibun no, Omai jishin no 13 and passim.

ERRATA.

Wherever in this volume the French û occurs, it should **be i doubled**, except in the case of uu,— oo–oo. The Roman **numbers below** refer to the pages in the *Introductory Remarks on Grammar*, **and the** Arabic figures to the lines of the same.

Page	Line	For	Read
II	5	Shiman	Shinau
	12	kai-fut	kai, fut
IV	2	verb.	verb
	12	⸨ tskuremash'	⸨ tskuremas'
		⸩ tani mono	⸩ tanimono
V	20	fire-Both	fire, both
	39	office,	office.
VI	33	ni-wa	Ni-wa
VII	19	naran. Appending	naran, appending
VIII	4	ama-nguno	Ama-nguno.
	11	Kiki wa	Kiku wa
	22	Kiki-ni-wa	Kiku-ni-wa
	31	イヘド or モ &c.	イヘドモ or
X	12	Sashiatta	Sashiatatte
	17	Horobi, to go to	Horobi, **to go** to ruin
	23	Moda	Monda
XI	33	Yunte	Iute or Itte
	40	Sh'te, going	Sh'te, doing
XII	7	dzongimas'	dzonjimas'
XIII	16	are be regarded	it be regarded
XIV	4	**to** speak. The phrase	to speak; the phrase
	12	coplula	copula
	35	Yomi	Yome
XV	43	Vorwal	vowel
XVI	20	Kuru, to bite	Kuu, to bite
	21	Tsuru & Tsurareau	Tszru & Tszrareru
	22	Tszreu	Tszreru
XVI	23	Tszseu	Tszreru
	26	S'kurareru	S'kuwareru
XVII	9	boues-the	bones, the
XVIII	13	Harae, to pay	Harai, to pay
XIX	13	Moyowananda	Mayowananda
	16	Kurunanda	Kurananda
	26	Tski, to	Tske
	27	Tobinakatta	Tobanakatta

ERRATA.

Page	Line	For	Read
xx	1	dz	dzi
	9	brielfly	briefly
	19	Ttasz	Itasz
	19	Ttashimas'	Itashimas'
	21	Kikaemas	Kikoemas'
xxi	29	miako	Miako
xxii	22	Dikineba	Dekineba
	42	kaisanu	Kaisanu
xxiii	5	although it	although. It
	13	mine domoshiru.	minedomo shiru,
	14	kikane	Kikane
	24	examples	example
xxiv	40	Gozarimaszeba	Gozarimaszreba.
	41	Aremash'tareba	Arimash'tareba
xxv	3	Arimash'oö, keredomo	Arimash'oö keredomo
xxvi	13	mimaszedomo	mimaszre domo.
xxvii	2	purpose as mi ni	purpose, as mi ni.
	12	preceeding	preceding
	26	Korosareraidearoö	Korosareru de aroö
	35	Keredomo	Keredomo
	37	Korosarareba	Korosarureba
xxviii	4	Korosare taroö ka	Korosare taroö ka
	9	*Infinitive*, ni	*Infinitive* Korosare ni
	15	Korosamash'te	Korosaremash'te
	32	Misatareba	Misctareba
xxviii	42	Miserataraba	Misetaraba
xxix	22	mi v. r. taku	mi v.r. and taku
xxx	16	pharse	phrase
	21	naru maimono	narumai mono
	22	Moshisoni	Moshi sono
	23	mode of the verbs	mode of the verb
	33	Miako kakaide	Miako Kakaide,
	38	Kakadzniita	Kakadz ni ita
	40	Kakadzniyoö	Kakadzni iyoö
xxxi	4	Kakiwashimai	Kaki wa shimai
	5	Kakaredomo	Kakaredomo
	9	**Kakiwashimai**	Kaki wa shimai
	23	Kakimai	Kakemai
	26	Kakanaideiru ko'.	Kakanai de iru ka?
	34	Infinative	Infinitive
	39	Kakanaidz	Kakanai de

ERRATA.

Page	Line	For	Read
XXXII	15	Koto e &c.	Koko e &c
	19	seru	senu
	19	Musabori toni	Musabori toru
	35	dame	tame
XLI	5	nako	naku
	12	puerite	puerile
	27	tszou	tszru
	31	Tattomer	Tattomu
XLIV	20	at a time, Two	at a time, two
XLV	8	Ichi man bu do san	Jchi man bu no san
	26	Tanamoro	Tammono
	40	Keme	Kome
XLVI	34	latter	later
XLVII	6	machiru	mahiru
	12	ken nichi	kon nichi
	12	to day mioō	to day, Mioō nichi
	15	nichi	nichi
	16	Shi 四 nichi	Shi 四 and nichi
	21	ochi (twice)	ichi
	32	Insoka	Misoka
	38	toka	to ka
LI	5	nouns	noun
	16	sadomete	Sadamete
LII	7	Kosh'ko ni	Kash'ko ni
	42	from words	form-words
LIII	36	nete	nite
LIV	3	Sote	Soto
	32	causility	causality
LV	22	haredomo	naredomo
LVI	31	and in often	and is often
LIX	38	Akiredo	Akindo
LX	99	tozi ni	tszi ni
LXI	30	more	mere
LXII	1	Kukimas'	Kakimas'

ERRATA.

The first numbers below refer to the No. of the sentence in the *Alphabetical Part*, and the next to the 1st, or 2nd, form of the same.

No.		For	Read
25	2	biyaku dztsz	biyaku dora &c.
16		ukeai ni	uke ni
49	1. 2.	ni jiu nin ni	ni jiu nin ni
51	1. 2.	フデウ ヤス ケ	フデヲケ オス
53	1	ャ ヶ	
66	2	ウャ	ウマ
74	1	ウウタ クシ カケクラ	ワウタクシ カケリテ
79	1		
"	2	ヨニ	ヨリ
83	2	タマヱ	オマヱ
87	1. 2.	no ano (ア)	soô. サウ.
89	1. 2.	itsz ni	itsz tsz ni
98	1. 2.	Nip'pon h'to.	Nip'pon no h'to,
126		get	yet
151	2	イレハ	イレロ
152	1	クテ	キテ
169	1. 2.	sam bu ni	sam bu no ni
170	2	Watak'shi no	Watak'shini
173	1	o yu ki	o ide
180		バン tomi ni	バン tomo ni
190		sh' te	sh'-te
193	1	ts' ka-t-te	ts'-ka-t-te
201	2	ko-o	go-o
255		confesses	confessed
269	2	do-ro-bo	do-ro-bo-o
271	2	me-da	me da
275	1	to-o-ri	do-o-ri
286	2	クゼ	クビ
287	1	ヱエ	ヱエ
413	1	i-ta mi-ma-s'	i-ta-mi-ma-s'.
417	2	so n na-ni	so-n-na-ni
420	2	wa-ka ra &c.	wa-ka-ra-na-kat-ta-
424	1	nu-ki-ta'-i	nu-ki-ta-i
431	1. 2.	ch'-o	ch'-o-o
432	1. 2.	ri-o	ri-o-o
449	2	o-no	a-no
468	1. 2.	モ mo	モウ mo-o
469	1. 2.	モ mo	モウ mo-o

ERRATA.

No.		For	Read
470	1	ko-to mo ko-n-ni-n	ko-to moò k'a-n-ni-n.
482	2	shi-ra-nu	shi-re-nu
499	1. 2.	Ko-re wo	ko-re wa
506	1	o ki-ka-se-te	ki-ka-se-te.
511	2	to-no	so-no
525	2	u-ke-a-i	u-ke-a-e
527	1. 2.	ta-bi-ta-bi	o-ri-o-ri
531	2.	ma-sh'-te-ya-ro-o.	ma-sh'-te ya-ro-o
532	1.	no-o-shi-me-sh'-ta.	na-o-shi-ma-sh'-ta
539	2	ツカス	スカス
545	2	wa-shi	wa-shi no
559	2	ne	ni
569	1	to-ke	to-ki
569	2	to-no	so-no
585	2	uttae ni szru	uttaeru
588	1	ts'-ku-na-i-ma-sh'-o-o	Ts'-ku-no-i-ma-sh'-o-o.
589	1	ts'kaemash'oò	ts'kaimash'oò
590	1.	torimasooo	torimashioò
591	1.	h'te	k'te
608	1. 2.	Tam-mei	Ham-mei
608	1. 2.	ch'o-mei	ch'o-me
630	2	sa-o	so-o
658	1. 2.	sz-he-te	sz-be-te
663	1. 2.	after "Nani ni" insert	de-mo
668	**2**	ta-ke-te	ts'-ke-te
673	**2**	ma-shi-da	mashi da
682	1. **2**.	a-z'-ko-ni	ko-ko ni
687		ha ji-me-te	ha-ji-me-te
694	1. 2.	ku-sz-re-te	ku-dz-re-te
699	2	ts'-ka-n	ts'-ka-nu
705	2	to o-ku	to-o-ku
710	1	デ & de	へ & e
711	2	ni-no-ru	ni no-ru
713	1. 2.	ko-o-j'-o-o	ko-to-ba
717	2.	ya-mi-ko-mo	ya-ta-ra ni
722	1. 2.	ts'-ke-na ke-re-ba.	ts'-ke na-ke-ri-ba
724		yu-u	i-u
732	1.	odori hane **maszru**	odorimaszru
739	1	tsz-me-ta-o	tsz-me-to-o
743	1. 2.	koshirai sai	koshirae sae
749	1.	koshirairu	koshiraeru

ERRATA.

No.		For	Read
754	2.	no ko-to	ko-to no
759	1.	ko-to	ko-to nga
767	1.	ka-i-zo-ku	ka-i-zo-ku nga
774	1.	ka-ji-da	ka-ji da
788	1.	i-i-ka-nge-n na	i-i-ka-nge-n-na
790		after "wild boars"	are abundant in the market in winter.
791	1	Yo-ro-pa	Yo-o-ro-pa
792		ngo-ku	ko-ku
792		wo-o-sa-me-ru	wo.o-sa-me-ru
793	2.	hi-ni	hini
797		yudzri j'o⁶mon	ko-ke-n-j'-o-o
816	2.	a-ta ra-nu	a-ta ra-nu
822	1.	ge ji-ki	ge-ji-ki
823	1.	ta-ka-o	ta-ko-o
831	1.	∨ ﾉ	ﾘ ﾉ
855	1.	yo-ro-shi-i	yo-ro-shi-u
864	1.	oboshimeshi	oboshimesz
865		kimono	kimono wo
868	1.	wo-o	o-o
884	2.	shi-ro-ki	shi-ro ki
885		hanashinasare	hanashi nasare
890	2.	ma-shi-da	ma-shi da
900	1. 2.	mo-u	mo-o
902	2.	ho-n-to	ho-n-to-o
912	1	mo-o-na-ji	mo o-na-ji
932	1.	ga	go
932	2.	e-sz nga-ta	e-sz-nga-ta
960	2.	nga-s'-ko-shi	nga s'-ko-shi
962		ch'-o-do	ch'-o-o-do
963	2.	yo-ri-a-chi	yo-ri a-chi
975	2.	da	aru
993	1.	a-ngo-ri	a-nga-ri
1002	1. 2.	ri-o	ri-o-o
1004	2.	ta-che-ngi-e	ta-chi-ngi-e
1008	2.	ya-ke-da	ya-ke da
1013	1. 2.	ch'-o-do	ch'-o-o-do
1026	1. 2.	,,	,,
1030	1.	tsz-yo-o	tsz-u-yo-o
1030	2.	tsz-yo-e	tsz-u-yo-o
1035	1.	gozarimas'	gozarimasenu

ERRATA.

No		For	Read
1040		mo	mo-o
1110	1.	nasarimas'k	nasarimas'
1115	2.	i-ku-ta	i-ku-ra
1243	1.	ka-yo o-na	ka-yo-o-na
1265	1.	naremas'	narimas'

Dialogues.

Page	No. of sentence	For	Read
175	F. 17.	cha wa	cha wo
"	"	ngurai, kaitai	ngurai kaitai
177	M. 29.	kooeki	koŏeki
178	N. 39.	ド ナ	ド ラ
178	F. 44.	ヤウク & ウモイマス omoimas',	オヲク & オモイマス omoimas'
179	F. 8.	ナイ	ナニ
"	N. 9.	ガン	ギン
180	F. 16.	uraremash'oŏ	uremash'oŏ
181	E. 20.	kito & トツア	kiito & トッタ
"	N. 23	ソノ	ソレ
"	N. 25.	s'oŏ	soŏ
182	F. 26.	hoŏyun totte.	hoŏyuñ totte
183	Line 1.	E. 30.	F. 30.
"	F. 30.	i-re-te イレテ アチラレス	sh'te シテ アケラレヌ
"	Line 15.	F. 33.	N. 31.
186	N. 21.	mino	mi no,
190	F. 48.	son, h'yoku & ジ	soŏ, hyaku & シ
192	N. 59.	kara & カラ	kura & クラ
"	S. 2.	カナ	カ子
194	B. 1.	チイト	チット
195	B. 5.	nangmochi	nangamochi
"	B. 13.	dz to & ズウト	dzito & ズイト
196	S. 18.	セウシマス	モウシマス

Weights and Measures.

Page	Line	For	Read
197	18	1266 Ft.	12.960 Ft.
198		after "written" insert	半兩勿
199		zeni	zeni,

ERRATA.

Index and Vocabulary.

Page	Line of 1st col.	Line of 2nd col.	For	Read
203	1		Pak'san.	Tak'san.
,,	12		Jtashimas'	Itashimas'
,,	14		moō sh'te	moōsh'te
,,	15		Szozmeru	Szszmeru
,,		12	931	1093
204	20		under "ancient" insert anchored, before "akari wo orosh'ta.	
,,	39		mono	mo no
,,		24	koōē ki	koōēki
,,		31	kik'e	kike
205	4		dzketemamotte	dzkete mamotte
,,	32		Ts wo atta	Te wo utta
,,		29	Atatamarimes'	Atatamarimes'
,,		39	Konomai	Kono mai
206	15		ji	ii
,,	21		Ita	Ha
,,	36		763	673
,,	47		kolo	koto
,,		1	niszru	ni szru
,,		14	kun	kuii
207	10		Yabarimash'ta	Yaburimash'ta
,,	20		After "Build", &c. insert 673	
,,	33		ku dasare	kudasare
,,	37		Toiu	To iu
207	40		Ts'kurara ru	Ts'kurareru
208	36		Nakasete	Makasete
,,		31	234	334
,,		38	Poōjin	Toō jin
208		43	Nok'kei	Nik'kei
209	5		Tammons	Tammono
,,	11		Coffe and	Coffee, and erase Coppee.
,,	15		Samun	Samuii
,,	17		755	739
,,		9	Hara kin'sep'p'uku	harakirui, Sep'puku
,,		21	omowaremai	omowaremas'
,,		23	Somuiti	Somouite

ERRATA.

Page	Line of 1st. col.	Line of 2nd. col.	For	Read
210	7		in	iu
,,	9		Hanera	Haneru
,,	25		seiki	seikio
,,	36		yndzri j'oŏmon	koken'j'oŏ
,,		5	46.	460.
211	1		1109.	1153.
,,	44		(with it)	(wish it)
,,		10	1007.	1006,
,,		22	in	ni
,,		42	257	277
212	2		akiru	ahiru
,,	18		k'unte	kujite
,,	29		Jikangennarioŏji	Iikangenna riooji
,,		17	Anaji	Onaji
,,		26	Dzchi	dzchi
,,		29	184—dele.	
,,		32	144.	141.
,,		41	827	887
213	19		Sangate	Sangatte
,,	34		Ichitan	Ichiban
,,	43		Yukeo	yuku
,,		14	ariwa	arewa
214	10		kakarimaseru	kakarimasenu
,,	31		Iioŏ	Jioŏ
214		9	osorote	osorete
215	15		H'ts	H'to
,,		11	141	241
,,		42	575	595
216	42		yohu	yoku
,,		22	888	858
,,		35	Heemaszru	Haemaszru
,,		42	776	766
217	8		Ts	Te
,,		41	52.	53.
218	45		364	1244.
,,		34	Mada	made
,,		43	Ika hodo	Ik'ka hodo
219	9		Watah'shi	Watak'shi
,,	31		expressedly	expressed by
,,	33		591	941
,,		19	Itama	Itamu

ERRATA.

For	Line of 1st col.	Line of 2nd col.	For	Read
219		23	209.	309.
,,		36	21.	821.
220		11	Tamar	Tama
,,		13	637.	657.
,,		16	gerund ive,	gerundive
,,		20	Ch'odo	Ch'oŏdo
,,		22	Sahi	Saka
221	18		oŏhina	Oŏkina
		27	1115.	115.
222		13	After "shishi" insert	718.
		36	Tamangnszri	Tamangsiszri
223		4	349 dele.	
,,		9	nasarete	nasareta
,,		30	795.	725.
,,		41	kawarieoo	kawari wo
,,		42	Ts'kunaimash'oŏ	Ts'kunoimash'oŏ
224		43	kaman	kamau
225	11		637 & 638	737 & 738.
,,	21		ne	ue
,,		22	938	738.
		27	621	641.
226	9		Itasz made mo	Itsz made mo
,,	44		Tammei	Hamme
,,		4	Mahiou	Mahiru
,,		43	toöyun	toöyuŭ
227	12		Once	One
,,		5	1269	1268.
,,		17	33	533.
,,		27	nasaremash'te	nasaremash'ta
		32	tozita	tszita
228	5		kahits'ke	kakits'ke
,,	20		Hairimas'	Haraimas'
,,	36		1087.	1070.
,,	40		yoridori	yoridori
		25	41.	40.
229	12		782	778.
230	2		Dehimasen'	Dekimasen'
230		2	iru	iro
,,		13	954.	594.
,,		38	123.	127.
,,		39	in	iu

ERRATA.

Page.	Line of 1st col.	Line of 2nd col.	For	Read
232		35	After "ashamed" &c.	668.
233	14		969.	979.
,,	47		927.	937.
,,		13	943.	942.
234	16		Idzn	Idzri
,,		3	655.	656.
235	9		after "shiro	872.
,,		26	673.	763.
235		43	after "expressed".	797.
236		40	468.	465,
,,		46	kamawaru	kamawanu
239	31		574.	572.
,,	33		574.	572.
,,	7	7	sh'ta ni **Dele.**	
,,		27	574.	572.
240	40		oyoba	oyobu
241	12		manidemo	nanidemo
,,		16	oõmu kashi	Oõmukashi.
,,		28	Dara	Dare
242		45	1164.	662.

www.ingramcontent.com/pod-product-compliance
Lightning Source LLC
Chambersburg PA
CBHW030735230426
43667CB00007B/718